PUBLICATIONS

OF THE

NAVY RECORDS SOCIETY

VOL. 154

CHATHAM DOCKYARD, 1815–1865

The NAVY RECORDS SOCIETY was established in 1893 for the purpose of printing unpublished manuscripts and rare works of naval interest. The Society is open to all who are interested in naval history, and any person wishing to become a member should apply to the Hon. Secretary, Pangbourne College, Pangbourne, Berks., R98 8LA. The annual subscription is £30, which entitles the member to receive one free copy of each work issued by the Society in that year, and to buy earlier issues at much reduced prices.

SUBSCRIPTIONS and orders for back volumes should be sent to the Membership Secretary, 8 Hawthorn Way, Lindford, Hants GU35 0RB.

THE COUNCIL OF THE NAVY RECORDS SOCIETY wish it to be clearly understood that they are not answerable for any opinions and observations which may appear in the Society's publications. For these the editors of the several works are entirely responsible.

CHATHAM DOCKYARD, 1815–1865

The Industrial Transformation

Edited by

PHILIP MACDOUGALL

PUBLISHED BY ASHGATE
FOR THE NAVY RECORDS SOCIETY
2009

Crown copyright material is reproduced by permission of The Stationery Office.

Published by
Ashgate Publishing Limited
Wey Court East
Union Road
Farnham
Surrey GU9 7PT
England

Ashgate Publishing Company
Suite 420
101 Cherry Street
Burlington, VT 05401–4405
USA

Ashgate website: http://www.ashgate.com

British Library Cataloguing in Publication Data

Chatham Dockyard, 1815–1865 : the industrial transformation. – (Navy Records Society publications)
    1. Chatham Dockyard (Great Britain) – History – 19th century 2. Shipyards – England – Chatham (Kent) – History – 19th century 3. Shipbuilding industry – Great Britain – History – 19th century 4. Naval architecture – Great Britain – History – 19th century
    I. MacDougall, Philip II. Navy Records Society (Great Britain)
    623.8'3'0942232

Library of Congress Catalog Card Number: 2008936584

ISBN 978–0–7546–6597–7

Printed on acid-free paper

Typeset in Times by Manton Typesetters, Louth, Lincolnshire, UK.

Mixed Sources
Product group from well-managed forests and other controlled sources
www.fsc.org Cert no. SA-COC-1565
© 1996 Forest Stewardship Council
FSC

Printed and bound in Great Britain by
MPG Books Ltd, Bodmin, Cornwall.

CONTENTS

ABBREVIATIONS

Add Mss	Additional manuscripts
ADM	Admiralty
BL	British Library
CHA	Chatham Dockyard
Cumbria R.O.	Cumbria Record Office
MEPO	Metropolitan Police
NMM	National Maritime Museum
PC	Privy Council
POR	Portsmouth Dockyard
RNM	Royal Naval Museum
SRO	Scottish Record Office
TNA	The National Archives of the United Kingdom

PREFACE

A great deal has been written about the actions of seagoing fleets, the individuals who commanded them and the vessels that made up those fleets. In contrast, the organisational infrastructure necessary for the purpose of building and preparing warships for the fleet has often been ignored. It was this failure to recognise an important aspect of naval history that first spurred me into several decades of researching and writing the history of naval dockyards. In Britain, which had the first industrial revolution, the royal dockyards could boast a civilian workforce that was considerably larger than that of any other industrial enterprise long before the industrial take-off. By the end of the Napoleonic Wars, the seven home yards of the Royal Navy employed a workforce of nearly 16,000 men and even some women. Even among industrial and social historians this scale of employment has often been ignored. Yet, on account of their size, the dockyards add much to our understanding of developing social processes. For it was within those yards that a system of recruitment, training and supervision of a large-scale workforce was pioneered. At the same time the artisans and labourers of the yards developed their own particular response to the means by which they were managed, attempting to ensure their own interests were protected and acknowledged.

My entry into the field of dockyard research was eased by the seminal work of Michael Oppenheim on Tudor and early Stuart naval adminis-tration, of John Ehrman on the navy of the late seventeenth century, and of Daniel Baugh on naval administration during the early eighteenth century.[1] By fully integrating the function and working of the dockyards into their overall research, these three naval historians established the importance of the yards while indicating necessary directions for future research. Publications by the Navy Records Society added depth to my knowledge by issuing two volumes of collected documents edited by Baugh and Merriman. While the former revisited and underpinned his

---

[1]Daniel Baugh, *British Naval Administration in the Age of Walpole* (Princeton, 1965); John Ehrman, *The Navy in the War of William III* (Cambridge University Press, 1963); Michael Oppenheim, *A History of the Administration of the Royal Navy and of Merchant Shipping in Relation to the Navy* (1896; reprinted Temple Smith, 1988).

earlier publication, expanding his time frame, Merriman examined naval administration, including the dockyards, during the age of Queen Anne (1702–14).[1] Later but also of importance were the works of Roger Morriss and Jonathan Coad. Both focussed specifically on the royal dockyards, Morriss undertaking an in-depth study of the wartime period 1793–1815 while Coad, in two illustrated books, concentrated on the architecture of the yards.[2] More recently, attention has been given to a long-neglected area of dockyard research, that of the nineteenth century. In his work on the final years of the sailing navy, Andrew Lambert examined the naval dockyards in the period after the Napoleonic Wars; J.M. Haas included the nineteenth century in his study of management at different periods in the history of the yards; and in 2004 David Evans looked at the technology represented by the facilities of the yards created in the period 1830–1906.[3] All three examined the dockyards in the early to mid nineteenth century and their work has much to commend it. However, they still left gaps. The period was one of dramatic change, and these writers were unable to give their full attention to a series of administrative reforms which with new technology had a dramatic impact upon the workforce.

The purpose of this volume is to provide a more full understanding of the difficulties faced by the dockyards during this period of far-reaching change. In part, it is built upon my doctoral thesis that looked at the abolition of the Navy Board in 1832.[4] However the present work goes much further. By concentrating on one naval dockyard and providing the documents relating to a whole series of reforms this study is able to examine how the day-to-day running of a major centre of industrial production changed in the period 1815–1865. The choice of Chatham was no coincidence. It was the yard that introduced the royal dockyards to the technology of the twentieth century. The private yards had long had experience of building ironclads and steam-powered vessels, the naval dockyards had not. There was every possibility that the work of building and maintaining ironclad warships would be diverted from the state-owned royal dockyards and turned over to the private sector. The Admiralty decision to make Chatham the location for building *Achilles*,

---

[1]D.A. Baugh, ed., *Naval Administration* (NRS, Vol. 120, 1977), R.D. Merriman, ed., *Queen Anne's Navy* (NRS, Vol. 103, 1961).

[2]R. Morriss, *The Royal Dockyards during the Revolutionary and Napoleonic Wars* (Leicester, 1983); J. Coad, *Historic Architecture of the Royal Navy* (London, 1983); J. Coad, *The Royal Dockyards 1690–1850. Architecture and Engineering Works of the Sailing Navy* (Aldershot, 1989).

[3]A. Lambert, *The Last Sailing Battlefleet* (London, 1991); David Evans, *Building the Steam Navy. Dockyard Technology and the Creation of the Victorian Battle Fleet, 1830–1906* (London, 2004).

[4]Philip MacDougall, 'Somerset Place to Whitehall: Reforming the Civil Departments of the Navy' (PhD thesis, University of Kent at Canterbury, 1994).

the first iron ship to be built in a royal dockyard, placed that yard at the forefront of technological change. For at that time neither Chatham, nor any other royal dockyard, was equipped to undertake this task. Had Chatham failed to complete the task satisfactorily, the future of the royal dockyards might have been very different.

The source material for this volume has been drawn principally from the National Archives at Kew and the National Maritime Museum at Greenwich. Their holdings for research into the history of the royal dockyards are invaluable. For the National Maritime Museum contains correspondence between the Admiralty and the Navy Board, the records of the Resident Commissioner, Captain Superintendent and officers at Chatham, while the National Archives holds the records of the Navy Board and Admiralty including internal correspondence, discussion papers and minutes. Unfortunately, the holdings of the National Archives have suffered from injudicious early weeding that has severely reduced the sources for the period following the abolition of the Navy Board. However, additional sources for the completion of the volume were found in the British Library, including its newspaper library, the library of Chatham Dockyard Historic Trust, Cumbria Record Office, Rochester Bridge Trust, Royal Naval Museum, and Scottish Record Office. To the Lord Chancellor and the trustees of the museums mentioned above, I make acknowledgement for permission to make quotations from the records they hold. To the staff of all these institutions I wish to extend my thanks for the courtesy and efficiency with which they consistently responded to the research I conducted for this volume.

INTRODUCTION

The selected documents in this volume provide an insight into the workings of a naval dockyard during a period of transformation. The years 1815 to 1865 were the ones in which the naval dockyards fully harnessed the use of steam and made the conversion from constructing ships of timber to those of iron. At Chatham, these changes were particularly apparent. In 1815, apart from a newly completed sawmill, the yard was entirely devoid of steam machinery. By the end of the period, the yard situation was very different. Not only was it building ships designed to accommodate steam engines but, throughout the yard, steam-powered engines had been installed in various workshops and centres of manufacture and were used for powering pumps for draining the docks. As for the transition to iron shipbuilding, this was a far more dramatic process. Throughout the period, those in the smithery were employed in the manufacture of increasing amounts of ironwork, producing items for use in ships' hulls together with fittings for all classes of vessels. Nonetheless, this was no real preparation for the construction of a 9,800-ton iron battleship, the task that confronted Chatham in 1860. The final product, completed in September 1864, was *Achilles*, the first such ship to be built in any royal dockyard – a vessel that signalled a new direction, not only for Chatham, but for all the naval dockyards.

The adoption of steam machinery combined with the decision to undertake iron shipbuilding at Chatham inevitably had a dramatic impact upon all those employed at the dockyard. To keep pace with the increase of steam engines, an ever expanding number of mechanists and machine-minders had to be employed, culminating in the appointment of a Chief Engineer at the head of a separate department. At the same time, other groups of workers found themselves possessing skills that were now better performed by steam-powered machinery. Among these were sawyers and scavelmen. The former were unable to compete with the speed and efficiency of the powered saws of Brunel's mill while the latter, hitherto responsible for the clearing and drainage of the docks, were made redundant with the introduction of steam pumps. However, such changes were nothing more than a ripple compared with the revolution in ship construction methods brought about by the laying down of *Achilles*. No longer was it the semi-skilled who were at risk. It was the yard's elite, the shipwrights, who were now threatened. Able to undertake any demand placed upon them when constructing ships of timber, they were at a loss when they came to ships of iron. Yet, from the Admiralty's point of view, they possessed something of even greater value being less confrontational when it came to the expression of grievances, they invariably resorted to the petition, using a procedure for its submission that the Admiralty had itself established. In contrast the metal workers, by whom they were being replaced, evinced a workplace militancy that had not been witnessed in the yards since the beginning of the century. In an attempt to assert their position, a strike by the newly employed metalworkers resulted in their permanent dismissal from the yard. To replace them, those newly dismissed (and about to be dismissed) shipwrights were invited to learn the skills of ironworking, a task to which they rapidly adapted.

Often neglected, but no less important, was the impact of these changes upon the environment of the yard. The clatter of steam-powered machinery now reverberated around the various factories and workshops within which they had been installed. Outside, the sounds of hammering on metal and various industrial pollutants were also transforming dockyard life. Dickens, in revisiting the yard after nearly fifty years' absence, was particularly struck by these changes, emphasising the distinctly different sounds that were produced by those engaged upon the construction of *Achilles*.

However, the changes impacting upon Chatham were not simply restricted to the issue of technology. The year 1816, the first full year of peace following the defeat of Napoleon, was one in which the yard was attempting to adapt to the new situation. Rather than being readied for a return to sea, now most vessels were being prepared for moorings in the ordinary, with the maintenance of these same vessels soon to be the yard's most important task. At the same time, government demands for economies, noisily supported by opposition radicals and Whigs in Parliament, meant the Navy Board was under pressure to reduce dockyard expenditure. At Chatham, this was to result in a near-50 per cent reduction in workforce numbers, a reduction eventually completed in 1833. A further aspect of this period of retrenchment was a series of administrative changes, the intensity of these increasing upon the accession of the Whigs in 1831. While earlier reforms had principally been aimed at financial economy, those of the 1830s were much more political in nature, the Whigs having fostered a long-term desire to abolish the Navy Board.

A further important theme that runs through this period is the consideration given to the long-term future of the yard at Chatham. In the years immediately prior to 1815 the dockyard had been under threat of closure. John Rennie, who was frequently consulted by the Navy Board, advocated that an alternative dockyard be built at Northfleet. Few could disagree with his argument for closure, the Medway having become increasingly difficult to navigate as a result of shoaling. That Chatham survived the threat of closure was, initially, a result of the huge costs involved in the construction of a new yard. More pertinent to its long-term survival was the fortuitous arrival of the steam dredger, this proving a remarkably effective tool in maintaining a navigable channel from Chatham to the mouth of the Medway. The dockyard, having acquired a secure future, was nevertheless subject to a number of calls for general improvements. Rennie, having accepted that expenditure upon Chatham was worthwhile, proposed a re-routing of the Medway, so that the area of the river immediately in front of the yard could be converted into an enclosed basin. This scheme was never adopted, however, such ideas remained. William Scamp, the Admiralty's Chief Assistant of Engineering Works, advocated the scheme that eventually transformed St Mary's Island into a massive extension far greater in size than that of the original area of the dockyard.

The final decision to undertake this huge project, together with the completion of *Achilles*, dictates the end point of this volume. To go beyond 1865 would have been to enter a very different dockyard, a dockyard that had been entirely transformed by the developments of the preceding fifty years. The intention here is to examine the period of transition and the impact it had upon both the facilities at Chatham and those employed within the yard. The extension belonged to a new era and there is no need to examine the period of its construction or later use. So, too, with the construction of iron ships at Chatham. But it was in the preceding forty years that those employed in the dockyard had acquired the necessary skills. This volume indicates how their environment changed and how they adapted to the new form of work.

TOWARDS *ACHILLES*: SHIPBUILDING AND REPAIR

Throughout the period 1815 to 1865, the primary tasks undertaken by Chatham dockyard were those of constructing new ships and of undertaking large-scale repairs on older vessels. In common with most other yards, Chatham also undertook a multiplicity of further duties. Among these were the fitting and re-fitting of ships [29, 37], the care and maintenance of vessels moored in the ordinary [37] and minor repairs on operational warships. With regard to the latter, Chatham was not especially suited. In part, this was because of its great distance from the sea but also a result of the declining depth of the Medway. The river, during much of this period, was subject to considerable shoaling, there being an insufficient depth both for the larger ships of the ordinary and for rapid, trouble-free passages between the dockyard and the open sea. It was recognition of these problems that prompted John Deas Thomson, a member of the Navy Board, to submit to Lord Melville in 1829 a recommendation that Chatham should be strictly confined to those duties to which it was geographically suited [31]. However, the idea of Chatham specialising in building and large-scale repairs, was not adopted at this time and the yard continued to perform a mixture of duties throughout the nineteenth century.

The Admiralty, whenever a new vessel was to be constructed, took the initial decision with instructions forwarded to Chatham by either the Navy Board (prior to its abolition in 1832) or the Admiralty Office (after 1832). Such orders were often accompanied by a set of drawings, although on occasions it might be a simple notification, with drawings sent nearer to the time of construction [56, 57, 73]. On being informed that a new ship was to be built, the Master Shipwright, whose department oversaw both construction and repair work, would consider the facilities and manpower that would be required. Of course, the administrators in London already had an awareness of docks and slips likely to be available, sometimes precisely stipulating which facility was to be used [12, 14, 28]. The choice of Chatham for construction of a new vessel was not always contingent upon the availability of a particular dock or slip; instead it might result from an accumulation of the necessary building materials at that yard [17]. Vessels constructed at Chatham varied considerably. In earlier years, the yard had been associated with the building of larger battleships of 74 guns and upward but after 1815 the construction of these vessels was less frequently required. Indeed, between 1815 and 1865, Chatham built less than thirty such vessels of which the 120-gun *Royal George* [28] and the 120-gun *Waterloo* [52, 59] were the largest. Instead, the yard concentrated on a range of middle-sized vessels [57] and relatively diminutive corvettes [17], brigs [33, 34] and bomb vessels [18]. In addition, the dockyard built a number of packets for the Post Office [50, 51] as well as fitting out the 'Dreadnought' hospital ship for merchant seamen [42].[1]

Building plans were drawn to a scale of 1 to 24 or 1 to 48. When they arrived they were passed to the shipwrights of the mould loft where they were projected full-scale onto the floor [55]. From these, joiners used fir battens to make the moulds employed by the shipwrights engaged on the building of a new ship to form the curves of the timbers. Apart from shipwrights and joiners, others closely involved in the construction stage were sawyers, caulkers and carvers. The sawyers, working either in sawpits or at the sawmill, were responsible for preparing the timbers. Once the planking had been fitted both to the decks and hull, caulkers ensured complete water-tightness by driving strips of oakum into the seams [14]. The carvers were responsible for such work as the figurehead fitted to the bow sometime before launching [5].

The length of time taken to construct a warship varied considerably, dependent both on the size of the vessel and the urgency with which she was required. To complete a ship within one year (313 working days) to a state where she was ready to enter the ordinary, it was estimated that 167 shipwrights would be needed for a 120-gun first rate and 37 for a paddle sloop [62]. However, completion dates could be dramatically deferred if alterations were made to the original plans while a vessel was still building [30, 32]. The future longevity of a new ship was dependent upon the quality of workmanship [58, 61] and the methods used to season and protect its timbers during the construction stage. For this reason, those conducting an official visitation to the dockyard would make a point of inspecting and commenting upon ships under construction [9] with consequent new orders [1]. In 1835, for instance, concern was expressed about overuse of the spike iron in caulking, which could have damaged a hull. As a result, use of this tool was considerably restricted [60]. Another fear was the alleged practice of workmen profiting from the embezzlement of bolts by the removal of the central section to create the so-called 'devil's bolt' [41].

---

[1]A full list of ships built or ordered to be built at Chatham between 1815 and 1865 will be found as Appendix 1.

The launch of a ship was an important occasion and one that had to be performed with great care [38]. If the ship to be launched was a particularly large vessel, huge crowds were drawn to the vicinity to witness the event [59]. Furthermore, a full report would appear in local and other newspapers, popular journals also carrying engravings [52, 59]. Once a vessel was successfully launched, a brief note of the event, was always sent to London by the yard Commissioner (Captain Superintendent from 1832), with details of her dimensions and draft [39]. However, despite George Parkin's assertion of having overseen the launch of 'a great number of vessels without accident' [38], things did not always go according to plan. In particular, there was a problem with *Powerful* in 1826 when George Parkin was Master Shipwright [23]. After being launched into the Medway from a building slip, a new vessel, if of timber construction, was taken into dry dock for coppering. Of course, not all ships were built on a slipway; some were constructed in dry dock: these vessels were not 'launched' but 'floated-out' (having, if necessary, already been coppered) [81]. Finally, the ship passed out of the hands of the Master Shipwright's department and into the hands of the Master Attendant, whose department looked after ships moored in harbour and rigged them ready for sea.

As well as constructing new ships, the Master Shipwright's department was responsible for the repair of ships in dry dock. Often, the docking of a ship would be the result of a survey of the ships in the ordinary and a report of a vessel's deficiencies to the Admiralty [8, 21]. All vessels – including those specifically sent to Chatham [12], port guard ships [22] and revenue vessels [2] as well as ships held in the ordinary – were regularly surveyed [8]. Having received a report of the survey, the Admiralty took the decision as to the work to be undertaken [28]. The most common reason for docking was the removal and renewal of copper sheathing [25, 26]; others included repairs to damage sustained by a vessel [24] and dismantling a ship once it had reached the end of its useful life [15, 66]. In giving attention to the underside of a ship's hull, any defective timbers were replaced and the vessel re-caulked. If coppering was the reason for docking, a vessel could be refloated in a matter of weeks. But occupation of a dry dock was frequently longer, for Chatham was suited to large-scale repairs [21]. Unfortunately, the work of repair was not always performed to the standard required. Questions were raised over the quality of caulking undertaken on *Spartiate* in 1825 [19, 20] and a series of questions were raised in 1835 about work on *Hastings* [58, 61]. Docking and undocking was a fairly routine business, but it did occasionally result in an accident [48], and delays occurred in 1841 as a result of the river icing over [63].

A somewhat different duty fell upon the Master Shipwright's department during the early 1830s when one of the yard shipwrights was commissioned to construct a model of the seventeenth-century warship *Sovereign of the Seas* [47]. Another shipwright was directed to join the staff of the model room at Somerset House [45].

Often, during the years of peace that followed the French Wars, newly launched or repaired ships would be brought into the ordinary where they joined a number of other vessels awaiting a future call to duty. It was normal for such vessels to be roofed to provide them with protection from the elements [10, 27, 29]. In 1832, new instructions were issued as to the roofing of vessels: only the waist was to be covered [46], the weather decks to receive instead a protective coating of tar and tallow [49]. By then, dry rot was thought to be best combated by keeping ships in a more open state with quantities of water introduced for the purpose of creating a moist environment [44].

Ships held in the ordinary, if deemed in need of extensive repair could, as noted, be dry-docked [13, 16]. However, all other repairs were undertaken in the harbour by teams of workmen [6]. Besides warships awaiting a return to duty, there were a number of other ships that were the concern of those employed in the ordinary. These included *Argonaut*, the Medway hospital ship until 1828 [3], several convict [16] and receiving hulks [43] and those vessels employed on harbour service [13]. Normally, such work was carefully planned in advance but emergencies occasionally upset the routine [34, 35, 36].

Throughout the period 1815 to 1865, the dockyard at Chatham was continually adapting to both minor and major changes in the design of ships as well as to the introduction of new materials and machinery [40]. Design changes included the reshaping and strengthening of warships by the adoption of Robert Seppings's round stern [4]. Following the conclusion of the Napoleonic Wars, most ships under construction and vessels undergoing major repair were provided with this new design feature [11, 373]. It had been Robert Seppings, as a result of his experience while Master Shipwright at Chatham, who had also proposed diagonal framing and the construction of masts in sections and these were further features of vessels under construction at the yard during the immediate post-war period [7].

The transfer to steam and iron produced new challenges. In the 1830s, a number of small paddle steamers were built [56, 64, 65], which included steam packets for the Post Office, such as *Gulnare* [50, 51]. The dockyard, at that time, was not involved in the construction of steam machinery; this was supplied either by Boulton & Watt [56] or Penn & Son [67, 71]. The existence of a large purpose-built government steam yard at Woolwich also resulted in much of the repair work on such machinery being performed away from Chatham. However, some engineering was carried out there. Chatham fitted the engines of some paddle steamers and constructed or modified such parts as boilers and paddle wheels [53, 54, 64, 69]; it also gave trial to such machinery once it was installed [68, 70]. Of greater significance was the conversion to iron shipbuilding. This gave Chatham a new area of specialisation that was not to be challenged by any other yard until later in the century. Already, there had been a steady increase in the use of iron in the hulls and fixings of ships, leading to an increase in the number of millwrights employed at the yard [70]. As a result, Chatham developed a workforce of considerable expertise, prompting the Admiralty to use individual experts beyond the confines of that yard [72]. It was for this reason that Chatham became the first government yard to begin construction of iron battleships with two very dissimilar vessels emerging from the yard. The first to be launched, in September 1862, was *Royal Oak*, a conventional 90-gun warship that had been radically redesigned while in frame, to facilitate the addition of iron cladding [76, 77]. The second was *Achilles*, the first true iron-hulled battleship to be launched in a royal dockyard. Interest in the progress of this second vessel was immense; every detail of her progress was recorded in both the local, national and specialist press [74, 75, 78]. Difficulties encountered when she was floated out of dock in December 1863 [81] may have contributed to later signs of part of her hull having corroded [83]. Prior to the launch of *Achilles*, a second ironclad battleship, *Bellerophon*, was laid down. Similar interest was shown in her progress [79, 80], with newspapers reporting delays arising from difficulties in the supply of materials and the means by which these were overcome [82].

1. Navy Board to Admiralty: ship construction

[TNA, ADM106/2267]   28 June 1815

When ships are set up on the slips exposed to the weather, the Spring has been chosen as the best time for commencing operations in planking, the caulking of the wales and bottom has been deferred until the ships have been about to be launched and the painting (except upon the weather works) has been postponed as long as possible. The precaution of a temporary housing in midships and every other means of keeping the ships dry by caulking the topside weather decks &c have also been resorted to.

To promote a circulation of air for the seasoning of the timber, a great proportion of the treenails has been omitted as long as possible, some strakes of plank left out, wind sails introduced into the hold and louvered boards fitted in the ships' ports. The system of covering over the docks and slips, which has been of late partially introduced, will no doubt effectively contribute to the duration of ships built and repaired by sheltering the frames as well as the converted materials and it will not only add to the comfort of the workmen but will also afford considerable facility in building and repairing ships. The rapid decay, which of late years has taken place in many ships built and repaired in the King's and Merchant Yards, may be attributed to the following causes: the want of a sufficient store of seasoned timber, the scarcity of English oak (a great difficulty which has rendered it necessary to substitute fir timber) and the necessity of fitting newly built and repaired ships for service without allowing sufficient time for seasoning them and also the want of a sufficient number of slips and docks at the dockyards to meet the increased demand for ships of war and to permit the frames &c to stand a sufficient time to season.

Within a few years several important changes have taken place in the mode of constructing ships that we expect will be found not only to give strength to the fabric but prevent premature decay by affording a free circulation of air in the upper parts, but this is not likely to be attended to with the important advantages expected, if care be not taken (when the ships are in commission) to keep the shelf pieces clear and the openings free from dirt, as has been done while they were building.

Having detailed the modes which have been adopted by us for the preservation of HM Ships, we beg to apprise their Lordships that every means in our power have been resorted to, to forward this desirable object, and we trust that by a steady perseverance in these plans and the experience which time will give of their effects, together with the adoption of any further improvements that may occur or be suggested to us, the durability of His Majesty's Ships will be much increased.

2. *Navy Board to Commissioner Barlow: ship surveys*

[NMM, CHA/F/29]   16 May 1816

Rear-Admiral Sir Charles Rawley having represented to us that he has found it necessary, with the concurrence of the Lords Commissioners of the Admiralty, to send to your port some of the revenue vessels, which cannot be conveniently surveyed, &c at Sheerness. We have to desire you will cause a regular survey and report to be made on such of the vessels the Admiral may order to proceed to Chatham, and that you will give directions to the officers of the yard to furnish them with such stores as may be applied for by the Admiral, who has been instructed by the Lords Commissioners of the Admiralty to cause an extra proportion of small stores to be supplied to them, to be lodged in the customs houses of their respective ports of rendezvous, for their future use.

3. *Navy Board to Commissioner Barlow: estimate*

[NMM, CHA/F/29]   24 May 1816

The Commissioners for Transports &c. having informed us that the pipes required by Dr. Douglas to be laid down in the *Argonaut* hospital ship for the conveyance of hot and cold water to the different wards of the hospital would certainly be a convenience, but before they can recommend it being done, they wish it to be ascertained what would be the expense of the work. We desire, with reference to your letter of the 17th inst., that you will cause an estimate to be prepared and transmitted to us for their information.

4. *Navy Board to Commissioner Barlow: ship design*

[NMM, CHA/E/126]   27 June 1816

The Lords Commissioners of the Admiralty having by their Order of the 13th inst. approved of the general adoption of the round stern suggested by Commissioner Seppings in the construction of His Majesty's ships. These are to direct and acquaint you, pursuant to their Lordships' directions, to cause all ships of the line and frigates to be built with round sterns accordingly and also to put round sterns to such as may be repaired provided the repair may be such an extent as to justify the alteration. To enable you to do which, drawings are in preparation and will be sent to you for your guidance.

5.   *Chatham Yard Officers to Navy Board: prices*

[TNA, ADM106/1824]   13 May 1818

Agreeably to the directions contained in your general letter of the 25th July 1816, we herewith transmit sketches for the heads of the *Blanche*, *Brisk*, and *Bustard*, for your Honourable Boards' approbation and directions thereon. The carvers prices for cutting them is as follows – vizt.

Rate	Guns			
5	46	*Blanche*	Standing Figure £20 as per estimate for ships of her class transmitted your Honble Board 9th July 1816.	
			Bust	£6. 0. 0d
Brig	10	*Brisk*	Bust	£3. 0. 0d
Brig	10	*Bustard*	Bust	£3. 0. 0d

6.   *Commissioner Barlow to Navy Board: caulkers*

[TNA, ADM106/1816]   26 November 1818

I have received your letter of the 10th instant, acquainting me that the committee of the board, on the late visitation of the yards, has stated to you, that it is their decided opinion that it will be good economy, and tend much to the general convenience of the service, if two or three caulkers were entered and borne on board the ordinary depot at each port, for the purpose of being employed in performing small jobs on board the ships in ordinary whenever they may be required, in order to prevent the necessity of sending men from the dockyard, who may perhaps take with them more hands than are actually required for work, that they may assist in rowing off the boat; – and desiring that I will consult the Captain Superintending the Ordinary, and let you know upon what terms I can engage caulkers for the service.

In reply, I have to acquaint you that I can engage them on the following terms vizt.

To receive the pay of a caulker of a 3rd Rate, vizt £2.6.0 per month, and to be victualled.

Requesting your further directions hereon.

7. *Navy Board to Chatham Yard Officers: mast construction*

[NMM, CHA/F/32]   21 December 1818

Having had under consideration the plan suggested by Commissioner Seppings for making top masts for ships of the line, by the adoption of which the following advantages will be gained while considerable inconvenience and expense in procuring an article always difficult to be obtained will be obviated.

1stly. Sticks of 9 to 10 feet shorter may be applied for main top masts and from 8 to 9 feet shorter for fore top masts, and by running the butt so much higher [*indecipherable*] will work from ¾ to 1 inch more in the upper quarters where they generally fall off.

2ndly. Sticks that are crooked may, by taking out the scarph from the lower part and cutting off the top, be applied as regular tops.

3rdly. Sticks that are knotting at the upper part, and thereby impracticable for topmasts on the present system may, by the principle in question, be brought in use as topmasts.

4thly. Sticks that taper suddenly at the upper part, in most circumstances, may be made into topmasts by the reduction in length, which this principle admits of.

5thly. It is not unusual therefore for the top mast to give way in the fid holes, shieves &tc, such top masts may again be made serviceable by adopting the principle.

We acquaint you that models will be sent for your guidance for making topmasts upon this principle and, when you have seen them, we direct you to send an account of the sticks in store at your yard, fit to be made into topmasts, on the principle in question.

8. *Navy Board to Commissioner Barlow: ships in ordinary*

[NMM, CHA/F/33]   27 March 1819

The Lords Commissioners of the Admiralty having had under consideration our report upon the state of the Fleet founded upon the recent examination into the condition of the ships and vessels at the several ports, have been pleased, by their order of the 13th instant, to give us instructions to the following effect. These we communicate for your and the officers' information and guidance and we desire that the same be attended to in the most careful and effectual manner. Viz.

In the ensuing Summer and during the Summer months of every succeeding year, an accurate examination is to be made of each individual ship in the state in which she may be lying, by the Commissioners of the several ports, taking to their assistance the Captain of the ordinary, the Master Shipwright of the yard or his assistant, and any other officers of the yard or ordinary who the Commissioner may think proper to call upon.

The Commissioner is to be authorized to open the ships in any small degree when he may think it necessary to his investigation. If he sees or has reason to suspect that the opening must be carried to any considerable or expensive extent, he is to apprise us in order that we may give directions in the matter as shall appear necessary.

The reports of these surveys are to contain the opinion of the Commissioners, and the other officers of the state of each individual ship and the nature of the repair, which she may appear to require, and the length of time she may be expected to last for service at sea with, and without such repair. Also her comparative state, with that in which she was when last surveyed, and generally all such particulars as may tend to bring before their Lordships the most full and accurate view of the condition of the Fleet.

These surveys are to be made at such times during the three Summer months as may suit the convenience and other duties of the Commissioners and officers who are to attend them, so as to enable us to transmit the reports to their Lordships by the 1st of October in each year; and the commissioners are to understand that they will be held deeply responsible for the accuracy of the surveys and reports, and their Lordships cannot doubt that these officers will give their most zealous attention to so very important a subject.

These surveys are not to be considered as in any degree diminishing the responsibility of the yard officers as to the state of the Fleet, nor are they to interfere with any visitation or examination that we or the Surveyor of the Navy may think proper and have been accustomed to make; and if it should happen that either of the Surveyors should be at the port when such examination is in progress, it should be proper that he should assist in it.

For your guidance in making comparative statements next Summer we enclose the reports made by the Surveying Officers last year of the condition of several line of battle ships at your port; and we desire that their suggestions for opening the said ships in order to arrest the progress of dry rot, which has been observed in many of them and which the surveying officers appear to suppose may, in an early stage be checked, if not entirely removed by the admission of atmospheric air, be adopted if not already done.

9. *Navy Board Committee of Visitation: report*

[TNA, ADM106/3233] 30 September 1819

The *Trafalgar* and *Prince Regent* building in this yard were inspected, particularly with regard to the formation of their sterns. Some observations were made with regard to the angles which may be formed in pointing the guns in the after parts in both ships, and the advantages of those in the ship with the round stern were very manifest. The ships appeared in excellent condition and the timbers were seasoned.

It was stated by the Master Shipwright that timber was much wanted in the dockyard, particularly for the line of battleships building, and he was instructed in all cases to give timely notice that supplies may be hastened.

It was noticed that none of the timber which, has been received from the Stratfield Saye Estate, has been found fit to be cut into thick stuff, being too small, but that the timber is good.

10. *Navy Board Committee of Visitation: minute*

[TNA, ADM106/3234] 25 July 1820

The roof over the *Achilles* is in a very incomplete state from the want of nails to fasten the roof and we request that you will give orders for this being hastened.

11. *Commissioner Cunningham to Navy Board: circular sterns*

[TNA, ADM106/1828]   2 March 1824

Agreeably to your letter of the 22nd ultimo I send you on the other side hereof, a list of the ships of the line and frigates which have been built or repaired with circular sterns at this yard; and also those in hand building and repairing with such sterns.

[*Obverse*]

Rate	Guns		
1	120	*Regent*	Built and fitted for sea.
5	46	*Diana*	Building
5	45	*Thames*	Building.
3	78	*Revenge*	Repaired and fitted for sea.
3	74	*Gloucester*	Repaired and fitted for sea.
5	42	*Owen Glendower*	Repaired and refitted for sea.
3	78	*Achilles*	Repaired.
1	120	*Royal George*	Building
2	84	*Formidable*	Building
2	84	*Powerful*	Building
5	46	*Unicorn*	Building
5	46	*Mermaid*	Building
3	74	*Alfred*	Repairing
5	46	*Africaine*	Ordered to be built and
5	46	*Mercury*	the principal part of the timber materials converted for constructing them with circular sterns.

12. *Commissioner Cunningham to Navy Board: docking*

[TNA, ADM106/1829]   27 July 1824

I have to acknowledge receipt of your letter of the 26th instant acquainting me that you have directed the *Minotaur* to be navigated to this yard from Sheerness and that her masts be unstepped and conveyed in her.

Should it be intended to lay them on her deck they must be removed previous to her coming into dock, which can only be done by raising sheers, and it will be attended with equal or even more expense and time than dismantling her in the first instance.

I therefore suggest that the main and mizzen mast may be hung on one side of the ship and the foremast and bowsprit on the other, unless you see no objection to them being towed up.

[Appended note]
Direct the Sheerness officers to cause these masts to be taken out and towed up to Chatham. Acquaint the commissioner at Chatham that we have given these directions and they are to be taken out of the water as soon as they may arrive. J.T[*ucker*].

13. *Commissioner Cunningham to Navy Board: sheer hulk*

[TNA, ADM106/1829]   29 July 1824

I acquaint you the officers report that on examining the bottom of the Chatham sheer hulk in the fourth dock they find the caulking very slack, and in consequence, they are proceeding to take off the whole of the copper which has been on upwards of eleven years.

14. *Commissioner Cunningham to Navy Board: launch*

[TNA, ADM106/1830]   21 February 1825

With reference to your letter of the 19th inst. and signifying that His Majesty's ship *Formidable* will shortly be launched.
    I acquaint you, the shipwright officers report that this ship is not as yet caulked, and there are other works remaining to be performed, before she can be put into the water. I therefore request to be informed whether her completion is to be proceeded with.

[Appended note]
To proceed on getting the ship ready for launching, doing the caulking last thing.

15. *Commissioner Cunningham to Navy Board: ship breaking*

[TNA, ADM106/1831]   2 July 1825

In return to your letter of 8th ultimo I acquaint you that the officers propose taking His Majesty's ship *Glory* carefully to pieces at the rate of eight shillings and six pence per ton, exclusive of the deduction of 20 per cent there from, which sum is to cover all common labour, also the expense of taking off the copper from her bottom.

16. *Commissioner Cunningham to Navy Board: repairs*

[TNA, ADM106/1831]	26 August 1825

It being intended to put the *Mermaid* out of the fourth dock on Tuesday next, and as the *Euryalus*, now fitting for the reception of convicts, has been on shore, carried away part of her false keel; the officers propose, that she may be taken into that dock and the whole of the false keel taken off, which will lessen her draught of water, and enable them to examine and report the condition of the copper put on her bottom by way of experiment. Waiting your instructions.

[*Appended note*]
Approve.

17. *Navy Board to Board of Admiralty: new construction*

[TNA, ADM106/2289]	13 October 1825

The timber in store at Chatham being applicable to the construction of an 18-gun corvette, we request you to acquaint the Lords Commissioners of the Admiralty that we would propose that a vessel of that class be built at that yard accordingly and we send herewith a draft estimating to the Rylandes, but of increased tonnage so as to bring her to the same size as other corvettes.

18. *Commissioner Cunningham to Navy Board: completion*

[TNA, ADM106/1831]	21 December 1825

I acquaint you, that His Majesty's bomb vessel, *Sulphur* building in this yard is nearly completed and it is proposed that she will be finished and launched on the 26th of next month.

19.   *Commissioner of Chatham Dockyard to Navy Board: caulking*

[TNA, ADM106/1832]   16 January 1826

In return to your letter of the 11th inst., desiring me to ascertain the name of the persons who were employed to caulk the parts of the *Spartiate* therein alluded to, and of the superintending officers on the occasion. I enclose for your information the copy of the shipwright officers' report on the subject.

[Appended note]
Two workmen have been discharged. It is not in our power to mark their misconduct on the way they deserve but we think it necessary he should caution the superintending officers now in the yard acquainting them against the reoccurrence of neglect and upon them to express the utmost vigilance in satisfying a so highly important a work as the caulking of H.M. Ships.

20.   *Yard Officers to Commissioner Cunningham: caulking*

[TNA, ADM106/1832]   16 January 1826

In obedience to the Honourable Navy Board's directions of the 11th instant, respecting the leaks in the *Spartiate*'s bottom. We beg leave to acquaint you, that the work complained of was horsed up an additional thread, and in some places two threads of oakum added, during which time the ship was suspended. The work complained of was in the birth of John Lowdall 2nd on the starboard side and on the larboard side in the birth of Abraham Earith. Both these men were discharged at the reduction, which took place on the 8th January 1825 per Navy Board's letters of the 6th January 1825.

Mr Canham was the Foreman who had the superintendence of the works. We have to observe that he was a very steady and correct man, and of good judgment in his profession, and he never if practicable, suffered a seam in the bottom of a ship to be paid until he had examined it. He was superannuated at his request in June last. In addition to the Foreman, who had charge of the work and carpenters in this ship, the caulking was attended by the carpenter of the *Powerful*, Mr. Storey on the starboard side, and the Carpenter of the *Alfred*, Mr Thomas on the larboard side. Both very steady, correct men and of good judgment in their profession. The sub-measurer who measured this work was Mr Thomas Rule.

We are at a loss to account for the deficiency complained of in the seams as the ship was tight in her bottom when she came to this port and was also very tight after undocking, and remained so until she sailed out of port on the 29th August 1823.

21. *Commissioner Cunningham to Navy Board: docking*

[TNA, ADM106/1832]   15 March 1826

In return to your letter of the 20th ult., I acquaint you, the officers report that they have opened His Majesty's ship *Tribune* and surveyed her and find that to put her in condition for three years at sea, it will be necessary to take her into a dock, and give her between a small and middling repair, which could not be provided in less time than seven months after taken in hand.

22. *Commissioner Cunningham to Navy Board: docking of guard ships*

[TNA, ADM106/1832]   27 April 1826

With reference to your letter of the 28th November 1822, signifying the directions of the Lords Commissioners of the Admiralty to cause the guard ships at the several ports to be docked from time to time as opportunities offer, to have their bottoms examined; I beg to acquaint you that the *Prince Regent* guard ship has been afloat three years, and that she cannot be taken into the dock here without having the rigging stripped, her masts taken out and the hold cleared, which would be attended with expense and inconvenience. I therefore suggest she may be navigated to Sheerness for the purpose and where she can be taken into a dock all standing.

[Appended note]
2 May.   This proposal is submitted for the consideration of the Board. Should be done in the Summer after the return of the *Gloucester*. Surveyor.

23. *Commissioner Cunningham to Navy Board: launch*

[TNA, ADM106/1833]   10 July 1826

Desire the Commissioner will inform the Master Attendant that we consider the arrangement and mode of proceeding in bringing up the

Powerful after being launched was injudicious by letting go the heavy anchor in the bows almost immediately after the ship was off the slip and a lighter one abaft at the same time. With respect to letting an anchor abaft, it is the first application of the kind that we ever heard of in launching and it also appears to us that the snapper was made of ropes of too large a size. As it is clear from the state of the ship that she has received considerable injury by the mode practised we think that this method of bringing up a ship so soon after she has left the slip should not again be put in practice.

The usual mode at the other yards is never to let an anchor go until a ship has run into the tideway. Even this is seldom necessary as ships launched before high water naturally tend to run up the river, this with judicious disproportion at the helm frequently renders the letting go an anchor unnecessary as the hawser used in launching usually brings the ship to the place required.

24. *Commissioner Cunningham to Navy Board: grounding of* Prince Regent

[TNA, ADM106/1834]   18 January 1827

In reply to your letter of the 16th respecting His Majesty's ship *Prince Regent* having parted from her moorings in a gale of wind on the 14th inst., I beg to acquaint you for the information of the Lords Commissioners of the Admiralty, that from the best information I can obtain, it appears that both the bittings of the moorings broke at the same time, which the officers of the yard considered was occasioned by the great pressure of the ship upon them in a heavy gust of wind ...

25. *Commissioner Cunningham to Navy Board: corrosion*

[TNA, ADM106/1834]   25 January 1827

The officers having reported to me on inspecting the copper sheathing upon the bottom of His Majesty's ship *Menelaus* they find several of the sheets very much corroded, in consequence of which, and in consideration of it being on nearly eight years, I have authorised the officers to proceed in taking it off, to prevent a delay to the service.

26. *Commissioner Cunningham to Navy Board: copper sheathing*

[TNA, ADM106/1834]   18 May 1827

In obedience to the Honourable Navy Board's general letter of the 7th June 1824 which directs that whenever a ship shall be docked, the copper sheathing of which has been protected agreeable to the suggestion of Sir Humphrey Davy, a very particular report shall be made on the state of the copper sheathing.

We have to acquaint you that upon docking His Majesty's ship *Brazen*, we found that barnacles of an immense size had attached themselves in clusters to the copper sheathing in the vicinity of the protectors. The shore barnacles are so unusually large that we suppose they must have been on the ship when she arrived here in December last. To give a better idea of their appearance, we have prepared a sketch of those about one protector, which we here forth transmit.

After the tide had subsided and the ship's bottom had been scrubbed and washed we proceeded to an examination of the copper sheathing, the greater part of which was put on at Portsmouth in April 1819 – but some of it was shifted in 1824 at that port, when the protectors were fitted, which is in better condition than the rest, yet evidently in a more advanced state of decomposition than copper which we shall hereafter allude to. And we should say from the uniform and actual wear of the copper on the *Brazen*, that its durability has not been prolonged by the application of the protectors – indeed the sheets upon which the protectors were fixed are more decayed than those adjacent, or even those most distant from the protectors.

From the result of this experiment we may venture to offer our opinion that no beneficial effect will occur by following up Sir Humphrey Davy's suggestion to preserve the copper sheathing of ships. In giving this opinion we beg to state that we have not come to a hasty conclusion, but grounded it upon very substantial data, the result of a minute inspection of the copper sheathing on the bottom of His Majesty's ship *Undaunted*. This ship had been afloat in this river nearly nine years, and upon being docked on the 11th instant, we found the whole of the copper sheathing, with the exception of about twenty sheets on different parts of the bottom, to be still good and serviceable, and would have, to all appearances, continued so for many years longer, had it not been thought expedient to strip it off to examine the plank of the bottom and the caulking. The few sheets that were corroded were generally of a bright red colour when the ship was docked, and eaten through: their premature decay could not have been influenced by the situation as the sheets immediately surrounding them remained perfectly good and covered with a fine coating of verdigris.

This is not a solitary incidence of the durability of copper on ships in this river. We have many such on record; and believe that if the copper be good and pure, it will stand the effect of water for years, without injury: but the more saline the water, the more rapidly will it destroy the copper, as was the case with that on the bottom of the *Brazen*, which ship had been employed on the coast of Africa. We have forwarded specimens of the copper herein alluded to by an examination of which it will be perceived that to which the protectors were applied is more foul with marine matter, and more corroded and rough on the surface, though on a seagoing ship, than that which was unprotected and on a ship lying in the harbour.

The protectors were decomposed in a great degree and contained little else than oxide of iron.

27.   *Commissioner Cunningham to Navy Board: ship roofing*

[TNA, ADM106/1835]   13 October 1827

The Master Attendant and the Harbour Pilot having represented to me that the transporting of the *Royal George* to Sheerness with the housing over her would be attended with extreme risk and danger at this season of the year when the days are short and strong and sudden winds prevail.

I suggest the propriety of the materials for the Roof being fitted here but not put up until the ship gets to Sheerness, which was done on the removal of the *Trafalgar*, now the *Camperdown*.

[Appended note]
Desire the Commissioners will state whether this opinion applies only to the stability of the ship after she has on board the large quantity of iron ballast and trunks fitted with water, which is usual when ships are laid up in ordinary but we have no objection to the roof being put up at Sheerness.

28.   *Commissioner Cunningham to Navy Board: docking*

[TNA, ADM106/1835]   1 November 1827

With reference to my letter of the 25th and 30th ultimo, I acquaint you that the officers propose that the *Royal George* be succeeded in the fourth dock by the *Clio* and *Basilisk*; the former for the examination of her bottom in consequence of her having been ashore and carried away her rudder; and the latter to examine the copper sheathing of her bottom and replace it with new if necessary, she being reported to be in a very leaky condition.

29. *Commissioner Cunningham to Navy Board: ship fitting*

[TNA, ADM106/1835]   29 November 1827

The port admiral having requested by his letter of this date that the fore cabin of His Majesty's ship [*Royal George*] may be fitted for a court martial room to prevent the inconvenience which he states to have been experienced at the late courts-martial held on board her, by the crowd pressing upon the members thereof; I beg to be informed whether the cabin in question is to be fitted as requested by the Admiral.

30. *Commissioner Cunningham to Navy Board: quarter galleries*

[TNA, ADM106/1838]   2 January 1829

Adverting to your letters of the 20th and 27th ultimos. to prepare certain models forthwith of the quarter galleries of a line of battleship and a frigate, showing the timbers of that part of the frames as well as the decks, agreeable to the proposals of Vice Admiral Sir H. Blackwood, and in the meanwhile to suspend all works on this part of ships building and repairing.

I request you will inform me whether these works are to be suspended on the following ships building viz. 2nd rate 84 guns *Monarch*, 5th rate 46-guns *Europa*, 5th rate 46-guns *Thalia*, 5th rate 46-guns *Penelope*, *Monarch* and *Europa* in a very forward state of completion, *Thalia* wholly planked, *Penelope* planked in part. As the Vice-Admiral has been on board, he is of opinion from their advanced state of completion, there is no necessity for suspending the said works, to carry into effect the proposal, as it will be attended with a great expense to take down that which is already in place and re-build others upon his plan.

[*Appended* note]
Apply to Admiralty to proceed with plans.

31. *Navy Board Commissioner John Deas Thomson to First Lord:*
specialisation of Yards

[SRO, GD51/2/1017]   25 January 1829

Considering Deptford therefore, as the only depot for the receipt & future
distribution of all manufactured stores, indeed for stores of every
description, not immediately calculated, for the construction and repairs
of ships (which latter are usually delivered at the different building yards,
out of the ships in which they are imported) and that the building
establishment may without inconvenience be removed to Woolwich. If
the fitting of convicts ships and transports be performed by contract, then
Woolwich may be strictly confined to the building and large repair of
ships and the same principle be extended to Chatham, including the
reduction of one of the two civil officers there.

The internal regulation of the civil officers of Deptford, Woolwich and
Chatham, arising out of the alterations now projected, would require
immediate and minute attention. The establishment at Pembroke, to which
Woolwich and Chatham would be thus nearly assimilated would require
no alteration whatsoever.

These three yards are thus placed on nearly the same footing, whereby
the expense of a commissioner and his consequent establishment is saved.
Any necessary reference from Sheerness on contracts and payments being
made to the resident commissioner at Chatham, are made in the same way
as from Woolwich to the Board in town.

The ships built or having undergone large repairs at Woolwich and
Chatham would then drop down to Sheerness, as their port of outfit, in
the same manner as the ships built at Pembroke now go round to
Plymouth, with this essential difference, that those from Woolwich and
Chatham would be fitted with their masts, yards, sails &c which the
establishment at Pembroke does not afford the means of doing.

32. *Commissioner Cunningham to Navy Board: ships' galleries*

[TNA, ADM106/1838]   18 May 1829

In reply to your letter of the 15th inst. inquiring to be informed when the
two models directed by the Hon Navy Board's letter of the 20th December
last, addressed to the resident commissioner, to be prepared according to
vice-admiral Sir H. Blackwood's proposal, will be completed.

I beg to acquaint you, that the model of the frigate is finished and that
the model of the first rate will be completed about the middle of next
month.

I have further to observe that the duplicates are not yet taken in hand, Sir H. Blackwood having directed that the two men sent from Woolwich should proceed with a first rate on the same scale with the rudder outside the counter, which they have commenced conformably to the Honourable Board's verbal commands when asked at the yard that I should 'follow the Admiral's orders respecting the models'.

[*Appended note*]
Acquaint Sir H.B.[1] that the Comptroller and Surveyor have stated that the verbal directions given by them to the Master Shipwright was to re-make such alterations in the two models to be formed under his direction as he might point out and that they did not authorise anything being done contrary to the directions received from the LCA, namely to complete two models only. With respect to the orders arising from the death of Rose the modeller it appears that the Master Shipwright immediately supplied in his place the best man that that yard could furnish; and orders were given to send from Woolwich the man borne as a modeller the moment the Comptroller received Sir HB's private note requesting such assistance. When this person, considered the most perfect in his line, was rejected, the man named by Sir Henry was ordered to proceed to Chatham.

33. *Master Shipwright to Navy Board: ship alterations*

[TNA, ADM106/1838]   23 August 1829

The plan and sketch which accompanied your letter of the 12th instant for our future guidance for fitting the chain plates of the 10 gun brig appropriated for the packet service, it appears that the bulwarks are to be lowered 9 inches. We have forwarded for the inspection of the Honourable Board a sketch showing the bulwark as at present fitted in midships and at the beaks of the round house and foc'sle being agreeable to the directions given by general letter of 30 May 1827 and also the gun whale and new position of the ports in red. And as the works of the top sides of the *Delight* are all completed and caulked and the ring and eye bolts to be driven and also the foc'sle, we deem it proper to ask if it is the intention of the Hon[ble] Board that these alterations be made in this vessel, and if so to what extent forward and aft. Should however, the hon[ble] board decide on not altering the bulwark in this instant, we beg to know if the channels are to be raised to the gunwales as per sketch alluded sent on the 12th instant.

[1]Vice Admiral Sir Henry Blackwood.

34. *Commissioner J.M. Lewis of Sheerness Dockyard to Navy Board: capsizing of convict hulk*

[TNA, ADM106/1839]   16 October 1829

I regret to have to acquaint you for the information of the Board that about one o'clock this morning the *Dolphin* convict ship at this yard owing to her adherence to the mud at low water filled in part from her lower deck scuppers as the tide rose. At the time this was discovered by the Master, she had several feet of water in her. The prisoners were got out immediately in the best manner that circumstance admitted and owing to the prompt and efficient assistance afforded by Commander Gregory, superintending the ordinary here, who was upon the spot with his boats and people in a few minutes after the alarm was given and who attended all night. It is mainly to be attributed that out of the 500 convicts on board, only <u>three</u> were drowned, and that all of the remainder, who all behaved in a very orderly manner, were safely lodged in the *Canada* convict hospital ship. With the assistance of the *Powerful* craft, which are lashed to her, there is every probability of her being righted this tide as it rises.

Colonel Savage, Commandant of the Marines, sent effective detachments to the Corps, as a guard, and to assist, in the event of the prisoners making an attempt to escape, but which I do not find to have been the case.

I enclose for the further information for the Board, a report made to me by the officers of this yard on the subject, having arrived here from Sheerness as soon as possible after I heard of the accident.

PS Having waited at the yard until high water I have to assume that the ship has been raised between four and five feet only but that it is hoped that the efforts that will be made tomorrow will be more successful.

35. *Chatham Yard Officers to Navy Board: capsized convict hulk*

[TNA, ADM106/1839]   16 October 1829

We beg to report that in consequence of the *Dolphin* hulk adhering to the mud in which she was embedded she did not rise with the flowing of the tide last night and a great quantity of water found its way through the holes of the privies on the orlop and upon her righting afterwards she went over upon her larboard side and it was only with very great difficulty that the prisoners were got out from the lower deck, three of whom were drowned. We have further to state that we are making every preparation necessary for righting the hulk this tide.

36.   *Chatham Yard Officers to Navy Board: report on convict hulk*

[TNA, ADM106/1839]   19 October 1829

In obedience to the Controller's directions to this yard on the 17th instant we beg to report that we have minutely examined the *Dolphin* convict ship. She is now perfectly upright and the water all pumped out and the mud all pumped out and we do now discover that she has sustained no injury by falling over, neither are there any leaks perceptible. Under these circumstances, we are of opinion that it will not be necessary to take her into dock.

37.   *Chatham Yard Officers to Navy Board: coppering*

[TNA, ADM106/1839]   6 November 1829

We beg to state that the copper bottom of the *Cumberland* fitting for a convict hulk, has been on nearly sixteen years, and in consequence of which, we have stripped off two strakes at the seat of water and find the caulking quite decayed and slack, and the plank in many places defective and will require shifting.

We therefore suggest the propriety of taking off the whole of the copper, in order to examine and re-caulk the bottom, to make the ship efficient for the number of years she may be probably required for the service she is intended, and to re-copper her bottom with the serviceable sheets, placing Messrs. Abbott's thin felt under the same to keep out the worm.

38.   *Master Shipwright to Navy Board: mode of launching ships*

[TNA, ADM106/1839]   19 November 1829

In reply to your letter of the 5th instant (received during my absence on leave) acquainting me that Mr James Peake, student of naval architecture of this yard, has requested that his plan for the launching of ships, as shown by the enclosures, may be adopted at the launch of the *Thalia*, and desiring me to report whether I see any objection to a compliance with Mr Peake's wishes.

I beg to state for the information of the Commissioners of the Navy, that it is well known that a ship when in the water, and particularly, when light, will alter her form in consequence of the aft and fore part being so much finer than in midships, and more particularly so are the French ships, and the *Thalia*. Under these circumstances, if a ship will alter her form in the water, what must be expected if the after body is not properly supported for the five or six hours she must necessarily stand in that state during the time the blocks are splitting and taking out from under her, prior to moving from the slip into the water. And from practice for several years past, it has been considered advisable to lengthen the bilge ways and substitute additional poppets, by which means, a similar support is given to the ship during the time she sits in the bilgeways, to that she receives when resting on the blocks in the dock. This has proved of very essential benefit by the ships going so much more easily off the slips into the water, than they formerly did with the short bilge ways and the after body so slightly supported.

From the foregoing observation produced by practical knowledge in the very great number of ships and vessels that I have launched and that without any accident (like those of several ships and vessels that have had bilge ways fitted and hove up on the slips for repair) and having now the same materials to transfer to the *Thalia*, with which the *Penelope* was launched a short time since, and several other frigates before her.

I therefore do not consider it would be to the advantage of his Majesty's service, or any credit, to deviate from that mode of launching ships, which has hitherto been found perfectly safe and satisfactory, by adopting the mode proposed by Mr Peake, which to say the least, can only be attended with great risk and danger, without any adequate advantage to be derived thereby.

[Appended note]
24 November 1829. The material being already provided on the plan we would recommend that they be applied to launch the *Thalia* but we cannot agree with Mr. Parkin that a ship sustained by the system recommended by Mr Peake cannot be properly secured forward and aft. Should there be any fear, as expressed by Mr Peake a perpendicular shore aft will remedy the danger. The plan is intended to be applied only to frigates and small vessels. RS [*Robert Seppings*]

39.   *Commissioner Cunningham to Navy Board: ship dimensions*

[TNA, ADM106/1839]   27 November 1829

In pursuance of the Honourable Navy Board's directions of the 4th January 1812 and the 12th March 1824, I beg to report as follows the dimensions, draft of water &c of His Majesty's Packet *Delight*, launched this day from the Mast House Slip viz.

Nature of the Ship	feet and inches
Length in the deck	90ft 2in
Keel for tonnage	72ft 6in
Breadth extreme from outside	24ft 9in
for tonnage	24ft 7in
moulded	24ft 1in
Depth in Hold	11ft 0in
Burthen in tons	233⁸/₉₄
False Keel	8in
Draft of water bilgeways	8ft 0in
abaft	10ft 2in

40. *Navy Board Secretary to Chatham Yard Officers: power capstans*

[NMM, CHA/H/1]   29 March 1830

I have the command of the Commissioners of the Navy to acquaint you that their Lords Commissioners of the Admiralty have directed that all power capstans for His Majesty's Ships be constructed on Captain Phillips' recently improved plan, but the great number of ships of all classes, which appear to be already supplied with power capstans, induce their Lordships to suspend their former orders to supply them to all ships building or requiring a large repair &c.

In the event however of a ship having the old plain capstan being commissioned and of the captain wishing to have a power capstan – their Lordships direct that it may be allowed by exchanging it with the power capstans of some ship of the same class in ordinary, providing the application be made in time to prevent any delay in the fitting of the ship.

41. *Chatham Yard Officers to Navy Board: embezzlement of copper bolts*

[TNA, ADM106/1840]   19 October 1830

In obedience to the directions of the Navy Board contained in your letter of the 22nd and 31st of last month (taking to our assistance the agent to the solicitor of the Admiralty and Navy) we proceeded to examine the several persons charged with having had any share, either directly or indirectly, in the embezzlement of copper &tc which have been going on in this yard, as well as to investigate all the circumstances connected therewith: taking for our government for the more effectually executing the Board's commands, the several instructions in your letter of the 22nd of last month.

We have completed the examination of the several persons charged with participation either directly or indirectly as well as many witnesses competent to furnish information, or elucidate doubts and have proceeded with a careful examination by the shipwright officers of the fastenings of the ships building or under repair. On the 3rd instant the Comptroller of His Majesty's Navy arrived and proceeded immediately to a full investigation of all of the matters connected with the subject of the Board's several orders to us. And to the Comptroller we delivered by his direction a list of the persons charged with having had any share, either directly or indirectly, in the embezzlement referred to, with our opinion of their respective guilt or innocence.

On the 6th the Comptroller, having finished his investigation, we were informed by him that nothing remained for the officers to do but to proceed with an examination of the fastenings, which has been done. The result of a comparative statement of the numbers drawn out of the store, with the numbers driven on such of the various works as could be got at for counting, we transmit herewith for the Board's information, noticing there is too much reason to believe that the excess drawn from the store beyond the numbers driven, have been embezzled.

From a careful examination of the fastenings of the ship that is building or under repair, the shipwright officers have ascertained the number of bolts that have been driven and they have not detected any false workmanship by the driving of what are called 'Devil Bolts'.

Annexed to the account of bolts counted in the works of these ships we have placed the name of the foreman, or other person who counted them, no one of whom was employed on the works he examined.

Anterior to the month of October last, the notes for the issue of copper did not express the particular services for which the bolts were collectively drawn. We are, therefore, on that account, incapable of complying with that part of the Board's command that directs us to report whether the articles drawn were of the exact sort and quantity requisite to the purpose of the works upon which the person drawing them was employed.

42.   *Chatham Yard Officers to Navy Board: fitting of hospital ship*

[TNA, ADM106/1841]   28 May 1831

In reply to the directions contained in your letter of yesterdays date, we beg to report that there is a considerable quantity of bulkheads and

materials of that kind here suitable for the interior fitting of the
Dreadnought as a hospital ship, which we deem worthwhile sending to
Woolwich.

43.   *Chatham Yard Officers to Navy Board: docking*

[TNA, ADM106/1841]   8 June 1831

In obedience to the directions contained in your letter of 3rd inst., we beg
to report that we were induced to recommend that the *Namur* receiving
hulk be taken into dock, in consequence of her very leaky state and
apparently defective condition, she being nearly thirty years older than
either the *Sirius* or *Terpsichore*, which ships proved in so bad a state when
taken to pieces as to excite our astonishment that they had not sunken at
their moorings.

44.   *Admiralty to Superintendent Gordon: preservation of ships in*
ordinary

[TNA, ADM222/1]   20 September 1832

It appears to be the opinion of many dock yard officers and also of those
naval officers entrusted with the care of the ordinary, that the deterioration
of His Majesty's Ships is much hastened by the practice at present adopted
of endeavouring to keep the internal parts of the hold dry, and being
myself persuaded that the decay instanced in the *Belle Ile* and *Bellona* at
Plymouth arises principally from this cause. I am induced, after much
consideration, to believe that the contrary course would prove a salutary
measure for the preservation of ships when laid up.

   I therefore propose that if their Lordships, upon due consideration of
a subject so important, concur in this opinion, that the Superintendents at
the several yards be directed to cause a sufficient quantity of water to be
admitted into every ship laid up in ordinary as will keep the interior
saturated with moisture as high as the original floor heads amidships on
as many ships as their Lordships may think fit to try this experiment
upon.

[Appended note]
Sir James Gordon to make a minute enquiry and ascertain whether the
Minotaur and *Defence* are among the ships whose holds are saturated
or considered to be perfectly dry and whether either of them have their
lower tier of trucks in. If they should have their trucks in, he is to report

what ships in ordinary are perfectly dry and which have not their trucks.

45.   *Surveyor General's Minute: employment of model maker*

[TNA, ADM222/1]   25 September 1832

Recommended that Richard Banniwell, shipwright in Chatham Yard, be employed in the Model Room at Somerset House during the absence of Elwell now about to proceed to Italy on duty connected with timber.

46.   *Surveyor General's Minute: roofing of ships in ordinary*

[TNA, ADM222/1]   27 October 1832

Recommended that the Superintendents of the several dockyards be acquainted that it is their Lordships intention that ships laid up in ordinary in future are not to have roofs placed over them except in the waist and the drawings of the sections of the roof are now preparing for the officers' guidance.

47.   *Surveyor General's Minute: ship model*

[TNA, ADM222/1]   30 October 1832

Recommended that Captain Superintendent Sir James Gordon at Chatham be directed to cause the model of the *Sovereign of the Seas*, which was being made by William Bournvill, to be forwarded to Somerset House for completion and that it be carefully packed during his leisure hours for conveyance.

48.   *Acting Superintendent King to Board of Admiralty: an undocking problem*

[TNA, ADM1/3392]   5 May 1833

I beg leave to report to you for the information of My Lords Commissioners of the Admiralty that the *Howe* was put out of dock yesterday. On this occasion I directed that 200 casks should be secured under her bottom (in case of a slack tide that would have prevented her going out of dock). In consequence of the cables that were passed round her, well under her bilge stretching the casks on each side slipped up to the waters edge, when the after part of the ship was at the narrowest part of the dock, so that it was necessary to stave in a number of the casks, by cutting the rest adrift from the swifters.[1] She was released, but not before 20 or 30 sheets of copper had been rubbed off. The ship however sustained no injury beyond this.

49.   *Admiralty to Superintendent Gordon: protection of ships' decks*

[NMM, CHA/H/6]   6 May 1833

I am commanded by My Lords Commissioners of the Admiralty to signify their directions to you to cause the weather decks of all ships not housed over to be paid with a composition made of the following ingredients: Stockholm tar with tallow, mixed in equal proportions and to be laid on as soon as possible when the decks are perfectly dry.

50.   *Admiralty to Superintendent Gordon: construction of Post Office packet*

[NMM, CHA/H/6]   30 May 1833

I am commanded by My Lords Commissioners of the Admiralty to signify their directions to you to cause a Steam Packet for the use of the Post Office to be laid down in Chatham Yard according to the drawings and dimensions which were sent to you yesterday. She is to be built under the immediate superintendence of Mr Spillar, the foreman, and every exertion is to be used to complete her in three months without employing the workmen beyond the present working hours of the yard and no more than five days in the week. A very accurate account is to be kept of the whole expense.

51.   *Admiralty to Superintendent Gordon: naming of Post Office packet*

[NMM, CHA/H/6]   12 June 1833

I am commanded by My Lords Commissioners of the Admiralty to acquaint you that the Post Master General has named the steam packet building at Chatham for the Holyhead station the *Gulnare*.

---

[1]Lengths of rope that completely encircled the ship.

52.   *Superintendent Gordon to Admiralty: launching*

[TNA, ADM1/3393]   18 June 1833

I beg leave to report to you, for the information of the Lords Commissioners of the Admiralty, that His Majesty's Ship *Waterloo* has been launched from the first slip in this yard this day.

53.   *Superintendent Gordon to Admiralty: prices*

[TNA, ADM1/3393]   22 June 1833

The officers of this yard having addressed to me the enclosed letter proposing a price for fitting paddles to steam vessels, and which they suggest may be allowed to the workmen of this yard, who have been thus employed on the *Dee*; I beg leave to submit the same for the consideration for my Lords Commissioners of the Admiralty, and venture to suggest that as many steam vessels have been fitted out at Woolwich, the officers of that yard may be called upon to state the rates they have allowed for the workers of this description.

[*Enclosure of 21 June 1833 signed by W. Hone Willis and William Morphin*]
Having fitted the *Dee* steam vessel with paddles, for which we have not any price in the Scheme of Task and Job, we propose 7d per foot superficial to make and complete such work and that the people employed on the *Dee* be paid for the work done at that rate.

54.   *Superintendent Samuel Warren of Woolwich Dockyard to Admiralty: observations on a proposal*

[TNA, ADM1/3393]   25 June 1833

With reference to your directions of yesterday's date to report upon the enclosed letter from Captain Superintendent Sir James Gordon submitting a proposition for paying the workmen of Chatham yard 7d per foot for making and completing paddle boards to steam vessels.

I beg leave to enclose for the information of the Rt. Hon My Lord Commissioners of the Admiralty a letter from the officers stating that at this yard the workmen have been allowed 3½d per foot for making the board but that they have been fitted by day work.

55.   *Yard Officers to Superintendent Gordon: new mould loft floor*

[TNA, ADM1/3396]   12 September 1833

We beg to submit that the mould loft floor be now laid, as the store will furnish us with suitable materials and not having a ship now laid on nor at present the prospect of one, before the work can be completed, its present state being such as to render it quite necessary. – Following is an estimate of the expense of the same:

Materials	£379	14s	9d
Workmanship	£ 92	5s	0d
Casuals	£ 20	0s	0d
Total	£491	19s	9d

[*Appended notes*]
For the Board's decision. Understand from Captain Symons there was a floor at Chatham ready for laying, it not being wanted it was to be sent to Pembroke.

Cannot recommend that the mould loft floor at Chatham be removed at present but the new flooring ordered to be prepared is to be laid by to season.

56.   *Admiralty Minute: new ship construction*

[TNA, ADM222/3]   2 October 1833

Recommended that Captain Superintendent Sir James A. Gordon at Chatham be directed to make preparations for building a steam vessel to be named the 'Blazer' on the same slip from which the *Gulnare* has been launched. That he be acquainted that she is to be built under the superintendence of Mr Spiller keeping an exact account of her expense [*sic*] and that she is to be built in three months if possible.

Drawings will be forwarded immediately and also that Messr Boulton & Watt be directed to provide engines and boilers similar to those for the *Tartarus* with the cylinders placed before the shafts.

57. *Admiralty Minute: new ship construction*

[TNA, ADM222/3]   7 October 1833

Recommended that Captain Superintendent Sir James A. Gordon at Chatham be informed that the *Goliath* of 80 guns, *Cumberland* of 70 guns and the *Active* of 36 guns, are to be built in the yard, and the drawings for them are in progress. In the meantime, he is to direct the officers to lay aside timber of proper sidings for them.

58. *Surveyor General's Minute: lax workmanship*

[TNA, ADM222/4]   22 January 1834

Observing by the progress received this morning from Chatham that the period for completing the *Hastings* is again delayed another month; notwithstanding she was reported ready for sea May last, and the employment of the following numbers of men on her since she was ordered to be prepared for service by the Lordships on the 9th ultimo.

First week ending the 14th December 1833   13 Shipwrights, 1 Caulker
Second week ending 21st December 1833   6 Shipwrights, 9 Caulkers
Third week ending 28th December 1833   41 Shipwrights,
                                              5 Caulkers
Fourth week ending 4th January 1834   87 Shipwrights,
                                             14 Caulkers, 6 Joiners,
                                             18 Smiths, 2 Sawyers
Fifth week ending 11th January 1834   90 Shipwrights,
                                             17 Caulkers, 14 Joiners,
                                             23 Smiths, 2 Sawyers
Sixth week ending 18 January 1834   127 Shipwrights,
                                              8 Caulkers, 24 Joiners,
                                             18 Smiths, 2 Sawyers

or 2,730 men for one day.

Independent of the men employed on her capstans &c and those for the rigging &c and sails I cannot refrain from detailing these circumstances and enclosing for their Lordships further information of the enquiries that I thought it necessary to institute on the receipt of the Progresses on the 2nd and 8th instance with the officers' answers thereto and to call the serious attention of their Lordships to the great laxity which appears to prevail in the shipwrights department of the yard in carrying their Lordships orders into effect.

59.   Description of Launch

[The Saturday Magazine]   8 February 1834

It may be uninteresting to premise, that when a ship is laid down or built, she is supported by a strong platform of oak, resting on a stone foundation, which are laid with progressive inclination to the water, on the opposite side of her keel to which they are parallel. On the surface of this slope or declivity are placed two corresponding range of planks, which form the base of a frame, termed a *cradle*, whose upper part lies next to the bottom of the ship, to which it is securely attached. Thus, the lower surface of the cradle, conforming exactly to that of the frame below, lies flat upon it lengthways, under the opposite side of the ship's bottom; and, as the former is intended to slide downwards upon the latter, carrying the ship along with it, the planes or surface of both are well greased with tallow and soap.

The necessary preparation for the launch having been made, all the blocks and wedges by which the ship was previously supported are driven out from below the keel, except perhaps five or six, which are left at the upper end of the slip; when her weight then gradually subsides on the platforms, which are accordingly called the *ways*. Formerly, the blocks and wedges were all driven out, and the ship was then held alone by stout oak bars, shod with irons called 'dog-shores', till the proper time for launching (when the cradle is entirely free to move along the sliding planks); but accidents have sometimes occurred, a few blocks are now left, as previously stated, to check the vessel on her course downwards. The last operation is to let the dog-shores fall; the ship then hangs for a few seconds, in consequence of the pressure of the remaining blocks, and, if after a short time she does not move, the workmen, who are all ready, strike at these blocks, which the weight of the ship instantly oversets, and she glides downwards into the water along the sliding ways, which are generally prolonged under its surface to a sufficient depth, to float her as soon as she reaches their furthest extremity.

One of the finest launches ever witnessed at Chatham was that of the *WATERLOO*, a first rate of 120 guns, which appropriately took place on the last anniversary of the glorious triumph of British arms. On that occasion, the scene in the vicinity of the dockyard, and on the broad and glistening surface of the Medway, was splendid and imposing. Every spot which could command a view of the launch, was densely covered with masses of human beings; and the river, which was crowded with yachts, steamers from the metropolis, and boats of almost every class, decked with flags and colours, seemed absolutely 'instinct with life'. As the moment drew nigh, the eyes of the vast congregation of spectators became riveted on the stern of *Waterloo*, which was the only part not concealed by the lofty-roof of the building slip. A slight agitation seemed at last to move the people; the interest deepened, and the silence became profound and breathless: then the heavy discharge of a single gun boomed impressively on the ear – a deafening shout burst from the multitude – the huge structure moved! The 'shores' or bars which held it, had been removed, the ceremony of naming was performed with the accustomed formalities, and the magnificent *Waterloo*, as depicted in our engraving, glided majestically into her home on the world of waters, amidst the roaring of artillery, a perfect model of symmetry and strength. And then the sympathies of the spectators were differently affected. The swell produced by the sudden plunging of so vast a body into the water, was necessarily considerable; and as the noble ship swung round with her formidable broadside, several boats were swamped, and human lives perilled. The shouting of the multitude was again hushed, but the excitement, though painful, was only transitory; in a few minutes, the gigantic vessel was securely moored alongside the *Southampton* frigate, lying in ordinary, without the occurrence of a single serious accident.

60.   *Admiralty to Superintendent Gordon: use of spike iron*

[NMM, CHA/H/10]   19 May 1834

The Lords Commissioners of the Admiralty having had their attention called to the alarming and destructive use to which the spike iron has been used by the caulkers to whom they attribute a want of proper attention in its application, I am commanded by their Lordships to signify their direction to you to cause the present general use of this instrument to be discontinued in the top sides, wales, waterways and decks, except under the express sanction of the Master Shipwright or his Assistant, who with the Foreman on the survey or inspection of the ship, should alone give direction when the spike iron should be used, and the inspector is to be held responsible for the least deviation from the orders which he may receive.

   Their Lordships desire you will impress strongly on the minds of the shipwright officers the very great importance of this duty which their Lordships hope will prevent the necessity of continuing into extensive repairs, and their injunctions are to be strictly observed in respect to the ships now bringing forward, particularly the *Barham*.

61. *Surveyor General to Board of Admiralty: poor workmanship*

[TNA, ADM222/6]   11 February 1835

Algerine. After being completely fitted out at Chatham in August 1834. On her arrival at Plymouth it was found necessary to caulk the upper deck.

Buffalo, timber ship. Fitted completely at Chatham for bringing home New Zealand spars also for carrying female convicts to New South Wales. On the ship's arrival at Woolwich to take the convicts on board the decks were found so defective and leaky that it was necessary to cover them with felt and to be dubbed with 2 inch fir deal. The expense of doing this was £312. Their Lordships were pleased to institute an inquiry as to whose neglect the defective workmanship was occasioned.

Winchester, Chatham for survey, 5 July 1833, reported she would require two-thirds of a very small repair at an estimated expense of materials £2913; workmanship £811 being at the rate of ten weeks at about 80 men. Upon the survey the ship was ordered to be prepared on the 10th July. In consequence of the *Winchester* having been completely refitted and re-coppered at Portsmouth in 1831 it was fully considered that the above survey was correct and that very little was required to be done to her apart from refit for re-commission. She was therefore taken into dock for this purpose in September 1833 but owing to the men being otherwise engaged she could not be taken in hand before May 1834 and their Lordships relying on the representation of the said survey were pleased to put her into commission on the 7th June when it was actually found necessary to employ the following numbers of men to complete her independent of those on her masts, yards, sails and stores.

But then being 18 weeks averaging 208 men each week instead of 10 weeks averaging 80 men each week thereby proving a want of great professional judgment in the shipwright officers who stated that in their opinion the defects might be made good at an expense of £811 for workmanship whereas it appears by the actual result of the number of men employed that at least £3800 has been expended on workmanship above.

Thalia. Launched on the 12th January 1830 and ordered to be brought forward in consequence of the Superintendent's letter of 21st February stating that she could be got ready immediately. Taken into dock 26th February. Undocked 23rd May. The following numbers of men were actually employed to fit her: 20677 being 32 weeks at an average of 65 man-days.

Hastings. Was taken into dock in February 1833 for the purpose of being fitted for service at sea. Undocked 3rd and reported 7 May 1833 completely ready so far as the housing would admit. Upon the faith of the above report their Lordships on the 9th December 1833 desired that she should forthwith be prepared for commission which the officers stated the following day would be ready to receive men in fourteen days but upon progress it took the following time a number of men to complete her being 12 weeks averaging 140 men per week. Observing during this period that the officers were entered into various very extensive repairs and alterations after the ship had been represented to be quite ready. I called upon the Superintendent on the 2nd and 8th of January for an explanation of the subject which being anything but satisfactory I considered it my duty to enclose the whole of the correspondence for the information of their Lordships and at the same time calling upon serious attention to the very great laxity which appears to prevail in the shipwrights' department at that yard in carrying their Lordships orders in effect.

62.   *Superintendent Clavell to Admiralty: employment of shipwrights*

[TNA, ADM1/3411]   24 May 1838

An account showing the number of shipwrights required to build a ship in one year (313 days) of the same size as each of those named, complete for a state of ordinary.

No. of guns	Name of ship	No. of men
120	*Waterloo*	167
92	*London*	144.5
80	*Goliath*	136
84	*Monarch*	138
70	*Cumberland*	126
74	*Hercules*	111
46	*Eurotos*	64
36	*Castor*	66
36	*Active*	71
28	*Rainbow*	35
18	*Scout*	32

16	*Wanderer*	29
6	*Lapwing*	15.5
	Phoenix	42.5
	Blazer	37

63. *Admiralty to Superintendent Clavell: icing of river*

[NMM, CHA/H/38]   9 February 1841

I have received and laid before my Lord Commissioners of the Admiralty your letter of the 8th Inst reporting that in consequence of the quantity of ice in the river, it has been found impracticable to undock either the *London, Formidable* or *Ardent*.

64. *Admiralty to Superintendent Clavell: boiler linings*

[NMM, CHA/H/39]   5 April 1841

I am commanded by my Lord Commissioners of the Admiralty to acquaint you that the following quantity of materials will be required for lining the boilers of the *Growler* & I am to desire that you will cause the same to be provided at the saw mills forthwith for seasoning.

vizt fir	Thick (inches)	Wide (inches)	Length (feet)
	2	6	23
	"	7	12
	"	9	14
	"	"	17
	"	"	25
	"	10	17
	"	"	29

65. *Admiralty to Superintendent Clavell: frames for paddle steamers*

[NMM, CHA/H/39]   6 April 1841

The Captain Superintendent at Chatham is informed for the officers guidance that the frames of the *Bulldog* and *Virago* steam vessels are to be provided similar to the *Growler*; but to suspend converting the top timbers to be placed near the sponsons and paddle boxes, until their Lordships have decided on the engines with which they are to be fitted.

66. *Admiralty to Superintendent Clavell: ship breaking*

[NMM, CHA/H/39]   12 April 1841

Having laid before my Lord Commissioners of the Admiralty your letter of the 1st instant – I am commanded by their Lordships to signify their direction to you to cause *Redoubtable* to be taken to pieces by task work at unlimited hours and earnings, allowing the workmen the sum of 6/6d per ton for the same as therein proposed.

67. *Admiralty to Superintendent Clavell: engine gear*

[NMM, CHA/H/39]   13 April 1841

With reference to the officers report of the 12th instant I have to request you will cause the steam engine gear required, to be received from Messrs. Penn & Son for which they will be paid the price mentioned in their letter of the 9th instant viz. £9..18..0d.

68. *Superintendent Richards to Steam Department: trial of machinery*

[TNA, ADM85/7]   26 January 1851

Trial of *Horatio*. Chatham Yard, 26th January 1851. In obedience to your memo of the 24th inst. desiring me to take charge of the *Horatio* for the purpose of carrying their Lordships orders for a further trial of the machinery of the vessel I have the honour to report that at 3pm on the 24th inst. we left this port in the *Horatio*, she drawing 19ft 1in aft and 17ft 2in forward, and anchored in Salt Pan Reach at 5.30 in twelve fathoms of water. The next morning, at 7.30, we weighed and proceeded to the Nore light vessel where we commenced the first trial, proceeding to the Mouse light vessel, making 25 revolutions, with the tide in favour, at the rate of 3 miles per hour, with 23 revolutions at the rate of 4, 5 and 6 per hour with 32 revolutions 6 and 4. The distance run between these stations being seven and three quarters of a mile, which was accomplished in 55 minutes, but no steam blowing off. The Mouse to the Nore with the tide against, in 1 hour and 18 minutes making 34, 35 and 28 revolutions, but no steam blowing off.

Second trial: from the Nore to the Mouse with slack tide in favour, in 45 minutes, with an average of 40 revolutions, the steam blowing off at starting.

From the Mouse to the Nore slack tide against, in 55 minutes and 10 seconds.

Third trial: from the Nore to the Mouse with flood tide against, in 58 minutes and 40 seconds, making from 36 to 39 revolutions, working expensively.

From the Mouse to the Nore with flood tide in favour in 49 minutes and 30 seconds, averaging 38 revolutions with no steam blowing off. I beg to observe that steam was got up to blowing off before starting from the stations on the second and third trials but never kept up through the whole distance. We returned to this port at 6pm last evening, leaving *Horatio* at her moorings in Chatham Reach. Thomas Lain, Master Attendant.

Trial of *Horatio*, Chatham Yard, 23 January 1851. No. 14. Sir, I have the honour to report that in compliance with their Lordships directions 25th September last for the trial of the *Horatio* for the purpose of testing her machinery;– that ship, in charge of the Master Attendant, left Chatham yesterday at 1pm and returned again to her moorings again at half past five.

I regret to state that the trial does not appear to have been satisfactory, as shown in the enclosed reports from the Master Attendant, and Chief Engineer of the yard, who accompanied him, as did also Mr. Hughes from Somerset House and Mr. Seward. I have directed the *Horatio* to be held in readiness for further trial, at the earliest day, should their lordships be pleased to order.

[*Enclosure 1. Letter No.14. Trial of* Horatio. *Report of Alex Lawrie, Chief Engineer, Chatham Yard, 23 January 1851*]
I beg to report that we left the moorings at 1.10 p.m. drawing 17ft forward and 18ft.11in. aft and proceeded down the River against a flood tide on trial making 33 revolutions, speed of 7 knots; with 30 revolutions 6; with 27 revolutions 6; with 23 revolutions 4. I further beg to state that we were one hour and 50 minutes from abreast of Upnor Castle, to abreast of the Garrison Point at Sheerness. Distance about eleven miles.

During this trial we were at most times short of steam. With respect to her helm she answers well.

[*Enclosure 2. Letter No. 15. Report of Alex Lawrie. Chatham Yard, 23 November 1851*]
I have the honour to report that on the trial of H.M.S. *Horatio* yesterday difficulty was experienced in keeping up the steam and on this account as well as the frequent pruning of the boilers only 33 revolutions were obtained out of the engines, the screw shaft not having attained the ordinary velocity. I am not yet able to state whether the alterations made

by Messrs Seward & Co. will have the affect of preventing the heating of the main shaft.

69. *Yard Officers to Superintendent Richards: machinery alterations*

[TNA PRO ADM85/7] 10 February 1852

Referring to your minute of 27th ult., respecting the ventilation of the after stoke hold of the *Barracouta* on which Mr Dinner was to communicate. We beg to state that we are now removing the after bulk head, in accordance with the drawings sent on the 17th of that month; but we are uncertain whether this comprises all that is to be done. If not, we require further information.

70. *Yard Officers to Superintendent Richards: millwrights*

[TNA, ADM85/7] 10 February 1852

In reference to your minute of the 23rd instant, respecting the proportion of smiths, joiners &c to the number of shipwrights; we beg to say that having for several years past felt extreme inconvenience from the restricted number of smiths, we are desirous of a considerable increase in this branch of workmen, from the former proportion of 1 to 4½ to that of 1 to 3½.

The immense increase of ironwork by the introduction of steam ships and the use of iron in the hull and fittings of all classes of vessels – and this, not only in quantity, but also of much more elaborate workmanship – the greatly increased demand for sea stores – such as iron bound blocks &c and, in this yard, the average employment of 4 or 5 smiths on the works pertaining to the Chief Engineer – are reasons for the increased proportions we have recommended.

With respect to joiners – the old proportion of 1 to 6 shipwrights (or 75 men) exclusive of the man employed superintending the planing machine, will we think suffice, having now the advantage of the mortising and tenoning machines lately introduced.

In the Chief Engineer's department the increase of millwrights should be from 1 to 17 to 1 to 13 and of plumbers and braziers from 2 to 89 to 2 to 75. It is proposed to include 2 brass fitters and 2 metal turners, in the increase of millwrights and as the increased demand for manufactured lead, in addition to the ordinary increase of labour, employs more labourers than formerly, it would be very advantageous were six ordinary labourers added to the present establishment of labourers at the millwrights' shop.

71. *Fitting Out of Frigate*

[*Illustrated London News*]   25 February 1854

The fitting out of this truly noble ship for the war in the East, as depicted on the preceding page, presents an air of order, precision, and regularity, intermingled with bustling excitement, which is very striking; and, echoing as are our Dockyards with, 'the busy note of preparation,' neither of them supplies a more interesting illustration than that which we have selected.

The *Euryalus*, Capt. Ramsay, is a 51-gun screw frigate, of 400 horse power. Her extreme beam is 50 feet; extreme length, 245 feet; between perpendiculars, 212 feet; tonnage, 2356 feet.

On the 17th ult. she had her steam up, and worked her trunk engines, by John Penn and Son, for two hours, at moorings, in the Medway. At one o'clock next day, she left Chatham, for the purpose of being tried at the measured distance between Nore and Mouse Lights, when her speed was ascertained as ten knots per hour; the engines working admirably, and making from 58 to 61 revolutions per minute. She anchored about five o'clock, pm, at Sheerness; and next morning proceeded under steam to Chatham, for the purpose of being made completely ready for sea at the port where she was fitted, and had her engines put on board.

In the accompanying picture the guns are on board; but carpenters, shipwrights, sailors, &c, are busy – some placing fire-buckets, cutlasses, shot, &c, in their proper positions near the guns; others stowing away the sails; whilst others are employed at the rigging; and at the moment we write, the engineers are hard at work, as are also dockyard artificers.

The *Euryalus* is now lying in dock bending her sails, and hoisting her boats in. She will come out of Dock on Tuesday next, and proceed to Gillingham to take her powder in; and she will be in the Downs to form one of the Baltic squadron on or before the 6th March.

72. *Isaac Cockell to Master Shipwright: request to be made overseer*

[TNA, ADM89/1]   9 January 1856

As contracts are being issued for the building of iron vessels, I beg respectfully to offer myself as a candidate for the position of overseer for such vessels, and having been engaged at iron ship building for 2 years previous to my entry in the dockyard in 1843, have thought it would not be presuming too much, to suppose that I understood the nature of that work as well as most men engaged in a dockyard.

And also beg leave to state that during the 13 years that I have been in the service, 4 years were passed at the ship's side, and 9 years as draftsmen and modeller, in which time I have produced the under mentioned models: *Tiger, Nankin, Hood, Orion* & *Euryalus* and have also passed an examination for an Inspector, in all of which I have endeavoured to deserve your approbation.

I therefore humbly solicit your kind patronage with a view to obtain the above named position or any other promotion you may think me deserving.

73. *Admiralty to Superintendent Goldsmith: drawings*

[NMM, CHA/H/40]   10 November 1860

The Captain Superintendent at Chatham is informed that the sheer drawings and mid ship section of the iron frigate to be built at that yard will be forwarded today for the officer's guidance.

74. *Progress on* Achilles

[*Chatham News and North Kent Spectator*]   1 February 1862

The building of the *Achilles*, 50, 6,079 tons, 1,250-horse power, is rapidly progressing in No.2 dock in Chatham Yard, although considerable delay has been occasioned by the difficulty, which is still experienced, of obtaining an adequate supply of iron of the quality expected. The description of iron now most urgently needed for the carrying on of the work in hand are the longitudinal plates, and of these, the greater portion which have up to the present time been received from the different contractors, has been rejected, having failed under the severe tests which are applied immediately the iron is received at the yard, in order to ascertain the quality of the metal. The strain which the iron supplied for the building of this vessel is expected to bear is 19 tons across the grain and 22 tons with it, in addition to which it is taken to the smithery, where it is subjected to different trials, – such as bending both in a cold state and under the influence of heat, punching, and in other ways, which render it almost impossible for metal which is not of the very best, both as to the material and manufacture, to find its way into the ship. Practical men, however, say that the tests which are applied, although tending to ensure the rejection of any iron but that of the best quality, are strictly fair towards the contractors, as they are not greater than good metal may be reasonably be expected to bear, and the price paid by Government is in advance of the market value of the article. A good proportion of the iron ribs of the *Achilles* have now been raised into position, but had it not been for the difficulty above alluded to, it is probable that at the present time there would have been four times the number of hands employed upon her, and that her framing would have been nearly or perhaps quite completed.

75. *Progress in the construction of* Achilles

[*Illustrated London News*]   26 April 1862

The construction of this gigantic iron frigate, under the superintendence of Mr. O.W. Laing, the Master Shipwright of Chatham Dockyard, is proceeding with the greatest rapidity towards completion: the vessel is nearly in frame, and the progress day by day is something wonderful. The *Royal Oak* wooden frigate of 51 guns is now ready for plating; and the forward state of everything in connection with the new fleet at this establishment reflects the highest credit on all the officials connected with it. The stem of the *Achilles*, of which we give a profile view, is a splendid specimen of iron forging; it was furnished by the Thames Iron and Shipbuilding Company, the builders of the *Warrior* &c., and weighs upwards of twenty tons.

This vessel, and the new frigates now building – namely, the *Hector*, *Valiant*, *Agincourt*, *Northumberland*, and *Minotaur* – are all to be coated with 5½ inch iron plates, with ten inches of teak, and the same inner skin of wrought iron. In these it is hoped that reducing the teak backing and increasing the armour plate will add to the strength of the ship.

The Duke of Somerset, First Lord of the Admiralty, accompanied by his private secretary, Captain J. Moore, C.B., and Rear Admiral R. Spencer Robinson, Controller of the Navy, paid an official visit to Chatham Dockyard during last week. Their object was to inspect the iron ships now under construction, in order to ascertain the progress made with them. On arriving at the dockyard His Grace was met by Captain Fanshawe, superintendent, Mr. Laing, master shipbuilder, Commander Pope, master attendant, and the other principal officials of the establishment, who accompanied him to the dock in which the *Achilles* is building, where he spent a considerable time inspecting the works. After leaving the *Achilles* he proceeded to the extreme end of the building sheds to inspect the armour plated frigate *Royal Oak*, 50, now ready to receive her shield-plates. Instructions were given for every exertion to be used in completing this vessel, which, provided no delay arises in plating her, will be launched in August next, and about a month before the period formerly calculated upon. The works adjoining the *Royal Oak* shed, in which the machinery required to be used in preparing the armour-plates is to be erected, were inspected, after which a visit was paid to the *Bulwark*, 91, and the *Belvedera*, 51, ordered to be converted into armour-plated shield-ships.[1] His grace returned to the Admiralty in the afternoon.

76. *Bending of Armour Plates*

[*Chatham News and North Kent Spectator*]   24 May 1862

Some further experiments have been made today in this dockyard before Captain Superintendent E.G. Fanshawe and the principal officers for the establishment for the purpose of fully testing the capabilities of the powerful hydraulic machine, for bending armour plates, which has been erected in the factory alongside No. 2 Dock, by Messrs Westwood, Baillie, Campbell and Co. of London. The experiments today consisted of giving a twist of six inches to one of the cold plates. This was successfully and easily accomplished, the machine bearing the heavy strain which it was necessary to put upon it, in order to effect the bending of this mass of metal, in the most admirable manner; and during the whole of the proceedings not the slightest mishap of any kind was experienced. The two plates which were bent on Saturday, and which are intended for the amidships plates of the *Royal Oak*, 50, building on No. 7 slip, have been raised to-day into their destined positions by the aid of the powerful traveller, in order to be fitted to the ship's side. It is intended to place a layer of felt prepared with turpentine and tar between the planking of the vessel and her armour plates.

77. *Alterations to* Royal Oak

[*Chatham News and North Kent Spectator*]   7 June 1862

The Chief Constructor of the Navy, Isaac Watts, Esq., paid a visit to this dockyard today for the purpose of examining the plans for the proposed alteration to the bows of the iron-cased frigate *Royal Oak*, 50, building on No. 7 slip, by which it is intended to adapt her for service as a steam ram for running down any vessel which may be opposed to her in action. Mr. Watts was conducted over the *Royal Oak* by O. Laing, esq., Master Shipwright, and minutely inspected every part of the vessel, in the

---

[1]Both *Belvedera* and *Bulwark* were under construction at Chatham, the former laid down as a wooden steam screw decker and the latter as a screw frigate. The order referred to their conversion into ironclads, a task that was never completed. Both were cancelled prior to launching, *Belvedera* in December 1864 and *Bulwark* in March 1873.

construction of which he exhibited a lively interest. His attention was, however, principally directed to the matter, which occasioned his visit; but it is not known at present how far the suggestions for alterations to the bows of the ship will be acted upon. Two immense iron catheads, each weighing about two tons, are being forged for the *Royal Oak* at the smithery in the dockyard. Before leaving the yard, Mr. Watts cursorily inspected the *Pylades*, 21, and the *Racoon*, 22, undergoing repair in the 3rd and 4th docks, and spent a short time in looking over the immense iron frigate *Achilles*, building in No. 2 dock.

78. *Iron for* Achilles

[*Chatham News and North Kent Spectator*]   28 February 1863

During the last few days about two hundred tons of angle and plate iron, to be used in the construction of the *Achilles*, has been landed at the anchor wharf of the dockyard, sent by the contractors, Messrs Moser and Co., of London, and today several of Beale's patent armour plates for the same vessel have been received from the Parkgate Ironworks, Yorkshire.

79. *Construction of New Ironclad Ordered*

[*Chatham News and North Kent Spectator*]   10 October 1863

The new iron-plated steam ram which is to be constructed on No. 7 building slip is to be commenced as soon as the necessary hands can be spared from the other vessels building or undergoing repairs here. The ram, which is to be built from plans by Mr. E. Reed, Chief Constructor of the Navy, will be a different class to any ship now in service. The whole of the hull, from the main deck to several feet below the waterline, will be encased in heavy armour, and she will also be constructed with a formidable projecting stem, capable of doing great injury to an antagonist by running into her. It was expected the *Lord Warden* would be commenced on the 1st of the present month, but in consequence of the orders issued by the Admiralty to get the *Achilles* ready for undocking in December, the whole available force of mechanics in the yard has been placed on that frigate, and it is probable that the new ship will not be proceeded with until the beginning of November.

80.   *Commencement of New Ironclad*

[*Chatham News and North Kent Spectator*]   7 November 1863

The building of the new iron war frigate *Bellerophon*, which has just been commenced at Chatham dockyard, will inaugurate a new era in iron shipbuilding, the Lords of the Admiralty, having for the first time admitted the importance of having the vessels of our future iron fleet constructed on what is termed the double-bottom, or unsinkable principle, by which a complete revolution will be effected in the mode of constructing iron vessels of war.

The chief defect which has hitherto been experienced in our iron and iron-clad ships is the, until now, insurmountable difficulty experienced in rendering them a fit place for hundreds of officers and men to pass two or three years of their lives. Unlike a wooden vessel of war, the bottom of the iron ship is so weak – in comparison with its other parts – and so liable to injury, that unless the ship is divided internally into numerous individual compartments or chambers, a comparatively slight touch of rock, or other such injury below water, would expose her to the risk of almost instant destruction. It has, therefore, hitherto been found necessary to divide the *Warrior*, the *Achilles*, and our other iron-cased ships, into short lengths or sections, by means of water-tight bulkheads, running across them internally, the number of these in the *Achilles* being nearly twenty, extending from the bottom up to the deck on which the guns are placed. In addition to these transverse bulkheads there are many others in various parts of the ship, so that the whole interior is divided into some scores of separate compartments, into any of which the sea may be admitted by accident or design, without affecting to any great extent the floating properties of the ship.

The value of this system of construction as a means of security is obvious, but on the other hand it is attended by enormous disadvantages, the chief of which undoubtedly consists in the division of an iron ship into a number of isolated tanks, or airtight wells, in which there is little or no ventilation. This serious disadvantage is to be obviated in the new ship.

In the design for this vessel, for which the iron-work is now being prepared in Chatham Dockyard, the minute subdivisions of the interior of the ship have been altogether avoided, chiefly by the conjoint adoption under new circumstances and with suitable modifications, of two inventions, both of which have already been separately used with great success – namely the double bottom, which has proved of such immense value in the *Great Eastern*, and the 'unsinkable principle', which has been applied by Mr. Lungley, of Deptford, to the two Cape mail-steamers, the *Briton* and the *Roman*.

Throughout the entire central portion of the *Bellerophon*, in which the engines, boilers, magazines, &c are placed, the bottom of the ship will be double, the inner and outer bottoms, or hulls, being placed from three to four feet apart, in order that there may be ample space between for cleaning and painting both as often as may be desirable. As this space between the two bottoms will not be required for use, it will be divided into numerous water-tight compartments in the usual manner, and will consequently form a serious of buoyant cells, any one of which may be injured without the sea being admitted to the others or to the ship. Beyond the central portion of the vessel, at either end, Mr Lungley's plan will be introduced, the lower deck being used as an interior bottom, and the space below it made available for stowage by means of iron water-tight trunks, rising above the water-line. It is this combination of water-tight trunks with water-tight decks – the former being intended as a means for entering below the latter – which constitutes what is known as 'Lungley's unsinkable principle,' by aid of which not only is the division of the vessel into water-tight compartments accomplished without obstructing ventilation, but the vertical trunks themselves form, as will be readily understood, ventilating apparatus of the best possible kind. In addition to what has already been described, the *Bellerophon* will be constructed with water-tight internal walls, completing the double bottom, and thus will, in fact, be made a double ship from end to end. With this system of construction the necessity for internal bulkheads is almost entirely done away with.

81.   *Floating of* Achilles

[Hobbes, *Reminiscences and Notes*, p. 308[1]]   23 December 1863

On the 22nd the tide at Chatham was one of the highest that had occurred for years, and, had everything been arranged for it, she might have been launched at noon that day. That night, however, several hundred workmen began to make the usual preparations. But it was found that the caisson at the entrance to the dock could not be removed without great difficulty, and that the exit of the ship would also be impeded by the projecting ends of the dock itself, which it would be necessary to cut away. At midnight the tide was high again, and the *Achilles* floated, but could not be launched

---

[1]R.G. Hobbes, *Reminiscences and Notes of Seventy Years*, Vol II. *Civil Service and Royal Dockyards* (London, 1895).

in consequence of the removal of the impediments not having been completed. She was, therefore, unavoidably allowed again to settle down. During the night the wind changed from north to south, and kept back the tide, so that she could not be floated out the following afternoon, though everything was ready. All the hands employed on her, however, were ordered to stay in that night. At 11pm she was found to be afloat, and the order was given to haul her out of dock. Five steamers – the *Adder, Monkey, Bristler, Sheerness* and *Locust* – which had been waiting some hours with their steam up, immediately took her in tow, and the capstan being at the same time manned, the *Achilles* was successfully floated out of dock into the stream. But now a new mishap occurred. Near the entrance to the dock a bank of sand and mud had accumulated, and in consequence of the length of time the *Achilles* had been in dock, and the impossibility of removing the caisson, it had gone on increasing. At the moment the *Achilles* cleared the dock, the tide, which at that part of the harbour is always of great force, caught her broadside and forced her round on the sandbank, where she grounded. The tide had now ceased flowing, and it was greatly feared that with the falling tide it would be impossible to get her off. Notwithstanding the united efforts of the five steamers, she at first defied all attempts to remove her; and it was only by the exertions of several hundred men, who manned the capstans on the sheer-hulk in the middle of the harbour, and the full steaming of the tugs, that she was ultimately got safely off the bank and taken to her moorings.

82. *Construction Delays*

[*The Times,* London]   6 August 1864

The delays which have taken place in the progress of the iron-clad frigate *Bellerophon,* 14, 4246 tons now building at Chatham Dockyard, in consequence of the non-supply of angle and plate iron from the contractors, are likely to be effectually remedied, arrangements have been completed by which at least 100 tons of iron will be sent into the dockyard weekly by Messrs. Cheney and Co., who have the contract for supplying that description of iron for the vessel. Notwithstanding, however, the delays which have taken place in the construction of *Bellerophon,* which are attributable solely to the non-delivery of the requisite material from the contractors, the most marked progress has been made on the construction of the frigate, which will not occupy one half the time in building that was consumed in the construction of the *Achilles,* built at the same dockyard. The works connected with the *Bellerophon* are watched with the keenest interest by some of the most eminent shipbuilders in this and other countries, several of whom have inspected the frigate since she has been in frame. Now that the works are sufficiently advanced to enable an opinion to be formed on the class of vessel the *Bellerophon* is intended to prove, it is impossible to fail observing that a totally new and highly economical mode of iron shipbuilding has been introduced by her designers. The great improvement already observable is the enormous reduction effected in the amount of expensive smith's work. The extent to which complicated and costly forge work has been insisted upon in all previous iron-cased ships has afforded incessant grounds of complaint by the contractors who built *Black Prince*, *Warrior*, *Hector*, *Defence*, and other similar ships, and it now appears pretty certain that the quantity of work of this kind which was actually performed in the *Achilles* at Chatham Dockyard has tended to make an exceedingly costly vessel. Hitherto the greatest defect in all iron ships has been the local weakness of their bottoms, which has usually rendered comparatively trifling mishaps fatal to them, while wooden ships meeting with the same casualties, frequently escape with but temporary, and more often trifling, injury. The usual mode of correcting this defect is by the introduction of water-tight bulkheads across the ship. This plan may have proved useful in the mercantile marine, but it interferes so seriously with the accommodation and ventilation of ships of war as to be an unsatisfactory remedy for the defect alluded to. In the *Bellerophon* the evil has been boldly met by the introduction of a complete double bottom, somewhat resembling in principle that of the *Great Eastern*, but far more complete and perfect in its arrangement. The system of longitudinal girders, found to answer so well in the latter ship, has also been adopted in the *Bellerophon*; but while the longitudinal frames constituted the sole, or nearly sole, bottom plating of the great ship, a strong and rigid system of transverse frames has been brought to its support in the *Bellerophon*, thus rendering her bottom stronger and more secure from injury than that of any other iron ship afloat.

83.   *Superintendent, Devonport Dockyard to Admiralty:* Achilles
exhibiting signs of corrosion

[TNA, ADM135/2]   16 January 1865

1st That the *Achilles'* bottom is corroded in many places at the bow, where the chain cable has apparently abrased [*sic*] the stem, and the plates on both sides, on some of which places oxide of iron has formed in small protuberances projecting nearly an ⅛th of an inch from the bottom, on scraping these off the iron was found to be but very slightly injured, which no doubt is to be accounted for from the time the action of the salt water has been in operation.

2nd Corrosion is also very apparent in several places where the shores were set when the ship was previously docked, although the precaution of placing paper under the shores was resorted to, to avoid injury.

3rd Considerable oxidization has taken place on the stern, and rudder posts, the keel immediately under the aperture as well as the projecting part of the stern tube, and rudder, and also on the edge of the bilge pieces, and discharge pipes, where it is evident the function of the water has washed off the composition, and left the iron perfectly bare. There are also numerous other places on the bottom where there are formations of rust, but as a rule the edges of the plates and rivets are free from oxidation. On an examination of the whole it is certain that the iron has received very little, or no injury up to the present time, but had the Ship remained in the water for a much longer period, it is probable that the plates would have been much deteriorated, especially in the neighbourhood of the screw, where galvanic action would be likely to take place.

2

IMPROVING THE FACILITIES

In a report presented to the Board of Admiralty in August 1814, John Rennie highlighted three specific limitations upon the value of Chatham as a dockyard, all of them requiring immediate attention [84]. The three problems to which he referred were the difficulties and hazards of navigating the Medway, the shallowness of the dry docks and the poor arrangement of the yard. To correct these shortcomings, over the next fifty years, the Admiralty expended a great deal of time and effort. Rennie's all-encompassing and immediate solution, the transformation of Limehouse and Chatham Reaches into a massive enclosed basin for the mooring of ships in a controlled level of water, was never adopted. However, it was an idea to which he returned in 1821 [105].

The hazards of navigating the river primarily resulted from an inadequate depth of water and the existence of numerous treacherous shoals. Furthermore, there was considerable evidence to show that the problem was getting worse [95]. Identified as a major factor in the process of shallowing was the existence of Rochester Bridge and its immense stone supports (or starlings). This reduced the flow of the current and inhibited the natural scouring of accumulated silt [96]. Much attention was, therefore, given to a complete replacement of the bridge [93, 99]. Other factors, either actual or potential, were also examined and commented upon throughout the period [93, 117, 118]. Despite the partial rebuilding of Rochester Bridge, the reshaping of the dockyard wall [87, 117, 120] and the removal of a number of further obstacles that contributed to a reduction in the flow of the Medway, it was ultimately the utilisation of more efficient dredgers [89, 112, 119] and use of paddle steamers for the towing of ships [116] that made the greatest contribution to improved navigation of the Medway. However, the problem still existed in 1857 [120].

The second problem to which Rennie alluded in his submission of 1814 was the shallowness of the dry docks and their poor state of upkeep. At the time the Admiralty agreed that all dry docks should undergo a thorough repair and improvement. At the same time, Rennie suggested the construction of a series of new docks. The Admiralty accepted the need for one new dock. This was built between Nos 2 and 3 docks [88].

Although preparatory work began in 1816, the first stone was not laid until March 1818 [98]. The dock, while under construction, was subject to a Navy Board inspection in September 1819 [100], with the new dock finally completed in 1821 [104]. The new dock was given floors 4ft below the low-tide level, allowing it to accommodate the largest warships of the day. This necessitated the introduction of steam pumping. Amongst those employed on these works were convicts [112], some of who were also employed on work connected with mud dredging [108]. Both the Admiralty and Rennie expected an earlier completion date for the new No. 3 dry dock and the contractors, Usborne Benson & Co., were frequently accused of causing unnecessary delays [90, 97, 102]. Following completion of the No. 3 dock, work commenced on lengthening and improving Nos 1 and 2 docks [104, 107]. Again, there were complaints about the tardiness of the work undertaken by Usborne Benson & Co. [106, 109, 110]. To save costs, and ensure the docks were adequately pumped, the steam machinery built for the first new stone dock was also used for pumping the other docks [115].

The third problem to which Rennie had alluded in his comments of 1814 was the deficiency of space for the storage of timber and other materials. To his mind, the solution was for all matters relating to shipbuilding to be transferred to the Frindsbury side of the river, so providing additional storage space for timber dedicated to this task. The Admiralty, for its part, preferred to increase the existing area of the dockyard. It rejected the idea of extending across the river and carried out a series of purchases of adjoining marshlands that lay within the parish of Gillingham. These purchases included St Mary's Marshes (also known as Finsborough Marsh) [85, 91, 103]. The intention at this stage was to use the new land for timber storage and the deposit of mud dredged from the River Medway [103]. Later, however, this purchased land formed the basis for a further extension of the dockyard as projected by William Scamp [120].

Concurrent with these improvements was the provision of roofs to the various docks and slips. The value of roofing was outlined to the Admiralty in a report of 1817 [92]. At Chatham, the work of covering the slips and docks began in 1816, when work commenced on the first dock and second slip [86]. Over the years, a large number of the docks and slips were eventually covered, the work performed in fits and starts [94, 113]. The present No. 3 slip, with its surviving timber roof, was not covered until 1838 but the style of its roof was in many respects similar to that over the No. 2 slip [114]. The adjoining 4, 5 and 6 slipcovers, also extant, are very different in style. Designed by Captain Thomas R. Mould of the Royal Engineers, they are of cast and wrought iron construction with a corrugated ironclad roof. The final slip to be covered at Chatham, the No. 7, was a considerable further advance in design. Authorised in 1851, it was designed by G.T. Green. Again, of iron construction, it incorporated travelling cranes operating on rails built into the roof structure.[1]

A further improvement to the shipbuilding and repair facilities at Chatham was undertaken between 1856 and 1858. This was the lengthening of No. 2 dock, a move necessitated by the increasing size of ships using the facilities at Chatham [122]. Even with this extension, however, further lengthening was essential, prior to the laying down of *Achilles*. This was achieved by cutting away the altars at the head of the dock. Another change to this area of the dockyard was the construction of a series of working sheds between Nos 1 and 2 docks [123, 126, 132] and the conversion of No. 1 dock into a work area. To achieve the latter, the existing roof to the dock was removed and a new floor installed to support heavy machinery [124, 125]. With the laying down of *Royal Oak*, further alterations to the facilities were required; a new plating shop was built adjacent to the No. 7 slip [135] and new machinery installed [131, 132]. Among contractors employed in these various undertakings were Grissels, who built the sheds between Nos. 1 and 2 docks [128, 130] and Foords of Rochester who were employed on both the plating shop and conversion of No. 1 dock [136, 137] while convicts were employed on constructing a tramway [137].

The decision to construct at Chatham the first ironclad battleship to be built in a royal dockyard not only projected the yard into the forefront of naval technology but also ensured that Chatham would lead other yards in the construction of new classes of battleship until the end of the century. This was partly because of its proximity to the skilled ironworkers employed along the Thames. However, Chatham lacked one of the essential features of a modern dockyard, an enclosed basin for the fitting out of large ships. Instead, any ship constructed at Chatham had to be completed in the tidal waters of the River Medway. However, following works begun in 1856 upon a new extension to the yard, thought was being given to the possible construction of a basin. These works had begun in a small way. Initially, it was simply intended to build embankments upon the newly acquired Finsborough (St Mary's) Marsh [111] for the construction of a few additional docks and slips. But the original plan was altered following the adoption of a much larger scheme proposed in January 1857 by William Scamp, Deputy Director of Works to the Admiralty [120]. The plan required the acquisition of further land, namely

---

[1]J. Coad, *The Royal Dockyards 1690–1850: Architecture and Engineering Works of the Sailing Navy* (Aldershot, 1989), p. 116.

St Mary's Island and St Mary's Creek [127]: the creek to be widened and converted into a line of basins, the island to house a vast factory building. The laying down of *Achilles* strengthened the case for Scamp's proposal. The area of the subsequently completed extension was first marked out in December 1860 [129] with the costs of completing the necessary river wall and embankment estimated at £902,000 [133]. An enabling Act was passed in July 1861 [134] and convicts were soon undertaking excavation work on the area designated for the basins [138, 140]. As construction proceeded, a number of alterations were introduced into the original design concept, but they never departed radically from Scamp's outline proposal set out in January 1857 [121, 139, 140]. By July 1865, as a result of both the forwardness of the works and their complexity, Colonel Sir Andrew Clark, Director of Engineering and Architectural Works, suggested that a competent officer, drawn from the ranks of the Royal Engineers, be appointed as overall supervisor [141].

84.   *John Rennie to Admiralty: defects of yard*

[Rennie, *Treatise on Harbours*, pp. 46–8.[1]]   27 August 1814

Having been employed by the Honourable Commissioners of the Navy, by letter dated the 29th November last, to give my opinion respecting a reference to them from Sir Robert Barlow, concerning the improvement of the river front at Chatham Dockyard, according to a line proposed by Mr Parkin, the Master Shipwright at that place, I was led to take a view not only of the subject immediately referred to my consideration, but also of the general defects of the dockyard itself, in as far as regards the building, repairing, and fitting out of ships of war, and the navigation of the Medway to and from it; the result of which I request you will have the goodness to lay before the Lords Commissioners of the Admiralty. The dockyard at Chatham, like those of Woolwich and Deptford, was established at a time when our ships of war were of much smaller burthen than they are at present, and when the depth of water in these respective rivers was greater, as may be seen by comparing the soundings taken a century ago with those that are now on the survey of the Thames and Medway. Had a dockyard been made on the Isle of Grain, by the side of the Salt-Pan Reach, those of Chatham and Sheerness would have been rendered unnecessary, as a dockyard at Northfleet would have also rendered those of Deptford and Woolwich. By two establishments the public expense would not only have been lessened, but the capacity of two such yards to carry on the business of the Navy would have been more than four times that of the present yards, and the access by water to and from them would never have been interrupted except in the most severe storms – an advantage which their Lordships are better able to appreciate than I can. Greatly as I would prefer a dockyard on the Isle of Grain to those of Chatham and Sheerness, these dockyards are so situated that they are capable of great improvement, and some of their most serious defects can be lessened, if not wholly removed; not so with those of Deptford and Woolwich – as no ingenuity or expense is capable of removing the serious objections against them; the only effectual remedy is a dockyard at Northfleet, on a scale capable of performing the business of both those yards.

The improvement now going forward at Sheerness will remove many of the evils attending that yard, and in other respects render it very complete; and if their Lordships shall be pleased to sanction what I am about to propose for the improvement of the dockyard at Chatham, some of the objections to that yard will in like manner be removed, and its

[1]John Rennie, *Treatise on Harbours* (London, 1895).

capacity for the building, repairing, fitting out, and keeping ships in ordinary, greatly increased. The evils attending the situation and construction of Chatham Dockyard are –

First, The difficulty and hazard of navigating large ships to and from it, and the insufficiency of water to keep them afloat in front of the dockyard.

Secondly, The shallowness of the dry docks, and their bad state of repair.

Thirdly, The arrangement of the yard, arising in a great measure from the want of room to deposit timber and other materials in the places most convenient for their conversion and use.

With regard to the first objection, I believe it is greatly allowed, that the largest ships of war can at all times in moderate weather get to the head of Long Reach, and it is seldom that they are prevented from getting to the head of Gillingham Reach, where the water is deep and the channel of the river wide; but from the head of Gillingham Reach, along Sovereign, Cockham, Chatham, and Bridge Reaches, the channel of the river is not only very crooked and narrow, but in many places exceedingly shallow; the great detention and hazard, therefore, of bringing ships up the Medway lies between Gillingham Reach and the dockyard, but even when they have got over this difficulty and hazard of the navigation, the water is so shallow in Chatham Reach, except in certain places which are generally occupied by ships fitting out, or those waiting for repair, and the river itself is so narrow, that it becomes exceedingly difficult for large vessels to navigate along these Reaches.

Secondly, The shallowness of the dry docks at Chatham has long been a subject of serious complaint.

At the first	17ft.	11in.	at springs, and	13ft.	10in.	at neaps
At the second	18	3	do	14	9	do
At the third	17	9	do	14	3	do
At the fourth	17	11	do	14	5	do

So that in neither of these docks is there sufficient depth of water for first or second rate ships of war, even at the highest spring tides, when docked, they are obliged to be heaved upon the blocks from 2½ to 3½ feet high; and at neap tides no ship of the line can be docked at Chatham.

Lastly, with respect to the arrangements, the deficiency is evident to every one who examines them; the timber is obliged to be stacked wherever room can be found to lay it, by which the expense of teams becomes very heavy. The principal part of the spars are kept in a mud pond fenced off from the Medway, which, with the floating bridge erected by the Board of Ordnance, obstructs the current and occasions a great deposition of mud; and these are again assisted by projection of the landing jetty in front of the dockyard. I might have gone into more detail, but it would extend this Report too far; and besides, it is a more fit subject for a separate Report, in case their Lordships shall approve of the plan I have to propose.

To remedy the evils I have stated, as far as the nature of the case appears to me to admit, I propose to make a new channel or cut for the River Medway, from the bend below Rochester Bridge, opposite Frindsbury church to Upnor Castle, forming a regular sweep, that it may join in an easy curve with the head of Cockhouse [*sic*] Reach, and to throw a dam across the old channel, from the north-east corner of Rochester Marshes to the Frindsbury side between the two shipyards, and another across at the north end of the dockyard and above the Ordnance floating-bridge, thus making the old river between the north end of the dockyard and the north-east point of Rochester Marshes into a wet dock, which, taking the surface covered at low water, will be upwards of 150 acres, leaving a space of land between the new proposed cut and the present channel of the river, on the Frindsbury side, of nearly the same extent, and which I proposed shall be purchased and taken into the dockyard.

At the northern end of the dockyard I propose that a new cut shall be made from the dock I have described, across Frindsbury to Gillingham Marshes, south of the line of St. Mary's Creek to the head of Gillingham Reach adjoining the fort, and at its lower end I propose a lock to communicate with the Medway, having a small basin at the head for the convenience of vessels going into or out of the dock or Medway.

The entrance of the proposed wet dock being at the head of Gillingham Reach will be generally, if not always, accessible, and I think I may confidently affirm that the detention and hazard of the navigation between Sheerness and Chatham will be in a great measure removed, – supposing even that the River Medway shall remain, in regard to depth, as it is now; but as by the new cut from near Upnor Castle to the land below Rochester Bridge the river will be much straitened and many of the impediments and obstructions to the flow of the tide avoided, there can therefore be no doubt that a greater quantity of tidal water will be thrown upwards than there now is, and this must again return to the sea; in like manner the land-freshes of the Medway will have a more free discharge than they now have, and consequently will pass off with great rapidity. The combined effects of these will no doubt deepen the river between the head of Gillingham Reach and Long Reach, and thereby further lessen the difficulties and detention in the navigation of these reaches.

As to the second head, namely, the shallowness of the dry docks, the plan I propose will not alter them; but as the docks are generally in a bad state, they must undergo a thorough repair, and when this is done, it will be the proper time to lay the floor of them sufficiently deep to take the largest ships to which their respective lengths are adapted; and such additional docks may be made as the demands of the public service may require, which perhaps may be to double the number of the existing docks.

As to the third and last head, namely, the arrangement of the yard, this in the present yard is much better than could have been expected, when the extent of work generally performed in it is compared with the extent of its surface. The total surface of Chatham Dockyard is short of eighty acres, in which there is no less than four dry docks, four slips for ships of the line, and three for lesser vessels, a set of saw mills for timber, with the necessary timber-fields, mast-houses, storehouses, ropery, smithery, commissioner's and officers' houses and gardens, with all the other conveniences appertaining to such an establishment; the consequence of which is, that the timber is obliged to be deposited wherever space can be found to lay it; and the stacks are of such a length as to render it extremely difficult and very tedious to get the pieces of timber wanted in the progress of building and repairing ships. I therefore propose that the present slips at Chatham Dockyard shall be converted into dry docks, and that every necessary building or appendage connected with the dry docks shall be retained in the present dockyard; but that the building of ships, the timber-fields, mast-ponds &c. shall be established on the opposite sides, where there is sufficient extent of ground for any purpose that may be required.

I am not aware in the execution of the plan I have proposed there can be any opposition from private individuals, except what may arise from the inhabitants of Chatham, in case it may be deemed expedient to prevent them from navigating up the canal from the head of Gillingham Reach to their own wharfs; if, however, this should be denied to them, and perhaps it may be right that it should be, a lock may be made at the upper end of the wet dock for their purpose alone, which will give them free access at all times to their wharfs.

As to the drainage of the streets, houses, &c., this may be done either by carrying a main sewer under the river into another, which should be made from the new intended building ground into the new proposed cut, or it may be carried into the river by Rochester Marshes; this, however, and other points will have to be considered, should their Lordships approve of the general outline and principles of the scheme, and order a regular survey, plan, estimates, &c. to be made. In the interim I have annexed a plan taken from the Master Attendant's chart of the Medway, in which the general outline of my proposed improvements are delineated; but this, no doubt, will be subject to considerable alterations in making a regular survey and laying down the whole to scale. It may perhaps be imagined that during the execution of the plan I propose, great inconvenience will be experienced and much interruption given to the operations of the dockyard; this, however, will not be the case; the whole will be executed, except the two dams, without the smallest interruption to the navigation or to any of the operations of the dockyard; and when the two dams are about to be executed, ships will pass through the canal to and from the dockyard in the like manner as they will do when the works are completed; unless, therefore, some annoyance of mud, which will be naturally moved while the dams are putting in and the mouths of the cut ballasting out, no other inconvenience will be experienced; this mud must, of course, be taken out by a mud machine.

85. *Commissioner Barlow to Admiralty: land purchase*

[TNA, ADM106/1815]   22 February 1815

In answer to your letter of the 31st of October last, acquainting me, that you have transmitted to the Lords Commissioners of the Admiralty a copy of my letter of the 18th of the same month recommending, for the reasons therein given, the purchase of some marshland adjacent to this dockyard, and the tenements thereon together with a plan of the lands in question, and that their Lordships had directed you to cause the lands and tenements described in the plan to be purchased for His Majesty's service provided the same can be obtained on reasonable terms; and desiring that I will enquire on what terms these lands can be obtained;

I have to acquaint you, that on the receipt of your said letter, I immediately proceeded to enquire in to the terms upon which the owners of the lands &c. in question will respectively agree to sell the same to the Crown. I have not, until now, obtained sufficient information to enable me to answer your letter.

The largest piece of fresh marsh, occupied by Thomas Baseden, and containing about 18 acres, and the sands in front are the property of John Strover Esq. and Mrs Elizabeth Strover who ask three thousand five hundred pounds for the purchase of them. Such purchase to be subject to the existing lease of the premises, of which eleven years were unexpired at Michaelmas last, and that the Crown should not be entitled to any rent for the remainder of the term.

The above terms appear to me to be exorbitant (indeed, I ought to add preposterous). I asked whether they were willing to submit the price to be paid for the lands in question, to the determination of two indifferent public persons, one to be nominated on the part of the Crown and the other by themselves but they have informed me that they must decline any such reference. It seems impracticable, therefore, to procure these lands for the public, by private negotiation, or in any other way than by Act of Parliament;

The other piece of fresh marsh, containing about seven acres, is the property of Mr. Simmons of Rochester who is willing to sell it to the Crown, and proposes to submit the price, to the determination of two indifferent persons, one to be nominated on the part of the Crown, and the other by himself;

The five tenements called Tom-All-Alone's are stated to be the property of Ann Hughes, the wife of John Hughes, a private soldier and a pensioner of the Chelsea Hospital, for her life, with reversion in fee to Robert Henge, her son by a former husband, and now settled at the colony of New South Wales. Hughes and his wife have mortgaged the life interest of the latter, and the mortgage is in possession under his security. Hughes, and his wife, resides in Ireland, but I cannot ascertain at what place. Nor have I been able to ascertain at what part of the colony of New South Wales, Robert Henge, the reversioner, resides. So that it seems impracticable, at present, and likely long to remain so, to procure these last mentioned premises for the public by private negotiation, or in any other way than by Act of Parliament.

86. *Commissioner Barlow to Admiralty: dock and slip roofs*

[NMM, CHA/F/27]   12 June 1815

The Master Shipwright of your yard having, in consequence of our warrant of the 20th ultimo directing roofs to be erected over the first slip and the first dock, recommends by his letter of the 8th instant that the Master House Carpenter should proceed to Woolwich to examine the roof that has been erected there, and to obtain any information respecting it that may be necessary, We acquaint you that we approve thereof, and desire you will give orders to the Master House Carpenter accordingly.

87 *John Rennie to Admiralty: sea wall*

[TNA, ADM106/3138]   19 July 1815

I took an opportunity on Saturday last the 15th inst. on my way from Sheerness to examine the line proposed by me in my report to your Honble

Board of the 10th of June 1814 for the new river wall at Chatham yard and I submitted to Commissioner Sir Robert Barlow the best mode which appeared to me of carrying the work into execution. I likewise stated to him that in so doing it would be necessary to deprive them of the use of the Dock No. 3 while the walls were building adjoining its entrance. When these were completed, it would in like manner be necessary to deprive them of Dock No. 4 while the walls were building adjoining its entrance and so on in succession for the slips Nos. 3, 4, 5 & 6. The inconvenience, which would by these proceedings be experienced while the works were carrying into execution, recalled to his recollection a plan, which had formerly been suggested, of making an additional dry dock in the space between the docks nos. 2 & 3, by which most of the above-enumerated inconveniences would be obviated. This objection appears to me so important, that I have thought it right to lay the same before your Honble Board previous to making out a plan and estimate of the wall as directed in your letter of the 6th.

If a dock is determined to be constructed between nos. 3 & 4 this should be done before the river wall is commenced. By this, substance would be provided for dock no. 3 before it is stopped and sufficient time would thereby be given not only to construct the river wall on each side of the docks nos. 3 & 4; but also to give them a thorough repair of which they stand greatly in need or to rebuild them entirely should it be deemed expedient so to do. I rather think this latter will be found most advantageous for the public service, as the cills are at present too high, by from three to four feet, and besides it would give additional facility to the docking and undocking of ships if their directions were to be considerably varied.

May I therefore request that your Honble Board will be pleased to take these suggestions into your consideration, and inform me of your determination on the subject.

88.   *John Rennie to Navy Board: estimate for new dock*

[TNA, ADM106/3138]   29 August 1815

Having by your letter of the 31st ultimo signified the approbation of the Lords Commissioners of the Admiralty to the suggestions made by me in my letter to your Honble Board dated the 19th ultimo namely, that it would in my opinion be advisable to make a new dock on the vacant ground between the docks nos. 2 and 3 at Chatham yard, previous to commencing the repairs of the docks nos. 3 and 4. I have according to your directions made out a design of a new dock for a first rate, together with a plan for a new river wall so far as it can with convenience be built previous to beginning the repair of the Dock no. 3. I have laid it down in such a direction as I hope will be found most suitable to the current of the flowing tide, at the time a ship ought to be docked or undocked. I have also made estimates and a specification of the dock river wall and steam engine for extracting the water while the dock and river wall is building, to be used afterwards to pump such water out of the dock as may remain at low water.

The size of the dock is conformable to dimensions furnished me by the Surveyor of the Navy. The floor is proposed to be 4 feet under the level of low water of an ordinary spring tide, which according to Mr Parkin's information rises 18½ feet, thus giving 22½ feet of depth at the high water of a spring tide, which I am informed will be sufficient not only to float a first rate but also admit of the proper sized blocks under her keel. At this time therefore there will be four feet of water to pump out of the dock at low water Spring Tides, and about nine feet at neap tides, and for this purpose a steam engine will be required. Were the plan of making a new cut for the Medway to be adopted, a large steam engine will be required because in this case, the whole contents of each dock would have to be pumped out. By this additional dock the number will be increased to five, there might at times be two ships docked the same tide. I presume it will be some years before this plan is carried into execution, I apprehend a much [lesser] steam engine will answer the purpose, and I think such a one as that now building at Sheerness will be quite sufficient. I have therefore estimated for an engine of that size and I have included the expense of working her while the Dock and River Wall is under execution.

I have made the estimate of the dock under three different suppositions:

First, supposing the whole of the alters, floor and entrance to be made of Aberdeen granite. In which case the probable expense of the dock, admitting the whole to be set on piles, which from Mr Parkin's borings I fear will be necessary, amount to £143,000. The steam engine, engine house, well and drain, amounts to £14,700; and working her for two years while these works are in hand £2000.

The river wall for 340 feet in length, supposing it to be faced with granite I have estimated at £25,724 making a total of £185,424.

Second, if the floor entrance and river wall is done with Dundee or Craigleith stone, there will be a saving of £16,000.

Third, if the floor of the dock is made with timber in place of stone there will be a further saving of £5000. But the granite for the purpose of a dock is so superior to all other kinds of stone that I submit to your Honble Board the propriety of adopting it, even at the extra expense I have estimated.

I have made no estimate for an extension of the river wall the whole length of the dockyard because this depends on the general repair and extension of the dock nos. 3 and 4 and also on the slips, mast houses and other matters. It would require a general plan for the whole before this could be accurately determined. What I have now done will when finished form a part of that general plan, so that there will be time enough to arrange the whole. While this dock and wall is in hand, and until it is completed, the extension of the river wall and repair of the docks could not be undertaken without very materially interrupting the general business of the yard. I may however, observe, that I have kept the estimates of what I now propose high, and the dimensions of the stone in the inverted arch and alters of the dock are larger than necessary, so that I would fain hope the cost will rather fall short than exceed the amount of the Estimate. As the steam engine will suffice for the whole, as well as a part of the cofferdam and piles, these expenses so far will be saved in whatever repairs the other docks and river wall may require.

[*Appended note*]
1 September 1815. The Board determined that the dock should be built of granite stone and that the work shall be done by contract.

89. *Admiralty to Commissioner Barlow: dredging*

[NMM, CHA/F/29] 29 January 1816

With reference to your letter dated the 1st June last, in which you stated that the Steam Engine vessel sent from Woolwich might be employed with advantage at your port in raising mud until the end of the year, and probably much longer. We acquaint you that Commissioner Cunningham has expressed to us, that it is absolutely necessary that she should return to Woolwich immediately. We therefore desire you will send her round without delay.

90.   *Navy Board, to Usborne Benson & Co.: land purchase*

[TNA, ADM106/3138]   2 September 1816

On his return from viewing the works you have undertaken at Chatham yard, Mr Rennie has represented to us that you are not proceeding with the excavation of the dock with proper expedition, although every facility has been allowed you; that a considerable quantity of the beech timber delivered for bearing piles is so cracked and ill shaped that it must be immediately removed; that no stone is yet delivered for the works. From all which circumstances he concludes that unless much greater exertions are made, there is no probability of the works being completed within the prescribed period. We have therefore to call your attention to these particulars, and to desire that the utmost dispatch may be used in forwarding the said works. We have directed the officers to point out to you the beech timber that is not fit for bearing piles and desire that it may be removed without delay.

91.   *Navy Board to Admiralty: purchase of land*

[TNA, ADM106/2273]   25 June 1817

Commissioner Sir Robert Barlow having represented to us the expediency of purchasing certain lands in the vicinity of Chatham Yard under the Act of last year – and it appearing to us from the statement that delay will only occasion an increase of the purchase owing to the improvement the lands are daily acquiring. We request you submit to the Lord Commissioners of the Admiralty our reply in reference to Mr Barrow's letter of this subject dated 10 March 1815 by which we were directed to suspend all negotiations for these marshes for the present. It may now be advantageous to the public that we should be authorised to treat with the parties, or if necessary call a jury for the purpose of assessing the value of the salt marshes and such other grounds as may be considered necessary for the convenience of His Majesty's service.

We send herewith for their Lordships information an account of the several pieces of ground and buildings it may from time to time be desirable to purchase. We would only recommend taking the salt marsh land if the rest of the property can be obtained on very eligible terms.

[Appended note]
Lands and houses at Chatham proposed to be vested in the Crown:

Fresh Marsh   18 acres   0 rods   39 perches
Salt Marsh   7 acres   2 rods   3 perches
Both belonging to Elizabeth Strover of Brompton (widow) and Samuel Roger Strover (Capt. of Bombay Artillery now in the East Indies). On lease from them to Peter King and released by him to John Baseden.

Fresh Marshes 7 acres 1 rod 35 perches
Belonging to John Simmons and in the occupation of John Bader junior.

Two tenements belonging to Richard Webb of Luton near Chatham.

Five tenements lately belonging to Ann Hughes
She took them under the will of her father Robert Simmons of Brompton in Gillingham, dated 7 May 1776 and proved in the Probate Court of Canterbury 14 June 1776. She died on 23 May 1816 in Ireland, leaving 4 or 5 children by her last husband, Hughes, a Chelsea Pensioner, and Richard Finch by her former husband. The residences of her children are now not known and would be very difficult to find out.

One tenement belonging to Thomas Clark.

One tenement belonging to Thomas Elvey

One tenement belonging to George Clerk

One tenement belonging to James Clerk

One tenement belonging to the denizens of Thomas Milton

92. *Navy Board to Admiralty: covering of docks and slips*

[NMM, ADM/BP/376]   25 October 1817

The ships lately repaired and newly built show no indication of decay, as was formerly the case, and there are strong grounds for believing that the present mode of seasoning the frames and building under cover will completely subdue the dry rot … We feel it to be our duty to urge in the strongest manner the propriety of covering all the slips and such of the docks as may not be required for the occasional docking of masted ships; and so much importance do we attach to this measure that we think it should take precedence over all other objects because there is none other that can compare with it as so immediately and permanently affecting the public purse.

93.   *Comptroller's Minute: navigation of Medway*

[BL, Add Ms 41,367]   November 1817

Not finding Mr Nicholson at Rochester I[1] proceeded with Sir Robert Barlow, and Mr Seppings to the lock above Aylesford, being one of the great evils so justly represented by Mr Nicholson, as tending to the injury of the River Medway in consequence of it preventing the natural and needful flow of the tide to its accustomed extent, which was formerly not less than four miles above the lock, and of a breadth varying from 50, to 80 feet, so that the water, of which the River is so deprived twice in twenty-four hours, must certainly amount to many millions of tons, and the injury to be apprehended to the public establishments at Chatham. The general navigation of the River Medway, from the want of that quantity of back water, which is so essential in preventing an accumulation of mud, is a subject of much interest and will call for early and serious consideration.

The remedies suggested in Mr Nicholson's excellent letter might diminish the evils: the allowing the tide to flow in and return four days of the Spring tide of each month and occasionally keeping open the gates and sluices (that at proper times the river may have the full benefit of the land floods). I am, however, much inclined to think that the only complete remedy will be the total removal of the lock, by which private interest will be made to yield to the public good. From what I hear of the state of the navigation to Maidstone, perhaps the proportion of the locks would be satisfied with a moderate sum by way of compensation and the neighbourhood might accommodate themselves to the inconvenience by arranging their exports and imports so as to meet the Spring tide every fortnight or use smaller vessels so as to navigate the river during the neap tides. It may however be difficult to accomplish so desirable an object without giving rise to much complaint and therefore the procuring the opening of the gates occasionally should be required of the proprietors of the locks for a time by way of experiment.

The cutting of a straight channel through the marsh by Burham Church would not be difficult or expensive. Some more competent judge should examine and report upon the probable effect of taking from the great bend in the river its usual strength of current, by being in a great degree directed

[1]Sir Thomas Byam Martin.

into the straights cut and if the bend in question should thereby fill up, it will deprive the river of still more water than at present.

But nothing appears more injurious than the bridge at Rochester built as it is with very broad starlings and arches of small space. If the bad tendency of it is considered by those who are better able to form a correct opinion it may perhaps be found advisable with a view of economy and the general advantage of the river, at once to construct a new bridge, in a line with the main street of Rochester and Strood, at the public expense and for which an Act of Parliament might immediately secure an ample interest for the advances, by levying a toll on the present bridge.

94. *Navy Board to Commissioner Barlow: docks and slip covers*

[NMM, CHA/F/30]   5 November 1817

With reference to the officers letter of the 4th inst., we have to desire that you will order the Master House Carpenter of your yard to proceed to Woolwich yard to see the manner in which the temporary roofs are constructed over the docks and slips in that yard for the guidance of the officers of your yard in carrying into effect our warrant of the 1st Instant for erecting temporary roofs over the docks and slips.

95. *Commissioner Barlow to Bridge Wardens: navigation of Medway*

[NMM, CHA/F/31]   10 January 1818

That the depth of the channel of the River Medway, has been for many years gradually diminishing, is a fact so generally admitted, that to adduce proof of it would be to occupy your time unnecessarily.

The following extract from the report of Mr. Rennie, the Civil Engineer, addressed to the Commissioners for Revising the Civil Affairs of the Navy, under the date of the 14th May 1807, I have but too much reason to believe is a true statement of the case:

'By a plan with soundings taken in the year 1724, It appears that the greatest depth at moorings in west of Gillingham Reach was 27 feet, the least 17 feet; in east Gillingham the greatest soundings at the moorings were 19 feet, the least 16 feet; In Cockham Wood Reach the soundings were 17 feet, & the least 12 feet. From Chatham Quay to Upnor Castle the greatest soundings were 23 feet, the least 11 feet; and from Rochester Bridge to Chatham Quay the greatest soundings were 20 feet, the least 13 feet.

Since the year 1724 several of the moorings have become more shallow, as appears by the soundings on the plan furnished by your Honble Board, taken by the Master Attendant of Chatham Dockyard in the year 1803; when the greatest soundings in East Gillingham Reach were 29 feet and the last 20 feet; but these soundings extend lower down than those of 1724. In Sovereign or West Gillingham Reach the greatest soundings were 26 feet; the least 15 feet. In Cockham Wood Reach the greatest soundings were 16 feet.'

96.   *Commissioner Barlow to Bridge Wardens, quoting John Rennie's report of 14 May 1807: navigation of Medway*

[Rochester Bridge Trust, Ms. 214]   20 January 1818

If Rochester Bridge had been pulled down some years since, and a new one built in the line of the streets through Strood and Rochester, with piers of suitable dimensions, instead of repairing the old one, the large starlings of which act as a dam, and prevent the tide from flowing up to the extent it otherwise would do, the depth of water in front of Chatham, Rochester, and in Cockham Wood Reach, would have been greatly improved. The trustees unfortunately determined on repairing the old bridge. This nuisance still remains and no advantage whatever has been gained. Unless, therefore, something is done to preserve at least, if not to improve the navigation of the Medway, the soundings will go on diminishing in depth and the dockyard will become less useful. In its present state, vessels of large draught of water must have all their guns and stores taken out before they can come up the dockyard and be dismasted before they can be taken into the dock.

97.   *John Rennie to Navy Board: construction of stone dock*

[TNA, ADM 106/3138]   21 March 1818

I visited the new works going on in Chatham yard on the 13th when I was in hopes to have seen considerable progress made since I visited that yard in October last. I found that the whole quantity of work done was not more than might have been done in half the time. If much greater exertions are not made in future, the dock will not be completed for several years to come. Sir Robert Barlow seems much dissatisfied with their slow proceedings and I think with great reason. There is much interruption occasioned to the operations of the yard by so much of the space being occupied with stone and other materials. I therefore beg leave to recommend to your Honourable Board to use such measures as may seem best calculated to hasten the business whereby a considerable sum will be saved to the public in the pumping of water, superintendence and the facility which will thereby be gained by the use of this dock.

98. *Laying of First Stone of New Dock*

[*Kentish Gazette*] 31 March 1818

Saturday noon the first stone of the new dock, in Chatham yard, was laid, and some ceremony took place in consequence. Miss Barlow, attended by her father, Sir Robert Barlow, the Commissioner, and several ladies and gentlemen, had the honour to set the appointed stone in its bed, first placing thereunder several new pieces of the current coin. At the request of Miss Barlow the Commissioner made a very suitable speech on the occasion. There was a good dinner afterwards given to the workmen, by the employers, at the Navy Hotel.

99. *Description of New Bridge*

[*Kentish Gazette*] 19 May 1818

Lord Melville arrived at Chatham in the Commissioner's yacht, a few days since, where he was met by the Earl of Romney, and since this consultation between the noble lords, it has been ascertained that a new bridge is certainly to be erected across the Medway at Rochester. It is to consist of five arches only, instead of eleven as the old one is now constructed. This will be a great means to keep the river clear of mud, and every other precaution is to be taken to prevent the choking up of the river, all impediments are to be removed, the moorings are to be placed differently, and the ships lying in the stream are to swing in the tide as before.

100. *Navy Board Committee of Visitation: stone dock*

[TNA, ADM 106/3233] 30 September 1819

First visited the new dock constructing and found everything going on well, that the number of workmen were now sufficient and that there was no want of stone or other materials for proceeding with the works.

Mr Rennie was here present and the subject of drawing the dock and providing the new gates that will be wanted in January next having been discussed, the mode of drawing was approved. Mr Richards, the Clerk of the Works, was directed to inspect the models for the gates intended for the tunnel to the mast pond in Sheerness yard and to provide models for those wanted for the dock at Chatham. The committee were of the opinion that it would be most desirable to advertise for a contract for the whole of the gates wanted at both yards that were considered of sufficient magnitude to induce the Masters of the first respectability to offer tenders.

The Committee having observed that it was intended to let additional alters upon the broad alters now forming in the dock which will be attended with very considerable expense without producing any adequate advantage, and having consulted Mr Rennie on the subject, who concurred in opinion with the Committee, that they might be dispensed with, it was determined that directions should be given to the officers for that purpose.

101.   *Navy Board to Commissioner Barlow: employment of convicts*

[NMM, CHA/F/33]   7 December 1819

In return to your letter of the 29th ultimo, we acquaint you that we have determined that the convicts employed at your yard shall work by task on all occasions. We therefore desire you will order the officers to prepare such a scheme as will enable the men with full exertion to earn four pence a day while pile driving and three pence a day when excavating: a moiety of which earnings is to be paid to them, and the remainder reserved until the time of their liberation.

We also desire you will order an allowance of two pints of beer and four ounces of bread to be made to each convict while so employed and direct the issuing of the beer at fixed periods during the working hours by the tapster, with whom we wish to make an arrangement for the supply of both articles.

102.   *Navy Board to Commissioner Barlow: abstract of correspondence*

[TNA, ADM 106/3138]   21 March 1820

29 August 1816.   Mr Rennie stated that the contractors were not proceeding with the excavation with proper expedition – that a quantity of the beech timber for piles was unfit and that no stone was yet delivered.

5 September 1816. Usborne & Co stated in reply to that complaint, that it was necessary that they should have a double railway and be allowed to carry the earth away in barges not only to the marshes but to other ground.

10 September 1816. Chatham officers reported that this should not be granted. The want of instruments having been the principal cause of delay and that the cofferdam is proceeding very slowly.

28 September 1816. Usborne & Co was desired to increase the number of their wagons and barges to expedite the excavation; also to hasten the completion of the dam.

1 October 1816. Chatham officers in answer to a second question from the Board whether a double railway could not be allowed, state that the contractor had not taken full advantage of the single railway, and that a double one would interfere with the works of the yard.

10 December 1816. Mr Rennie reports his having been at Chatham to examine a slip, which had happened in the excavation. To his report thereon, he adds 'that the proceedings of the contractors hitherto have been dilatory in the extreme, by the delay in the completion of the coffer dam. Not only has a considerable sum been expended in pumping water but no part of the excavation is yet ready for piling'.

13 December 1816. The Board informed Messrs Usborne & Co that they should enforce the penalty of their bond unless they make greater exertions.

18 December 1816. Usborne & Co in answer that they had no order for the coffer dam till late in July, and have been impeded by the weather and want of timber.

10 January 1817. Mr. Rennie in reply, states that the dam ought to have been completed in October; not withstanding those circumstances.

28 February 1817. Usborne & Co complains that after being called upon to use greater exertion, the expenditure for the year is to be limited to £45,000.

17 March 1817. The Board, after writing to Mr Rennie, informed them that they were surprised at receiving this remonstrance, the coffer dam being not yet completed, and it being uncertain when it will be, whereby

a great expense arises which might otherwise be saved; and observed to them that their proceedings had been irregular and ill arranged and had the appearance of wishing to cover the ground with materials without performing any effective part of the work.

18 March 1817.   Mr Rennie announced that they were proceeding with more regularity than hitherto, and had delivered better stone.

16 June 1817.   Chatham officers report, that the ground at the head of the dock had given way. This they attributed to the want of energy in the contractors the dam having been completed only the week before – which prevented them from keeping the work properly drained – in addition to which some of the contractors men have left work, their wages having been reduced.

8 September 1817.   Chatham officers report that another large slip of the ground into the dock had taken place.
    Mr Rennie, who had been desired to proceed to the spot, reports that this as well as other similar accidents was owing to the softness of the soil. The only effectual remedy is to perform the work with the utmost expedition, but the contractors have never used proper exertions.

4 October 1817.   Mr Rennie, having been furnished with report made by Chatham officers of the proceedings of the Contractors since the commencement of the work, states that 'if matters do not mend the execution of the dock will cost as much, if not more, than the tenders of other parties amounted to, and submits that it might be beneficial to the public to take the work from Usborne & Co.'

20 October 1817.   Mr Rennie having again visited Chatham and had all the papers with him, states his opinion to be confirmed that the Board had it in their power to take the work out of the contractors hands – but he does not consider it advisable – the contractors having made arrangements which are likely to prove satisfactory.

11 March 1818.   Mr Rennie informs the Board that having visited the yard he finds no more work has been done, than might have been in half the time, by hastening it a considerable sum will be saved in pumping &c &c.

16 March 1818.   Usborne & Co, in reply, states that the delay has not originated with them. They having been desired to limit their operations, but have been occasioned by occurrences not under their control.

1 April 1818.   Chatham officers report that no obstacle has been thrown in the way of the contractors by them. There has been only a trifling delay by the stopping of the engine.

23 May 1818.   Chatham officers report, that the works are partially stopped for want of a drawing of the alteration intended in the head of the dock.

25 May 1818.   Usborne & Co to the same effect.

26 May 1818.   Drawing sent.

29 July 1818.   Chatham officers report that there are not as many men employed as might be with advantage owing to the scarcity of bricks and the whole sum voted for the year (£70,000) will not be expended.

31 July 1818.   Usborne & Co explains the want of bricks and request to be allowed to use some from the works at Chetney Hills, which was granted.

20 May 1819.   Sir Robert Barlow complained of the slow progress occasioned by the want of stone.

20 August 1819.   Mr Rennie states that since he last visited the dock there has not been done one fourth of the work that ought and unless much greater exertions are made, the money voted will not be expended during the present year.

25 August 1819.   Usborne & Co explain that they were not aware of any delay but there might have been for want of some particular shaped stones which have now arrived.

103.   *Navy Board to Admiralty: purchase of marshlands*

[TNA, ADM106/2281]   24 May 1821

In our letter to you of the 18 May 1820 we adverted to the several claims which had been sent up by the individuals to Finsborough Marsh in the vicinity of Chatham dockyard (for the purchase of which we obtained the sanction of the Lords Commissioners of the Admiralty on the 12th July 1819) and we submitted the propriety of procuring an Act of Parliament, authorising the purchase.

In answer to that letter their Lordships were pleased to signify to us by Mr Barrow's letter of 1st July, that they concurred in the opinions expressed in a note dated the 1st June from Mr Bickwell to the Comptroller of the Navy, which opinion was in favour of treating with the several claimants and effecting the purchase without application to Parliament to vest lands in the Crown. This, as Mr Bickwell observed, foundered on the necessity of their being taken for the public service and therefore he apprehended that some difficulty might arise to the passing of a Bill as to Finsborough Marsh.

The course recommended by Mr Bickwell had however been tried before. We submitted that proposal by our letter of 18th May 1820, and we have now to request you to signify to their Lordships that it having been represented to us by Commissioner Sir Robert Barlow that circumstances had transpired, which induced him to suppose that the marsh might at one time have belonged to the Crown. We, on the 4th September last desired Mr Bickwell to inquire into the ancient state of it and endeavoured to procure proof of any acts of ownership that might have been exercised thereon by the Crown within the space of sixty years past and to lay the result before the Counsel for the Affairs of the Admiralty and the Navy for his opinion whether there are grounds for instituting proceedings by information of intrusion or otherwise for recovering possession of the marsh.

Mr Jervis' opinion on the case having been cordially obtained we enclose a copy of it by which their Lordships will perceive that he does not deem it proper to lay claim to the marsh for the King but advises the passing of a vesting act similar to that of 44th George III cap 79 for the purpose of being ultimately purchased but which Act will require many additional clauses.

Mr Bickwell, in transmitting to us that opinion, has suggested that if it shall be determined to apply to Parliament the marsh might be included in the Bill now in preparation for the purchase of Blue Town. As it is essentially necessary and convenient for the deposit of the timber now lying afloat in the Medway and other stores we beg to recommend that the measures now suggested by Mr Jervis and Mr Bickwell be taken to obtain possession of Finsborough Marsh.

104. *Navy Board to Admiralty: dock entrance*

[TNA, ADM106/2281] 25 May 1821

In consequence of the formation of the new dry dock in Chatham Yard and the alteration that has been made in the line of the river wall, it has become necessary to make a new entrance to the old dock (number two) in the accompanying drawing of the docks in that yard.

It is proposed by Mr Rennie that the new entrance shall be 4 feet 3 inches deeper than the present entrance – that is the same depth as the entrance to the new dock (no. 3).

To the adoption of that proposal however, the Surveyors of the Navy, who are well acquainted with the docks at Chatham, feel objection, considering that one dock of the depth of number three is sufficient for the port of Chatham, more especially as there are three docks capable of receiving first rates in progress at Sheerness, and apprehending that difficulties would arise in digging the foundations lower, and that it would be attempted not only with very great expense, but will endanger ships docking by the seal of the gate being so much lower than the flap of the dock.

105. *John Rennie to First Lord: proposal for enlarging dockyard*

[Rennie, *Treatise on Harbours*, pp. 48–50.]   1 September 1821

In my letter to the Board of Admiralty, dated the 27th August, 1814, I described to their Lordships a plan which had occurred to me of improving and enlarging Chatham yard so as to render it fit for receiving the largest ships of His Majesty's Navy, and docking and undocking them at all times of tide, and also of enabling the largest ships of the Royal Navy to get to and from it.

This plan was to make a cut for the River Medway, to commence at the lower end of Bridge Reach, in the parish of Frindsbury, to the said River at Upnor Castle, and to dam up the old channel at Rochester Marshes and at the north end of the dockyard, so as to convert the whole of the space between the embankments into a wet dock, from which north end of the yard a canal was proposed to be made across the Marshes to the head of Gillingham Reach, where it was to enter the Medway by a lock capable of receiving the largest ships, having a basin within the lock where vessels gong to sea might wait until wind and tide served, or those bound for the dockyard might come in with the flowing tide, and remain in the basin until ready to be moved up the canal into the wet dock in front of Chatham yard. In order that vessels employed in the trade of Chatham might have a ready communication with the Medway without passing through that part of the wet dock used for the public service, a short canal was proposed to be made across part of Rochester Marsh with a lock in it, to form a communication with Bridge Reach.

The plan upon which the above scheme was formed was made by the Master-Attendant at Chatham Yard. The plan was perhaps tolerably correct as far as the river for navigation is concerned, but by no means as to the land. No estimate accompanied my report of August 1814, though I believe afterwards one was formed, no copy of which was kept by me. It now however, turns out, from the actual survey, that the hill to be cut through in the parish of Frindsbury is both higher and wider than I was led to believe at that time. This, although it does not in any degree affect the practicability of the project, increases the estimate beyond what your Lordship seems to have made up in your mind; though, as the great bulk of the work can be done by convicts, it may not, perhaps, in your Lordship's estimation, materially affect the question.

The plan which I have the honour to present for your Lordship's consideration is laid down in a survey, both of the River Medway and the grounds it embraces, with great care, and which I have no doubt is very correct. The new cut for the Medway is proposed to be 600 feet [*wide*] at the surface or level of an ordinary spring tide, 400 feet at bottom, and 20 feet deep at low water. These dimensions at the upper end are the full size of the present river. At the lower end it is proposed to be 750 feet wide, and of the same depth. The quantity of land this cut will occupy, including its slopes and banks will be about 85 acres, and the land lying between it and the Medway is about 160 acres more, making in all at this place about 245 acres.

The old channel of the Medway included within its banks is 243 acres, and will form a wet dock of that size.

The quantity of land, which the canal and basin at Gillingham Reach will occupy, is about 60 acres, and the canal at Rochester Marshes about 2 acres

The purchase of 245 acres, as valued by Mr
Giles, including Bindley's ship yard, is   £54,536   14s   0d

The purchase of the land for the canal and basin
at Gillingham Reach, taking 60 acres only, will be £6,000   0s   0d

The purchase of land and premises on Rochester
Marsh   £ 1,463   0s   0d

But if the whole of Frindsbury Marsh is to be purchased, as also that of Rochester, the value, as in Mr Giles's schedule, would be £75,829 6s 6d. I apprehend, however, what I have stated above will be all that can be required.

The works more immediately connected with the dockyard I propose to make on the largest scale that the service can require. The canal to

Gillingham Reach is proposed to be made 300 feet wide and 30 feet deep, so that ships of the largest class can pass through it even at neap tides and when they get up to the Medway at Gillingham Reach, they will meet with no detention there. The basin adjoining the entrance lock I propose to be made 1000 feet long and 450 feet wide and of the same depth as the canal. The lock into the Medway to have 28 feet of water at neap tides and the communication lock between the canal and basin to have the same depth of water as in the basin. By means of this lock, the water in the wet dock and canal will always be kept nearly at the same level, i.e. of spring tides. I do not apprehend the waste of water between a spring and a neap tide will ever exceed a foot on the surface, so that the water from the basin may be used to secure the entrance of the lock without affecting the general level of the water in front of the dockyard. When a change of water in the dock is required, it can be let through the canal at Rochester in spring-tides, and out at Gillingham, by which all fear respecting the evils arising from stagnant water will be remitted.

Objections will in all probability arise to this plan from the inhabitants of Chatham, under the apprehension that their sewers will be obstructed. To remove this inconvenience, it is proposed to make an intercepting sewer, to convey the water from Chatham into the Medway below Rochester, at which place, by the new cut, the surface at low water will fall quite as low as it now is at Chatham. By the improved current, the soil and mud will be effectually swept away, which, owing to the great depth of the Medway where it is now discharged, this not the case, as much of it settles, and is very detrimental to navigation.

Another mode of performing this work might be to make a sewer along the river-side of Chatham, to intercept the soil. From this it might be conveyed under the river in a cast-iron pipe, and by a sewer along Frindsbury Marshes to the Medway, above Upnor Castle. This mode, however, would be more expensive than the former, and probably not more effective.

The probable cost of the respective works I have named, the calculations of which have been made with great care, is, however, great, as appears by the annexed estimate, amounting to £685,812. Of this sum, at least £350,000 is for earthwork, nearly all of which can be done by convicts. The balance, namely, £335,812, would be consumed in materials, purchase of property, and labour of regular artificers.

With this your Lordship will receive a small plan of the work; the large plan will be ready for your Lordship when you return to London.

[Enclosure]
Extract of the probable expense of making a new cut for the River Medway, from the lower end of Bridge Reach, Rochester, to near Upnor

Castle, and for a dam across the river at Bridge Reach, and another at the lower end of Chatham Reach, and a canal to Gillingham Reach, having a basin with entrance and communication locks.

To 3,019,573 cubic yards of cutting through the chalk hill in Frindsbury, for the new channel of the River, the chalk to be deposited on the marshes	at 1s	£150,978	13s	0d
To 2,739,000 cubic yards of cutting in the marshes for the said river, the earth to be in like manner deposited in the river	at 9d	£102,712	10s	0d
To 198,442 cubic yards of earth to form the bank across the river at Bridge Reach	at 9d	£7,441	11s	6d
To 493,000 do. to form the bank across the river at the lower end of Chatham Reach	at 9d	£18,487	10s	0d
To 1,064,500 cubic yards of cutting in the canal and basin to Gillingham	at 9d	£39,918	15s	0d
To coffer-dam at Gillingham Reach		£19,475	0s	0d
To an entrance lock, with wing walls at do.		£122,570	0s	0d
To communication lock between the canal and basin		£58,835	0s	0d
To lock and cut at Rochester Marsh		£16,766	13s	4d
To a sewer for the drainage of Rochester and Chatham		£537,185	12s	10d
To steam engines and pumps for pumping the water while the works are in hand		£15,000	0s	0d
To towing paths for canal		£5,000	0s	0d
To contingencies		£56,626	7s	2d

To the purchase of land and premises   £62,000   0s   0d

                                              £685,812   0s   0d

106.   *Navy Board to Admiralty: escalating costs*

[TNA, ADM 106/2287]   18 March 1824

The expense of constructing the entrance to the dock number two at Chatham being likely to exceed the estimates made by the late Mr Rennie to a very considerable amount, we are anxious to call the attention of the Lords Commissioners of the Admiralty to the subject before the work is further proceeded with and at the same time to submit for their Lordships' consideration the expediency of adopting some other course respecting it.

Mr Rennie estimated for the entrance to this dock a sum that amounted to £19,000 and it appears to us upon reference to a line drawn and marked by his own hand in the plan, his calculation was made with a view only to the construction of as much masonry as would extend inward to the distance of less than fifty feet from the face of the river wall.

The excavation of the upper surface of the entrance has however, been carried to a distance of 96 feet, which the Clerk of the Works has informed us was done by the verbal directions of the late Mr Rennie. If the measuring is also to be so extended, it follows that the expense will be much greater than their Lordships have hitherto sanctioned.

The Messrs Rennies do not consider that the excavations have been carried further than was intended. We however, entertain a different opinion, not seeing any reason why the late Mr Rennie should send us a plan of the dock regularly set off by scale, and the only part not being a correct relative proportion should be the line in question, which as it was to fix the boundary of the work at present to be expected, seemed to require the greater accuracy. We think we are borne out in our opinion that this line did mark the extent to which Mr Rennie intended to proceed, because his estimate of that part of the work amounted only to £19,000 while the sum now expended for the entrance, besides what has already been paid amounts to £34,678.

The sum paid for the dock, lately finished amounts to £182,286. If so large a part of the dock No 2 is to be completed, as now contemplated (being one-third of the whole dock), including the most expensive and difficult part of the works, to which a culvert or drain must necessarily be added, it may reasonably be assured that the plan as understood by the Clerk of the Works, and approved by Messrs Rennie, will cost upwards of £60,000 instead of £19,000. The execution has hitherto cost £1,138 but if the work is pursued: 4,500 cubic yards of earth will need to be removed.

In considering this subject it is proper to bear in mind that unless it is ultimately intended to build an entire new dock, the greater part of the expense now proposed for the entrance will be unnecessary.

107. *Commissioner Cunningham to Navy Board: construction of caisson*

[TNA, ADM 106/1829]   18 December 1824

With reference to your letter of the 17th ultimo to afford every facility carrying on the works at the dock no. 2, in the course of the ensuing year, I acquaint you that it will be necessary to construct a caisson for this dock as soon as possible. It is therefore proposed that one may be built in the groove of the new dock, if the entrance of which is similar to the new dock, in order that it may be ready to be floated into its place by the time the masonry of the latter is completed.

108. *Commissioner Cunningham to Navy Board: mud shoals*

[TNA, ADM 106/1830]   10 February 1825

I have received your letter of 31st ultimo and 9th instant, desiring to know whether it may not be practicable to accommodate a sufficient number of convicts on board the present hulk, for the purpose of being employed in the removal of shoals in the river, without fitting the *Conway* for the temporary accommodation of the men and also to be informed of the smallest number of the prisoners necessary to be employed upon the particular service.

In return to which I have to acquaint you that it will require 200 men at least to perform this work with advantage to the service to be employed in the description of barges alluded to in my letter of the 5th of August last. Upon consulting with the person in charge of the prisoners I learn this additional number of men cannot be accommodated on board the present convict hulk. It will consequently become necessary that a vessel should be fitted merely for the convicts to be lodged on board in security. No fire hearth or extra fittings will be required, with the exception of the iron gratings to secure the parts &c &c as the provisions will be prepared on board the *Dolphin*, and the other necessary assistance rendered from that ship.

Having directed the officers to report to me the expense of fitting the *Conway* for the service in question, they report that on a further consideration of the subject, they are of opinion that it should be more advantageous to the public to fit the *Wye* for the purpose, she having a spar deck, and being in other respects similar to the *Conway* excepting that her hull is not so valuable nor are her masts on board. The fitting of either vessel will be for coppering the bottom £558 0s 0d and fitting for prisoners £442. 0s. 0d. Total £1,000. Although it is intended to place the ship upon the mud with the *Dolphin*, they [the officers] do not apprehend that the worms would, in the course of two or three years, affect a material injury to the bottom of the ship if she is taken first into dock and her bottom paid with mineral pitch instead of coppering her. I find that either of these ships can be taken into the mast pond drain for the purpose of having the bottom paid with mineral pitch as above suggested.

109. *Commissioner Cunningham to Navy Board: progress of works*

[TNA, ADM 106/1830] 12 July 1825

Adverting to my former correspondence relative to the works carrying on in this yard at the Dock No. 2, I think it proper to acquaint you that, not withstanding, there are only thirteen masons employed thereon. It appears by a report from the Master Shipwright that the quantity of stone in hand is not more than sufficient to keep them employed for about a fortnight but that the contractors stated to him on Saturday last another vessel was loading with that article and might be shortly expected. I suggest the propriety of the contractors being urged to send timely supplies of stone, in order that no impediment on that account, may take place in carrying on the works in question, with the few hands that are employed upon them.

110. *Usborne and Benson to Navy Board: problems encountered*

[TNA, ADM 106/1832] 28 March 1826

We have not only agreed to pay a great advance in freight considerably beyond any persons to induce a supply of stone, but we are also paying a higher price for the article. If the Honourable Board would be kind enough to refer to our letters they would find we have already suffered considerable loss by the delays we have experienced for want of orders and other circumstances to which we are sorry again to refer. In fact it must be evident to yourselves that having a reserve of £8000 in keeping up a large expensive establishment and these works being the only remaining concern we are jointly engaged in, it must therefore be clear to every person, that it is our interest, and also would be much to our convenience, to finish the business in order that we might settle the accounts finally. We cannot therefore conceive what has given rise to the complaints, as the officers on the works cannot but be aware that we are doing all that men can do to give satisfaction and up to the middle of last year no complaints were made. With regard to more masons being taken on, we beg leave to state, that we must be allowed to be the best judges on that head. We think it is not fairly represented to the Honourable Board that more masons could be employed with [*the*] present quantity of stone because there are many stones on the ground that it would be imprudent to work until the other courses arrive and which arises from the extreme difficulty in procuring, the peculiar form of many of them. We have, however, to give satisfaction, taken on more masons and we are in daily expectation of two vessels arriving with stone. We have taken every precaution human foresight can devise for the supply of that article, and as it arrives we will take care to augment the number of workmen in proportion, as a few more cargoes will bring in all the courses regularly. We sincerely trust that a short period will finally complete the business.

111. *Commissioner Cunningham to Navy Board: land for depositing of mud*

[TNA, ADM 106/1833]   20 November 1826

With reference to my letter of 18 March last relative to the purchase of several pieces of land therein alluded to; I beg to suggest that some measure may be taken therein, and particularly as it respects St. Mary's or Finsborough Marsh, it being the only eligible place wherein the mud that is raised out of this harbour can be deposited. This marsh is overflowed at high water; spring tides, except where it has been raised by the mud which has been laid upon it and there still being a great quantity of soil which must be removed away. When the coffer dam and the old wall in front of the dock are taken up, and which if deposited on the marsh in question, will continue to raise it and eventually make it good land and consequently enhance its value. It may therefore be advisable to secure the land before the principal proprietors make such a plea for demanding an extravagant sum for the purchase of it.

112. *Commissioner Cunningham to Navy Board: dredging expenses*

[TNA, ADM 106/1836]   26 June 1828

Expense of steam, mud engine, punts, boats &c. and the hire of barges specified

1815	£1,118		Includes the expense of building two mud barges.
1816			
1817	£65	19s	
1818	£946	5s	2d	Includes the expense of building two mud barges.
1819	£790	7s	11d
1820	£70	3s	7d
1821	£50	4s	
1822	£57	14s	9d
1823	£135	6s	8d
1824	£691	10s	7d
1825	£989	1s	6d
1826	£652	0s	3d
1827	£126	16s	7d
1828	£95	0s	4d

Wages and victualling of the steam mud engines, labour of yard and convicts

1815	514.	6s	3d
1816	635.	0s	1d
1817	668	7s	3d
1818	1504	3s	2d
1819	1494	9s	11d
1820	1784	17s	5d
1821	1151	4s	4d
1822	768	2s	1d
1823	918	5s	6d
1824	1411	4s	7d
1825	1885	0s	8d
1826	1162	3s	8d
1827	687	13s	10d
1828	698	4s	6d

113.   *Chatham Yard Officers to Navy Board: estimates*

[TNA, ADM 106/1837]   17 October 1828

By the workmen of the Dockyard –

To remove the cofferdam in front of entrance to new stone dock, including for clearing away remaining part of jetty, and for erecting new landing place.

Estimate of such sums as may be necessary for completing
the Works   £1,500

Money that will be laid out during the year 1829   £1,500

For repairing in part the north and south sides of North Mast Pond Walls.

Estimate of such sums as may be necessary for completing
the Works   £860

Money that will be laid out during the year 1829   £860

Erect a new roof over dock no. 2 and copper the same.

Estimate of such sums as may be necessary for completing
the Works   £6,850

Money that will be laid out during the year 1829   £3,425

114.   *Commissioner Cunningham to Navy Board: dock roof*

[TNA, ADM 106/1837]   22 November 1828

In return to your letter of the 18th instant adverting to the officers' estimates of the 17th ultimo of the probable expense of the new works at this yard in the year 1829. I acquaint you that, in calculating the estimated sum of £650 for the completion of the roof over the Dock No. 2, it was contemplated to paper it, and that through error copper was inserted.

115. *Commissioner Cunningham to Navy Board: introduction of steam pump*

[TNA, ADM 106/1838]   23 April 1829

The shipwright officers having represented to me that it is attended with considerable labour and expense to keep the first, third and fourth docks clear of water in consequence of it being under the necessity of pumping them out by hand. Not only this expense might be saved, but also that of making a dam every time a ship is docked, if three culvert drains were constructed: namely one to lead from the first to the second dock, one from the fourth to the third dock and one from the third to the new stone dock, by which the water may be pumped out by the lift engine. It would be the means of keeping it in a proper state by its more frequent use, as it is now often put in motion without any other advantage than that of keeping the machinery in order.

116. *Master Attendant to Superintendent Gordon: employment of steam vessels*

[TNA, ADM 1/3386]   8 November 1832

In consequence of your minute of this day I have consulted with my assistant and harbour pilots on the subject of taking the *Iphigenia* and *Warrior* to the Thames. We are of the opinion that at this season of the year it would not be safe to employ less than fifty men on the *Warrior* and thirty on the *Iphigenia*. We do not recommend that these ships be jury rigged but that two small topgallant mast sails and gear, which are already provided and kept in readiness in the rigging house, shall be put on board to assist them in their passage as circumstances will admit, which suggestion if approved of can be carried into effect without any increased expense.

The employment of two steam vessels in the above service will not only lessen the risk of their navigation but from the increased expedition derived from them, there would be a saving of expense so far as the wages of the men and their extra allowances are concerned.

117.   *William Ranger (contractor) to Civil Architect of the Navy:*
reconstruction of No. 4 dock

[TNA, ADM 1/3502]   22 December 1834

I have received your amended instructions respecting the proposed new dock and river wall with steps at His Majesty's yard Chatham and as under. I beg to subjoin the result of my calculations and the amount for which I am willing to execute the several works –

Amount for the dock, river wall with steps complete	£9,020
Timber for piles of dam and wall	495
Driving piles, stages and shoring	485
Breaking up the slip, excavating and clearing the dock of old timber	1,000
Building the caisson of old materials	500
Total amount	£11,500

I hereby agree to perform the several works for the above sum of eleven thousand five hundred pounds – and in every respect to your entire satisfaction.

118.   *Master Attendant to Superintendent Clavell: proposed landing*
place

[TNA, ADM 1/3404]   3 May 1837

In reply to the Admiralty order of the 24th I most respectfully bid to state that I have carefully examined the place pointed out by the inhabitants of Chatham where they wish to erect a jetty or landing place for their steam boat passengers. I find the shore or flat runs so far into the river at that place, that a pier carried out to low water at marked spring tides would in some degree impede the navigation of the river. On examining the shore I find that at about 110 fathoms to the westward, at a place called Joslins Wharf, that an open jetty might be erected without doing any harm to the river or its navigation provided that all communication with it to be strictly confined to the extreme end and nothing to be allowed to take the ground near or either end of it.

119. *Architects' Department to Admiralty: estimated costs for dredging of the river in 1842*

[TNA, ADM 1/5521]

Cleaning mud and forming a groin to prevent further accumulation, opposite the dockyard.

The shoaling of the River Medway – particularly at the naval anchorage, and opposite the dockyard – has long been a subject of anxious solicitude – various plans have been proposed, but in general they involve the consideration, of large sums of money.

The present mode is to clear away the mud by dredging – and to form a groin on the side of the river opposite the dockyard, which will have the effect of diverting the stream more into the centre of the channel, and of narrowing the channel, so as to increase the scouring power of the stream.

£4,000

120. *Report of Deputy Director of Works: proposed extension*

[RNM, Portsmouth Mss 286 (previously Da 0126)]   8 January 1857

St. Mary's Creek and St. Mary's Island

The most important question for consideration is the appropriation of St. Mary's Creek and St. Mary's Island. The accumulation of mud in front of the yard, requiring constant dredging, is chiefly in consequence of this creek. If permitted to be open, the inconvenience from mud will continue and the sides will be required to be embanked. Though this might be done, and the inconvenience and annual expense perpetuated, yet St. Mary's Island must be so separated from the yard as to create a still further inconvenience and annual expense. Here I must remark that the great principle, which should govern the arrangement of the naval establishments, is usually overlooked; as from the manner in which the establishments have been created, and from time to time extended, the great question of economising labour has been entirely lost sight of. The largest and most important establishment is the most defective in this respect. The consequence must be an annual waste, and, what is of much greater importance; the establishments are not adapted for performing the pressing duties required of them during war with the requisite dispatch.

To shorten the distance from Chatham yard to Sheerness yard, and to make available for yard duties the larger water space with a greater depth of water at Gillingham Reach, must be advantages favourable to the scheme for adding St. Mary's Creek and St. Mary's island to the establishment.

The removal of old Rochester Bridge will probably add to the depth of water in front of the yard but annual dredging will not be prevented so long as the passage through St. Mary's Creek is continued.

Mast House

There is not a mast house in the service that is properly adapted to the duties of mast making, nor is it usual to employ the mast houses as stores. Thus, in converting the rough timber; in applying the timber in a converted state for mast making; and depositing the mast when made, in the store (probably in a position that will require an equal amount of labour in taking it out again) an enormous expense and loss of time must be incurred. To facilitate such important duties I would suggest that all the work of mast making, from the rough balk, should be done in the mast houses; that the mast house should be the mast and spar store; that all the masts and spars of a ship should be stowed together in berths and that properly constructed travellers should be provided for the removing, and depositing, such large masses with facility and great dispatch. Provision should be made also, for preparing, repairing and stowing, tops and cross trees. For such an arrangement the mast house will require to be about 270 feet in breadth.

Boat House and Store

But for improvements at Devonport and Sheerness – now in progress (though not equal to the wants of the service) it might with truth be stated that every establishment is greatly deficient in accommodation for boats, both as regards working space and stowage. The building not long ago constructed at Portsmouth at a great cost, is totally unsuited either for a working boathouse or a boat store. At Sheerness there must always be in store a large number of boats, and the boats must be repaired; but I am not aware that it is necessary to build boats at Sheerness, except for employing the men when not required for repairs.

At Chatham a boat building establishment may probably with advantage be provided; to be used chiefly as a boat building establishment in which improvements may be introduced – for selecting and sawing timber – for an improved application of labour – and by the employment of machinery.

Timber (Oak)

A much larger quantity of oak timber is deposited at Chatham in the rough tree than at any other establishment. The ground recently occupied by such timber was equal to 10 acres. The timber sheds generally are in a dilapidated state.

Opinions have been, and still are, divided as to the method that should be adopted for stowing and seasoning timber for shipbuilding.

It would appear to be desirable that this, and some other large questions touching dockyard management should be set at rest in a satisfactory manner.

The stacking of timber by either of the methods now in use is attended with an expense in labour for stacking and un-stacking that is but imperfectly understood. To stack timber in such a manner as to apply the moulds, and to enable the timber to be selected with certainty, avoiding the great labour of un-stacking and re-stacking is difficult and probably impracticable, so long as it is considered essential to stack timber horizontally. Should an unobjectionable method of stacking timber perpendicularly be devised, all these advantages would be secured.

Under the most favourable circumstances a very large space for timber converted and un-converted will be required at Chatham and for which St. Mary's Island is favourable.

Timber (Fir)

It has been the practice for a long time to deposit the valuable timber from which masts and spars are prepared, in mast ponds and mast locks. This method was doubtless introduced from a supposition that timber immersed in water is preserved from decay. This is no doubt the case so long as the timber is immersed but I never yet saw a mast pond or a mast lock, in which a very large portion of the balks are not all or in part exposed. For the present, mast ponds and mast locks can scarcely be dispensed with, notwithstanding the damage the timber sustains from exposure and worms.

The method recently patented by Dr. Bourcherie, a French chemist, may probably lead to useful results. The subject of the preservation of timber is of immense importance and worthy of a very careful investigation.

The Basins

Economical construction, by using inexpensive materials and convict labour, offer inducements for providing at Chatham [through the use of

St Mary's Creek] ample basin space useful at all times but essentially necessary to meet the demands of a great war.

At Deptford some basin space is being added while at Woolwich the basin space was twice increased. After the works were commenced at Sheerness, much more basin space [was and still] is required. At Portsmouth, though 100 feet was added to the breadth of the basin during the time the works were in progress, yet this establishment is still deficient in basin space. At Devonport the basin will chiefly be used as a boat basin and at Keyham a suggestion that I made some years ago for increasing the north basin from 700 to 1000 feet, was approved from a conviction that more basin space would be required. Having all these examples, it would be a great misfortune should another mistake be made at Chatham.

Slips

The preparations now nearly completed for hauling up the gunboats at Haslar are likely to prove as efficient for the purpose as I had anticipated. To have a large number of vessels at all times in a state of efficiency, ready for use, is of itself an advantage of some value. Taking into consideration that vessels may be repaired – their machinery may be repaired – and if necessary vessels may be constructed at those establishments without any obstruction to the duties of the larger establishments – the benefits that must result from such a scheme will be found at all times great; but for war incalculable.

I propose to construct the slips a few feet only below the surface of the ground, as at Haslar. To avoid the incline it is proposed to lift the vessels by water in a lock and to place them on the cradle in a cradling dock.

The draught of the batteries is about 8 feet. The lock will require to be constructed to about 10 or 12 feet only below high water neap tides. This will admit of vessels up to the frigate class, light, at spring tides or larger vessels in a launching state being taken to or from the slips.

Should this suggestion be entertained, this is a work on which the convicts may be at once employed. As the whole of the work may be done by convict labour, and as inexpensive materials only will be necessary, it may be accomplished at a comparatively small cost (should it be practicable to make arrangements for advantageously employing the convicts).

Stores and Present Mast Ponds

Should the site proposed for this mast pond be entertained, the site of one of the present mast ponds is well adopted for a great central store house

– the excavated space forming a basement storey. It may be expedient to remove the present saw mills, though under the disadvantage of having to lift the timber 30 feet above the coping level; but so long as the saw mills remain as at present, the mast pond into which the tunnel enters will be required in connection with them.

Anchors, Mooring Anchors, and Mooring Buoys

The present position of the anchors at Chatham is not ill adapted for use – but the existing method of stowing the anchors at all the establishments is most objectionable.

Observing at Woolwich about eighteen years ago, the great loss of time and the liability to accident; I suggested a method for removing the objections, and which was approved by the Board. It has only been attempted (imperfectly) at Portsmouth.

By the old method the anchors are stowed against wooden rails supported by wooden posts. Usually three, and sometimes four anchors on each side are lashed by chains or ropes to the rails, sometimes in such manner as to require all the anchors to be laid down – and usually three – to get out that nearest the rail.

I proposed that the anchors should be stacked under a pre-constructed traveller, in such manner that the Anchor required should be taken from the stack leaving all the others untouched.

I am not aware why this obvious improvement has not been generally adopted, both for anchors and mooring buoys.

The method may be adapted to the present anchor wharf if continued or to the new site as proposed.

Factory Buildings

Two designs are laid down for the Factory – one adhering nearly to the plan of the Keyham Factory as to the general arrangements. The other is, I think, an improved arrangement for the fitting and erecting shops and boiler shop, being nearly on the plan as recently introduced at Sheerness yard.

The alterations – and which are considered at Sheerness, great improvements – consist in having (for boiler making) the work of punching, shearing, riveting, smiths' work, and furnace work in immediate connexion with the boilers. For the fitting and erecting shops, the space for erecting is in the middle of the shop and the fitters' work and tools are immediately contiguous to the space for erecting. For boiler making, fitting and erecting great facilities are afforded for promoting dispatch and accuracy.

Coaling

The subject of receiving coal from colliers, and depositing the coal in ships of war of all classes, with the requisite facility and dispatch (though first submitted for consideration in 1843) has not advanced to the state of perfection that is necessary.

For ordinary cases, with the assistance of hydraulic cranes, coaling at one side of the ship may generally be sufficient. For war it is doubtful if the desired dispatch can be secured except by coaling at both sides of the ship at the same time and with this view the arrangements for Chatham have been made.

Roads, Tram Roads and Railroads

About eight years ago in consequence of the defective state of the paving of the yards generally, it was determined to introduce a system of stone tram roads. This has been done to some extent at Woolwich, Chatham, Portsmouth and Devonport, and to a small extent at Deptford and Sheerness.

About £25,000 has been expended (including the sums provided for this year) on stone tram roads.

The stone tram roads are no doubt a great improvement. It may be a question, however, if a more efficient system of roadways for the large establishments, especially for Chatham, if extended, may not be introduced – less expensive in first cost and repairing – more economical, by reducing the great expense of teams – and promoting dispatch. For the small establishments a method may be adopted for using the available materials for the yards (and this should be promoted for all practical purposes) capable of being repaired at a small cost; but for Chatham a simple method of railroads is, I think, quite necessary for promoting dispatch and economy.

An extension of the North Kent Railway to Dover is in progress of construction; a branch is commenced, or will be immediately commenced, to Sheerness. To a communication with Sheerness yard I have already alluded; a communication with Chatham yard would also appear to be quite necessary; though it may be questionable – from the direction of the line – whether the advantages to the Dockyard have been sufficiently secured.

A line of rails in communication with the main line should be taken through Chatham yard and to the Marine Barracks. A communication will then be formed by railroad from London to Deptford, Woolwich, Chatham, Sheerness, Deal, Dover and Portsmouth.

River Walls, River Boundary, and Basin Walls

For this extensive work – if only on the most limited scale – a method of construction of the most simple and inexpensive kind capable of being executed by a well-organised system of convict labour, should be adopted; as explained in my report dated August 1855.

For the Boundary of St. Mary's Island I would recommend a sloping embankment, faced with Kentish Rag Stone; both for dispatch and economy.

The improvement of the water space and river generally, should be carefully considered in laying down the new line of embankment.

The River Medway, Dredging &c

The state of the River Medway from Rochester Bridge to Sheerness Yard may not appear to be a subject essentially necessary to be attended to in dealing with the subject of Chatham yard improvements. Chatham Reach, Cockham Reach, Sovereign Reach and Gillingham Reach, are the great basin boundary of the Admiralty land – whether that land may be appropriated as proposed by the large scheme or not – and nearly the whole of the distance may be required for mooring ships in ordinary.

The whole space of flat surface between the rising-ground on both sides is a series of small islands. The ditches and tidal water courses continually enlarging carrying off into the bed of the river, and from the bed of the river to the Nore, just enough of the surface of the soil to cause a greater amount of destruction at every succeeding tide.

Besides the evils resulting from the constant removal of surface soil, there are tidal streams and boundary irregularities that must cause serious damage to a tidal river in which a great depth of water is so essentially necessary – such for instance as the junction of Pinup Reach, Long Reach and South Yantlet Creek.

The importance of this river would appear to suggest the propriety of dealing with that part forming the boundary of naval property at once.

Convict Labour

By a judicious method of employing the convicts, and one, which I believe may without difficulty be introduced; the whole scheme, large as it may appear, may be carried out to completion within a moderate time, and at a small cost.

I stated in a report dated August 1855, that the dispatch with which the extensive works proposed at Chatham can be executed, and the cost of such works, must depend on three things

1st.   The description of materials to be used in the works.

2nd.   The method to be adopted in applying the materials to the works.

3rd.   The method to be adopted for employing, in the most advantageous manner, the convict labour.

As regards the employment of convicts I made the following remarks. In the employment of convicts I have long taken great interest not only from observation but also from giving directions for management of works where convicts are employed. Though I believe improvements have been effected at Gibraltar, and more particularly at Bermuda, yet I entertain a strong opinion that the convict has not yet been made efficiently available. What appear to be wanting are a general system of mechanical management and a method of qualifying men and applying their labour to duties for which they are practically qualified.

The general management as regards the discipline of convicts will necessarily require being under the control of the convict department but the direction of the men in the execution of their duties may, I imagine, be under the control of this department.

This being established, a method should be adopted for raising the men from a state of worthlessness to useful labourers, from labourers to artificers, and from artificers to leading men. I most successfully adopted a similar method for qualifying men for executing difficult engineering and other works of great magnitude at a foreign station; and some years ago prepared a form for the guidance of officers in accomplishing the same object with convicts at Gibraltar and Bermuda, and which is still successful in use.

Before commencing the work on a large scale, I would suggest that this question should be carefully determined, and a system established by which a proper amount of labour will be secured for promoting the work; and the men generally will be improved by knowing the value of their labour.

I have confined my remarks chiefly to the extension; but it is impossible to overlook the fact that the existing arrangements of the yard are most defective, whether considered with reference to the most limited or the most extensive scheme.

121. *Director of Works to Secretary of the Admiralty: employment of convicts*

[TNA, ADM1/5703] 6 July 1858

In compliance with the Board's orders, I have personally communicated with the Superintendent at Chatham regarding the employment of convicts and also with the Governor of the prison; and from information obtained from them and from the report of the superintending civil engineer, I find that the total number of convicts for which employment is required is from 750 to 800.

On the day of my visit, and for some time previous, the total number actually employed by the Admiralty was 700.

Of these, <u>183</u> were employed on work in connection with the improvement of the yard by convict labour and <u>76</u> under the Clerk of Works, leaving <u>441</u> employed on 15 distinct miscellaneous duties in the dockyard.

It is in regard to the latter that the Governor desires to find more suitable employment.

The Governor stated that he would not object to a certain number, say 250, being employed in the dockyard for a time, though as a general rule, it was very desirable to get them to work in larger numbers.

If therefore suitable work for some 300 more convicts could be found, the present requirements of the case would be sufficiently met.

As the new river wall works proceed, further employment, to a small extent, say for 50 more, will be found; but I cannot find any means of employing the remaining 250 without breaking ground on a new site.

Under these circumstances, I beg to refer to works ordered in Admiralty Order of the 19th March 1858 and suspended by Admiralty Order of 3rd April 1858. This work comprises the forming of an embankment along the riverfront of St Mary's Island. It is of an inexpensive character (about £200 per one hundred brick yards) and it is particularly suited for the employment of a considerable number of convicts, as it consists almost wholly of labour forming the embankment and setting the facing of old materials. I presume this embankment must be made sooner or later, whatever may be made of St Mary's Island in order to preserve it against the erosion caused by the action of the tide, waves and steamers.

Further, as will be seen from the report of the Acting Superintending Civil Engineer, the probable expenditure on account of the work sanctioned in Admiralty Order of the 3rd April 1858 will be about £475 only, whereas permission is made in the Estimates of the current year for an expenditure of £10,000 – finally, this work would at once have given profitable employment to about 250 men.

For the above reasons I beg to recommend that the embankment of St Mary's Island, as approved in Admiralty Order of 19th March 1858, be now taken in hand. I believe this Order will practically meet the present requirement of the Home Office for the suitable employment of convicts.

122.   *Re-opening of No. 2 Dock*

[Illustrated London News]   13 November 1858

The dock recently completed at Chatham, known as No. 2 dock, of which we give an engraving on page 445, was commenced in October, 1855, and completed in October of the present year. It was built by Messrs. J. and C. Rigby, from the designs of the director of engineering and architectural works of the Admiralty. The dimensions of the dock are as follows:–

Length from the caisson to the coping	395 feet
Length on the floor from caisson to head of dock	360
Depth from coping to floor	31
Width on the floor	30
Width between coping	85

The floor of the dock is constructed with Cornish and Devonshire granite, bedded on brickwork in cement, which is laid on a thick bed of concrete. The sides are also built with the same description of granite, filled in at the back with brickwork laid in cement, and backed with concrete of great thickness; it is also provided with slides at the head and sides.

123.   *Controller of the Navy to Superintendent Goldsmith: building sheds*

[NMM, CHA/H/104]   5 October 1860

The Captain Superintendent at Chatham is requested to direct the officers to report with the least possible delay, whether they see any objection to the erection of sheds between Nos. 1 and 2 Docks as shown in the accompanying tracing and to the appropriation of the site now occupied by the temporary Smithery and Coal Store for a Smithery for the purpose of building the iron ship.

124. *Controller of the Navy to Superintendent Goldsmith: building sheds*

[NMM, CHA/H/104]   10 October 1860

As the proposed new sheds will greatly crowd the very confined working space about the dock, and as the construction for 'levelling slabs' will effectually prevent any extension of the dock in that direction, it is referred for the reports of the officers, whether it would not be better as a temporary arrangement to fill up the dock (No. 1) to substitute an iron roof, and then use the whole space under the dock roof as a working yard in connection with No. 2 Dock.

125. *Surveyor to Board of Admiralty: building sheds*

[TNA, ADM92/21]   23 October 1860

With reference to the enclosed correspondence respecting the site in Chatham yard proposed for the erection of sheds for forges, furnaces &c for the purpose of building an iron ship of the 'Warrior' class in No. 2 Dock, I am of opinion that the most convenient position will be between Nos. 1 and 2 Dock and I therefore submit that the necessary steps be taken with a view to the work being performed as soon as possible.

126. *Controller of the Navy to Superintendent Goldsmith: building sheds*

[NMM, CHA/H/104]   6 November 1860

With reference to the arrangements in progress for the construction of the iron cased ship; My Lords direct that you will cause so much of the old roof of No. 1 Dock to be taken away as will prevent danger from fire. You will however report whether you consider it desirable to retain a portion of the roof as a cover for men to work under.

127. *Planned Dockyard Extension*

[*Chatham News and North Kent Spectator*]   10 November 1860

Any doubt as to the intention to make a large extension of our Dockyard is now removed. In the next session of Parliament, Government will apply for powers to enclose St. Mary's Island, to divert the St. Mary's Creek stream, to stop up certain roads, abolish wharves and a ferry, and to perform all such acts as are necessary for carrying out a scheme for a great enlargement of the Dockyard.

This is an important fact for our Towns. An augmentation of our Dockyard must, in the first place, cause a great increase in the amount of employment, and sensibly swell the amount of expenditure of various kinds in the Towns. With an enlarged Dockyard must come increased employment for officers, clerks, artificers, labourers; a larger demand for residencies, increased trade, augmented prosperity for the locality. It is believed that these Towns are making an advance in almost every direction; and this scheme, if carried into effect, will give a great impetus to that progress. We may expect other public works to follow. We know that we are to have more fortifications, – involving a fresh outlay on labour to no inconsiderable extent, and a subsequent augmentation of the number of military stationed here. Coincidentally with this increase of general expenditure, arising from outlay of public money, we may look for a considerable relief in the poor-rates of a large portion of the district by a Government contribution for property owned by the State – which ought, indeed, in equity, always to have contributed towards the parish rates.

Though, unfortunately, of late the Towns, in common with most places, have suffered from the generally depressed state of trade, and the failure of a Kentish staple – hops, and though they will, like other towns, feel the effects of the short harvest, we may reasonably expect that, from the greatly increased Government expenditure – a kind of expenditure on which the locality must greatly depend at all times – which we may look for in the future we may safely prophesy a large increase in the prosperity of our Towns.

128. *Director of Engineering and Architectural Works to
Superintendent Goldsmith: building sheds*

[NMM, CHA/H/104]   3 December 1860

The Board, having accepted Mr Grissel's tender for constructing sheds near No. 2 Dock, Mr Grissell has been instructed to proceed with the work.

The Clerk of the Works is requested to set out the lines of the sheds in the yard and make the necessary preparations for proceeding with the work as expeditiously as possible.

129. *Admiralty to Superintendent Goldsmith: building sheds*

[NMM, CHA/H/104]   13 December 1860

Mr. MacDonnel is required to have stakes driven showing the line of the new river wall crossing the end of St. Mary's Creek and meeting with the new embankment, and to prepare a plan showing details of the junction between the wall and embankment, the line of stakes are required to be driven nearly in accordance with the original plan, but with a view to forming the crosses to the most perfect lines that may be practicable.

130. *Admiralty to Superintendent Goldsmith: smithery roof*

[NMM, CHA/H/105]   11 February 1861

My Lords have been pleased to accept the tender of Messrs. Grissell to erect an iron roof over the new smithery according to plans &c. at the cost of £682 – the works to be completed in three weeks.

131. *Report to Admiralty by Master Shipwright and Chief Engineer: slotting machine*

[NMM, CHA/H/105]   12 February 1861

We have carefully examined the sketches and specifications of the proposed slotting machine and consider Smith, Beacock and Tanents much the best but not sufficiently so to account for the great difference in price vizt. £300. Under these circumstances we propose that the tender of Mr. Collier may be accepted. We have to request that a sketch and specifications of the machine selected may be forwarded for our guidance.

132. *Admiralty to Superintendent of Chatham Dockyard: roof over smithery*

[NMM, CHA/H/105]   14 March 1861

The Captain Superintendent at Chatham is requested to cause the old copper store at the yard to be vacated and prepared for the machinery wanted for building the *Achilles*.

133. *G.T. Greene to Admiralty: estimated costs*

[TNA, ADM1/5838]   6 May 1861

For completing the river wall and embankment to the extent as shown on plan, including coffer dams for executing the work within, free from water, and for hired labour necessarily required and superintendence.

£85,000

For the materials to be purchased for constructing the locks, basins and docks, including the hired labour necessarily required and super-intendence.

£500,000

For the purchase of materials for factory buildings, including hired labour necessarily required, and superintendence, but omitting factory machinery and tools of every description.

£180,000

For caissons or bridges, bollards, capstans, foundations for sheers, penstocks, culverts and wharves.

£82,000

For the purchase of tools, plant &tc for the works generally

£10,000

Add probable cost of dredging the river below the entrance locks to a mean depth of 27 feet at half tides and a width of 600 feet.

£ 45,000

Total   £902,000

134. *Enlargement of Chatham Dockyard*

[The Chatham Dockyard Act, 1861, 24 & 25 Victoria XLI, 351]
                                                        22 July 1861

When the Commissioners [of the Admiralty] shall have acquired or purchased in perpetuity the Fundus or Soil of St. Mary's Creek, other wise Swinborough Creek, in the parishes of Chatham and Gillingham, or one of them, in the County of Kent, and of any other inlet shown on the said Plans [deposited with the Clerk of the Peace for Kent] or one of them, and have compensated the Mayor and Aldermen and Company of Free Dredgers of the City of Rochester for the destruction of the fishery in the said creeks, or any or either of them, it shall be lawful for the Commissioners, without any writ being issued or other legal proceeding being adopted, to embank and stop up both or either of the ends of such creeks, or of any or either of them, the fundus or soil of which shall have been so purchased or acquired, and in respect of which compensation for the destruction of the said fishery shall have been made as aforesaid, and to reclaim the fundus or soil, and divert the waters of such creeks or any or either of them, and to abolish the ferry across the River Medway from the hard or landing place called Prince's Bridge to and from the opposite shore of the said River at Upnor and to stop up and abolish the highway, carriageway, and footpath passing on the outside of or adjacent to the eastern and northern boundary walls of Her Majesty's Dockyard at Chatham, extending from the lower end of Westcourt Street in the town of Brompton in the parish of Chatham in the County of Kent to the said hard or landing place called Prince's Bridge and the ends nearest the said highway, carriageway, and footpath of all ways leading into, across, or from the said highway, carriageway, and footpath, passing on the outside of or adjacent to the said boundary walls, and also all ways over, through, or across any of the lands acquired or to be acquired under the provisions of this Act, and also to abolish the hards or landing places at Prince's Bridge and Gillingham Bridge, and the parish wharf near thereto, or any or either of them, or any part or parts thereof; and the fundus or soil of the said Creeks and each of them, when so purchased or acquired respectively as aforesaid, and of the said hards and landing places, and the said highway, carriageway, and footpath, shall vest absolutely and exclusively in the Commissioners, as is herein provided with respect to lands purchased, taken, or acquired by the Commissioners under this Act; and it shall be lawful for the Commissioners to make such openings in the embankments or walls of the said creeks, or any or either of them, at any time or times, as they the Commissioners may deem expedient for Her Majesty's Service.

135. *Sheds for Metalworking Machinery*

[*Chatham News and North Kent Spectator*]   15 February 1862

Preparations are being made for the erection of a shed at the lower end of the dockyard similar to the ones alongside the No. 2 Dock. When completed it will be furnished with machinery of the most powerful description for drilling, bending and otherwise preparing the heavy armour plates with which the *Royal Oak* and *Achilles*, now in course of construction, are to be covered.

136. *Improvements to Dockyard Facilities*

[*Chatham News and North Kent Spectator*]   22 February 1862

In order to provide increased facilities at Chatham Dockyard for constructing the iron and iron-plated vessels now building, as well as those intended to be built, at the naval establishment, the Lords of the Admiralty have decided on expending a considerable sum during the present year in the improvement and enlargement of the dockyard, in addition to the large sum voted last year for the formation of new docks and basins, and the erection of an additional factory and other buildings. The principal works in connection with the enlargement of the dockyard will be executed by convicts. The second dock, in which the iron steamer *Achilles*, 50, is under construction, will be improved at a cost of about £3,500, which sum will be expended in the construction of a new caisson at the entrance, £1000 having already been voted for this purpose. It is also intended to enlarge the workshops used by the mechanics and artisans employed on the *Achilles*, at an estimated cost of £1000.

Their Lordships have also given directions for the enlargement of the millwrights' yard and premises so as to admit of a greater number of hands being employed in the connexion with that department, should their services be suddenly required. The erection of a large workshop on the space adjoining the slip on which the *Royal Oak* is building the works connected with which have already been commenced by Messrs. Foord and Sons, the contractors, will involve an outlay of upwards of £3000, including the machinery required in armour plating the wooden ships.

Directions have also been given for erecting additional quarters for the metropolitan police force employed in the dockyard, at an estimated cost of £3000. The total sum that it is intended to expend during the present year in the improvement of Chatham Dockyard, excluding the large amount already voted for that purpose, is nearly £50,000.

A considerable addition is to be made to the number of mechanics employed on the *Achilles*, provision having been made for employing 1,051 hands on that vessel during the present year in order that she may be completed in the shortest possible time. The sum taken in the estimates for wages for the hired workmen engaged on the iron ships this year is £74,310. Provision has also been made for the entry of hired artificers and labourers at Chatham Dockyard and the other dockyards for a period of four months, to be employed exclusively on the repair of ship, the sum required for this purpose being £30,000.

137. *Construction of Tramway*

[*Chatham News and North Kent Spectator*] 26 April 1862

A party of shipwrights are now employed in forming a tramway across No. 1 Dock which has been substantially floored over, and the roof of which has been considerably extended, thus forming a vast workshop in which the sections of the iron frigate *Achilles*, 50, are temporarily fitted together, previous to being lowered into the next dock where she is being built. No. 1 Dock will for some considerable time be unfit for accommodation of vessels, as it is in the hands of the government contractor Messrs. Foord and Sons of Rochester, who are lengthening and improving the entrance. When the tramway is completed it will be furnished with long carriages, and will be used for transporting the heavy iron plates to the adjoining factory, where machinery of the most powerful description is in the course of erection for preparing them for the ship's side. In about a week's time every preparation will be completed and a commencement will be made to prepare the plates for the *Royal Oak*, 50, which is building on No. 7 slip.

138. *Inspection of New Works*

[*Chatham News and North Kent Spectator*] 10 December 1864

Today [6 December 1864], the Lords of the Admiralty paid an official visit to the dockyard and naval establishments at Chatham arriving from Whitehall by the morning express train. The members of the Board present comprised the Duke of Somerset, K.G., senior Lord, Vice-Admiral the Hon. Sir F.W. Grey, K.C.B., Rear-Admiral C. Eden, C.B., Rear-Admiral R.S. Robinson, Controller of the Navy, and Captain R. Hall, private secretary to the First Lord. The visit was made in connection with the Estimates which are now in course of preparation for the ensuing year, and for this purpose it was found requisite to inspect the works now in actual progress at Chatham Dockyard as well as the works contemplated, in order to decide on those which will be carried out, together with the probable sum necessary to be taken for the purpose in the estimates.

After transacting some official business with the heads of departments, their Lordships, accompanied by Capt. Stewart, C.B., the superintendent of the establishment, and the officials, made a tour of the shipbuilding department of the Dockyard. They directed their exclusive attention to the ironclad frigate *Bellerophon*, 14, 1,000 horse power, and *Lord Warden*, 24, 1,000 horse power, which are the only two vessels now in hand, the work on the whole of the other ships having been suspended for some years past. The *Bellerophon* is about one-fourth completed, but, from the rate of progress already made and the number of additional hands placed upon her, there is little doubt that she will be finished and afloat before the close of the approaching year. Their Lordships were conducted over the principal parts of the vessel by Mr. Thornton, the Master Shipwright, and they afterwards proceeded to the other end of the Dockyard to the shed under which the *Lord Warden* ironclad ship is under construction. The progress made in this vessel appears to be more marked than in the case of the *Bellerophon*, but both are expected to be completed about the same time. Upwards of 2,000 hands are employed on the two vessels, and provision will be made in the estimates for that number to be continued until both frigates are out of hand.

After completing their inspection of the shipbuilding department, their Lordships next gave their attention to the department of works, which, in consequence of the magnitude of the improvements for the enlargement and extension of the Dockyard, absorbs a considerable portion of the sum yearly voted for the Chatham naval establishments. The principal of the works now in progress are those in connexion with the formation of the new docks, factories, workshops, and other buildings at the eastern extremity of the present Dockyard, on the site of St. Mary's Island, the whole extent of which, as well as some of the adjacent land acquired by the Crown, has been absorbed for that purpose, the entire new works extending over an area of 300 acres. The present Dockyard covers an area of 100 acres, so that the additional space will enlarge Chatham Dockyard to four times its existing size.

Accompanied by Mr. Bernays, principal civil engineer at Chatham, under whose directions the extension works are being carried out, their Lordships traversed the greater portion of the island, and spent some time in the inspection of the various portions of the works on which the hands engaged on the undertaking are employed. Up to the present time the work has been mainly carried on by convicts, of whom there are 800 to 1000 daily employed on St. Mary's Island. Already the first of the three basins, which will cover, in the aggregate, a space of nearly 100 acres, or more than double the whole of the existing basin accommodation in England, is getting well forward, although there is still a considerable amount of excavation to be made before the required depth is reached. The principal factory is also under construction, and here again the work is getting well forward. This building will be 1,000 feet in length by 500 feet in breadth, while the whole of the new factory buildings and workshops will cover an area of 12 acres. The original estimate of the entire works was £902,000, but only a comparatively insignificant portion of that amount has already been voted, and at the present rate of progress few persons of the present generation will see the extension works at Chatham completed to the original design.

139. *Director of Works to Board of Admiralty: description of proposed extension*

[TNA, ADM1/5913]   21 March 1865

The works designed for the extension of Chatham Dockyard were originally intended, for the most part, to be executed by convict labour alone, and were estimated at £943,876.

The slow progress of these works, inseparable from their execution by prison labour, together with the necessity for an early completion of an establishment within the estuary of the Thames, where iron-clad ships can be built and repaired, have led to the determination to employ civil labour more largely.

With this object the original estimate has been increased by £306,124, making a total of £1,250,000.

The design consists of enclosing, by an embankment, the whole of the island and flats of St. Mary, extending from the northern end of the present dockyard river wall on the Medway, following the bend of the river northerly, and thence to the eastward to a point opposite the village of Gillingham, an area of 380 acres, of which 74 acres are deep water space, consisting of three basins, constructed on the natural line of the creek or branch of the Medway, which separates St. Mary's Island from the mainland.

The largest, which is to the eastward, communicating with the Medway by locks into Gillingham Reach, is the 'fitting-out basin' of 33 acres, with 30 feet depth of water at high water neaps, and wharfage frontage of 5,800 feet.

The second, with an entrance from the last, closed by a caisson, is the 'Factory Basin' of 20 acres, and a wharfage space of 3,750 feet, with proposed factory extending along its southern front.

On its northern side, forming a novel and special feature in the general project, a camber, with berths in connection, on which iron vessels, of about 3,500 tons, can be placed out of the water, has been designed; but its adoption has not received any official sanction, nor has its cost been included in any of the estimates; but some provision or other of a similar kind will, doubtless, be much wanted for iron vessels when in reserve.

The 'western or repairing basin,' connected also with the last, opens into the Medway, and has a water space of 21 acres, with 3,500 feet of wharfage.

These two latter basins have also 30 feet at high water neaps.

At the south side of the 'repairing basin' are four graving docks, 420 feet in length on the blocks, with 28 feet 6 inches over the sill at high water neaps, and 31 feet 6 inches at high water springs.

These works were commenced in 1856.

Since then about one half of the embankment and 2,000 feet of the river wall on the west have been completed, the walls of the 'repairing basin' commenced, and the foundation of a portion of the factory buildings are in.

The expenditure in the execution of these works, including about £33,000 for civil labour, will, up to the 31st instant, amount to £153,880.

For the further execution of this extension, I recommend that separate tenders for the execution, by contract, of the following works, be invited: –

First. For construction of the 'repairing basin' with two of the docks: this tender to include offers for their execution at a lump sum, or by a schedule of prices.

Second. The construction of the 'factory basin': also at a lump sum, or by a schedule of prices.

Third. The execution of the factory buildings on a schedule of prices.

These should form one contract, or three separate contracts, at the option of my Lords.

For these contracts the Admiralty will furnish bricks and Portland stone.

The approximate cost, including materials provided by the Admiralty, amounts to £610,000.

The time to be stated in the contract for the execution of the 'repairing basin,' the two docks and 'factory basin' should not exceed four years, and they should be completed by the autumn of 1869.

The factory buildings should not take more than two years to build.

This will allow time for the shafting, machinery, and other fittings to be fixed in the factory ready for use when the two basins and the two docks are complete.

Contracts for dredging the Medway from 'Folly Point,' through Gillingham Reach to the lock entrance, to a mean depth of 27 feet at half tides, and to a width of 600 feet, forming part of the original design provided for in the first estimate, need not be called for until 1866.

Should it be decided to have the works above named (the repairing basin, two docks, factory basin, and factory buildings) executed by contract, the prisoners may be employed during the same time:

1. In the completion of the river wall.
2. In the construction of the embankment.
3. The lock entrance and dam.
4. The fitting-out basin.
5. The public wharf at Gillingham.
6. The foundation of ground and roads.
7. Brick making.

By this arrangement the works proposed to be done by the prisoners may be far advanced when those proposed to be executed by contract will be completed and a large part of the extension available for use.

By the arrangement I have suggested, whilst no very large sum will come in course of payment during the financial year 1865–66, provision will have to be made for payment of not less than £580,000 in the four years following, in addition to £40,000 a year for the employment of convicts, and £15,000 a year for three years for dredging the Medway, or a total (including £70,000, the amount in Estimates 1865–66) of £855,000.

The distribution of this amount, as required to meet the expenditure on the various works, will probably be as follows: –

In 1865–66:
Payment on account of contracts	£30,000
Employment of prison labour	£40,000

In 1866–67
Contracts	£150,000
Convicts	£40,000

In 1867–68
Contracts	£150,000
Convicts	£40,000
Dredging	£15,000

In 1868–69
Contracts	£200,000
Convicts	£40,000
Dredging	£15,000

In 1869–70

Contracts	£80,000
Convicts	£40,000
Dredging	£15,000

Accepting these amounts as the probable expenditure in the years named, a balance of £241,120 will remain of the original estimate to provide, by convict labour, for the completion of the 'fitting-out basin' and the two remaining docks.

140.   *First Secretary of the Admiralty to Treasury: estimate of expenses for extension*

[TNA, ADM1/5913]   29 March 1865

Having reference to your letter of the 9th instant, respecting works, the cost of which is spread over a series of years, I am commanded by the Lords Commissioners of the Admiralty to acquaint you, for the Lords Commissioners of Her Majesty's Treasury, that the principal works referred to, for which provision is sought in the Estimates for 1865–66, are the extensions to the Dockyards at Portsmouth and Chatham. My Lords will make a further communication to the Treasury as to the nature of the proposed contracts for Portsmouth; but the arrangements in connection with the extension of Chatham Yard, for which they think Parliamentary authority should be given, so far as they relate to contracts spread over future years, are as follows:–

The works in progress, or which it has been decided to execute, consist of three basins, four docks, a factory, the embankment of the river, and a river wall, besides the dredging of the river, and the forming of the ground and roads.

My Lords contemplate, for the present, employing convicts on the embankment, the river walls, the fitting-out basin, and the lock entrances, and the formation of the ground and roads. Simultaneously, the construction of the repairing and factory basins, two of the docks, and the factory buildings would be proceeded with under contract.

The probable amount of the contracts for these purposes is estimated at £610,000, which my Lords propose to spread over a period of four years (or within five financial years), as follows:–

1865–66	£30,000
1866–67	£150,000
1867–68	£150,000

| 1868–69 | £200,000 |
| 1869–70 | £80,000 |

The expenditure in connection with convicts during that period would be £40,000 a year, and in addition about £150,000 a year would be required for dredging in the last three named years.

The total expenditure from the 1st April next to the financial year 1869–70, would be, therefore, £855,000, leaving on the gross estimate £241,120 for subsequent years. This would be applied to the completion of the fitting out basin and the construction of the two remaining docks by convict labour.

Such being the general nature of the arrangement contemplated by my Lords, they hope that an authority may be obtained for an expenditure of £610,000, in one or more contracts, spread over the period 1865 to 1869.

141.   *Director of Works to Secretary of the Admiralty: appointment of superintending officer*

[TNA, ADM1/5939]   12 July 1865

Bearing in view the magnitude of the extension works at Chatham, the combination of free and convict labour with the many difficulties which arise from it and the number and extent of the proposed contracts, I have come to the conclusion that to carry out their execution with the utmost efficiency necessitated their supervision by an officer, not only of high professional qualifications but also of such standing as to give additional weight to his position.

I beg therefore now to submit that an officer of the Royal Engineers should be especially selected and appointed to superintend the whole of the extension works.

He should, in addition, have placed under him the ordinary works in the dockyard at Chatham and Sheerness, as well as the Marine Barracks and Naval Hospital at Chatham, thus forming the whole into what may be considered the Chatham district.

In making this submission I have to state I am not so much actuated by any feeling of disqualification at the manner in which Mr Bernays (who will still remain on the works, in his present position as Assistant Civil Engineer without any diminution of income), has performed his duties at Chatham, as by the belief that he has not that experience or peculiar qualification which an officer under such heavy responsibilities as are involved in these works should possess.

Should my Lords approve of this proposal I would suggest that the income of the officers to be appointed should be £750 with a right to the occupancy of the house in Chatham dockyard built for the Superintending Royal Engineer, now occupied by Mr Rivers, Clerk of Works, who should be assigned the house recently built for the Master Rope Maker now vacant.

3
MANUFACTURING AND THE MOVE TO STEAM POWER

The manufacturing side of Chatham dockyard underwent considerable change during the years 1815 to 1865. At the outset of this period it was heavily dependent on muscle power, with no operating steam engines installed in any of the centres of manufacture. By 1865, all but a few specialised crafts had witnessed the impact of steam. Also, the nature of materials under manufacture was changing [173, 191] with new factories and workshops, designed from the outset to make full use of steam-powered machinery, beginning to operate [163, 190]. However, development during this period was piecemeal, lacking overall and co-ordinated planning [195].

The revolution in steam was already forging ahead in 1815, with construction underway of Marc Brunel's mechanically powered wood mills. The building work was mostly undertaken by the yard's work force [155]. Upon completion, the mills transformed the process of timber plank manufacture, able to process quantities from a variety of types of timber at considerable speed [172] both for Chatham and other yards [152, 171]. As a result, only a small number of sawyers were retained, these either on a reduced rate of pay, undertaking work in connection with the operation of the mill or carrying out tasks too complex for the saws of the wood mill [196]. Although designed by Marc Brunel, the man responsible for overseeing the completion of the mill was a Mr Ellicombe, upon whom Brunel placed much trust [148]. However, on the appointment of a Master Sawyer of the Mills [144], Ellicombe was considered by the Commissioners at the Navy Board as surplus to requirements [146, 147, 149]. The totality of the finished design, encompassing not only eight sets of circular powered saws but also a canal for the easy movement of newly arrived timber and an overhead rail system which directly connected the mill to an area for the storage of planks, attracted visiting dignitaries [145] and much published praise [150, 184]. Not surprisingly, it was subject to an inspection by the Commissioners of the Navy Board shortly after its completion [164].

Having been designed to meet the demands of the war-time navy, the wood mills were soon producing more sawn timber than required, leading to part of the building being considered for conversion to storage [157].

113

The upper floor accommodated a duplicate set of the block-making machines [142, 143] – Brunel's other contribution to Britain's naval dockyards. The wood mill and its machinery were put to a multiplicity of uses. Indeed, the steam engine was used to power treenail mooting machinery [161] and for pumping water both for the dockyard and nearby Royal Marine Barracks and subsequently the new Melville Hospital that was built opposite the Main Gate [169]. In 1834, it was also proposed that the same engine be used for powering lathes [180, 181]. Despite the early acclaim, William Scamp in 1857 chose to criticise both the location and construction of the mill [195].

The processes involved in the manufacture of rope before the adoption of steam were given in the report of an inspection of the ropery carried out by the Commissioners of the Navy Board in 1823 [166]. The ropery should have been subject to steam power in 1811 when new jack wheels, constructed by Henry Maudslay, were first brought into use. These were operated by a continuous rope pulley that was designed to be mechanically rather than manually powered. But it was not until 1837 that this form of power was introduced to the laying floor [182, 183] with mechanisation of the spinning process following a few years later [186]. However, the interim period, prior to the introduction of steam, was not without innovation and progress [170, 176, 177, 178, 186, 187]. On two occasions the Master Rope Maker at Chatham was asked to report his observations on machinery and methods employed in French naval yards, with a view to introducing superior processes to the ropery at Chatham [151, 154, 179]. It was the introduction of machinery, especially that associated with the spinning of yarn, that resulted in an initial deskilling of the male work force [198] and an eventual decision to admit female labour, a matter that was under consideration in 1864 [201].

In 1817, J. Weekes, the leading man of plumbers, suggested that a mill for milling lead should be built at Chatham. The proposal was fully investigated [156, 158, 159, 160] and resulted in the construction of a combined lead and paint mill. The Navy Board already had plans for a new painters' shop [153], but extended it to accommodate the new lead mill [162]. Construction of this building took place between 1817 and 1819 [156, 158, 159, 162, 163] with the object of meeting the paint and lead requirements of all the naval dockyards [174]. The siting of this structure was also later criticised by William Scamp in 1857 [195].

The smithery benefited from the introduction of steam power, with steam operating the tilt hammer used in constructing the largest anchors from 1843 [188, 189]. Hitherto, the smithery had been able to meet all of the demands for ironwork [194]. However, the move to iron-hulled vessels meant that the smithery had to be supplemented by new workshops and a metal mill, which acquired a 50 cwt steam hammer during the early 1850s [193]. In his *Reminiscences and Notes*, R.G. Hobbes describes the workings of the metal mill, together with other manufacturing workshops in the yard. Although not published until 1895, his descriptions refer approximately to the year 1849 [190, 191].

A problem confronting the dockyard upon the introduction of steam machinery was the frequent delay in the arrival of new or replacement machinery. The dockyard purchased this machinery from, and initially had repairs undertaken by, manufacturers such as Henry Maudslay [168, 175]. As the engines within the dockyard multiplied, ever more specialists were recruited to maintain the machinery. The fairly insignificant number of skilled mechanics employed in the early part of the century [165] grew quite considerably, with most machinery eventually repaired in-house [197]. However, even by mid-century, the numbers directly employed at Chatham were insufficient to meet all needs, additional boilermakers having to be borrowed from other yards [192]. Further recruitment continued, and by the late-1850s a new department had been created, known as the department of the Chief Engineer [194]. In 1857, when a further increase in this department's establishment was requested, the following manufacturing areas of the yard were listed as relying on steam machinery: the oar makers' shop, cement mills, ropery, lead and paint mills, saw mill and metal mill [196].

Despite the rapid changes taking place within manufacturing, these branches of the yard were ill prepared for construction of the iron-built battleship, *Achilles*. All major components had to be manufactured by outside contractors, with Messrs Rigby and Beardmore making the stern frame and the Thames Iron Shipbuilding Company the stern and knee pieces. Other companies involved in the supply of armour plating and other ironwork were Mare and Co., Moser and Sons and the Bowling Green Iron Company. However, the use of contractors was not considered a successful experience [199], a factor that reinforced the decision to extend the dockyard on to St Mary's Island. Here were to be included a number of new or expanded areas of manufacture, although these were not to become available to the Admiralty until the early 1880s.

142.   *Navy Board to Commissioner Barlow: block-making machinery*

[NMM, CHA/F/27]   20 December 1815

Mr. Brunel having been employed to make a duplicate set of machinery in the block mill at Portsmouth, to be applied in the event of any accident happening to the machinery at present in use. He having recommended that the machines so provided may be deposited in the room immediately over the boilers of the steam engine over the sawmill in Chatham yard, which room is entirely proof against fire and particularly eligible, on account of its temperature, for the reception and preservation of iron work liable to rust. We desire, as the place pointed out appears from the heat to be fit for the deposit of iron articles, and is represented as inapplicable for a working shop or office, that you will cause these block machines to be deposited there; if you see no objection.

143.   *Commissioner Barlow to Navy Board: block-making machinery*

[TNA, ADM106/1815]   29 December 1815

In reply to your Letter of yesterday's date desiring that a duplicate set of block machinery, which Mr. Brunel has been employed to make for the block mill at Portsmouth, be deposited in the room immediately over the boilers of the steam engine for the sawmill in this yard, if I see no objection thereto.

I beg to acquaint you that I am not aware of any objection to the said machinery being so deposited, and I will give directions accordingly and for the same being taken proper care of.

144.   *Order-in-Council: appointment of Sawmill Master*

[TNA, PC2/197]   30 January 1816

The water works connected with the steam engine and sawmill recently erected in Chatham yard being now in a complete state fit to be applied in case of fire to the purpose of forcing water through various parts of the yard; and these works; having on account of their connection with the machinery comprising the sawmill, certain arrangements and combinations adapted to the object as well as the situation, the Principal Officers and Commissioners of the Navy have recommended that a Master of the Mill should be appointed to have the superintendence and management of the machinery and other works connected with it, including all the water works and pipes about the yard, and that he should be allowed a salary of two hundred and fifty pounds per annum, being the same salary as is allowed to most of the master workmen in His Majesty's Yards.

And as we agree in opinion with them of the expedience in this appointment, we beg leave with all humility to propose to your Royal Highness that a Master of the saw mill for the purposes before stated, may be appointed accordingly with an established salary of two hundred and fifty pounds per annum.

His Royal Highness the Prince Regent having taken the said memorial into consideration was pleased, in the name of His Majesty, and by and with the advice of His Majesty's Privy Council, to approve what is therein proposed, and to order, as it is hereby ordered to, that a said Master of the Sawmill for the purposes stated in the said memorial be appointed accordingly with an established salary of two hundred and fifty pounds per annum. And the Right Honourable the Lords Commissioners of the Admiralty are to give the necessary directions herein accordingly.

145. *Royal Visit*

[*Kentish Gazette*]   12 March 1816

On Saturday morning about 10 o'clock the Archduke, attended by Prince Esterhazy, the American Ambassador, visited Chatham Dock Yard, and were received, under a salute from the cannon on the lines, by Commissioner Sir Robert Barlow, who was in readiness to attend and conduct them through the yard. Every part worthy of notice was pointed out to them, particularly the sawmill, which they inspected very attentively for a considerable time; the Archduke John being very inquisitive, and noted in writing many observations. The inspection of the Dock Yard being finished, after taking some refreshments at the Commissioner's House, their Imperial Highnesses accompanied Colonel Pasley to the floating bridges, in order to view a torpedo,[1] which had been placed in readiness on the Medway.

---

[1]Colonel Pasley (later Major General Sir Charles Pasley) of the Royal Engineers was a pioneer in underwater warfare and was, in the years immediately following the Napoleonic Wars, carrying out experiments with underwater diving bells as a means of attaching explosives to the supporting structure of bridges. It is one of these diving bells which is here described as a 'torpedo'. In 2001 a plaque to Sir Charles Pasley was unveiled within the Historic Dockyard at Chatham.

146.   *Navy Board to Commissioner Barlow: dismissal of sawmill*
superintendent

[NMM, CHA/F/29]   23 April 1816

We have to desire that you will inform us whether in your opinion the attendance of Mr. Ellicombe to superintend the works connected with the saw mills at Chatham may not now be dispensed with in consequence of the forward state of those works particularly as we conceive that Mr Bacon, the Master of the saw mills must now be fully competent to undertake that superintendence himself.

147.   *Navy Board to Commissioner Barlow: dismissal of sawmill*
superintendent

[NMM, CHA/F/29]   9 May 1816

We have to acknowledge the receipt of your letter dated the 2nd instant in which you state that you are not aware of the necessity for the further attendance of Mr. Ellicombe to superintend the works connected with the sawmills, and we desire that you will signify to Mr. Ellicombe that his services are no longer required at Chatham.

148.   *Marc Brunel to Navy Board: objection to dismissal*

[NMM CHA/F/29]   23 May 1816

In reference to your communication of the 9th inst. which I received on my return from the continent, informing me that you have desired Commissioner Sir Robert Barlow to signify to Mr. Ellicombe, that his services were no longer required at Chatham to superintend the works connected with the sawmill. I beg to observe that I cannot but express my surprise at the nature of the communication, no less than at the manner [in which] it is conveyed.

Had I been asked whether his services were required for superintending the work already connected with the sawmill, or were necessary to it, I should not have hesitated on the answer I should have had to return. But when I took over what Mr Ellicombe has had to do, and what he has to do, for establishing the carriage now preparing and also for disposing the means and connecting the powers whereby the timber is to be conveyed to and fro and spread over the ground; I should easily have accounted how far the abilities and services of that gentleman were necessary for the establishment, had I been honoured from you, with a previous application such as my situation and the confidence I have hitherto been honoured with, had given me a right to expect at the hands on the honourable Navy Board.

If for so short a period as 2 or 3 weeks, Mr. Ellicombe's exertions and labours have not been so actively and usefully employed as they were before, it is because others have not been so expeditious in the executions of the works they had to perform, as I had expected. The work I allude to, namely that which is intended to convey the power through the whole course of the railway is ready to be forwarded to Chatham.

If at this period, I am deprived of the services of Mr. Ellicombe to effect that which I have imparted to him during the gradual progress of that undertaking, or in the course of correspondence that has subsisted between both him and myself, I shall be under the necessity of making more frequent journeys to and from Chatham, a circumstance attended with great inconvenience to me and of greater expense to the public than Mr. Ellicombe's charges could possibly have been.

Mr. Ellicombe's services have not been continued by me, solely for superintending the sawmill; but for directing the execution of the work in general, and for giving them the effect they should arrive at, before they can be left to the management of others – The manner he has already acquitted himself of the trust placed in him, justifies, in a very satisfactory way, the choice I have made. No part of the work evinces greater proof of his abilities and judgement than the manner in which the timber lifting apparatus has been put up and put into action.

What remains to be fixed cannot be combined with the existing works, nor connected as it should be, unless I have the entire management of the concern as I have hitherto had, and unless I have the choice of the instruments I think necessary to my purpose.

Mr. Ellicombe being from his superior education – liberal connections, and from his uncommon acquirements fitted, in every respect, I trust that your Honourable Board has no personal objection to him, [and that] he will be allowed to continue where he is, in the character of my confidential agent, in superintending my Chatham engagements, until I have completed it, waiting for your Honourable Board's directions and instructions.

149.   *Navy Board to Commissioner Barlow: retention of sawmill*
superintendent

[NMM, CHA/F/29]   30 May 1816

In consequence of your letter of the 24th inst., we have consented to Mr Ellicombe remaining a further time in the superintendence of the works of the sawmill at your yard, but we have desired Mr Brunel to let us know how much longer it is likely that Mr. Ellicombe's attendance there will be absolutely necessary, and we have to request that you will satisfy yourself and make us acquainted with the necessity that exists for continuing his services at the public expense, under the directions of Mr. Brunel.

150.   *Description of the Sawmill*

[Wildash, *The History and Antiquities of Rochester*, p. 73.[1]]   1817

At the northeast extremity of the yard some new works have lately been constructed, commonly called the sawmills, projected and executed by that modest and persevering mechanic, Mr. Brunel, who has effected as much for the mechanic arts as any man of his time. These sawmills, as the name imports, are employed in converting the fir timber used in the service of the yard into planks or boards; and are erected on an eminence about 35 feet above the level of the lowest part of the yard. To the ground on the north side of the mill; which is appropriated to the stowage of timber, balks are floated from the river by means of a canal which runs open about 250 feet; this canal on entering the rising ground becomes a tunnel in length about 300 feet, and empties itself into an elliptical basin the length of which is 90 feet, the breadth 72 feet, and the depth 44 feet. The operation of raising the timber from this basin is worthy of observation; and the steady, though quick motion with which it ascends is truly astonishing. We have witnessed a balk of 60 feet long, and 16 inches square, raised to the top of the standard 60 feet in the space of 60 seconds! The sawmill is constructed on a very extensive scale; and the mechanism of it may be reduced to three principal things; the first, that is the saw drawn up and down as long as is necessary, by a motion communicated to the wheel by steam; the second, that the timber to be cut into boards is advanced by a uniform motion to receive the strokes of the saw; for here the wood is to meet the saw, and not the saw to follow the wood, therefore the motion of the wood and that of the saw

---

[1]W.T. Wildash, *The History and Antiquities of Rochester* (Rochester, 1817).

immediately depends the one on the other; the third, that where the saw has cut through the whole length of the piece, the whole machine stops of itself, and remains immovable; lest having no obstacle to surmount, the moving power should turn the wheel with too great velocity, and break some part of the machine.

151. *Admiralty to Commissioner Barlow: rope making*

[NMM, CHA/F/30]   1 January 1817

The Lords Commissioners of the Admiralty having referred to us the accompanying letter from Mr. Pennell, His Majesty's consul at Bordeaux, inclosing copies of a 'process verbal' and a proposal for communicating a new discovery relative to cordage, adopted at the dockyard at Rochefort, which he has received from M. Dufourg. We desire that you will consider the proposal, and report to us your opinion thereon, for the information of the Lords Commissioners of the Admiralty. At the same time we have to observe, that to increase the number of strands in a rope, appears to us to be calculated to weaken the rope and to render it less strong than one made of strands but containing equal number of yarns.

[*Enclosure:*
Letter from W. Pennell, British Consul Office, Bordeaux, to Secretary of the Admiralty, 31 August 1816]
I have the honour to transmit herewith, for the information of the Right Honourable the Lords Commissioners of the Admiralty, copies of a 'Process Verbal' and a proposal for communicating a new discovery relative to cordage adopted at the dockyard at Rochefort, which I have lately received from Monsr Dufourg, and which he states to have already transmitted for the consideration of their Lordships in the month of June last, but has not received any reply.

Should their Lordships, on a perusal of those documents, deem the proposal or the discovery therein alluded to, worthy of their consideration, or that I should witness the process and make a report thereon, I have to request you will be pleased to communicate to me their instructions.

[*Enclosure:*
Letter from Monsieur Dufourg to Secretary of the Admiralty, 20 June 1816]
The protection & encouragement, which the English government is always ready to grant to those discoveries which tend to the perfection of art or of science, embolden me to address your Lordships, in order to solicit you

to present to the Admiralty my proposal of the disclosure of two new methods, both relative to the art of rope making, and yielding results equally economical and advantageous.

The first of the processes consists in a new method of laying ropes for the use of the Navy, the results of which are, that they acquire 15 per cent more strength, with a saving, at the same time, of about 12 per cent in weight, compared to that of cordage made after the usual manner of rope makers, and manufactured of the same materials, with the same number of threads, and in ropes of equal length, with only a very small difference in the thickness, which does not lose more than a thirtieth part.

The second of these processes consists of double machinery [sic] for laying ropes with a saving of 75 per cent in the expense of workmanship with respect to the laying only, for the expense of spinning is still the same as before.

It is generally the practice (at least in France) to lay the ropes one-third, sometimes upwards of one-third, namely at seven-nineteenths and between seven-nineteenths and one third, for cables and hawsers and between one-third and one-quarter for running rigging.

The method, which I propose consists of laying them only between $\frac{1}{3}$ and $\frac{5}{17}$, between $\frac{1}{3}$ and $\frac{1}{4}$, between $\frac{5}{17}$ and $\frac{1}{4}$ and lastly at $\frac{1}{4}$ according to the different uses for which they are intended. They retain in other respects all the qualities of the ropes, laid above those proportions, that is to say, that they are as proper to last a long while, being as light, and in some measures more compressed than in others, since with equal threads they have a little less thickness. Consequently they are equally impenetrable by water, which has already been proved by experience, they have even this property in preference to other cordage: that they are stronger; more pliable; and less susceptible of yielding or stretching after they are once strained to the degree of tension which they should have (this is to be understood of the standing rigging). Lastly, they are not subjected to the defect of untwisting, therefore you need never fear that the strands will separate, that the threads will disunite and the cordage unravel, all which things entirely depend on the different degrees of laying the ropes have undergone during the process of their making.

152. *Marc Brunel to Admiralty: timber for other yards*

[TNA, ADM106/2272]   15 January 1817

With respect to the sawmills we beg leave to state that it is not only employed in cutting such articles for that yard which a saw mill can be applied [sic] but also for the other yards.

153.   *Chatham Yard Officers to Admiralty: new painters' shop*

[TNA, ADM106/2272]   15 January 1817

We transmit herewith plans, elevations and sections of a building proposed to be erected in His Majesty's Dockyard at Chatham for a painters shop in lieu of the present one which is in a very decayed state and also a plan of part of the yard showing by a red tinge the situation intended for the said building. The estimated expense for this building amounts to £5,685 and we desire you will be pleased to move the Lords Commissioners of the Admiralty to furnish us with their authority for erecting it in the present year.

154.   *Navy Board to Commissioner Barlow: experiments in rope making*

[NMM, CHA/F/30]   29 January 1817

With reference to that part of your report dated the 14th inst. on the proposal of Monsieur Dufourg relative to the manufacture of cordage in which you observe that all the experiments made with the breaking machine in Chatham yard tends to an inference contrary to the statements of M. Dufourg, that multiplying the strands essentially contributes to render the cordage stronger. We desire that you will answer to us the reports of the results of the experiment to which you allude, or if we have already been furnished with them, that you will point out their dates.

155.   *Navy Board to Commissioner Barlow: sawmill expenses*

[NMM, CHA/F/30]   17 February 1817

Expense of building the engine with a canal, tunnel &c by the people of the yard:

Cost of Materials used	£27,551
Cost of workmen	£13,764
Total	£41,315

156.   *Leading Man of Plumbers to Yard Officers: milling of lead*

[TNA, ADM106/1815]   24 February 1817

I conceive it to be part of my duty to use economy in the utmost in the consumption of His Majesty's stores and submit anything that may occur to me to you that may help attain that desirable object.

And as there is to be directed a large steam engine for pumping out the docks, and when not employed for that purpose, I beg leave to recommend a mill be attached to it for milling the old lead into sheets and pipes of all sizes for the use of all of His Majesty's Yards which may be done at the expense of about one shilling per cwt. Therefore, as the expenditure of this yard only is upward of 25 tons per annum in peace, and the other yards, calculating at the same proportion, the saving of expense in manufacturing will be very great, as the present price for doing it is seven shillings per cwt.

157.   *Marc Brunel to Navy Board: objection to use of mill for storage*

[NMM, CHA/F/30]   30 March 1817

It will perhaps be said that the spare area is as well calculated as any other part of the yard for the stowage of other material; but viewing it with all the advantages that are coupled with its present disposition, I would consider it would be as great a waste of its present means, as any part of the mill itself, if it was converted into a store.

158.   *Yard Officers to Commissioner Barlow: milling of lead*

[TNA, ADM106/1815]   20 April 1817

Agreeable to the directions in your minute contained in your minute on the accompanying letter from Mr Weekes, Master Plumber [*sic*], on the subject of attaching a mill to the steam engine to be erected in the yard, for pumping water from the docks to mill old lead into sheets, and for pipes of different sizes for His Majesty's several dockyards, pointing out saving of the expense in the re-manufacture of that article.

We beg to state that we are decidedly of opinion, if what Mr Weekes has submitted is put into execution it will tend greatly to the advantage of His Majesty's service.

159.   *Admiralty to Commissioner Barlow: milling of lead*

[NMM, CHA/F/30]   31 May 1817

We have acknowledged the receipt of your letter of 24th inst., inclosing a proposition made by Mr. J. Weekes, the plumber, for attaching to the steam engine which is to be erected for pumping water out of the docks, a mill for milling old lead into sheets and pipes. We desire you will let us know whether rollers can be attached to the sawmill for the purpose of milling lead, sending us a joint report thereon from Mr Bacon, the Master of the Mill, and Mr Weekes, whom you will desire to take the matter into consideration.

160.   *Chatham Yard Officers to Master Shipwright: milling of lead*

[TNA, ADM106/1815]   5 June 1817

Conformably to Commissioner Sir Robert Barlow's minute of the 1st inst directing us to take into consideration a report for the information of the Honourable Navy Board, jointly, whether rollers can be attached to the sawmill for the purpose of milling lead into sheets, pipes &c.

We beg to state that it is our opinion, that it will not be practical to attach rollers for that purpose to the present sawmill, in consequence of the steam engine not having power sufficient to carry the additional works. Should a sufficient power be provided, we are of opinion that the southeast wing of the sawmill could be then appropriated to that use.

161.   *Admiralty to Commissioner Barlow: treenail mooting machinery*

[NMM, CHA/E/126]   25 June 1817

We have received your letter of 21st inst., informing us that Mr. Beale has completed his treenail machinery attached to the sawmill in your yard. We direct you to prepare a scheme of task for mooting treenails by the machinery in question and submit the same for your approval.

162.   *Navy Board to Admiralty: milling of lead*

[TNA, ADM106/2273]   27 June 1817

We desire that you will please to acquaint the Lord Commissioners of the Admiralty that our attention has lately been directed to the considerable saving that the public would derive by re-manufacturing the old lead which arises in the King's Yard, a measure suggested by Mr J. Weekes a plumber of Chatham yard. We have also taken into consideration a suggestion made by Mr William Smith, the Foreman of Painters in Woolwich yard, that the paint for the use of the service be ground by machinery instead of by manual labour as heretofore. Having had before us a report from Mr Holl, Surveyor of Buildings, on the above subjects, and approving of his proposal that the twelve horse steam engine lately used in Sheerness yard for grinding cement should be removed to Chatham to be appropriated to the purpose of grinding paint and re-manufacturing old lead. We enclose a copy of his report to be laid before their Lordships and transmitting also the plans he has submitted for the new painters' shop at Chatham. Wherein recommendations proposed to be provided for the grinding of paint and rolling of lead and referring their Lordships to the Estimate contained in the enclosure of the expense (£5795) of the additional building and requisite machinery for the above service. We request to recommend to their Lordships the proposed machinery to be erected in Chatham yard.

163.   *Minutes of Navy Board Committee of Visitation: lead mill and paint shop*

[TNA, ADM106/3233]   30 September 1819

The committee inspected the lead mills and painters' shop now constructing and found them in a considerable state of forwardness, the Mill for rolling lead being complete and at work. It was suggested, and appeared necessary, to this committee, that a separate building should be appropriated for melting the lead to divest it of its impurities previously to it being carried to the mills to be cast into cakes for rolling. For this, a small building adjoining, which is now used as a lot house, seemed from its situation, to be well calculated. In the event of the north hemp house being raised, as is in contemplation, a part of it may be appropriated to supply the place of the lot house before mentioned.

164.   *Minutes of Navy Board Committee of Visitation: sawmill*

[TNA, ADM106/3233]   30 September 1819

The committee viewed the sawmills and machinery appertaining thereto for stacking timber &c. They were much satisfied with works going on there, the same being extremely well executed, seven of the sawing machines were at work and the whole eight may be worked.

The Master of the Mill was directed to prepare an account of the full particulars of the quantity of work, which may be executed.

165. *Commissioner Cunningham to Navy Board: millwrights*

[TNA, ADM106/1827]   1 August 1823

I have received your letter of the 29th ultimo desiring I will call upon the officers to revise the proposed establishment of the millwrights in this yard; and in return thereto I send you a copy of their report on this subject.

[Undated enclosure addressed to Cunningham and initialled R.G.]
I beg to state to the Board that there are 9 millwrights belonging to Portsmouth yard lent to Chatham and Sheerness, two to the former and seven to the latter yard.

The commissioner at Chatham has reported that an establishment of this description of workmen will be required in that yard after the new works which are carrying on shall be completed and that 6 is the smallest number of which it should consist. I would therefore suggest 4 of the millwrights lent to Sheerness should be removed to Chatham (to be replaced by four of the hired millwrights now at Chatham), which with the two at present employed there will form the establishment required. In order to allow of their receiving the same rates of pay as if they had continued in Portsmouth yard it will be necessary to place them in classes, two in each class. This arrangement will leave only one hired millwright in Chatham yard whose rate of pay I recommend will be that of the first class without any allowance of chip money.

The whole of the rates of pay however, hereunto mentioned, to be subject to the reduction of one fifth, being the reduction made from the established war rates of pay of the millwrights of Portsmouth yard.

166. *Navy Board Committee of Visitation: rope manufacture*

[TNA, ADM106/3237]   4 November 1823

The commencement of rope making is first to issue a quantity of hemp to each hatcheller who, having passed it several times over the hatchel or cone, retraces in his hands the clean long fibres called topped hemp which is set aside for the manufacture of rope above 3 inches. The part that is coned off by the hatcheller is collected together and sent to the dresser under the name of toppings. The dresser in the process of his business collects from the toppings a certain portion of hemp, which in some of the yards amounts to one-half, at others to only one-third. The hemp so obtained is called dressed hemp and the refuse is described as 'toppets'. At Portsmouth it is usual to collect from the toppings one-half the quantity of dressed hemp, for instance out of 9 lbs of toppings 4½ lbs of dressed hemp, while at Woolwich they take only one third. It is, therefore, clear that the better cordage ought to be made at Woolwich where less of the inferior part of the toppings is manufactured, but the Portsmouth method, as far as relates to the first cost, is the cheapest.

The next step is to give the topped and dressed hemp to the spinners to be spun into yarn. The quantity issued is 64 lbs to every four spinners, which is then divided into eight parts, each part intended to spin two threads and one quarter, but from not always being equally divided, it often happens that the yarn is spun into different sizes. To make this more intelligible, suppose that in the division of the 64 lbs one bundle is 9 lbs, another only 7, it follows that as the yarn must be of the same length, one must be thicker than the other. As the yarn, so different in size, might not, and probably would not be made up in the same rope so as to let the one compensate for the other, it must frequently occur that the ropes are greater or less than they were designed to be. It is therefore necessary to give general orders upon this head, directing that each spinner shall have a bundle of hemp to himself of the proper established weight, and that when delivered to him he is to take care to sort the quantity so as to have the yarn of equal size and strength.

With a view to greater expedition in making rope it is the practice in the King's yards to run the yarns in four instead of single. The meaning of this is that four yarns are put upon the reel together, and when brought into use for making rope the four are run through one hole in the minor or register plate instead of placing the yarn upon the reel single and when making it into rope giving each yarn a separate hole.

The method of running the yarn single is far preferable, as it then forms a straight line but to satisfy ourselves of the difference in the strength of cordage so made, than that made by the fours, we had some three inch rope made of each. The result of several experiments was decidedly in favour of the former.

The rope made of yarn runs single, sustained 15 hundredweight more than the other and as the fact of its 'greater strength appears to have been very well known by the rope makers' it is extraordinary that the frequent letters of reprobation written by the Board upon the subject of feeble cordage issued to the ships, this circumstance was never pointed out as the cause.

It is stated that if yarn is run single it will be very tedious. This we admit, but a remedy has been suggested which we have reason to think will enable us to adopt the plan, and at the same time to make much greater quantity of rope in the dock yards than at any former period, even to the extent of nearly one half more. To affect this desirable object, it will be necessary to have a small steam engine of six-horse power in each yard for the double purpose of tarring the yarn, and what is technically termed forming the strands by the equalising machine. The expense of tarring the yarn by horses is 2s per haul, each haul consisting of 400 yarns, and as it is usual to tar 20 hauls in a day, the expense amounts to £2 per diem.

In war the tarring is four days in the week, in peace on an average a little more than one.

The forming the strands by the Huddart steam engine will affect a saving of nearly one-third of the expense of making rope; or in other words, it will enable five men, who now make two ropes to make thirteen and the same charge for wages, namely 5/3d each man.

It would also be proper to direct the wheel frames in the several yards to be moved up to the spinning floors by which there will be an opportunity of applying the wheel frames to two different sizes of strands at the same time and thereby afford the means of making a greater quantity of cordage.

We have no wish to propose any hasty measure founded upon speculative notions, which might lead to expense, without any certainty of alternative advantage and as there is already a steam engine at Portsmouth for the purpose of tarring yarn it requires only the addition of a shaft for the purpose of forming the strands. We therefore propose that Mr Parsons be sent to Portsmouth with directions to carry this plan into execution and if it is thought to propose the benefits we have pointed out the Board will be satisfied of the propriety of introducing the same system in the other yards.

The plan we have been recommending has reference to all rope down to 2 inches to be made by Mr Balfour's machinery. The rope of 2 inches or under, which is now made by a frame wheel, we propose should hereafter be made by a jack wheel of the motion from 12 and 14 to 1 inch, in addition to those of the present size now in use.

It is stated by Mr. Fenwick, the late Master Rope Maker, whose long experience in the toil of his profession and general intelligence is entitled to confidence, that the strength to be obtained by the more general use of jack wheels in making small rope will be equal to [*illegible*] and this too without any increased expense.

167.   *Commissioner Cunningham to Navy Board: commentary on submitted sawyers' petition*

[TNA, ADM106/1828]   10 March 1824

They beg to state to you the nature of the timber from it being kept under cover is very hard and more difficult to cut than formerly. They further beg to state that they labour under a greater disadvantage than any other yard on account of the sawmill, which deprives them of the best and lightest work of the yard.

168.   *Commissioner Cunningham to Navy Board: steam machinery problems*

[TNA, ADM106/1832]   19 January 1826

With reference to your letter of the 11th inst., desiring that one of the wrought iron boilers ordered in May last of Mr. Maudslay for the saw mill, be put up in lieu of the boilers sent from Mr. Lloyd, which on trial was found to be so badly made as to be quite unfit for use. I acquaint you that the boilers in question, have not yet been delivered by Mr. Maudslay, and request that they (or one of them) maybe sent into shore without further delay.

At present there is but one boiler to work the engine at the saw mill, and that, although said to work in May last, is now in so bad a condition, it is with the greatest difficulty a sufficient quantity of steam can be produced to impel the machinery; and without some prompt measures are pursued, it is expected that the sawing apparatus must stand still, for want of a boiler to work the steam engine.

[Appended note]
Write to Mr Maudslay most urgently as the sawmill will otherwise be at a standstill.

[Second appended note by Mr Taylor]
I have been to Mr Maudslay and seen the two boilers, he assures me they will be completed in ten days of which there appears to be no doubt as the ends only remain to be done. Submitted that the Commissioner be informed of this and Mr Maudslay that we depend on his assurance.

169. *Architect to Victualling Board: employment of saw mill engine*

[TNA, ADM114/40]   16 March 1827

I beg to lay before you the following information respecting the means of supplying water at Chatham Hospital for your guidance – The supply of water for the houses in the dock yard and for the Marine Barracks flows from a reservoir near the saw mill into which it is pumped by the engine – This Reservoir, being only 15 feet above the cill of the dock yard entrance gates is high enough to supply the Marine Barracks (which lies lower). It will not answer for the hospital, the Cistern of which is 60 feet above that level.

If therefore the supply is to be from the dock yard the water must be forced up by the engine, as high as the top of the building. The pipes will answer this purpose as far as the dock yard gates, and may be continued from there to the hospital premises. I should advise a puddled reservoir, to contain 500 tons of water, to be formed in the small piece of ground A annexed which is the only part of the government premises that is sufficiently high for the water to flow, thence to the level of the roofs of the pavilions where some of the cisterns are. The water will soften and exposure to the air in this reservoir and the supply will always be certain, whilst the most convenient times may be taken for renewing it by the engine in the course of the week.

It will be useless to alter the system of supply to the Marine Barracks because it would only add to the labour by lifting the water to an unnecessary height.

There is no doubt that the saw mill engine can perform this service at such hours. It would not be disadvantageous that it should be so, because the steam is always kept up. In the event of a fire with a main pipe along the side of the hospital and buildings the force of the engine could be applied which is far more efficient than the ordinary flow from the reservoir which however will be very desirable for the supplying of water for consumption.

I am not disposed to credit this report that the dock yard water is not good and find various opinions therein, but if that should be the case then the well in the garden at B may be deepened and enlarged and an engine of about 4 or 6 horse power may be put up hereafter to supply the Reservoir. The connection of pipes with this to the Dock Yard may be found advantageous to both parties in case of emergency at either place.

A sample of water from the well at the Ordnance Barracks, that of the dock yard and that of W. Baldocks close to the Hospital have been produced to be analysed.

170.   *Navy Board Committee of Visitation: quality of cordage*

[TNA, ADM106/3239]   25 September 1827

Mr Fenwick, the late Master Rope Maker at this Yard, having waited upon
the committee, the enquiries lately made at Plymouth and Portsmouth
respecting the quality of the cordage manufactured in the King's Yards,
was pursued and particularly with reference to the change in the mode of
manufacture introduced by Mr Parsons.

Mr Fenwick and the Master Rope Maker at the yard object to the use
of Parson's cylindrical roller and believes that the yarns when subjected
to its operation are injured in consequence of the twist in the yarns being
unequally affected by the preference so applied that the yarn is injured
also by friction being drawn through so many more hooks and rings than
were formally in use and further by the flat nippers now applied in the
process of tarring yarn, the Tar is not so equally pressed out as the concave
and convex nippers previously in use. On the last point the committee
recommended to the Board to call upon the officers of Portsmouth yard
to report the quantity of tar now used in tarring a certain number of hauls
of yarn, compared with the quantity used for the same number previously
to June 1823. Mr Fenwick and Mr Moxon further observed, with reference
to the friction of the yarns by being drawn through the hooks and rings,
that by this method the yarns were taken at once off the wheel, undisturbed
by any other process, and lay smoothly on the brackets until the haul was
tarred. The difference of opinion that prevails on this important subject
requires mature consideration. At the same time it is proper to observe
that complaints of the inferiority of the King's rope compared to that
manufactured in France and Spain prevailed before, as well as since, the
system of Mr Parson's was introduced.

171.   *Master Attendant to Navy Board: increased demand upon
sawmill*

[TNA, ADM106/1833]   11 October 1827

Averting to your letter of the 6th inst. desiring the sawmills may be worked
day and night for the intended dwellings at Fernando Po. I beg to acquaint
you that as there are not two sets of workmen in the yard capable of
working the mill and as strangers would do but little with the machinery
compared with the experienced men, they are of opinion that the men
usually employed in the saw mills work extra from daylight in the morning
until dark at night and on Sundays. They would cut more materials than

persons unaccustomed to the particular motions of the machinery in the night. They have further stated that the steam engine must be employed about three hours every night, when the sawmill is not at work, to pump water for the use of the dockyard, Royal Marines and convicts.

I beg to add that it has been judged expedient in order to prevent any delay, to arrange for workmen at the saw mill, with one millwright and shipwright to work until dark this evening and all day tomorrow (Sunday) and to come into the yard at half past four o'clock on Monday morning.

172. *Commissioner Cunningham to Navy Board: employment of saw mill*

[TNA, ADM106/1838]   5 March 1829

In return to your letter of the 10th ultimo, signifying that it appears expedient in that the sawmills should if possible be employed exclusively in cutting African timber into thick stuff and planks. I acquaint you that the officers report that in their opinion it is probable that 1560 loads of thick stuff and plank can be cut there per annum by employing four frames, it being necessary to continue the other three frames in cutting beams, waterways, deals scantlings &tc. The officers further state that £12 7s 9d is the probable rate per load, at which the said thick stuff and plank can be cut, having calculated the timber at the rate of £9 9s per load conformably to your letter of the 6th August 1828.

173. *Comptroller to First Lord: chain cable*

[BL, Add Ms 41,399]   19 January 1831

Upon the question you put as to the number of ships now in commission which use chain in preference to hempen cables I beg to refer you to letters from the Navy Board to the Admiralty dated 8 May 1821, 23 February 1822 and particularly to that of 12 May 1823 also 17 June 1824, 10 January & 6 April 1826 and 7 & 13 January 1829, all affording incontrovertible evidence of the utility and economy from the use of chain cables.

I find on referring to official documents that the average number of ships employed between 1821 and 1825 inclusive was 157 and that the annual average expenditure of cordage in the same period was about 3,050 tons.

Between 1826 and 1830, the annual average number of ships in commission was 180 and the yearly expenditure of cordage only about

2,500 tons, this evidently showing that owing to the extensive use of chain a considerable reduction of hempen cables (about 500 tons per annum) was effected although a quarter number of ships were employed than in the preceding years – and allowing for the difference I may fairly allow that the saving upon 180 ships would have been 180 tons of hemp or about £30,000 a year.

Besides the positive saving in a pecuniary point of view – politically it is of the utmost importance that this country should be rendered less dependent on Russia than hitherto for such an important article of supply, which in lieu, an opening has been made for the employment of a valuable substitute, the produce of this country.

174.   *Navy Board to Superintendent Gordon: milled lead*

[NMM, CHA/H/4]   26 November 1832

The milled lead, which the officers were directed by my letter of the 5th instant to send to Plymouth, being much wanted in that yard, I have to request the same be forwarded as soon as possible, particularly that of six pounds to a foot square.

175.   *Admiralty to Superintendent Gordon: boiler repair*

[NMM, CHA/H/4]   4 December 1832

In reply to your letter of the 30th ult. I request that you direct the officers to send the boiler belonging to the sawmill to Messrs Maudslay to be repaired.

176.   *Admiralty to Superintendent Gordon: tarring machine*

[NMM, CHA/H/6]   20 May 1833

I am commanded by My Lord Commissioners of the Admiralty to signify their directions to you to report upon the merits of a machine for tarring yarn invented by Mr Joseph Parsons, Master Rope Maker at Portsmouth Dock Yard.

177. *Superintendent Gordon to Admiralty: manufacture of cordage*

[TNA, ADM1/3395]   22 August 1833

My attention having of late been much directed to the mode in which the rope makers are employed I beg to submit for the consideration of my Lords Commissioners of the Admiralty the absolute necessity there exists as a first step for ensuring the proper manufacture of cordage, that the spinners should be required to spin 4 threads an hour only, instead of five, and that the directions laid down in the 8th Report of the Board of Revision, page 88, as to the rope makers' hours of attendance, which, except when closing cables, or in other similar cases should be the same as those of the other workmen. From a careful perusal all the orders and correspondence on the subject, I am of the opinion that they have been enormously deviated from and should be forthwith strictly enforced instead of their being allowed to go home when their stint is finished, which is the present arrangement and which manifestly tends to the injury of the service. This is likely to induce the men to slight their work in order to get the day's work finished as soon as possible that they might quit the yard. The men employed laying, generally now go home before 3 and the spinners before 4 o'clock every day.

I also beg to inform you that it is my intention shortly to submit to their Lordships a proposal for a different mode of preparing the hemp and the yarn and for altering the amount of the required daily stint in making the various sorts of rope, with the view of remedying the defects so much complained of in the cordage manufactured in the dockyards.

[Appended note dated 5 September]
Approve of this suggestion being adopted at Chatham only and direct him to report the result for their Lordships information.

178. *Superintendent Gordon to Admiralty: inferior cordage*

[TNA, ADM1/3396]   4 October 1833

On enquiring into the causes which have led to the complaints of the inferiority of the cordage manufactured in the dockyards, two subjects have presented themselves most forcibly to me, as likely to have produced these results, first the mode of employing the workmen, and second the rules adopted in the manufacture of raw material into rope.

On the first point it appears that the workmen have for many years past been allowed to quit the yard as soon as their stint were finished; and it therefore followed that their particular attention was directed to get it done as soon as possible without paying that due regard to good workmanship which they ought. In place of this it appears that on 3 December 1822 twenty pounds per cent was ordered to be abated from the rope makers task scheme, but, to prevent their wages being reduced thereby they did twenty per cent more work in nearly the same number of hours as before and thus kept their wages precisely as they were. My Lords Commissioners of the Admiralty however, having been pleased by their order of the 6th inst. to direct that they should work the same number of hours as the other people and spin only 4 threads an hour and the ground of complaint on their heads is I think removed.

On the second point, the mode of manufacturing cordage, I am decidedly of the opinion that all cordage should be made from 35 or 40 thread yarn spun from hemp. The Master Rope Maker and foreman however, consider (although I do not agree with them) that large cables may still be made from 25-thread yarn manufactured from hatchelled hemp. It may be said, that the plan if adopted will prove very expensive, but if reference is made to the rate attained for the sale of old stores for toppets, it will be found that a very good price is likely to be given for the hemp used by the rope makers at this place as it will be of so much better quality than the toppets and the additional expense will surely not deserve consideration if it will remedy the evil complained of.

The proposal for what may be considered in future as a fair day's work for the various branches of rope makers, which has been drawn up by the Master and foreman of rope makers in this yard, is submitted herewith and which is calculated for the Summer hours labour and can of course be decreased in Winter in proportion to the decrease of working hours.

[*Enclosure*]
Chatham Yard. A proposition from the Master Rope Maker and Foreman of what may in future be considered a fair day's work for the various branches of rope making.

Hatchelling   7 bundles per man per day.
Parting   30 bundles per man per day.
Carrying   40 bundles per man per day.
Dressing hemp bands when covered three-quarters   50 cwt
Dressing hemp bands when not covered   100 cwt
Dressing hemp damaged   1lb 1qtr
Dressing hemp toppings including toppets weighed out and carried away three quarters and 7lbs
Yarn   1435 threads

179. *Admiralty to Superintendent Gordon: French rope manufactory. Copy of report produced by Superintendent of Portsmouth Dockyard*

[NMM, CHA/H/8]   8 October 1833

I beg leave to submit the method followed in manufacturing cordage at Cherbourg. The men employed in cleaning the hemp for spinning take out eight per cent, they do not top the hemp so no toppings are produced. The method they follow when hatchelling, is that they throw one end of the hemp in the hatchel and continue to draw the hemp through their hand until about 7 lbs are drawn through. They then turn a small head at each end of it after which it is taken to the spinner who puts it round his body, not over his shoulder, for spinning. And to prevent his hemp from falling down, he ties an apron round his waist, the ends of which he brings over for the hemp to rest in. He then goes to the wheel, hooks on his hemp, and commences spinning his yarn from the hemp in front of his body (not from the ends). He spins two yarns in the hook, each yarn 3 lbs of hemp & of 182 fathoms in length, which he follows up whilst it is being reeled on a reel which is placed behind the spinning wheel, passes through two nippers which smooth the yarn and give it a smooth appearance.

The method of tarring the yarn I did not see, only saw the tar heated, which by thermometers was at 145 degrees. The rope maker said it was fit for tarring the yarns. They tar one yarn at a time, their general practice is to tar the yarn at the time the spinner follows his yarn. When spun the yarn is drawn through the tar, which is in a copper placed between the spinning wheel and the reel on which the yarns are reeled. They heat the tar by steam, after the yarns have passed through the tar copper two lizards or nippers are put round the yarn by drawing the yarn through the nippers it takes off superfluous tar from the yarn. This is done by two men employed to reel and guide the yarns on the reels with the man guiding having a hole in a piece of wood. The yarn passes through the hole to the reel, which he guides from one side of the reel to the other. They reel from two to three cwt of yarn when tarred on each reel.

The yarns, when wanted to make cordage, is reeled from the reel on to the bobbins, the length required to make the cordage. The bobbins are then placed in the frame, each yarn having a separate hole in the register plate, which holes are formed in circles round the plate. The yarns are put through the plate into the tubes, which tube is calculated in size to receive the number of yarns to form the ropes for strand or cable. Then the machine for applying the twist is brought too, the yarns are hooked on a pinion. The rope for drawing is put round the regulating plates for applying the portion of twist by which the yarns are formed into a strand.

The men then commence drawing the rope which draws the machine forward by which the yarns are drawn from off the bobbins through the tube, which tube being small consolidates the yarn by which a smooth surface is brought on the strand which improves the appearance of the cordage. When the length is formed to make the rope or cable strand, the strand form is cut off the machine and brought back again, by which only one strand is formed at a time. During the operation of forming the strand the quantity of twist is applied by the machine to form the yarn to an angle of 27 degrees and before the top is put into lay the strands into rope an additional twist is applied to form the yarns to the angle of 37 degrees. They then commence to lay the ropes.

180. *Surveyor of Navy to Admiralty: powering of turning lathe*

[TNA, ADM222/4]   22 January 1834

Recommended that the spare power not at present used in the machinery at the sawmills at Chatham be applied to a turning lathe for spindles of capstans and for iron and woodwork, which are at present effected by manual labour.

[*Marginal note*]
This measure is very desirable but I do not know if there is any lathe at Chatham applicable to the purpose. I would submit that the officers report on the measure requisite to be taken, and the means they have applicable thereto and an estimate of such parts as they can form a judgment of.

181. *Admiralty to Superintendent Gordon: powering of turning lathe*

[NMM, CHA/H/9]   24 March 1834

I am commanded by My Lords Commissioners of the Admiralty to acquaint you that they approve of applying the spare power, not at present used by the machinery at the sawmills, for turning spindles of capstans and other iron and woodwork, and for drilling holes in iron knees &c as mentioned in your letter of the 22nd inst.

182.   *Architect to Superintendent of Chatham Dockyard: engine house for ropery*

[TNA, ADM1/3502]   2 March 1836

The engine house will be conveniently situated within the space between the present tarring house and the adjoining building where there is a space of 40 feet by 20 feet. The building may be formed, the boilers set and the chimney erected by the workmen of the yard at an expense of about £500. The engine will perform all that is required and the tar be heated by steam on the spinning floor as Mr Ewart will explain.

183.   *Superintendent Gordon to Admiralty: engine house for ropery*

[TNA, ADM1/3404]   20 February 1837

The enclosed I beg leave to submit for the consideration of My Lords Commissioners of the Admiralty a letter from the officers of this yard proposing that assistance be rendered to Boulton & Watt in fixing the spare boiler of the 14 horse engine at the ropery, stating that the millwrights are so fully occupied that one can not be spared for the purpose and I beg leave to add that although their Lordships were pleased to sanction on the 4th of November last the employment of two extra millwrights and to introduce extra boys in the rope jacks, the officers have only been able to obtain the services of one man.

184.   *Description of the Sawmill*

[Wright, *Topography of Rochester, Chatham* (Chatham, 1838), p. 73.[1]]   1838

The sawmills are situated at the northeast extremity of the dockyard. They are erected on rising ground about thirty-five feet above the level of the lowest part of the yard, and are enclosed in a room ninety feet square, roofed in by a light covering constructed of wood and wrought-iron. The machinery comprises eight saw-frames, and two circular benches, with windlasses and capstans, which feed the frames; to work which an excellent thirty-horse power steam-engine is employed. These frames again are wholly independent of one another, and each of them formed to admit of from one to thirty saws, inserted or removable at pleasure,

[1]I.G. Wright, *Topography of Rochester, Chatham, Strood, Brompton &c* (Chatham Hill, 1838).

according to the number of planks required to be obtained out of a beam of timber, which, moreover can, by their arrangement, be procured of various thickness if necessary.

The ground on the north side of the mills is appropriated to the stowage of the timber, to which balks are floated from the river by means of a canal running open to the extent of about 250 feet, till it enters the rising ground, when it becomes a tunnel 300 feet in length, and discharges itself into an elliptical basin ninety feet long, seventy-two feet broad, and forty-four feet deep, from whence the timber is raised to the saws with extraordinary velocity by the machine of the mills.

There is also a room appointed to models of blocks, and is a very handsome exhibition.

The whole of these admirable contrivances were projected and executed by the ingenious Mr. Brunel, of Thames tunnel celebrity.

185. *Admiralty to Superintendent Clavell: millwrights*

[NMM, CHA/H/35] 8 June 1840

It appears that the Commissioner has 'begged to be allowed to retain the two millwrights entered for the repair of yard steam machinery at the ropery'. I am commanded by My Lords Commissioners of the Admiralty to say that they have no objection, provided the estimate will meet the expense.

186. *Admiralty to Superintendent Clavell: chain power*

[NMM, CHA/H/35] 14 August 1840

I am commanded by My Lords Commissioners of the Admiralty to acquaint you that they have directed the civil architect to make arrangements for applying chain power to turn the spinning wheels at the ropery at Chatham according to a plan suggested him by Mr Fincham.

187. *Admiralty to Superintendent Shirreff: hauling off yarn*

[NMM, CHA/H/38] 6 January 1841

I am commanded by My Lords Commissioners of the Admiralty to acquaint you that they have ordered Mr Chapman, the Master Rope Maker of Deptford Yard, to repair to Chatham with the model of a plan for warping off a haul of yarn in a large reel & to communicate with you & the officers of the ropery relative to the advantages and application of it. He is ordered also to ascertain whether the new winches lately made at Deptford can be advantageously worked at Chatham by the supply of yarn at Deptford.

Their Lordships desire you will give Mr Chapman every information and assistance he may require toward the adoption of his plan & provided no material objection can be shown against it (of which their Lordships are to be immediately apprized) you are to cause a large reel in the plan of Mr Chapman's model & of the dimensions he should recommend, to be completed [as] expeditiously as possible at Chatham for the purpose of facilitating the supply of rope yarn for the machinery at Deptford & Mr Chapman is to arrange with the officers at Chatham the position & mode in which it may be desirable to fix it.

You are to report to their Lordships on the foregoing points & to inform me as soon as the reel is completed, when directions will be given for its erection.

188. *Admiralty to Superintendent Shirreff: tilt hammer*

[NMM, CHA/H/38]   24 February 1841

The sum of £4,309 being proposed in the Estimates for the ensuing year for a steam engine tilt hammer and Hercules hammer for the smithery at Chatham, I am commanded by My Lords Commissioners of the Admiralty to signify their directions to you to transmit drawing and specifications in order that tenders may be called for & the work put in hand as soon as possible after the estimate shall be passed.

189. *Architect to Admiralty: estimate*

[TNA, ADM1/5521]   1842

With the exception of Woolwich, the smitheries in the different dockyards have, until lately, been totally unprovided with machinery; all work being executed by sheer manual labour. In every private establishment, of any importance, machinery is extensively used and its great efficiency and economy tested beyond all doubt. At Sheerness and Portsmouth, machinery has been applied with advantage and it is now proposed to extend it to Chatham and Plymouth. Moreover, as there is a deficiency of means, for making anchors, as the demand is great and only a limited supply can be obtained from contractors, additional anchor fires are required and the machinery [therefore] is rendered still more requisite.

£4,309

190.   *Description of the Rolling Mill*

[Hobbes, *Reminiscences and Notes*, pp. 120–21]   *c*.1849

Here were several great furnaces, and some gigantic machinery, together with the 'rollers' of various dimensions, between which the blocks of glowing metal taken from the furnaces were placed, and where they were rolled out into sheets of various length and thickness, or into rods which were afterwards cut into bolts, or turned into screws, rings, etc. We had, however, to take another opportunity to see the whole process [191]. It may be sufficient for the present to say that we learned that more than 3000 copper sheets, weighing upward of twelve tons, were required for sheathing a single line of battle ship, besides which the timbers were bound and riveted together with bolts of the same metal, of which most of the nails used in the construction were composed.

191.   *Description of the Manufacturing Departments*

[Hobbes, *Reminiscences and Notes*, pp. 143–8]   *c*.1849

The mechanical departments of the yard were of endless interest, and it was a pleasant change, when sometimes wearied with the monotony of my work, to rise from the desk and visit them. I loved to go to the smithery and watch the forging of the mighty anchors, and see the blows given whose thunder shook the solid earth around and might be heard afar off. Again and again I looked in at the metal mills. Let me describe the process of manufacturing the metal. It was formerly called *conversion*, as the copper was not smelted from the ores, but from old sheathing and bolts from ships, sent to Chatham from all the other Royal Dockyards. Many tons at a time were delivered at the metal mills, where a suitable reverberatory furnace was used to melt the copper in quantities of from four to five tons at a time, which quantity could be melted once or twice in the twenty-four hours as required, the work going on day and night without intermission from Monday to Saturday, three sets of men being employed. The furnace was charged at a side-doorway, which was a framework of iron filled with firebricks to resist the high temperature of the furnace during the 'firing'; this door was opened, by a weighted iron lever, as required for the addition of metal until the full charge was put in. If the copper was to be refined and taken out the same day, the front-door was closed, and 'firing' commenced, that is, renewed stoking, for the fire had been burning strongly during the whole of the charging process. With the doors closed and renewed stoking, the heat had become great and the copper was melting; the leading man therefore opened the door and introduced his 'rabble' to stir the mass so that all might be melted; closing this door, he opened the side-door and took out a sample, which he broke at a vice, and this guided him to the next step, which was to introduce into the molten metal 'the pole', commonly a piece of beech or oak from 20 to 30 feet long, and as large as the front-door would admit in diameter; making a fulcrum of the arch of the front-door, he lifted the outer end of the pole with his shoulder and forced the inner end down into the molten copper, which immediately boiled up into beautiful golden sprays; then, placing a board with a V cut to receive the pole, he rested, and the refining went on. Again and again, as the pole burned away, its outer end was lifted up and the end thrust further into the boiling copper, the refiner frequently taking small samples out and breaking them to ascertain the 'pitch' of the copper. The refining being sufficiently advanced, the pole was lowered and the side-door opened and, by a new process, cakes of metals that had been prepared, by another process, of sulphide of copper, were introduced into the 'charge,' and thoroughly stirred by the 'rabble,' causing further agitation; the metal was then skimmed with another 'rabble,' and with a small ladle a 'hammer-test' taken out, which the leading man carried to an anvil. While he held it, three men struck it with sledge-hammers until a plate about the size of a man's hand was beaten out, quite thin at the edges; he then quenched the plate in water, examined it carefully, and, if quite satisfied, took out from the furnace another small test, quenched it, nicked it, and bent it to cracking at the vice to see the grain of the copper; when, if up to 'touch pitch,' the 'ladling out' commenced, cast iron pots to receive the molten metal having already been prepared and arranged in front of the furnace, occupying three sides of a square. The pots were bottomless, but stood on thick slabs of cast iron, and, quickly as they could move, two men – or more when large cakes had to be cast – followed each other with ladles full of the molten copper, pouring it into pots. (The first round, being bottom plates, on the cast iron, were 'wasters,' and had to be returned to the refinery furnace the following day.) In the next round the metal for cakes to be rolled into sheets was cast, about eighty-four pounds to each cake, the men followed each other quickly, and pouring three ladles into each pot, which set rapidly; as soon as the round was completed, it began again at the starting-point, depositing cake upon cake until the leading man, who stood watching every ladleful of copper with a small iron paddle in his hand, ready to pick out any floating bit of charcoal or other impurity before the cake set, called a halt to stoke his fire and make another test of the metal; and, if it had gone back, he thrust in the pole again and covered the surface with charcoal; when ready, ladling was resumed, and continued until the whole charge of about five tons was taken out. This was allowed to remain to cool until the following morning, when the cakes had contracted sufficiently to lift from the pots. They were then separated with sledgehammers, trimmed with trimming-hammers, and stacked ready for the Rolling Mill. This completed the first, or refining process, and hereafter we will describe the rolling.

At other opportunities I visited the ropery (1,110 feet long), where cordage of every description was made, and the raw material, and every stage of manufacture might be seen. The hemp was chiefly supplied by Russia, the coarsest, strongest, and best being from St. Petersburg; Italian hemp also was used. Before being officially received it was tested; it was then carefully stowed and placed in the charge of the Storekeeper, from whom the quantities daily required for manufacture were drawn. It was next 'heckled' through fine spikes till the short threads, used for small cordage, and refuse, were drawn out of it; then it was weighed into small parcels of about 2½lb. each, called 'pigs', which were afterwards spun into 'yarns,' each yarn at this stage passing through a copper of boiling tar. The yarns were next spun into 'strands', each strand, to prevent embezzlement, having the Government mark inserted in coloured worsted through the whole length of the strand, the mark at Chatham being yellow, that at Portsmouth blue, that at Devonport red. Great ropes were *cable-laid* and *hawser-laid*, the former having three *large* strands, each of them containing three smaller strands, or nine strands in all, every one of them of 37 original yarns, altogether 333 yarns, a hawser-laid rope containing only three strands. The spinning was done in the Spinning-rooms, which were about 1000 feet long, the boys who ran to and fro with yarns covering many miles a day. The whole was under the Master Rope Maker, who was subordinate to the Master Attendant; in consultation with whom the work of each day was arranged and communicated the previous evening to the foremen, who was responsible for the quality of all hemp officially received, and for using the oldest hemp first; as well as for seeing that all candidates for entry in the ropery possessed the necessary qualifications before being placed upon the yard books, and instructing them in their various duties; and, as well as the Master Rope Maker, for using every precaution and vigilance to prevent accidents by fire among such inflammable materials.

Leaving the ropery, I occasionally turned to the left, and, passing some of those chain cables with which we had now become familiar, and which were gradually to some extent superseding such hempen cables as we have seen in course of manufacture, came out on the river side, fronting which were the great storehouses, containing, like those at Sheerness, immense quantities of stores of all kinds, neatly and systematically arranged; and, among the rest, ropes of all sizes, and great numbers of hempen cables, some of which were 28 inches in circumference and 120 fathoms long. The rigging and other articles of equipment for the dismantled ships lying in the Medway might be seen in compartments appropriated to them. All along the wharf outside were anchors of huge but varying sizes. Close at hand were the Lead and Paint Mills, where lead was milled, drawn out into pipes, etc., and the paint, immense quantities of which were used in the yard, ground and prepared.

Again and again, as I have said, I visited the metal mills, and now I will describe the process of 'rolling.' The 'tough cake' copper, refined, as we have seen, was taken by the workmen to the furnaces at the back of the 'rolls' – large revolving steel cylinders worked by gigantic machinery – which were charged by the day gang as soon as they arrived in the morning, one furnace with the cake copper so brought them, the other with plates previously produced; after stoking their fires, and while the heating was going on, they breakfasted; then, the heat being ready, the rolling was commenced. The first operation was called 'breaking down the cakes,' i.e., reducing them from about 1¾ inches to about three-eighths of an inch in thickness; the plate, withdrawn from the furnace red-hot, being passed by one workman between the rolls and returned to him over the top-roll to be passed through again and again, the rolls being at each pass brought closer together till the required dimensions by gauge were obtained; then the 'catcher' thrust the plate into a tank of water hard by to quench it and remove the oxide; this was continued until the whole 'charge' was rolled. The shearman next took the plates to the 'Lowmoor Shears', cut them into three equal parts, sheared them to size, and weighed them for making two finished sheets each; they were then returned to the furnace to be reheated, rolled again in the next heat to about one-third of their previous thickness, again returned to the furnace, and then, as they were taken out, doubled over, and passed again and again through the rolls till of the proper length. Once more they were taken by the shearman, who cut off the double end and any irregularities and immersed them in a tank of diluted sulphuric acid, which effectually removed all the oxide; they were then put on a rack to drip, and afterwards transferred to an inclined table over which a stream of water was continually running, washed with brushes, rinsed, and placed on a rack over a flue to dry.

192.   *Chief Engineer to Surveyor of Navy: steam machinery*

[TNA, ADM85/1]   5 June 1850

I beg to report that the under mentioned Steam Engine Boilers require repair:

Boiler at lead mill
Boiler at ropery
Boiler at smithery steam hammer
Boiler at metal mills
Boiler at sawmills

and I submit a set of boiler makers be lent from Woolwich for this purpose – so soon as these workmen arrive they may commence repairing.

[Appended notes]

6 June. The Captain Superintendent is requested to direct Mr Lawrie to report why these boilers cannot be repaired by the workmen of the yard.

Chatham Yard. 7 June. Millwrights are not accustomed with this species of work and there are no boiler makers attached to this yard. Hitherto it has been the practice to get workmen lent from Woolwich for that purpose, & I do not think it judicious to have these repairs executed by millwrights. Alexander Lawrie.

11 June. The Captain Superintendent is requested to cause these boilers to be repaired by the workmen of the yard. No difficulty seems to be experienced in other yards in executing the repairs of the boilers without the aid of boiler makers.

These boilers are to be repaired by the workmen of the yard. Captain Superintendent.

13 June. Acted. A. Lawrie.

193.   *Chief Engineer to Surveyor of Navy: new machinery*

[TNA, ADM85/1]   7 June 1850

As the sum of £330 has been allowed in the estimates 1850/1 for new machinery at this yard, I would submit that the 'small steam donkey to supply feed water to the two high pressure boilers for working 50 cwt steam hammer of new forge attached to metal mills' as proposed be demanded from Messrs Nasmith, Gaskell &c. Under the present arrangements the above boilers are to be supplied with feed water by hand pump & therefore the necessity of being furnished with a steam donkey as early as possible. I would further beg to be informed in what way the remaining portion of the £330 is to be appropriated.

194. *Chief Engineer to Surveyor of Navy: smiths and joiners*

[TNA, ADM85/1] 9 June 1850

In reference to your minute of the 23rd instant, respecting the proportion of smiths, joiners &c to the number of shipwrights; we beg to say that having for several years past felt extremely inconvenienced from the restricted number of smiths, we are desirous of a considerable increase in this branch of workmen: from the former proportion of one to four and a half, to that of one to three and a half.

The immense increase of iron work by the introduction of steam ships and the use of iron in the hull and fittings of all classes of vessels, and this not only in quantity but also of much more elaborate workmanship; the greatly increased demand for sea stores, such as iron bound blocks &c.; and in this yard the average employment of four or five smiths on the works pertaining to the Chief Engineer, are reasons for the increased proportions we have recommended.

With respect to joiners: the old proportion of one to six shipwrights (or 75 men), exclusive of the man employed in superintending the planing machine, will, we think suffice, having now the advantage of the mortising and tenoning machines lately introduced.

In the Chief Engineer's department the increase of millwrights should be from $\frac{1}{17}$th to $\frac{1}{13}$th, and of plumbers and braziers from $\frac{2}{89}$ to $\frac{2}{75}$. It is proposed to include two brass fitters and 2 metal turners in the increase of millwrights and as the increased demand for manufactured lead, in addition to the ordinary increase of labour, it will be very advantageous were 6 ordinary labourers added to the present establishment of labourers at the millwrights shop.

195. *Deputy Director of Works: report on manufacturing departments*

[RNM, Portsmouth Mss 286 (previously Da 0126)] 8 January 1857

The sawmills and all the arrangements in connexion with that establishment were no doubt a great mistake. Had the money so expended been employed in levelling the ground, a large addition might have been made to the yard, at no additional cost and a much more efficient and economical arrangement might have been provided for the saw-mills.

By the construction of the metal mills a very good smithery has been considerably damaged.

The present arrangement for manufacturing lead in sheet, lead pipes, paint, putty &c, are by no means equal to what should be provided, and the site is objectionable.

At some future time it may be found necessary to remove the saw mills to a more advantageous site; to increase the metal mills (and to make provision in connexion with the metal mills for manufacturing lead in sheets, pipes, paint &c.) and to construct a new smithery on the site of the present timber traveller. For all this the ground should be levelled.

The ground south of the sawmills is favourable for additional officers' houses.

The large piece of ground at the back of the ropery, including the gardens, might afford ample space for increasing the rope making establishment (including rope stores and hemp stores) – but for this the ground should be lowered.

The sail loft and sail stores &c will admit of extension and improvement – and should be in a more convenient position in reference to the basins.

196.   *Chief Engineer to Superintendent of Chatham Dockyard:*
artisans and labourers

[TNA, ADM89/3]   3 December 1857

Workmen at Millwrights' Shop
Single stationed   1
Leading men   1st class   1
                                2nd   1
Pattern makers   1st   –
                                2nd   –
Millwrights & fitters   1st   4
                                2nd   26

Apprenticed		3
Assistant fitters		4
Turners & machine men	1st	2
	2nd	2
Smiths	1st	–
	2nd	2
Hammer men		1
Founders	1st	2
	2nd	2
Turners in wood	1st	1
	2nd	5
Labourers at machine		14
Labourers at ordinary		7
Boys	1st	1 ⎫
	2nd	1 ⎭ All as messengers

Sawmills		
Leading men		1
Workmen	1st	12
	2nd	7
	3rd	6
At pit and saw	1st	1

Cement Mills		
Cooper		1
Calciner		1
Miller		1

Metal Mills and Sheathing Nail Shop		
Single stationed (writer)		1
Leading men	1st	1
	2nd	4
Workmen	1st	6
	2nd	11
	3rd	15
	4th	14
	5th	7
	6th	10
Boys	1st	–
	2nd	3
To study manufacture of metals		1

Plumbers and Braziers

Leading men	1st	–
	2nd	1
Workmen	1st	1
	2nd	9
Apprenticed		3

Braziers and Tinners

	1st	1
	2nd	1

Engine keepers	7
Stokers	7
Oar making machine	8
Single stationed labourers	5

197. *Chief Engineer to Superintendent Goldsmith: increased demands*

[TNA, ADM89/3]   3 December 1857

I beg to submit that the great increase in the number of ships fitted for service in this port, added to that of machinery in operation: oar making machines, cement mills, laying and spinning machines at ropery, lead and paint mills, saw and metal mills, as well as the manufacture of water closets for all the yards, always affording employment for millwrights and other mechanics, render it necessary in order to meet these demands, that the establishment of the Chief Engineer should comprise (in addition to the present establishments) the under mentioned classes:

At Millwrights' Shop

Millwrights	1st class	3
	2nd	3
Labourers ordinary		16

At Plumbers Shop

Copper smith	1

At Iron Foundry

Apprentice or boy	1

Decrease in present establishment of workmen at
Millwrights' shop consequent on the introduction of
treenail and oar making machine –

Wood turners   2

Decrease in Plumbers Shop   Plumber   1

The increase of men proposed and the workmen in plumber and brazier's
shop, placed on the 10 hour system, would in my opinion enable the Chief
Engineer's department to meet the current demands of the service.

198. *Surveyor of the Navy to Storekeeper General: apprentices*

[TNA, ADM89/3]   24 June 1858

The enclosed correspondence on the present system of entering house
boys and spinners' apprentices at Chatham, Portsmouth and Devonport
with a draft of a submission on this subject are referred for the information
of the Storekeeper General and for any observations he may wish to make
thereon, before being transmitted to their Lordships.

I would suggest that with reference to the present store of yarn, which
is below the establishment it would be a convenience to employ the
spinners' apprentices as rope makers, as far as possible and, for that
purpose, the proposed establishment of house boys might be completed
at once.

As the experiment is being tried at Chatham, of spinning yarn by
machinery – with a prospect of success, I see no objection to the spinners'
apprentices being part of the establishment of spinners.

199. *Controller of the Navy to Admiralty: manufactured items for*
Achilles *and* Black Prince

[TNA, ADM1/5840]   15 February 1863

All our contractors have complained that we require work of exceptionally
good character, such as some of them say is quite unusual in the trade.
Others, again, compare it to engine-making rather than ship-building work
and have made it the subject of claim for extra payment. After all this very
good extra work, which is so superior to ordinary (in their estimate), we
find watertight compartments leaking water faster than pumps can clear
them, false bottoms leaking, sluice doors and valves not acting, what other

term than slovenly can be given to work confessedly inferior to the very superior workmanship which has yet produced such as results as these?

200.   *Steam Spinning Jennies*

[*Chatham News and North Kent Spectator*]   3 September 1864

Some time ago the Lords Commissioners of the Admiralty decided that all rope made in this dockyard should be manufactured by steam. To carry this out it has been found necessary to have more accommodation for the erection of steam spinning jennies, and for that purpose the upper storey of the large hemp houses Nos. 1 & 2 in this dockyard have been converted into one large spinning room. Workmen are now busily employed in clearing out, repairing and otherwise fitting the hemp houses for the reception of steam machinery, which is expected to arrive here next month.

201.   *Inspection of Ropery*

[*Chatham News and North Kent Spectator*]   10 December 1864

Returning to the dockyard by the eastern entrance, the visitors [members of the Board of Admiralty] proceeded to the rope-making establishment, where some extensive alterations are in progress consequent on the introduction of the new spinning and other machines for dispensing with hand labour in the manufacture of the largest description of cables. A portion of the machinery has already been received at the dockyard but several of the largest machines are now in the course of manufacture by Messrs. Fairbairn of Leeds. It is still undecided whether to employ young women or lads to take charge of the machinery, but as a certain delicacy of touch as well as nimble fingers is required, it is probable that the Admiralty will break through the rule hitherto observed, and will introduce girls for employment in Chatham Dockyard. On completing their inspection of the ropery their Lordships adjourned to the official residence of Captain Stewart of the dockyard, where they partook of luncheon.

4

STORAGE, SECURITY AND MATERIALS

Storage

The late-eighteenth century had seen construction at Chatham of a number of either new or replacement storehouses, allowing the yard to enter the period under review with sufficient storage of a better quality than that available in the other yards. Thus, on only a few occasions after 1815 was administrative attention directed to the construction or repair of storage facilities, it being necessary to carry out repairs to the rigging house [216], the lower mast house [221] and the roof of the hemp house [214], and to increase the number of linseed oil storage cisterns in the painter's shop [217].

Of equal importance to the possession of adequate storage was its efficient use, so that materials were stored under ideal conditions. The over-ordering of stores had to be avoided, as material would perish if kept for too long. This was the first economy attended to at the end of the French Wars [203], but no consequent reduction in storehouse labourers was achieved immediately [204]. As for the means of storage, because of the great quantities held, that for timber and hemp was subject to much scrutiny. In November 1823, the entire rope-making process was reviewed, with the first half of the subsequent report directed to the best method of storing hemp [212]. Criticisms made in this report resulted in a strong written defence by Commissioner Cunningham [213]. A particular problem with the storage of hemp was its liability to overheat [206, 208], made worse if excessive amounts of train oil were applied during hatchelling [209]. The challenge was not simply in the preservation of the original raw material but in keeping that which was partly manufactured. Having been spun into yarn, it was first stored in the white yarn house before being immersed in a kettle of heated tar and transferred to the black yarn house [208]. To aid the preservation of the finished product, thought was given to the possibility of replacing tar with a mineral composition applied by a painting process [205].

The most advantageous means of storing and preserving timber were also frequently reviewed, for large amounts could be lost as a result of decay [255]. In 1815, the Navy Board issued instructions to each of the dockyard commissioners that outlined the best methods of preserving timber, with a summary of these instructions being sent to the Admiralty [255]. The report noted that the boiling of plank and thick stuff (plank over 4 inches thick) was occasionally undertaken. An alternative to the boiling of timber was to soak it and experiments were undertaken using salt water [202]. In 1833 an order was issued to discontinue the boiling and immersion of plank and timber [222], and greater efforts were made to store timber under cover [219]. To increase the availability of cover, orders were issued for the construction of more proper sheds where timber could be stacked to admit a free circulation of air [220].[1] At Chatham sheds were located in the extreme north of the yard. Few questions arose with the storage of other materials, although the value of storing old sails was raised [210].

Issuing and accounting for stores raised problems that had to be faced [260]. It was strictly laid down that all stores should be issued by age; the officers at Chatham were reminded that this should apply particularly to rigging and sails [259]. For the short-term storage of items required for ships under construction or repair, fitting or refitting in the harbour, a number of store cabins were located around the yard from which stores were issued on a daily basis. They, in turn, were supplied from the larger storehouses. These cabins, the Navy Board concluded, were uneconomic [211] giving thought to the construction of a new three-storey building, to be termed the 'present use storehouse', from which all stores should be issued [215]. However, this building was not pursued. Instead, two existing storehouses were utilised: one to issue stores for ships under construction and repair, the other to issue stores to vessels afloat. Attention was also given to an improved system of accounting by which stores were issued on production of a note signed by a foreman of the yard. At the end of each month, the foreman was required to submit to the Admiralty an abstract of stores used. This simplified the previous system in which the requisition notes of quartermen were sent to London every day [218]. The number of store men and issuers was also increased to permit those collecting stores to return to their place of work as quickly as possible [223].

---

[1]In 1771, following an Admiralty visitation to the yard at Chatham, the Earl of Sandwich, the First Lord of the Admiralty, had recommended the construction of four sets of timber seasoning sheds. This new range of sheds, all completed by 1774, was to supplement those built during the 1770s. For further details on these earlier sheds, see J. Coad, *The Royal Dockyards 1690–1850: Architecture and Engineering Works of the Sailing Navy* (Aldershot, 1989), pp. 127–8, and P. MacDougall, 'A Social History of Chatham Dockyard, 1770–1801' (Open University M Phil thesis, 1983), pp. 269–72.

202. *Annual Report on the State of the Navy: immersion of timber*

[TNA, ADM106/2272]   16 January 1817

We have reason to believe that immersion in salt water is a very good preventative to the decay of timber, and we would therefore recommend (if their Lordships should approve of this suggestion) that the timber when converted should be put into the water for a few months, and then placed under sheds until required for use.

By this arrangement a large proportion of the timber in each yard will be in constant process of seasoning and ships constructed of such material and built under cover we have reason to expect will prove durable fabrics, instead of beginning to perish as we have known in some instances almost before they are brought into service.

203. *Navy Board to Commissioner Barlow: economies*

[NMM, CHA/F/30]   23 January 1817

It being absolutely necessary that the expense of the current years, in every department of the naval service, should be limited as much as possible, we have particularly to call your attention to the state of the stores and to desire you will not only caution the officers not to demand greater quantities for the current services, or insert more in those columns of the periodical return in which the probable expenditure of the year will be stated, than they shall be of opinion, on mature consideration, but that you will also, before any demand for stores is transmitted to us, examine the same yourself in order to judge of the propriety of the qualities demanded and give such direction to officers on the occasion as you may deem necessary.

204. *Commissioner Barlow to Navy Board: reductions of storehouse labourers*

[NMM, CHA/F/30]   23 May 1817

I am humbly of opinion that in consequence of the storehouses being so detached it will be impossible to do with less than the number at present employed viz. 26 without having constant resort to yard labourers.

205. *Navy Board to Commissioner Barlow: preservation of rope*

[NMM, CHA/F/30]   26 June 1817

Mr. Thomas Grant, who resides at No. 1 Great St. Helens, having with his letter of the 20th inst. forwarded to us some specimens of rope painted with his mineral black composition, which rope he states will be found equally pliant with the same sort of rope not painted (a piece of which accompanies the specimen) and much stronger than it would be if tarred. We acquaint you that we have ordered these specimens to be sent to you and desire you will cause an experiment to be made of the paint, furnishing us with your opinion and observations thereon, particularly especially as it regards the strength and durability and its ability to crack and admit water.

206. *Questions placed by Navy Board Committee of Visitation to Ropeyard Officers*

[NMM, CHA/F/31]   22 July 1818

Is it usual to cut the bales of hemp after they are received, and if so, for what purpose?
We cut open the bales of hemp when received from ships, whenever we find from a long voyage, or leaks, that the hemp is in a hot state, in order that the heat may evaporate. When in good condition, we let it remain in bundles, as it is found to keep best.

Do you find the Hemp heated towards the bottom when stowed to a great height? Does it whilst so stowed, smell musty and do you consider that it is better to stow it in small quantities, for its better preservation?
Excepting when received hot, as above stated, we do not find it to heat after it is stowed in our warehouses about sixteen feet in height, which we think should not be exceeded. Consequently, when it does heat, it commences towards the bottom and ascends. It smells musty, and if there is not sufficient air to allow it to evaporate it condenses, and the top hemp becomes wet, which we always remove immediately and dry. Hemp may be stowed to the above height, the length of any storehouse, not a ground floor, without injury.

If hemp is at any time found damp and heated, does it recover its full strength on being exposed to the air? And if this is the case, should you think it advantageous to cover the hemp, so as to exclude it from the air?

At any time if found damp and heated, we cannot conceive it can ever recover its full strength, but when first imported, if it is in that state, it may by immediate care received, so that the deterioration shall be so small as hardly to be perceptible. But we still think it advantageous to cover it, being of that porous nature as to imbibe the moisture of a damp atmosphere and by alternate heat and cold, loses its vegetable substance, and becomes harsh and weak.

If it be thought not desirable to exclude hemp from the air, why is it necessary to cover the tarred yarn?
We consider it desirable to cover the tarred yarn, after it has been duly overset, and the heat evaporated, to prevent dust getting thereon; and the external air in time, from drying the inside of the piles. We here beg to add our opinion that hemp is preserved best in its raw state, but when it is spun into yarn, the tar thereof is its best preservative as the hot tar incorporates with the gum of the hemp and stops its vegetation, whereby we are not apprehensive of any heating afterwards taking place.

Is it desirable to increase the number of floors in the hemp house, or not to have any but the ground floor, and to store the whole in bulk?
It is desirable to increase the number of floors in our hemp houses. But we should never stow hemp upon a ground floor, as repeated experience has shown us, that it will imbibe the moisture the distance of some feet from the floor. We formerly had tons damaged by so doing.

207. *Report of Navy Board Committee of Visitation: storage of cordage*

[TNA, ADM106/3232]   23 July 1818

Mr Fenwick was questioned on the propriety of covering cordage as commended by the officers of Portsmouth and Plymouth and he gave his opinion that it is prejudicial to cover cordage deposited on the ground floor (an allusion particularly to the storehouses at Chatham) because if any damp gets into the cordage from the exhalation of the earth it cannot escape as it would without the covering, and consequently it condenses and ultimately, in his opinion, would destroy the cordage. That with respect to cordage in the upper part of the storehouses, he did not consider that the air admitted therein (which is not a continual current of air) can, in any respect, be injurious to it. He considers that hemp will preserve its strength longer in that state than in yarn and that white yarn will not be found desirable from its liability to heat and disintegration by vermin. He therefore considers it must be tarred if yarn is continued on the establishment.

208. *Navy Board to Commissioner Barlow: overheating of yarn*

[NMM, CHA/F/33]   5 January 1819

In consequence of a letter which we have received from the officers of your yard dated the 4th instant, informing us that a pile containing 96 hauls of white yard, coiled between the 1st October last and the 1st ult. was so hot in the centre that the thermometer stood at nearly one hundred degrees. We desire that you will cause this yarn to be tarred immediately, provided you consider the same to be necessary, and are satisfied that the degree of heat which has been discovered has not arisen from the want of sufficient care either in using the oil allowed for cleansing the hemp, or in stowing away the same in the hemp houses.

209. *Navy Board to Commissioner Barlow: oil dressing of hemp*

[NMM, CHA/F/33]   3 February 1819

We have received your letter of yesterday, informing us of the result of your enquiry into the means of applying the oil in dressing hemp. We desire that you will strictly forbid the applying it by the hand in future and that you will order the officers of the ropeyard to cause the oil to be put in future into a small jar or tub within reach of the workmen, who, after placing the hemp on the tool, are to dip a small birch broom into the oil and by striking it over the top of the hatchel, the oil will be generally distributed without the risk which has hitherto attended operations, and an uniform practice will prevail.

We request you will give your attention to this matter and direct the officers to report from time to time on the state of the white yarn (which they are to continue to manufacture) for our information.

210. *Committee of Visitation to Chatham Officers: old sails*

[TNA, ADM106/3234]   29 July 1820

We desire you will give us your opinion whether the old sails (appropriated to ships) now in store are likely to suffer any detriment from being kept; and whether you do not think they might be advantageous to be used for hammock cloths, bags, tarpaulin &c and to make new sails from time to time.

211. *Navy Board to all Dockyard Commissioners: storehouses*

[NMM, POR/G/5] 15 June 1822

The system of having numerous store cabins, as at present established in the various parts of the several dockyards, for supplying stores for the current service, appears to their Lordships to be objectionable, not only on account of the expense and the frequent employment it causes to clerks in taking account of their monthly remains, but also from its liability to fraud, and the facility with which the quartermen obtain whatever they please from these cabins, without rendering any account of their expenditure of the articles they must have taken. Their Lordships however are not prepared to say that these cabins can be at once wholly dispensed with. They would propose, that the several commissioners should have their attention called to the subject, and be directed to reduce gradually and with as little delay as may be practical without injury to the current service, the number of these store cabins. They may further recommend that, after due investigation and consideration of the subject, that each commissioner should be directed to state whether, in his opinion, by establishing two or three present use storehouses, in different parts of each yard, these very objectionable store cabins, as now managed, might not altogether be got rid of. In the meantime, stores should only be taken from these cabins by the authority of the foreman, under their signatures as at present by the quarterman, who should render an account of the application of them daily to the Master Shipwright's office.

Their Lordships deem it proper to add, as connected with this subject, that in their opinion the large storehouses which exist in each of the dockyards under the name of the 'present use storehouse' should be made that which the name implies: a store, in which articles of every description should be placed (as far at least as may be practicable), so that the issues of the day should be made as much as possible from this store only. It [*the present use store*] being replenished, from time to time, as might be necessary from the other storehouses, which would then only be required to be opened for the purpose of delivery out of them these occasional supplies for the present use store. If this regulation was put into practice, a store keeper's clerk, attending at this store to regulate and take an account of the issues from it, would be quite sufficient for the purpose, instead of it being found necessary as at present to employ storekeeper's clerks in different storehouses at the same time, throughout each day, and other clerks for the special purpose of issuing some particular species of stores.

212.   *Extract of Report following a Navy Board Inspection of Chatham and Portsmouth Ropeyards*

[TNA, ADM106/3237]   4 November 1823

It is surely necessary to remark that the first and essential requisite for good cordage is the certainty that none but hemp of the best quality should be received. If there is any mixture of an inferior sort, there can be no uniformity of strength in the rope and hence the necessity of extreme care in the receipt of this important article.

We have every reason to believe that the officers of the yard discharge their duty in the receipt of hemp with due fidelity to the public and fairness to the contractors, so that according to the agreement, none but good merchantable hemp is received. Governing themselves by this principle, we regret to find that the hemp of this year is not generally of a quality fit for the service and that much of it has been rejected, so that the Board will be disappointed in their desire to make up by the present importations for the deficiency of last year.

A careful selection has been made of the good hemp and we find upon a trial of its strength, compared with that received in 1813, that it is such as may be considered of a proper quality but the mixture of good and bad, in the different bundles, has induced us to suspect that the contractors are subject to some unfair dealing in Russia. We are strengthened in this suspicion by the opinion of those who have been long accustomed to the inspection of hemp, by whom it was particularly remarked that the bands by which the bundles were bound together, and the tiers of the layers, are two thirds heavier than usual, occasioned in general by the introduction in the middle of them of very inferior hemp, or what indeed may be more properly called tow. As the contract stipulates that the bundles shall be received and paid for as hemp of the first quality, it becomes necessary to have some early explanation from the contractors, and to apprise them of the suspicion we are led to entertain of some unfair dealing in Russia.

In sorting and selecting the serviceable hemp a considerable expense is incurred by the public, amounting at Portsmouth to £6.14s per diem on about 42 pounds on each layer. As the contractors are bound to deliver good merchantable hemp fit for the service, 'we think their failure to do so, and the consequent necessity of sorting it, ought not to be an expense chargeable on the public.'

The mode of preserving the hemp in the storehouses by guarding it from damp or currents of air has been pointed out by former committees of the Board. As we doubt whether the directions which have been given are acted upon in the same manner in all the yards we recommend that an order should be sent to each yard to see that the bundles are all thoroughly free from damp before they are lodged in the storehouse and that when there the whole be surrounded with canvas; the top left uncovered to let the heated air escape; and steps be taken so that the hemp is not in contact with the walls.

When so stowed away the windows should be opened in dry weather; occasionally the upper bundles thrown aside and those below brought to the top to guard against its heating.

A comparison of the quality and strength of the Italian hemp with that of Russia occupied much of our attention. The decided superiority of the former was proved by a variety of experiments, particulars of which will be found in our minutes. Without dwelling upon our report in a more minute detail on the strength of the two sorts of hemp, it will be sufficient to state that a piece of Italian rope of 3 inches in size sustained a strength of 3 hundredweight more than a piece of Riga rope of the same size. The experiment was made several times with nearly the same result and in the other sizes of Rope the same relative superiority was proved.

Our next object was to ascertain practically how far the opinion of the rope makers was correct as to the greater expense of dressing the Italian hemp. For this purpose two skilful hatchellers were employed, the one on 7lbs of Italian hemp and the other on 7lbs of Petersburg hemp. The operation of dressing each occupied two minutes; the loss on the Italian hemp (from the custom of not delivering it in so clean a state as the Russian) was one-third part, that of the Peterborough one-seventh.

The expense of dressing the Italian hemp is 5s per hundredweight that of the Peterborough 6d per hundredweight.

This loss, and the difference in price of dressing, is undoubtedly an objection to the use of Italian hemp and the extent to which we should otherwise oppose. We have thought it desirable to bring the subject under the consideration of the Board in the hope that the Italian hemp growers may be prevailed upon to clean their hemp as in Russia – which may be done without difficulty. In that case we should at once get rid of the loss, which we have described. We are not without hope that some means may be found of reducing the expense of dressing, which arises in a great quantity from the very great length of the Italian hemp, and the necessity of cutting, or breaking it, in order to let it spin off freely from the body of the rope maker.

At Portsmouth and Chatham there are proper machines for breaking Italian hemp. At the other yards it is cut. In the course of several experiments we made at Chatham the cut hemp appeared, in some instances, to be the strongest but we are not prepared to say that it is on the whole the best method.

The use of Italian hemp, in making boltrope for the sails, has been already ordered which is undoubtedly a great improvement. We think it should at once be extended to the rope for topsails, halyards and the lifts for the lower and topsail yards; all of which have much wear. The greater duration of the Italian hemp, when applied to such purposes, will nearly compensate for the increased expense before stated. It may indeed be a question whether it will not be a positive saving in point of expense, it appearing by a memorandum in the possession of Sir B Martin, taken from a letter which he received from an intelligent officer commanding a ship of the line in the Mediterranean, that a 5 inch rope, rove as a fore brace, manufactured at Naples and worked against a King's rope of the same size, rove on the opposite side, two of which were worn out, and it lasted as long as the third.

We are strongly inclined to recommend the more extended use of Italian hemp. It will encourage a greater attention to the growth and manufacture while a competition between the markets of Russia and Italy will give us the benefit of the exertions and improvement of both parties and tend to hold down the high prices to which this country has so often been subjected by the monopoly of Russia. We also recommend that all line and twine should be made of Italian hemp.

213. *Commissioner Cunningham to Navy Board: hemp storage*

[TNA, ADM106/1827]   30 December 1823

Averting to your letter of the 24th instant, on the subject of preserving the hemp in store; I beg to acquaint you that every attention is paid thereto, some of it is stowed against the sides of houses which are lined with board of a sufficient thickness to keep them dry, and where the sun comes upon it. As the bundles are open for inspection, it is stowed away loose, frequently opened for examination and has always been found in good condition. I therefore suggest whether it would not be unnecessary to follow the process of placing canvas behind the hemp so circumstanced, as described in the aforementioned letter, a measure which, in my opinion, and in the officers' opinion, will not add to the security of the hemp, or afford any further protection against damp, than the measures before described have been found to do.

[*Marginal notes*]
Acquaint him that as he appears so perfectly satisfied that the hemp stored as here described will be preserved in good condition we are willing to acquiesce in his suggestion that it should remain undisturbed but the regulations for the receipt of hemp in future should be carefully attended to.

214. *Commissioner Cunningham to Navy Board: hemp house*

[TNA, ADM106/1829] 2 December 1824

The roof of the old hemp house in this yard, which was raised one storey in the year 1813 having settled considerably, and caused several leaks to the detriment of the hemp that is stowed therein; I request you will order the Surveyor of Buildings to inspect the same immediately, in order that some steps may be taken for its security before the bad weather sets in.

[*Appended note*]
Mr. Taylor to take a convenient opportunity of visiting the yard when he may inspect the hemp house.

28 December. I have inspected the roof of this hemp house and find that in consequence of the hemp having been stowed in the upper floor and in the roof itself the weight has by the natural compression or sinking of the hemp fallen on the tie beams and timbers in the roof which was never intended. I am informed that it is requisite to continue to store the hemp in the manner (which has occasioned the fracture of the tie beams) in order to obtain sufficient room. If this be the case, the roof must be supported by storey posts under the tie beams as shown on the section enclosed and marked AA. It will also be requisite to introduce solid blocks of timber between the present storey posts and the substance of the floor. Taylor.

215. *Commissioner Cunningham to Navy Board: present use storehouse*

[TNA, ADM106/1829] 27 December 1824

I have received your letter of the 21st ultimo desiring to have a plan and estimate of a 'new present use storehouse' proposed to be erected in this yard; and a statement showing the expense of pulling down the old storehouse, the probable value of the materials if sold by auction, and whether any, and what part of such materials could be appropriated to the new building.

In return for which, I herewith send you plans (Nos. 1 and 2), the former showing the storehouse as proposed to be rebuilt with three storeys similar to the old one, and the latter with two storeys. I likewise forward a copy of the officers report, the estimated expense for taking down and rebuilding it, as also of the amount of serviceable articles that may be brought into use again, and showing the probable value of the old building materials if sold by auction. In transmitting these plans and estimates, I have to remark the storehouse proposed on plan number 2 appears to be the best calculated to answer the purpose required, as it will afford greater height and width in the rooms and can be erected at a less expense by £1,222 than shown on plan No. 1, as deduced from the following comparative estimates. Vizt.

Plan No.1
Expense of pulling down old storehouse	£	299	
Expense of rebuilding new storehouse	£12,694.	16s	6d
Deduct for useful materials	£	370	
Deduct for amount of supposed sale of			
unserviceable materials	£	758	
	£	1,123	
	£11,865		

Plan No.2
Estimate for building	£11,072	16s	6d
Add amount of useful materials in old building	£	370	
Deduct amount saved in labour pulling down if			
sold by auction	£	299	
Add £		71	
	£11,143.	16s	6d
Abate produce of sale, say	£	500	
	£10,643.	16s	6d
For building proposed on Plan 1	£11,865	16s	6d
For building proposed on Plan 2	£10,643	16s	6d
Difference	£	1,222	

216. *Commissioner Cunningham to Navy Board: rigging house*

[TNA, ADM106/1830]   4 June 1825

I have to acquaint you, the officers represent that the wood work between the crowns of the arches is decayed, upon which steps the pillars supporting the rigging house and store rooms above it; and in consequence thereof the floors and roof of the building have settled from 6 to 7 inches. They have taken measures to stop any further damage, and to set up the floors and roof of the said building, and after taking away the decayed timber between the crowns of the arches, they purpose putting down stone for the base of the pillars.

The officers also state that the lifting of the floors and roof of the building will be a work of considerable time and importance and as it requires the best workmen to perform the same, they propose that the men employed thereon be allowed the maximum of the house carpenters earnings, there being no prices in the scheme of task and job for this description of work.

[Appended note]
Acquaint the Commissioner that the arrangement appears judicious and that the Board approves of it being carried into effect.

217. *Commissioner Cunningham to Navy Board: linseed oil*

[TNA, ADM106/1834]   6 February 1827

The officers represent to me that having paint of various colours to manufacture for the whole of the Navy establishment, the average consumption of linseed oil has increased 20,000 gallons annually; and the present cistern under the painters shop will not contain more than 8,000 gallons, out of which quantity, they have frequently expended 6,000 gallons within three months. Should there be any delay after the expiration of the period in completing the quarterly demands for oil, any unforeseen occurrence taking place on the part of the contractors, the remaining stock of 2,000 gallons would very soon be exhausted. It is therefore proposed that three cisterns be made under the road in front of the painters' shop (as described by red lines on the accompanying sketch) which may be drawn off occasionally into the cistern under the present use shop and by that means always ensure good-old oil, as it not only improves in colour by keeping but also adds to the presentation of the work on which it is applied. The estimated expense of erecting

and leading the cisterns and fitting them with pipes, cocks &c is
£475.

218. *Navy Board to Storekeeper: accounting procedures*

[NMM, CHA/H/4]   3 February 1832

The Lords Commissioners of the Admiralty being desirous of reducing
the number of documents transmitted to this office relative to the issue of
stores for yard services as also the numerous entries thereof in the
storekeeper's ledger as well as facilitating the mode of determining the
value of stores supplied to each ship or service. I have to acquaint you
that it is under consideration that the following plan shall be forthwith
introduced at the several yards for that purpose.

First, a monthly abstract is to be formed of the stores issued to each
ship or service so as to determine the total quantity of each article issued.
A list of such stores is then to be prepared, showing the quantity, rate and
value of each article as well as the total expense for the month. This
account is to be prepared by the foreman or other officers responsible for
the issue of stores, who must satisfy themselves as to the correctness on
comparing the same with the demands he has made out for the said
stores.

Second, the above-mentioned monthly accounts are to be prepared
progressively day-to-day as the stores are issued. The accounts resulting
therefore to be considered as the vouchers the storekeeper will allow for
the issues.

Third, at the end of the month one general abstract is to be prepared
showing the quantities of the several articles with regard to ship or service.
Quantities are then to be entered in the ledger to the credit of the
storekeeper and the said abstract, with vouchers above mentioned,
transmitted to this office for examination.

Fourth, as regards to the timber articles, the plan already in operation
according to the regulations of December 1824, provides for making
monthly abstracts of the issues, which are therefore to be rated and valued
monthly instead of the daily notes being sent to this office.

With a view to the adoption of the above mentioned arrangement I have
to request that you give directions to the storekeeper to propose
immediately such form or forms of ruled paper as may appear best suited
for carrying the same into effect. And for the purpose of reducing the
number of vouchers in regard to stores issued to ships fitting out or
refitting, I have further to acquaint you that it is further proposed that one
voucher only, excepting in those cases where a part of the stores may be

supplied in one quarter and part in another, shall be transmitted, showing the whole of the supply to each ship and then the date of the completion of that supply.

219. *Admiralty to Master Shipwright: saturation of timbers*

[NMM, CHA/H/5] 21 March 1833

I am commanded by My Lord Commissioners of the Admiralty to signify their instruction to you to suspend the practice of saturating timber at least until all the means of placing sided timber under cover in a convenient manner for the admission of air shall be exhausted. Their Lordships further desire that you keep such a number of sawyers that you may think advisable constantly employed in the siding of timber applicable to ships' frames accessing only such compass timbers as may be best converted out of the rough stock and you are to place it separately in such places that it shall be available for use when wanted, allowing the oldest timber to be used first.

220. *Admiralty to Superintendent Gordon: timber storage*

[NMM, CHA/H/5] 29 March 1833

My Lord Commissioners of the Admiralty having called for the opinion of the several shipwright officers of the dockyards on the important question whether timber for ship building was improved, as to its duration, by steeping it for a certain time in salt water, a practice which has partially prevailed for several years past in consequence of orders from the late Navy Board, or whether its durability is more likely to be extended by keeping it under cover, properly placed and arranged so as to admit to a free circulation of air; and finding by the returns received, the general opinion is in favour of the latter plan, I am commanded by their Lordships to signify their directions to you to discontinue the practice of steeping in salt water, and to make preparations in the Dock Yard under your superintendence for stowing it under cover as aforesaid.

You are therefore to select at some convenient spot in the yard for the erection of a proper shed for this purpose, in which are to be deposited the Sided Timber, Thick Stuff, Plank, and Spars, and so arranged that any one piece can be conveniently drawn out when wanted without disturbing the rest, bearing in mind, that at the same time, that it is their Lordships particular desire that the oldest Timbers should first be made use of.

That with regard to the rough timber you are to see that it is not suffered to lay scattered about the Yard, but to be stacked in the most convenient situations, and classed in such a manner that the pieces most suitable for the purposes wanted may be got at with facility, without disturbing the stack, and you are likewise to take care that the pieces selected for conversion, whenever it can be done, be those that were first brought into the yard.

You are to make these arrangements gradually so as not to interrupt the ordinary operations of the yard without employing extra labour, or incurring any extra expense.

221.   *Superintendent Gordon to Admiralty: repairs to mast house*

[TNA, ADM1/3399]   5 November 1833

The officers in having represented to me in making up the accounts for the past month of the expense in buildings for the civil architect they find that the repair at the lower mast house has already exceeded the sum allowed for the estimates by £200 that has been caused by the building being in a much more defective state than could possibly have been anticipated and that the further sum of £150 will be required for completing the repairs which are now in hand. I beg to report the same for you for the information of the Lords Commissioners of the Admiralty and request that their Lordships will be pleased to authorize this extra expenditure which is absolutely necessary for the proper completion of the work, parts of the roof not being shut in.

222.   *Surveyor of Navy to Board of Admiralty: storage of timbers*

[TNA, ADM222/4]   16 August 1834

In reference to their Lordships circular of the 29th March 1833 directing the discontinuance of saturating timber in salt water I would recommend that the several superintendents be acquainted that it was their Lordships intention that the practice of boiling planks &c in salt water should also be done away with and that they should be directed to cause this intention to be coming into effect.

223. *Storekeeper to Superintendent Goldsmith: store men*

[TNA, ADM89/4]   7 December 1859

With reference to the Surveyor of the Navy's communication of the 2nd instant I beg to represent that in consequence of the great increase in the issue of timber and stores caused by the increased number of workmen in all classes, an additional timber issuer and two additional storehouse men are required to prevent the workmen being detained at the storehouses when they apply for stores.

[*Appended notes*]

9 December.
The Captain Superintendent at Chatham is informed for the officers' guidance that this proposal has been approved as a temporary arrangement but the employment of the persons on these services is to be dispensed with as soon as possible, and he is requested to cause the names of candidates for this situation to be transmitted as usual.
Surveyor.

Chatham Yard, 23 December 1859.
In pursuance of the Surveyor's minute of the 9th and his letter of the 7th instant and your directions thereon I beg to submit the names of candidates for the two temporary appointments of storehouse men in order that two of them may be appointed, observing that their names are placed in order of relative efficiency vizt.

> Charles Wragg, Labourer, aged 35. Service 7 years
> Henry David, Labourer age 25 service 3¼ years
> George Salmon, aged 32. 4 years service

And I have to add that after the most extended enquiries amongst and relative to the yard labourers I cannot hear of any others, who have not been pronounced ineligible, not professing a knowledge of the first four rules of arithmetic, which I hold to be an essential qualification for storehouse men, whose duties are similar to those of an assistant in an ironmonger or ships' chandlers shop.
Robert Laws, Storekeeper.

Chatham Yard, 24 December 1859.
Forwarded in reference to the Surveyor's minute of the 9th instant, I herewith return, observing that I have duly investigated these

recommendations. I consider two men are required in addition to the two extra storehouse men now employed, and conscientiously believe the selections have been influenced by no other motive than the public good.

G. Goldsmith, Captain Superintendent.

Security

During the eighteenth century numerous attempts had been made to prevent the loss of stores occurring both through opportunist theft of small items by the work force on a daily basis and through more organised night forays into the yard. However, no measurable success was ever achieved, with a great wealth of stores lost each year. Until 1833, in the front line of the battle against thieves, were those termed porters, warders, watchmen and rounders. Each had a specific role, with the porter usually located at the Main Gate and rounders conducting regular patrols. The warders had general duties, assisting porters during times when men were leaving the yard [228, 229] and holding the keys to various buildings, while watchmen undertook night duties [238]. An inspection of buildings was undertaken on Sundays when an additional employee checked the stores for any outbreak of fire [231]. This task was subsequently taken over by the officers of the yard working in unison with the patrolling warders [232]. The number of warders, watchmen and rounders tended to vary, influenced by the availability of a secondary security force, a military guard. After 1815, the size of the military guard was rapidly depleted [226] and the number of warders and watchmen expanded [224]. Members of this guard were drawn from the ranks of the Royal Marines or, if marines were unavailable, from one of the regiments posted to the nearby Chatham Barracks [235, 237]. Neither arrangement was particularly satisfactory, as those responsible for the security of the yard were all too often responsible for breaching that security [227, 233, 237]. To make the subsequent detection of stolen items easier, various materials, including rope and sailcloth, were marked [225, 236]. Those suspected of stealing dockyard stores were usually brought before the Commissioner of the yard who, as an appointed magistrate, had the right to conduct an examination [230, 233, 237].

    Although not adopted at the time, a proposal for the creation of a dockyard police force was made by Sir Thomas Byam Martin in August 1820 [234]. His proposal had clear similarities to, and may even have prompted, the scheme that was introduced into the dockyards in 1833. Immediately prior to the introduction of the latter scheme, the Admiralty commanded John Barrow to contact each of the dockyard superintendents to seek their comments [239]. Gordon's reply from Chatham has been lost, but he must have returned a particularly enthusiastic response, for it was Gordon who was asked to pioneer the scheme [240, 242, 243, 246]. The Chatham Superintendent went on to devise the wording of the oath [241], a code of instruction and details of how many serving officers would be required [244, 247]. All were completed early in the summer of 1833 and subsequently printed. The new policing arrangements were quickly extended to the other home yards [245]. This Dockyard Police Force was not entirely self-reliant, for it was dependent on the civilian work force to carry out additional fire watch duties [249]. Although an improvement on watchmen and warders, the new body survived only a short period. Despite attempts to improve its efficiency [248], it was superseded in December 1860 by a force entirely in the hands of the Metropolitan Police [250, 254]. A few members of the Dockyard Police Force were transferred to the new body [251], induced by the offer of improved accommodation [252] and the availability of medical treatment at the Royal Marine Infirmary [253].

224. *Navy Board to Commissioner Barlow: warders and watchmen*

[TNA, ADM106/3375]   29 April 1815

Col. D'Arcy, commanding the garrison of Chatham, having been under the necessity of further reducing the guard at the dockyard, in so much as the number of privates, which should consist of 135, is now no more than 64.

And Maj Gen Winter, Commandant of the Royal Marines, having been under the necessity of wholly withdrawing the detachment from dockyard duties; I have to request you will bring these circumstances under their Lordships' notice, in order, should it be thought proper, immediate steps may be taken to reinforce the garrison; and that you will inform their Lordships, that I have judged it expedient for the security of the dockyard to order an additional number of wardens by day and watchmen by night to be employed, until a sufficient military guard can be obtained.

225. *Commissioner Barlow to Admiralty: theft*

[TNA, ADM106/3375]   29 April 1815

We have received your letter of the 12th inst., with its enclosures, and acquaint you, that we approve of your having sentenced William Hilder and John Miller, yard labourers, to three months imprisonment in the house of correction at Maidstone for having in their possession some marked canvas.

226.   *Commissioner Barlow to Admiralty: withdrawal of military guard*

[TNA, ADM106/3375]   1 May 1815

In addition to my letter of 29th ultimo, I have to request you will inform their Lordships that the commanding officer of this garrison has, this day, been under the necessity of wholly withdrawing the military guard from this dockyard. In consequence, I have judged it expedient to order an additional number of warders by day and watchmen by night, to be employed, until the garrison can be reinforced, so as to be enabled to furnish a guard for the better security of the dockyard.

227.   *Commissioner Barlow to Navy Board: theft from yard*

[TNA, ADM106/1815]   18 December 1815

Nicholas Fitzpatrick, a private in the East India Company's Artillery, having been detected on leaving guard this morning with a piece of marked line in his hat and a quantity of wood in a handkerchief, was this day summarily convicted before me for the marked line and committed to Maidstone gaol to hard labour for three months.

228.   *Admiralty to Commissioner Barlow: mustering*

[NMM, CHA/F/29]   1 February 1816

It having been suggested to us that many of the valuable articles which are embezzled from the King's yards are probably carried out by the workmen when going to their dinner, the crowd at that time passing the gates preventing in many instances the possibility of detection by the officers & men stationed there. Being of opinion that if the workmen were mustered previously to their leaving the yard at dinner time, as they now are before going out in the evening time, an opportunity would be afforded for the warders &c at the gate to stop suspected persons. The passing of so great a mass of people at one time would be prevented and, when the others are all out, those men who the officers suppose to have King's stores concealed about them can be searched. The wardens making a daily report to you of the persons so stopped and of the result of their examination. We have to desire that you will state to us your opinion of this plan, by which we consider that the time lost to the men will be very trifling. [For] those first called it would be only a delay of four minutes and to those called last of not more than a quarter of an hour, which would be made up by their being last called in. You will also acquaint whether you have anything to suggest which in your opinion may be more likely to affect the object in view.

229. Commissioner Barlow to Admiralty: mustering

[NMM, CHA/F/29]   3 February 1816

Agreeable to the directions contained in your minute on the Navy Board's letter of the 1st instant, we beg to acquaint you that if the workmen were to be called out at their dinner times, they would not pass the gate in so great a crowd. If put into practice at this yard it would be attended with great inconvenience to the people, from the most of them living at such great distances from the yard, particularly in the winter months, when they are only allowed one hour to go home for their dinner.

230. Confession of John Ayres under Examination by Commissioner Barlow

[TNA, ADM106/1815]   12 March 1816

[John Ayres] who, on his oath, saith that in the month of April and May 1811 the *Terpsichore* lay in the Medway off Chatham yard as a receiving ship. That His Majesty's ship *Montague*, being then ordered to be paid off, came along side the *Terpsichore* at the latter end of April & was lashed to her. That about a fortnight or more after the *Montague* had been there and while she continued lashed to the *Terpsichore*, being about the beginning of May, John Williams then boatswain of the *Montague* and now of the *Namur* told examinant and William Allen Boatswain of the *Terpsichore* that he had some surplus stores in the *Montague* and wished to bring them on board the *Terpsichore*. They assented. He, at the same time, telling them that they should share in the produce of them [and] that soon afterwards and to the best of his recollection in the following night, some of the stores were taken out of the *Montague* and shared between the main deck and the lower deck in the fore part of the *Terpsichore*. A night or two afterwards, the remainder were brought & stowed in like manner. The said John Williams, and some of the *Montague*'s crew, got the stores out of her and put them on board the *Terpsichore* and stowed them there. The said William Allen, Robert Nicholson, carpenter of the *Terpsichore*, and examinant were present on each of the nights and saw it done.

The stores, so taken from the *Montague*, and stowed on the *Terpsichore*, consisted of a large quantity of junk (he thinks about three tons); a number of coils (to the best of his recollection fifteen) of new rope of from five inches to three and a half and eight bolts of new canvas. The stores were so removed two or three days before the *Montague* was paid off and when she was so, the crew did not go on board the *Terpsichore* but were drafted into other ships. There were on board the *Terpsichore*, at that time, only the examinant, the said William Allen, the said Robert Nicholson, & the boatswain's boy, whose present residence he does not know and whose name he does not recollect.

A few days after the stores were put on board the *Terpsichore*, the said John Williams and Robert Nicholson and Walter Burn (a leading man of the rope house in Chatham yard) took the junk on shore in a barge which either Williams or Nicholson had hired for that purpose. It was taken away at the fore part of the night. Examinant did not see this done (being on shore ill at the time) but he was told of it by the said Robert Nicholson, who also told him that the barge belonged to one Wheeler of Chatham. Wheeler, exam't believes, now lives at Maidstone, is a lame man and, as he thinks, a pensioner in Chatham yard.

Examinant never heard to whom the junk was sold or for how much. The said Robert Nicholson paid him and the said William Allen one pound a piece for their share of it and said that four guineas went to pay the barge hire. The new rope was cut up into lengths & the King's mark taken out of it by examinant and the said Allen, Nicholson & Williams on board the *Terpsichore*. It was conveyed ashore in bread bags by them all four and the said Walter Burn by night in various parcels. Examinant went twice himself in the *Terpsichore*'s boat accompanied by the said Allen, Nicholson & Williams with several parcels of it. They landed it at Holborn Hard in Chatham and there found Burn with some other men to his assistance ready to receive it. They took it to a dealer near the Golden Lion on the Brook, Chatham, who bought it off them. He does not know the dealer's name or person and being dark at the time would not know the house. They went to a public house near the dealer & he there came to them & paid the money for it; does not recollect how much, nor the sign of the possible house. He does not recollect how much he received for his share of the rope, but there was a reckoning among them about it.

The eight bolts of canvas wrapped in a hammock were taken ashore from the *Terpsichore* by John Appleby a rigger in Chatham yard on a shore boat in the night. Examinant does not know who sold the canvas or to whom, or for how much. He did not receive anything on account of it. The whole of the stores were taken from the *Terpsichore* within a fortnight or thereabouts after being put there from the *Montague*. The said Walter Burn was, as examinant believes, brought into the transaction by the said Robert Nicholson of whom he was an acquaintance. That the said John Appleby was brought into it by the said John Williams, of whom he had been a shipmate.

231. *Navy Board to Barlow: inspection of buildings*

[NMM, CHA/F/29]   28 October 1816

Commissioner Cunningham having called our attention to the expense which is incurred by the inspection every Sunday morning of the buildings in the several dockyards which contain combustible stores, the persons employed to inspect them being paid, under the authority of our general letter dated the 9th September 1812, two shillings and sixpence each Sunday, We acquaint you that in order to avoid this expense but still wishing to preserve the inspection and watching of the storehouses &c. We consider it proper that the Clerk of the Ropeyard or Master Rope maker should be required to visit the hemp houses &c. that the patrolling warders should be required to visit all the places at present visited by the foremen &c. and to make reports twice in the day of their examinations; We therefore desire you will give orders to that effect and should you think it useful that these rounders or warders should have access to the stores you will of course permit them.

232. *Navy Board to Commissioner Barlow: inspection of buildings*

[NMM, CHA/F/29]   17 December 1816

Having again had under consideration the object of the inspection of the yard buildings on Sundays for which directions were conveyed to you by our letter of 28th October last, we acquaint you that whatever orders you may issue respecting other buildings, we consider that the interior of the following should be inspected without fail every Sunday;

    Painters' shops and stores
    Oakum houses

Rope houses
Hemp houses
Hatchelling houses
Yarn and tar houses

We therefore desire that you will make the necessary arrangements for unlocking and relocking the said buildings at a suitable time in order that the officers of the ropeyard and the patrolling warders and rounders in the dockyard, may have access thereto. You will direct the Clerk of the Check to pay the person who may be employed to unlock and relock the doors in the ropeyard eighteen pence a day, on account of the extent of that service but we do not consider any allowance necessary as it respects the dockyard.

233. *Theft of Copper Bolts*

[*Kentish Gazette*]   31 March 1818

Saturday. A shipwright, named Denton, was committed to Maidstone Gaol, by Sir Robert Barlow, Commissioner of Chatham Dockyard, on strong suspicion of embezzling copper bolts. They were thrown over the dockyard wall in the night, and were discovered by the military guard, and brought to the dockyard next day. On an investigation it was discovered that Denton had left his duty as rounder (a superior kind of watchman) that very night, and had a few days before been provided from the store house with copper bolts, for his work at the slip where he was employed by day, similar in weight and otherwise to those found. As rounders have important trust, and are in possession of the night patrol, and have egress and regress to all parts of the yard and store houses; the most steady men and best character among the shipwrights are appointed to this office, and it will be much regretted should this man have betrayed his trust.

234. *Comptroller to First Lord: dockyard police force*

[SRO, GD51/2/993/1–2]   6 August 1820

With a view to the protection of the valuable property in the dockyards, and to the preservation of the peace of the several ports, it has occurred to me as highly expedient that something like a Dock Yard Police should be established in each yard; and I submit an arrangement which I conceive may place at the disposal of the commissioners of the ports a trustworthy and powerful body of men, who will always be within immediate call in the event of any disturbance, and a class of people upon whom it is presumed every reliance may be placed, from the manner in which I propose that they should be constituted.

First then I would recommend that about 800 or 1000 men (according to the magnitude of each establishment) should be selected from the several classes of artificers and workmen, making character and activity the guide in such choice and leaving it with the commissioners to see that the most scrupulous attention is paid to this very important and main point in the formation of such a body.

The persons so formed to be called 'Yard Constables' and to be sworn in the usual manner, and each furnished with a staff.

A quarterman of shipwrights (being persons always promoted on account of good character, conduct and abilities) may be appointed in the proportion of one to every one hundred 'Yard Constables'.

The whole to be under the direction of the Resident Commissioner who must necessarily be put into the commission of the place.

The constables so established shall be liable to be called upon to aid in the preservation of the peace of the town under any other magistrates than the Commissioner upon any sudden emergency but if time and circumstances permits, they shall wait the orders of the Commissioner before they place themselves at the disposal of any other magistrate.

My idea is that the good conduct and effective faithful services of the constables should be secured more by prospective benefit than present reward or rather by a combination of both.

I would therefore only propose to give the quartermen 10s and the inferior constables 5s each on the King's birthday, which for about 4,500 men will amount to £1,147 per annum.

When called into service, and so long as they continue upon duty as constables they shall have one shilling each per diem in addition to the maximum of the earnings of their respective classes or the highest rate of day pay if their class is not upon task and job work.

The wardens and watchmen of the yard shall always be selected from the 'Constables' and in consideration of their being men of the best character they shall have a preference in promotion, but subject in this respect to the opinion & choice of the Commissioner's officers and of the approval of the Navy Board in the usual manner.

As a further encouragement the quartermen and other constables shall be allowed to reckon one year of additional time in computing their superannuation for every six years that they may serve as constables, provided their conduct has been invariably steady and correct in the discharge of that duty, and which shall be certified by the officers, with the Commissioner's approval of their certificate.

According to the existing regulations no person is entitled to superannuation from a dockyard unless he shall have completed a servitude of twenty years, besides his apprenticeship, and as it is not probable that any man would hold the appointment of constable more than 12 years, it would in that case qualify him for superannuation after 18 years service. As the higher rate of superannuation can only be obtained by servitude of thirty-five years, he would according to any scheme be qualified after a period of 33 years.

The men are always anxious to avoid superannuation and therefore the being qualified at an earlier period will not occasion any material expense to the public, while the prospective advantage to the men, in case of sickness or declining health, will be of sufficient value to secure their good conduct. At the same time it will give the Commissioner and officers a very considerable and desirable influence over the whole body of the people, who will hope by proper conduct to recommend themselves to the situation of constables.

As a still further encouragement I would strongly advise that persons who shall have completed twelve years as constables shall, whenever they are superannuated, receive ten shillings per quarter, in addition to the amount of their superannuation, and which cannot be attended with much expense, even after twelve years, when it will first gradually come into operation.

Under the influence of such encouragement there can be no question as to the good conduct of the men and the consequent security, which will be afforded to the public establishments and the peace of the seaports in the event of any disturbance. I am not aware of any objection that can be made to the establishing such a body of constables, at so very small an expense.

The Commissioner and officers will, of course, be strictly charged not to grant any certificate to constables but upon strict proof of the deserving conduct of the men. They will also be enjoined to discharge any men from the office of constable whose conduct may at any time be exceptionable [sic], and men so discharged shall forfeit all the benefit of the regulations.

No man to be entered as a constable who is above 40 years of age.

235. *Commissioner Cunningham to Navy Board: military guard*

[TNA, ADM106/1828]   3 April 1824

In return to your letter of the 3rd instant I have to acquaint you that the following is the strength of the military guard sent to do duty in this yard viz.

Subalterns	2
Sergeants	3
Corporals	6
Drummers	2
Privates	87
	160

They are relieved from the garrison every twenty-four hours.

236. *Commissioner Cunningham to Navy Board: King's mark*

[TNA, ADM106/1828]   29 April 1824

Adverting to your letter of yesterday, directing that the yellow worsted be used at this yard in future, as the King's mark &tc., in cables, cordage, and bolt ropes; I have to request that the 10 cwt. demanded in the officers' last quarterly return No. 162 from the contractor (Mr Henry Mills) may be ordered of that colour, and also 5 cwt. in addition thereto, in lieu of the like quantity of white worsted in store here; and as the latter is of the colour ordered to be used at Woolwich yard, I beg to suggest that it be sent thither.

237. *Master Attendant (in Cunningham's absence) to Navy Board:*
theft of copper nails

[TNA ADM106/1835]   23 July 1827

I beg to transmit for your information the copies of depositions taken before the magistrates of Rochester against J. Welden a private of the Royal Marines at Chatham, at whose residence some copper nails and other articles were found on the 9th inst. bearing the King's mark. I request that your solicitor may receive instructions to prosecute for the offence.

[*Enclosure*]

18 July 1827. Taken before the Rev Alexander Brown, Rev. George Davis and Dr. Richard Simon Joynes. The examination of Abraham Plumber says: I am sergeant in the 1st or Chatham Division of the Royal Marines. The prisoner, John Welden, is a private Marine and belongs to the same division and to the 59th divisional company. On the 9th instant he was confined in the guard room of the Royal Marines barracks at Chatham on suspicion of stealing a pair of trousers from one of his comrades. The prisoner is a married man and does not usually sleep at the barracks. On that day I received directions to go to his lodgings and take thence all his clothes. He had a room in the house of Mrs. Rooke at Brompton in the parish of Chatham and I went thither and asked her to let me go to the prisoner's room and take away his clothes. She accompanied me to his room and told me it was occupied by the prisoner and his wife. I went with Mrs. Rooke into the room and gathered up all his clothes, which were lying about the room. In the same room there was a small box, the lid of which was shut but not locked. Upon opening it I found it contained a bag and some wearing apparel. The bag was thus marked, J. Welden. The weight being considerable I opened it and found it contained copper nails and other articles. Upon finding such property I desired Mrs. Rooke to call Thomas Silver (a private Marine who accompanied me) and upon his coming upstairs I delivered to him such bag with its content and we together and in each others company returned to headquarters and there I reported to Arthur Tuft, the colour sergeant, the discovery made and what had been found and taken from the prisoner's room. He and me in the presence of Silver examined such bag in Sergeant Tuft's room and ascertained that the articles contained therein consisted of copper and metal screws, nails bolts and other things marked with the broad arrow. The bag and those articles were then left with Arthur Tuft.

The examination of Charles Chandler Patterson in the County of Kent. Hatter who also being sworn says I am one of the Constables of the Parish of Chatham: On the 11th inst. I received from the witness, Sgt. Plume, a large quantity of King's stores consisting of 17lbs of metal deck nails, one new metal screw weighing ¾lb, several pieces of old copper bolt weighing 11lb, 2lbs of new coppering, 6oz of old metal and 1lb of old copper, each and every one of them marked with the broad arrow and also one dowling bit which several articles I took to the storekeeper's department on Saturday last, the 14th inst. for the purpose of these being accurately weighed and valued. I now produce the same stores and dowling bit together with a canvas bag marked with the prisoner's name and which bag he has admitted to me was his property. C.C. Patterson.

Before the Rev. George Davis, 20 July 1827. Examination of Mary Rooke, the wife of Cornelius Rooke of Chatham, labourer, who being duly sworn said: The prisoner John Welden during the last two months has, with his wife Mary Welden, resided in my father's dwelling house in Brompton and had the exclusive use of a chamber for which they agreed to pay me a weekly rent of 2s. He slept there on all occasions except when his duties prevented him doing so. He did not sleep there last Monday week, the 8th inst., as he was that night on guard in the dockyard. He told me to send his dinner there. The next day. Monday 9th, the prisoner came to my house. It was a little after noontime. He had upon his shoulder a canvas or duck bag, which I thought must be weighty because he perspired very much. The bag was about half full. He carried it up the stairs and, I suppose, into his room. All that he said upon coming in was, 'well here I am once more'. He remained upstairs a short time and then came down and had his dinner and then returned to his room and shortly afterwards left my house. Afterwards, on the afternoon of the same day, Sgt. Plume came to my house and enquired of the prisoner lodged in my house and I sent him up. Afterwards I followed and found him in the prisoner's room and in my presence the Sgt took out of the prisoner's box a bag being the same which he had the same day carried upstairs and on being opened I saw that it contained copper articles. The sergeant said that upon some of them the broad arrow was marked. The prisoner's wife had been absent from him. X (Mark of Mary Rooke).

238. *Commissioner Cunningham to Navy Board: reduction of watchmen*

[TNA, ADM106/1835]   2 October 1827

Having, in pursuance of your letter of the 13th September last, I have consulted the officers and duly considered the subject of watching and warding this yard. I cannot consistently, with a view to the due security thereof, recommend any reduction in the number of warders and watchmen at present employed; except that it should be considered two patrolling warders are sufficient for that duty. In which case, being three at present borne: one of them might be discharged.

With regard to the watchmen, the number employed each night has recently lessened in consequence of the increased number of warrant officers borne as supernumeraries upon the cheque, who take their turn in watching the dockyard at night, in diminution of an equal proportion of watchmen.

239. *Admiralty to Superintendent Gordon: specialised security force*

[NMM, CHA/H/5]   29 March 1833

My Lords Commissioners of the Admiralty having under their consideration the present mode of watching, warding and rounding in H.M. Dockyards and being of opinion that it is inefficient for the due protection of the public property in the yards and capable of improvement without incurring additional expense by setting apart a certain number of men to be exempted from labour and employed solely in the protection of the dockyard by day and night. I am commanded to call your particular attention to this subject; and having naturally considered the same, you are to report to me for their information, your opinion as to the most efficient plan to be adopted for affording that protection to that property which by too many proofs is subject to frequent depredation.

The principal points you will have to consider are as follows.

Whether a body of wardens and sub-wardens might not be established, to consist of young, able-bodied and trustworthy men, belonging to the yard, and exempted from all labour, to be formed into a Corps of Police and placed under the immediate control of the Superintendent. If this be your opinion: in what manner do you propose they be stationed or patrol along the line of the seawall or other parts of the dockyard? What number of men you would recommend as necessary to ensure a complete and efficient protection to the Yard?

What wages they ought to receive, bearing in mind however that the men now paid for watching and warding in your yard is considered by your Lordships to be fully ample and must not therefore in any arrangement you contemplate be exceeded? Whether or not some superior officer may not be placed at the head of this body of police, immediately under the control of and responsible to the superintendent, and what description of officer this should be?

240. *Secretary, Metropolitan Police to Admiralty: dockyard police force*
Forwarded to Admiral Superintendent Gordon

[NMM, CHA/H/6]   2 July 1833

The Commissioners of Police have the honour to return herewith the papers relating to the establishment of Police in His Majesty's Dock Yards forwarded therein by the desire of their Lords Commissioners of the

Admiralty and requesting the Commissioners of Police might offer any suggestions that might occur.

The Commissioners of Police do not feel confident to offer any as to the numbers proposed, not having seen the ground. The commissioners will therefore only observe that if the men are lodged without expense to them, a deduction equal to the rate they would have to pay for lodging themselves or approaching to that might they think be deducted from the amount of weekly pay. The price marked for the constables' truncheons is, in the opinion of the commissioners, much too high. Those furnished to the constables of the Metropolitan Police cost that sum originally, but a great part of that sum it now appears was for an unnecessary degree of painting, which would not again be sanctioned. They ought to be provided for at half the price.

241. *Admiralty to Superintendent Admiral Superintendent Gordon:*
police oath

[NMM, CHA/H/7] 20 July 1833

I do swear that I will well and truly serve our sovereign Lord the King in the office of Special Constable for His Majesty's Dock Yard and Arsenal at Chatham without favour or affection, malice or ill-well; and that I will to the best of my power cause the Peace to be kept, and all His Majesty's Stores and Property to be preserved from depredation and plunder; and I will prevent all offences against the persons and property of His Majesty's Subjects in the said Yard and Arsenal; and that while I continue to hold the said Office I will to the best of my skill and knowledge discharge all the duties thereof faithfully according to law. So help me God.

242. *Superintendent Gordon to Admiralty: policing*

[TNA, ADM1/3395] 11 August 1833

The police have been under instruction in their duty since the 26th ultimo but from the place I intended to lodge them in is not quite complete I have found it impossible to put them on permanent duty without being obliged to open the gates to admit in the reliefs to allow those going off duty to pass out in the middle of the night, which I do not consider advisable.

We have not yet received the clothing, I hope it will be sent down by the time the station house is ready. I much fear we must have three reliefs instead of two only, as it will be impossible for the latter to do the duty required by both day and night.

I know their Lordships' wish is that the police should be efficient, and, at the same time, the expense of it, if possible, should be kept within the estimated sum allowed for watching &c. on the old plan. In proposing the number of inspectors, sergeants and constables, I was therefore induced to keep within the sum allowed and did not pay attention to the fatigue that a man could daily undergo which experience and a more mature consideration of the subject has since better enabled me to estimate. I am now decidedly of opinion that, unless we have a sufficient force to give the men some additional relief every other day, their physical powers will not be equal to the performance of the duty.

The number of constables at Chatham is at present fixed at 28, and as there are 14 beats and posts by day, and 12 by night. Each man will have 12 hours duty in the 24, allowing only 2 men by night available for any casualty. I now propose to have in addition one inspector, one sergeant and 8 constables.

243. *Admiralty to Superintendent Gordon: report on new policing arrangement*

[TNA, ADM1/3396]   17 September 1833

In obedience to the commands of My Lords Commissioners of the Admiralty signified in that part of Mr Barrow's letter of the 2nd July last which directs me to send, for their Lordships' information, a weekly report stating the manner in which the system [*of Police*] works, before they adopt it generally in the rest of the dockyards.

I have to report that owing to the unavoidable delay which has arisen in fitting up the residence, and obtaining their clothing, the police force did not come on permanent duty until Monday the 9th, and then only in the day time; but, as far as I can judge, I beg to assure their Lordships that I am satisfied the system now introduced is very superior to the old one, and cannot, I should think, fail to work well.

As both the day and night duty was yesterday permanently undertaken by the police, I shall be able next week to give their Lordships a decided opinion on the merits of the night arrangement, as compared with the old system of watching.

[TNA, ADM1/3481]

244. *Comparative numbers of watchmen and wardens with new policing arrangement*

8 October 1833

Yards	Numbers								Amount		
	Watching and Warding[1]		Scale of Chatham and Sheerness			Proposed			Upon Old System of Watching and Warding	Police Force	
	Day	Night	Inspectors	Sergeants	Constables	Inspectors	Sergeants	Constables		As Established	As Proposed
Woolwich	7	15	3	3	25	3	3	30	£969	£1878	£2155
Chatham		**29**	**3**	**3**	**36**	**3**	**3**	**40**	**£1860**	**£2488**	**£2709**
Sheerness		34	3	3	25	3	3	30	£1810	£1878	£2155
Portsmouth	16	77	3	3	36	3	3	40	£3155	£2488	£2709
Plymouth	14	56	3	3	36	3	3	40	£2553	£2488	£2709
Pembroke			3	3	25	3	3	25	£1240	£1878	£1878
Total			18	18	183	18	18	205	£11587	£13098	£14315

[1]Warders not given for Chatham.

245. *Admiral Superintendent Gordon's* Code of Instruction *for Dockyard Police*

[TNA, ADM1/3398]   17 October 1833

In obedience to the command of My Lord Commissioners of the Admiralty signified in Mr Barrow's letter of the 16th inst. I beg leave to transmit herewith the original Code of Instructions drawn out by me for the police force and which was forwarded to me on the 2nd July by their Lordships.

[Enclosure]

A proposed detail of police force and beat by day and night laid down for the protection of His Majesty's Dockyard at Chatham.

The force to consist of the following officers, sergeants and police constables.

1   Warden and Director
2   Inspectors
2   Sergeants
28 Constables

The constables to be stationed on beats as follows:

Day Duty

Beats
No. 1.   From the upper gate to the paint and lead mills round the sheds adjoining the Captain-Superintendents garden down between the rope and storehouses to the rigging house and return. Note, this beat is strengthened by two sentinels.

No. 2.   From the guard house near the new stairs to the rigging house and return. This beat is strengthened by 4 sentinels.

No. 3.   Stationary at the principal landing stairs. Strengthened by 1 sentinel.

No. 4.   Stationary at the jetty head.

No. 5.   Stationary at the mast house drain. Strengthened by 3 sentinels.

No. 6.   Stationary at the convict ground and looking towards the boathouse slip.

No. 7.   From the boathouse drain to the reed house corner to the lower part of yard and return.

No. 8.   Stationary at the lower gate by day.

No. 9.   From the reed house around the boundary wall up to the lower point of the sawmill, down by the chip bins, round the timber sheds, down the Middle Road, round by the sea store boat house, by the plank houses, over the upper mast pond, up the Main Road to the lower part of the upper mast house and then by the brick layer's pound to the sawmill.

No. 10.   From the sawmills along the boundary wall to the Captain Superintendent's poultry yards, turning into the sail fields looking to the back part of the sail loft, down by the officers' gardens, turning by the officers' stables; down by the convicts' pound; back of the officers' houses; in front of the sail loft and pay office, round the Commissioner's garden and house, by the office to the clock store, looking to the joiners' shop and the smithery, along by the upper part of the mast house; the block house, glazier's shop, store cabin and pump house.

No. 11.   New ground outside the lower gate.

No. 12.   From the anchor wharf guard house along the wharf to the jetty head and return.

No. 13.   From the jetty head along the wall to the reed house corner and return.

Note: Nos. 12 and 13 patrols constantly by day along the wharfs to aid and assist and be in readiness to any call along the wharves looking to all docks and slips to the main road as they pass. By so doing the stationary men will always have assistance without leaving their respective posts.

No. 14.   To visit all the workshops.

Nos. 15 & 16.   In reserve at the gate.

Detail of the Day Duty
1 Inspector
1 Sergeant
16 Police constables

14 police constables on beats; 2 in reserve at the upper gate and the sergeant constantly going round the yard to visit his men. When the Inspector goes his rounds the Sergeant can come in and take charge of the gate so that there will be always two people at the gate with an officer.

The day and night duties may be exchanged monthly if thought necessary.

Statement of Pay Proposed:
Inspectors £100 yearly.
Sergeants £1. 2s 6d weekly.
Police constables 19s weekly.
Exclusive of clothing for sergeants and police constables.

Detail of Night Duty
1 Inspector
1 Sergeant
12 Constables who will be placed on beats as follows.

No. 1   From the guard house near the new stairs taking the anchor wharf as far as the Master Attendant's office and return.

No. 2   From the Master Attendant's office along the wall to the jetty head and return.

No. 3   From the jetty head stairs to the mast house slip and return.

No. 4   Stationed at the convict ground but to look particularly to the boathouse drain.

No. 5   From the mast house slip to the reed house.

Nos. 6 & 7   From the reed house lower corner of the wharf to the east corner of the land wall looking into the 26 timber sheds in front of the sea store boathouse.

No. 8   From the sea store boat house taking the main road to the lower part of the upper mast house crossing to the lower part of the sawmill, round the boundary wall to the Captain Superintendent's poultry yard, returning by the sail field back of the officers' gardens taking the Middle Road down to the cross road by the plank house over the upper mast pond and looking into all sheds and saw pits.

No. 9   From the upper side of the mast house looking into the blockhouse glazing shop and clock store round the Captain-Superintendent's house and garden in front of the sail loft and to look into the front and back of the officers' houses and converter's pound.

No. 10   The same as the day duty No. 1.

Nos. 11 & 12   Reserve at the gate.

Police Instructions

The following general instructions for the different ranks of the police force are not to be considered as containing rules of conduct applicable to every variety of circumstance that may occur in the performance of their duty; something must be, necessarily, left for the intelligence and discretion of individuals; and according to the degree in which they show themselves possessed of these qualities, and to their zeal, activity, and judgment, on all occasions, will be their claim for future reward.

It should be understood at the outset, that the principal object to be attained is 'The Prevention of Crime'.

To this great end every effort of the police is to be directed. The security of public and private property, the preservation of tranquillity, and good order, and all the other objects of a police establishment, will thus be better effected, than by the detection and punishment of offenders, after they have succeeded in committing crime. This should be constantly kept in mind, by every member of the police force, as the guide for his conduct. The officers and men, should endeavour to distinguish themselves by such vigilance and activity, as may render it extremely difficult, for any one to commit a crime, within the limits of the dockyard.

Conditions

The conditions, upon which each man is to be admitted into the police force, are stated here. That no complaint may be made hereafter upon these being enforced; but it is, at the same time, to be understood, that the Captain Superintendent is authorized to reserve to himself the power, subject to the approbation of the Lords Commissioners of the Admiralty, to alter or annul any of these conditions, and also to make such new rules, that he may deem expedient.

Articles
1. Each man shall devote his whole time to the police service.
2. He shall serve and reside, wherever he is appointed.
3. He shall promptly obey all lawful orders, which he may receive, from the persons placed in authority over him.
4. He shall conform himself to all the regulations that may be made, from time to time, for the good of the service.
5. He shall not, upon any occasion, or upon any pretence whatever, take Money from any person, without the express permission of the Captain Superintendent.
6. He shall furnish himself with new clothes, whenever the Captain Superintendent may direct; and he shall at all times appear in his complete police dress.

7. Such debts owed by him, as the Captain Superintendent shall direct to be paid, shall be paid, by him, forthwith.

8. He shall receive his pay weekly, on such days as shall be appointed.

9. His pay as police constable is nineteen shillings a week and in addition the following articles of clothing will be supplied him vizt.

> first year:
> 1 great coat
> 1 cape
> 1 badge to great coat
> 1 badge to cape coat
> 1 coat
> 1 pair of cloth trousers
> 1 pair of boots
> 1 pair of extra boots
> 1 hat
> 1 cover to hat
> 1 stock
> 1 embroidery to collar
> 1 button branch and stick
>
> Second Year
> 1 coat
> 1 pair of cloth trousers
> 1 pair of extra cloth trousers
> 1 pair of boots
> 1 extra pair of boots
> 1 hat
> 1 embroidery to collar

10. He shall not quit the police force, without giving a months notice; in case he quits, without giving such notice, all pay, then due to him, shall be forfeited; and if he be dismissed the police force, the whole of his pay then due, or unpaid, is forfeited.

11. Every man dismissed the police force, or who shall resign his situation, shall before he quits the service, deliver up every article of dress and appointments which have been supplied to him, and if any such articles have been, in the opinion of the Captain Superintendent, improperly used or damaged, a deduction of any pay due to the party shall be made, sufficient to make good the damage or supply a new article.

12. For any irregularity of conduct or neglect of duty, he shall, for every offence, be fined such portion of his pay as the Captain Superintendent may adjudge, and he shall be liable to immediate dismissal for unfitness, negligence, or misconduct, independently of their other punishment to which he may by law be subject. The Captain Superintendent may also, if he thinks fit, dismiss him, without assigning any reason.

Outline of General Duty

The police force will be formed into two divisions, one of which consisting of an inspector, sergeant, and a proportion of constables, will be always on duty.

The division on duty will be relieved at certain hours, according to the seasons of the year, of which due notice will be given.

The dockyard will be divided into beats, and their limits will be clearly defined and numbered.

An inspector, sergeant and as many constables as the Captain Superintendent may direct, will constantly live in the dockyard, in the residence provided for them, in order to render them speedily efficient in case their services of such as are off duty, should be required for any sudden emergency.

In case any constable should be absent, by sickness, or any other cause, his place is to be supplied by one of the reserve constables, at the division station.

The officers and men, who are off duty, are to consider themselves liable to be called on, at all times, and will always prepare themselves when prepared, at the shortest notice, and, when so ordered, they must sleep in their clothes, to be in complete readiness when called on. The names of the men on duty will be entered in a book at the division station, and opposite their names will be the number of their respective beat.

246. *Superintendent Gordon to Admiralty: dockyard police*

[TNA, ADM1/3399]   1 November 1833

With reference to the memorandum from the Accountant General (hereafter returned), which accompanied Mr Barrow's letter of the 29th ultimo, I beg leave to state that the augmentation of the police establishments at Chatham and Sheerness to their present numbers vizt.

	Chatham	Sheerness
Inspectors	3	3
Sergeants	3	3
Constables	36	25

247. *Printed instructions for Constables appointed to the Dockyard
Police Force*

[NMM, Library L67/277]   1834

1. Every police constable in the force may hope to rise to the superior
stations by activity, intelligence and good conduct. He must make it his
duty to recommend himself to notice by diligent discharge of his duties
and strict obedience to the commands of his superiors, recollecting that
he who has been accustomed to submit to discipline, will be considered
best qualified to command.

2. He is to devote the whole of his time and abilities to the service; he
is at all times to appear neat in his person and correctly dressed in the
established uniform; his demeanour must always be respectful towards
his superiors.

3. He must readily obey all orders and instructions of the director,
inspectors and sergeants of the police force, to which he belongs. If they
appear unlawful or improper, he may complain to the Admiral or Captain
Superintendent; but any refusal to perform any orders he may receive, or
negligence in doing it, will not be suffered.

4. When he is to go on duty, he will take care to be at the appointed
place, if not before, precisely at the prescribed hour. He is to fall in with
others of his party, and after being inspected, he is to be marched by his
Sergeant to the beat committed to his care. He will be held responsible
for the security of all property, particularly stores that may have been
placed under his charge, all of which he is carefully to deliver over to his
relief. He will also use his utmost exertions and authority for the
preservation of the peace and general good order during the time he is on
duty.

5. He will be expected to acquire such a knowledge of the workmen of
the yard, as will enable him to recognise their person.

6. He will be expected to see every part of his beat at least once in ten
minutes or a quarter of an hour. This regularity of moving through his
beat is not however to prevent his remaining at any particular place if his
presence there be necessary, to observe the conduct of any suspected
person, or for any other good reason; but he will be required to satisfy his
superior that there was a sufficient cause for such irregularity.

7.   He is not to suffer any stranger to walk about the yard, or go into any workshop, or ship, or vessel, building or repairing, without being properly attended by an officer in uniform, or producing a pass ticket. Should he discover any stranger without being so attended, he is to demand the ticket, in a civil manner. Should it not be produced, such stranger is to be sent to the Inspector on duty, for examination.

He is not however to interfere idly, or unnecessarily, but when required to act, he will do so, with decision and boldness, on all occasions; and he may always expect to receive the fullest support, in the proper exercise of his authority.

8.   If after the people have quitted the yard in the evening, there be discovered in the yard, or lurking in boats, by the wharfs or jetties, any person who have not the parole, they are to be taken into custody, and delivered into the charge of the nearest sentinel, until the arrival of the sergeant, who, if requisite, will request a sufficient force, from the military guard, to escort such persons to the station house, where they are to be examined by the Inspector, and kept in close custody until the morning.

9.   When women, children or other persons, are allowed to carry the breakfasts and dinners for the artificers and workmen, or military on guard, into the yard, he is not to allow them to loiter about, or stay longer than may be necessary. He is to direct all such persons to leave the yard immediately the people go to work or have finished their meal. If any such person should neglect so to do, he is to give them in charge to the nearest sentinel until the arrival of his sergeant, or a police constable, on the spot.

10.   He is not to allow the crews of any vessel lying at the wharfs, jetties, basins or cambers, to be straggling about the yard, nor on any pretence to suffer them to take chips or other articles, however trifling, for the use of their vessels. He is to be very careful that no person gain admittance to, or go from the yard, by a boat coming from alongside a ship or vessel. In either the above situations; he is also to take care that the crews of such ships or vessels are not allowed to come out of them, except during the working hours of the yard, without permission from the Admiral or Captain Superintendent.

11.   He is not to allow any person to enter or leave the yard, near his beat, by any other way than the dockyard gates, and such other places as may be established for that purpose. Neither is he, on any account whatever, to suffer any workman, or other person, employed in the dockyard, to leave it during the working hours, either by water or otherwise, without being satisfied, by the attendance of an officer, that such person is proceeding on the public service. If he should detect any

person attempting to leave the yard, without authority, such person is immediately to be arrested.

12.   He is not to suffer any foreigner to land, without special directions from his superior; nor any stranger, unless accompanied by an officer in uniform, or belonging to the yard. Neither is he to allow any officer, or other person to land, or take boat; nor are any stores to be landed or taken off, excepting at the places established for those purposes. The Constable stationed at each of the public landing-places in the yard is to keep the stairs clean and clear, and he is attentively to enforce all orders and regulations, with respect to the description of officers, or persons, who are allowed to land or embark at the different stairs, where he is stationed.

He is also to observe that none but King's boats are to be suffered to land, excepting such as may be employed in bringing stores. On Sundays no persons are to be allowed to land or take boats there except officers of the yard and of His Majesty's Ships; and the boats' crews are not to quit their boats and straggle about the yard.

No one is to be allowed to land after sunset, excepting officers in uniform, who may desire to see the Admiral or Captain Superintendent, or the other officers of the yard.

Officers having the number may likewise be allowed to embark until eleven o'clock, but after that hour the sanction of the Admiral or Captain Superintendent must be obtained. In such cases, no boat is to be permitted to remain alongside the stairs for more than five minutes.

13.   He is not to suffer any artificer, or other person, employed in the yard, to loiter about, nor is he to allow any person belonging to one department, to enter the workshop or houses of another department, without having business to transact there. In watching the conduct of persons, whose behaviour is such as to excite just suspicion, he is always to bear in mind, that the *prevention of crime* will be best attained, by making it evident that the persons are known and strictly watched, and that certain detection will follow any attempt to do wrong.

14.   When he takes any one into custody, he will give such person in charge to the nearest sentinel, or he may deliver over his prisoner to the sergeant. It may sometimes be desirable that he should accompany the party to the division station, in order to substantiate the charge, in which case, his place is to be immediately supplied by another constable. When he takes property from any one, he should not suffer it to be out of his sight until he delivers it to the inspector of his division, and receives from him a proper receipt of the same.

15.   He is to be very careful, during the loading or unloading of any vessel, that no stores be improperly conveyed or concealed on board. He

is to assist in examining and searching such as may have delivered their cargoes near his beat, previously to their leaving the wharfs and jetties, for the purpose of preventing the embezzlement of any government stores or property. If he should observe stores of any kind lying about, or improperly exposed either to injury or embezzlement, or if he should discover any doors or windows open, that ought to be shut, or any other negligence with respect to the security of stores, houses, &c., he is immediately to give notice thereof to the sergeant, in order that the storekeeper or other officer concerned may be informed thereof, the same being reported for the information of the Admiral or Captain Superintendent.

16. He is to be very careful that no stores be carried away from any wharfs or jetties within the limits of his beat, without a note or proper authority, agreeably to the regulations that may be made on that head. If from circumstances, he should doubt the propriety of any stores being carried afloat, or otherwise taken away, he is to inquire for what ship or service they are intended, and should not a satisfactory account be given, he is not to allow the stores to be removed, reporting the circumstance to the sergeant on duty. He is also to observe that no stores or materials are to be carried off by workmen for repairing or refitting vessels afloat, unless properly passed by the foreman.

17. He is to pick up all small articles, such as copper, iron, nails of all sorts, rings, &c., which may have been dropped by accident, or lying about the yard, and put them into a chest on his beat, which will be kept locked, and examined by the Inspector or Sergeant twice every day. Whatever stores may be found therein, an account thereof is to be entered in the property book, previously to their being returned to the storekeeper.

He is to be careful that no smuggled liquor, or contraband goods of any kind, be landed or lodged in the dockyard.

18. He is not to allow any one to smoke in the dockyard, or on board any vessel in dock, or on the slips. He is at all times, but more particularly in the evening, carefully to search all places on his beat liable to accident from fire, extinguishing all fires and lights he may discover, excepting such anchor fires, or fires in kilns as may be kept burning by authority, or in places where artificers may be still at work.

He is likewise, most strictly, to enforce all orders he may receive with respect to fires and lights on board vessels, within the limits of his beat.

19. In case of fire, or any other alarm, he is to give instant notice thereof, by springing [sic] his rattle, and sending information to the Admiral or Captain Superintendent, the police station and residence. No alarm bell is to be rung, without orders from the Admiral or Captain Superintendent.

He must inform himself of the situation of every fire cock in his beat and where the fire engines and hoses are kept. He must make himself perfectly acquainted with the mode of fixing on the hoses to the fire cocks and of using them.

For his exertions upon these and other occasions, the Admiral or Captain Superintendent may recommend him to the Lords Commissioners of the Admiralty for a reward; but on no pretence shall he receive a gratuity of a private nature from any person, for any thing relating to his duty. This will always be visited with instant dismissal.

20. He must ever bear in mind, that there is no qualification more indispensable, to a person in his situation, than a perfect command of temper, never suffering himself to be moved in the slightest degree, by any language or threat that may be used. He will do his duty in a quiet and determined manner; but in doing so, he is to be civil and attentive to all persons of every rank and class, as no insolence or incivility will be passed over.

248. *Admiralty to Superintendent Clavell: efficiency review*

[NMM, CHA/H/37]   12 November 1840

I am commanded by My Lords Commissioners of the Admiralty to acquaint you that the Commissioners of the Metropolitan Police intend sending two of their superior officers to Chatham Yard for the purpose of ascertaining what arrangements are necessary for making the police force of the yard more efficient, and I am to signify their Lordships directions to you to afford them every assistance in the prosecution of their enquiry.

249. *Superintendent Shirreff to Admiralty: fire procedure*

[TNA, ADM1/5521]   13 May 1842

With reference to the proposal contained in my letter of the 4th December last, that 8 or 10 shipwrights should sleep in the yard nightly to be in readiness with their tools in case of fire to cut off the communication with any adjacent buildings and also forwarding a station bill for the officers &c. I have the honour to submit, for the consideration of the Lords Commissioners of the Admiralty, the propriety of allowing the suggestion as to the shipwrights to be adopted.

250. *Demise of the Dockyard Police Force*

[Hobbes, *Reminiscences and Notes*, p. 207]

I have spoken of the dockyard police and their organization as a local force. That system continued to prevail until December, 1860, in all the yards except Deptford and Woolwich, which, being within the Metropolitan district, were under the charge of Superintendent F.M. Mallalieu, and the men of the Greenwich Division. Mr. Mallalieu had joined the police on the formation of the force by Sir Robert Peel in 1829; and from his long experience had learned the value of tact, discretion and kindness – qualities much required in dockyard police matters. Affairs had therefore gone more smoothly in the yards under his care than the rest; and it seemed desirable to the authorities that all the yards should be placed under his care. Accordingly in August 1860 an Act was passed which gave the other yards and kindred establishments into the custody of the Metropolitan Police; and ere the end of the year a detachment of that body was formed into five dockyard divisions: Woolwich, Portsmouth, Devonport, Chatham (including Sheerness), and Pembroke. Each division was placed in the charge of a superintendent, and Mr. Mallalieu was promoted to the rank of Inspecting Superintendent in general charge of the whole. His especial duty was to go from division to division periodically to see that one uniform system was carried out in all.

251. *Senior Police Commissioner Richard Mayne to Admiralty: admission into new policing body*

[TNA, MEPO1/58] 18 October 1860

The Metropolitan Police are to take charge of several dockyards as soon as arrangements can be made. Constables serving in the yards will be admitted into the Metropolitan Police if qualified and having good character.

252. *Admiralty to Superintendent Goldsmith: medical arrangements*

[NMM, CHA/H/140] 10 November 1860

My Lordships desire to acquaint you that they have approved of the Metropolitan Police force at the yard under your superintendence, being sent to the Royal Marine Infirmary in case of serious accidents, for medical treatment.

253. *Second Secretary of the Admiralty to Samuel Whitbread:*
premises

[TNA, MEPO1/58]   26 November 1860

The alteration of the premises for the occupation of police and carrying on the duties in the yards at Chatham and Sheerness are most urgent and the papers for the purpose are before the Admiralty. I request you will be so good as to cause the necessary sanctions to be given without delay. We shall be ready to undertake the police charge of both the yards on Monday next.

The Captain Superintendent in each yard affords all aid in his power by making necessary temporary arrangements.

254. *Senior Police Commissioner Richard Mayne to Admiralty:*
commencement of duties

[TNA, MEPO1/58]   5 December 1860

I have to acquaint you for the Lords Commissioners of the Admiralty that the Metropolitan Police force, commence their duties at Her Majesty's Dockyards at Chatham and Sheerness on Monday 3rd instant.

Materials

There was a constant search for new and better materials, with much attention directed to the supply of hemp and timber. Most hemp came from Russia, which was a potential enemy in time of war [173]. To obtain an alternative source of supply, experiments were undertaken to ascertain the strength of Italian and Chilean hemp [260, 262]. Another solution was to replace anchor cables of rope with chain cables, these having been first used by the navy in 1817 [173]. Timber was the most important of all shipbuilding materials throughout this period and new sources of supply were sought around the world [255, 266]. Different types of timber to those normally associated with the construction of British men-of-war were considered [265, 266], and there were numerous experiments to ascertain their strength and quality [263, 264].

Efforts were also made to give better protection to materials both in store and in use. A summary of instructions as to the best means of preserving timber when held in store was issued to resident commissioners in 1815 [255]. Five years later experiments were made in tarring oakum [256, 257]. In 1833, it was determined that ships in ordinary should no longer be moored with masts *in situ*, because masts deteriorated less rapidly if stored in one of the two yard mast ponds [261]. Further instructions for the better preservation of stores were issued in 1832 [259] when attention was also given to the prevention of corrosion in iron [258].

255. *Navy Board to Admiralty: timber preservation*

[TNA, ADM106/2267]   28 June 1815

In consequence of the directions of the Lord Commissioners of the Admiralty, signified to us by Mr. Barrow's letter of the 20th January 1812, to take into consideration the mode of stowing timber and of building ships and to communicate with the dockyard officers on the subject and to propose any plans that may occur to render H.M. Ships more durable. We have to request you to acquaint their Lordships that these circumstances have at all times occupied our serious consideration, and whenever representations have been made, or plans have occurred to us to forward this important object, we have directed the officers of the dockyards to put them into immediate practice.

The preservation of the store of timber we have considered of the greatest importance and therefore have taken precautions that it should be stowed in the best possible manner for its preservation and seasoning. The grounds over which it is put is strewed with ashes from the smith's forge (in order to prevent vegetation and absorption of moisture) and a considerable separation left between each piece of timber, for a circulation of air. These precautionary measures have also been adopted with regard to converted timber when it could not be kept under cover. It would no doubt be of considerable importance, from the facility it could give to the best conversion of timber, if it were placed in low piles, but the ground space at the dockyards will not permit this arrangement. When piles of timber have, from time to time, been broken, the logs have been canted and the defective parts cut out, and that side placed downwards, which mode has conduced its preservation.

The practice of boiling thick stuff and plank in order to season it more rapidly and to prevent its shrinkage has been resorted to upon some occasions; the use of oil and also paint made of white lead has also been had recourse to where two pieces of wood were in contact. The plans presented by individuals for the preservation of timber have also been tried (particularly those pointed out by Mr Sowerby). Whenever those plans promised to be attended with success, reports upon such experiments are directed to be made as the ships are examined.

In the use of several kinds of timber in ships attention has been had to place it in situations the most adapted to its quality and engagements have been entered into for supplies of timber (exclusive of those from the Baltic and North America) from different parts of the Globe, the quality of which was considered to be equal or superior to British Oak. With respect to timber intended to be brought into use, particular attention has been paid to removing the sap, which from the timber not having attained maturity, has been found to cause rapid decay and the growth of fungus.

256. *Navy Board to Chatham Yard Officers: oakum preparation*

[NMM, CHA/E/140]   22 August 1820

As it is highly desirable that the best method should be adopted in preparing oakum for caulking with a view to giving it greater durability, these are to direct and require you to cause some oakum to be spun in a proper manner, to pass through a kettle of mineral tar, and afterwards under the nippers. When so done, it is to be again picked and applied, while in a proper state for caulking, to that part of a ship's bottom which is always under water (or such other parts as have been found to occasion the most rapid decay of oakum). After a sufficient time has elapsed, you are to give us your opinion thereon compared with oakum, which has been prepared in the usual manner.

In carrying out this experiment you are to take to your assistance the Master Rope Maker, who is to join in the report and if any experiments have already been made, you are to inform us of the results.

257. *Navy Board to Admiralty: preserving oakum*

[TNA, ADM106/1839]   6 July 1829

In pursuance of the Honble Navy Board's general letter of 22nd August 1820, directing us to cause some oakum to be spun in a proper manner, to pass through a kettle of mineral tar and afterwards under the nippers, and when so done, to be again picked and applied while in a proper state, to that part of a ship's bottom which is always under water, or to such other parts as have been found to occasion the most rapid decay of oakum.

We beg to state that on the 2nd April 1821, the bottom of His Majesty's ship *Latona* was caulked as follows, with oakum so prepared: starboard side 18th and 19th seam from the keel, 30 feet from forward and 60 feet from aft; 11th seam under the wale 126 ft. forward from the counter rail – larboard side; 20th seam from the keel at 50 ft. from the stern post.

And we have to observe that on a most minute inspection of the bottom of the *Latona* now in dock, we find the caulking with the mineral tarred toppets appear much slacker than that caulked with oakum prepared in the usual manner. On a comparison with the two sorts of oakum, taken from the bottom of the said ship, as nearly to the same places as possible, it might be seen by reference to the specimen sent this day to the Navy Office for the Honble Navy Board's inspection, that the oakum tarred with mineral tar, is not in an equal state of preservation to that usually used and made from junk. Consequently, we consider the oakum prepared in mineral tar, not so durable for caulking as that prepared in the usual manner from junk.

258. *Navy Board to Chatham Yard Officers: oakum preparation*

[NMM, CHA/H/4] 10 March 1830

I am commanded by the Commissioners of the Navy to acquaint you that they have determined to make trial of a method of preserving iron from corrosion, proposed by Commander Sweeny and others, who have taken out a patent for the same; and that the *Hornet* building at your port, and the *Spider*, ordered to be built, have been selected for the purpose of the trial. It is the Board's intention that the *Hornet* shall be fastened with copper as usual, and the patent iron sheathing put over it, and that the *Spider* schooner shall be altogether fastened with the protected iron proposed by the inventors and have copper sheathing put over them in the usual manner. The bolts of the *Spider*, where the protected bolts are used, being 3 inches instead of 2½ inches, as before ordered, in order to let the ring in; and I am further to direct you to govern yourselves accordingly.

259. *Admiralty to Storekeeper: use of stores*

[NMM, CHA/H/4] 7 November 1832

My Lords Commissioners of the Admiralty having under their consideration the important question of the expenditure of naval stores and having observed that a different practice prevails in the several dockyards in the mode of issuing the same and being of opinion that it is highly expedient that one uniform practice should be established in all the dockyards both home and abroad, I am commanded to signify to you their Lordships direction that you take to your assistance the Master Attendant, the

Master Shipwright and Storekeeper Superintendent. Upon consultation with those officers, to select two storehouses, the most conveniently situated for the respective purposes, to which they are to be applied, to be arranged as present use storehouses in which articles of every description as far as may be practicable are to be placed. [They] are to be replenished from time to time as is necessary from the other storehouses and to be made as little as possible places of receipt of the deliveries by contractors [with] no issue being allowed to be made from the same store at which a receipt is going on. From one of which the issue of boatswain and carpenters' present use stores for the current demands of ships in commission and for the artificers working upon ships afloat, are to be made. The other [storehouse is] to be termed the 'central present use storehouse'.

If a suitable [boatswain and carpenters] store can be found, convenient for all parts of the yard, it is to be made the exclusive place of issue of the stores required for ships building or repairing or the other works of the dockyard. It being an important object to be kept in view that the officers, and those who come from time to time with proper authority, as it is convenient for the fitting of ships in commission to draw the stores allowed by the establishment, should be supplied and enabled to get them on board the ships without delay. Much of the facility with which this can be affected, depends on the situation of the storehouse from which the present use stores are to be drawn. You should be guided in the selection and internal distribution of this present use storehouse by what appears to be the most convenient arrangement, which the local circumstances of the yard afford for having the stores promptly supplied and easily conveyed on board the ships.

Considerations of a similar nature should determine the position of the central present use storehouse, it being desirable that it should be placed as much as possible in a central spot with reference to the situation of the different docks or building slips in the yard.

Their Lordships, in the consideration of the subject of the issue of stores, have naturally directed their attention to the necessity of providing for the due appropriation of them and feeling that the full attainment of this object must mainly depend upon the efficiency and integrity of the inferior officers and others entrusted with the superintendence of the artificers and by whom the demands upon the Storekeeper are sanctioned and who therefore are responsible for the proper application of the issues which by their authority are made, I have to signify to you their Lordships directions that you enforce, on all occasions, the strictest attention on their part to the wants of the service and the demands, which under their signature are made upon the Storekeeper. That such stores only be drawn as can be applied during the day to their works in hand, as nearly as may be. That you call it to be established as an invariable practice that when the artificers quit their work or the works of the day are ended, that the leading men of each gang of shipwrights shall collect all remains of issues that may not have been used. [They] shall deliver them over to the foremen superintending their respective divisions of the yard whose duty it is, practically, to watch the operations of the artificers in the execution of their work. [They] are to take such surplus stores into their own custody and to regulate the further demands of each service by the quantities of the remains thus given into their charge and to deposit each of the stores (except copper articles, which are always to be deposited in the storehouse) as will be required on the following day for the works in hand, in a chest of convenient size, which you are to take care is provided at each dockside, giving the key of it into the possession of the foreman. [You are to undertake] inspecting it occasionally at uncertain periods for the purpose of ascertaining that no unnecessary accumulation of stores is allowed to take place.

All remains of stores which may not be required at the completion of the particular service (or which may not be immediately wanted for the progress of the works for which they were issued) are invariably to be returned upon a return note by the foreman to the storehouse from whence they were drawn, where they are to be received into charge again and duly accounted for by the storekeeper.

In like measure you are to give particular directions to the Master Shipwright, his Assistant and foreman that a special care be taken when ships are surveyed and preparing for undergoing repairs or to be broken up. That an accurate account be made out of all copper bolts, fastenings and other serviceable stores, which may be removed from such ships by the shipwrights. Which account, when signed by the foreman, is to be delivered, together with the stores, into the most convenient storehouse, the clerk giving a receipt of the same and charging the Storekeeper with them in his daily account.

All the foremen or other officers on whose demands the stores are issued (and who will be held strictly responsible for the propriety of their expenditure) will be required at the end of each month to examine the monthly account, to be made out by the Storekeeper of the stores issued to them respectively. By comparing it carefully with the demands they have previously made for the stores, and after complete examination of it, verify the same by their signature. For this purpose, instead of sending up the issue notes to Somerset House, you are in future, as soon as the Storekeeper shall have returned them, and for the greater convenience of the foreman, you will keep them in separate parcels according to the signatures of those respective officers, until the monthly accounts, after which they may be disposed of as is most convenient.

Their Lordships having also in considering the subject of the issue of the stores in the dockyards taken into consideration the regulation contained in the 20th Article of the Storekeepers' Instructions requiring him to lay apart for ships in good condition all such boats, anchors and sails and other stores as may belong to them. [This] article of stores has, in some instances, remained for a length of time being appropriated to a particular ship, not brought forward for service at sea, and have thereby deteriorated. [At the same time,] stores of more recent manufacture have been provided and issued for ships, to which the appropriate stores might with advantage have been made applicable. Their Lordships considering that it will be expedient to obviate altogether the inconvenience occasioned by this practice, I have to signify to you their Lordships command that you cause the stores of the various articles heretofore appropriated in the manner referred to, to be kept up in classes or sorts without regard to particular ships, so as to ensure the issue of them for supplying the general wants of the service according to priority of date in their manufacture. That you cause such alteration to be made in the internal fittings of the storehouses as may be indispensably necessary for the convenience and arrangement and prompt issue of the stores upon this principle; always bearing in mind that the general establishment order to be provided for the ready equipment of the different class of ships in good condition in ordinary at your port is to be duly and regularly kept up.

260. *Admiralty to Superintendent Gordon: trials of Chilean hemp*

[NMM, CHA/H/4]   12 November 1832

Having agreed to receive from Mr Morris such part of the Chile hemp, about three or four tons, which the Master Rope Maker inspected in the London docks, that should be found in the usual inspection of receipt free from damage, at the rate of £30 per ton, I request you will give orders for the receipt of the same. [It is] to be immediately worked up into cordage and the strength of which is to be tried in the dockyard against rope made of the several other sorts of hemp (which may be in store) and the results reported on. The remainder of the cordage made of Chile hemp is to be issued at the earliest opportunity, reporting the name of the ship or ships to which it may be supplied.

261. *Admiralty to Superintendent Gordon: preservation of masts*

[NMM, CHA/H/5]   1 April 1833

In order to preserve ships' masts for a longer period than by placing them in ships intended for the ordinary, where they are found more speedily to deteriorate, it is the direction of the Lords Commissioners of the Admiralty, that in future ships so intended, shall not be masted and that their bowsprits only shall be kept on board, but not shipped. Further, when ships are brought forward for commissioning, as well as those in commission, which may require masts, if there should be any of the proper size in the ordinary, their Lordships desire that you will give the preference to those masts, and appropriate them to such ships. In all such cases you are to refer for their Lordships approval.

262. *Superintendent Gordon to Admiralty Secretary: trials of Italian hemp*

[TNA, ADM1/3397]   15 October 1833

I beg leave to inform you that I have sent the coach this evening to your address to be inspected by My Lords Commissioners of the Admiralty some specimens of the cordage made of fine yarn from Italian hemp (spun at the rate of 5 threads an hour) for the *Pandora*'s rigging. I regret to observe that it does not appear to be as even and well made as the specimen of French rope sent to me by their Lordships but I trust that when the rigging for the *Tribune* ordered to be prepared by Mr Barrow's letter of the 8th inst. is made, I shall be able to forward a more improved specimen from the men being allowed more time in its manufacture. The specimen of French rope will be returned by coach tonight.

263. *J.G. Dennison to Admiralty, forwarded to Superintendent Gordon by the Admiralty: experiments in relative strengths of timbers*

[NMM, CHA/H/10]   25 April 1834

My brother, who is, as you know, established at Chatham in the Government service as an engineer, among other pursuits of the service, has been making many experiments on the strength and qualities of various kinds of timber.

In order to carry forward these experiments, he wishes for permission to obtain from the dockyard, specimens of some of the foreign wood in use there. The whole supply he would ever require, would amount, so I suppose, to a very few feet of timber.

Perhaps you would, if you see no objection, to give authority in the dockyard that he might be afforded the facility required by my brother.

If you think the result of the experiments as to specific gravity of strengths of the various woods would be of any use or interest to you my brother would be very happy to communicate to you all that he has obtained.

264. *Admiralty to Superintendent Gordon: trials in relative strengths of timbers*

[NMM, CHA/H/10]   30 April 1834

I am commanded by My Lords Commissioners of the Admiralty to signify their direction to you to assist Lt Dennison of the Royal Engineers in the experiments in timber proposed in the accompanying letter, provided no unnecessary waste of timber and no labour of the artificers takes place.

265. *Admiralty to Superintendent Gordon: qualities of Italian and Polish larch*

[NMM, CHA/H/38]   5 January 1841

The Captain Superintendent at Chatham is requested to call upon the officers to report very fully on the respective qualities & dimensions of the Italian larch in comparison with other timbers, particularly as to the conversion & adaptation for shipbuilding purposes either in the construction of steam vessels or otherwise: stating for which purpose it is considered peculiarly applicable and whether it can be advantageously used as a substitute for English oak thick stuff and plank.

Also to make a similar report on Polish larch.

266. *Surveyor of Navy to Board of Admiralty: alternative timber supplies*

[TNA, ADM87/77]   8 October 1860

The increased and continually increasing demand for timber of all kinds, especially for the purpose of shipbuilding, & the consequent exhaustion of the forests which hitherto mainly supplied the demand, render it imperative that investigation be made in new regions, where forests are known to abound to ascertain how far they may be likely to yield timber equal or approaching in value, to European oak, or Indian or African teak.

My Lords Commissioners of the Admiralty desire the cooperation of Her Majesty's ministers & consuls abroad, of the Governors of Her Majesty's Colonies, of officers in the Army and Navy (especially medical officers, whose education has rendered them more or less familiar with botany & the products of plants) to aid in procuring samples of woods & all reliable information which may contribute to so important an object.

As the information required will naturally often relate to new kinds of woods, it is a matter of the greatest consequence that not only the vernacular or local (native) name of the tree be given, but its botanical name should be determined. For this purpose, specimens of leaf bearing branches about a foot or 6 inches long with flowers and fruit be procured & transmitted in a pressed and dried state.

Equally important it is that blocks, a foot square (much longer if a good opportunity occurs of transmitting them), should be [made] of such wood as are worthy of attention to the Admiralty, as samples of quality; these, bearing a number corresponding with that attached to the specimens, so as to verify them: and accompanied with every kind of information that can be obtained respecting them.

For example,

1. The general size of the tree, the height & thickness of the trunk below the branches, & the length & diameter of the principal limbs: also whether these limbs are crooked, so as to be useful for knees, or straight.

2. Remarks on the supposed quantity of trees in the country & the probable nature of the supply: the places of growth, whether near the sea or navigable rivers, or any ports convenient for shipment – stating whether facilities exist or may be created for procuring supplies & giving a rough estimate of getting a cargo on board ship at per load.

3. State the known uses in the country by natives or Europeans & the general character the tree bears for any useful purpose, especially in boat & shipbuilding.

4. If practicable, obtain the specific growth or weight of a very exactly cut cubic foot of the perfect wood of the tree, taken from the butt end, – the weight to be marked on the specimens; & these specimens sent home to be again weighed & measured when seasoned.

There is every reason to believe that in our own colonies, in western tropical Africa, in British Guiana & in Australia (particularly among the Blue Gum Trees) many hard and durable woods, approximating to the oak in quality, may be detected, if due enquiry were made. It is clearly as much to the interest of the colony that affords them, as to the mother country, which offers a reward for them that a searching investigation be made of their properties & uses & costs of transport. British colonies, we have reason to know, affords noble timber of the coniferous or pine, suitable for masts and spars, especially in the Douglas Pine (Abies Douglasii). Japan & North China possesses several kinds of oak. Botanists have detected 7 different kinds in Japan alone, but their commercial value, is as yet, totally unknown to us.

5

ECONOMICS, CUSTOM AND THE WORKFORCE

The ringing of a dockyard bell officially denoted both the length of the working day and the time of the mid-day lunch break [275, 295, 297, 304]. It was this same bell that was rung on Friday mornings to call the men to the pay office to collect their wages [323]. Upon entering the yard, both morning and afternoon, the workforce was formally mustered [297, 304]. The length of the working day varied by season, maximum use being made of daylight, although the working of overtime might extend these hours [272, 304]. Some differences in the working day existed between the yards prior to 1834 [304]. In all, six days were normally worked each week, although in June 1822 this total was temporarily reduced to five as a means of economising on the overall wage bill [296]. Four days in each year were given as holidays, these including the monarch's birthday [287]. When any of the agreed days fell on a Sunday, the following Monday was allowed as the holiday [301]. The launch day of a ship was given as an additional half-day holiday but only for those involved in its construction. An exceptional two-day holiday was given in August 1862 to allow dockyard employees to visit the Great Exhibition in London [326].

The end of the wars with France in 1815 made a considerable impact upon all those employed at Chatham. Whereas the two previous decades had been characterised by a degree of job security, an upward growth in workforce numbers and frequent overtime, the post-war period was to witness a complete reversal. A government forced to economise sought major cutbacks in the numbers employed and in paid working hours. However, neither the working of a five-day week nor the reduction in overtime followed closely upon the arrival of peace, a large amount of work having to be undertaken upon ships of the returning fleet. Indeed, the immediate post-war period witnessed an augmentation of numbers employed, with some, including the women of the colour loft, allowed overtime [268, 269].[1]

Post-war retrenchment only hit Chatham in March 1816. The Navy Board was forced to cut back levels of payment and hours worked [272]

---

[1]The colour loft during this period was the only employer of women, first claim to employment going to widows of those who had died in dockyard service.

and to begin a series of reductions in numbers employed [271]. Dismissals were to continue throughout the next twenty years [278, 282, 283, 284], with a final severe round after the economising Whig-led coalition achieved power in 1830 [294]. Only in 1854, upon the nation's entry into war with Russia, did recruitment at the yard once more begin to increase [319], a scale of employment that continued into the post-war period [322]. Those dockyard artisans and labourers who were laid off during the earlier period were given a week's wages in compensation [267] but were initially denied passage money to help them return to their original place of recruitment [283]. Only in 1825 was this reversed [284]. A further economy was achieved in 1830 by the termination of 'chip money' [291]. The shortfalls in labour that resulted from these many cutbacks were partly made up by the employment of convict labour. Housed on hulks moored in the River Medway, convicts undertook many of the unskilled tasks previously undertaken by teams of horses, scavelmen and labourers [290, 292].

In 1818, the Admiralty proposed a 20 per cent reduction in wage levels.[1] The Navy Board Comptroller chose to reject the idea, believing that a cut in wages would prove disastrous, the men seeing it as a 'breach of faith'. He maintained that, while nothing immediate might happen, it was likely the yard employees would 'retaliate when war shall again make us sensible of their consequence to the state'.[2] This fear of employee retaliation was based on sound historical evidence. Frequently, during periods of peace, the dockyard workforce had quiescently accepted government-imposed conditions, aware that their skills were little valued in such times. Upon the outset of war, however, their position was dramatically strengthened and Chatham had seen a number of major strikes that coincided with an initial period of hostility.[3] The Comptroller wished to avoid any possibility of such action in the future. In the meantime, workforce discontent was voiced through petitions, a time-honoured device, the use of which was encouraged by those in authority. Over the years, an approved procedure had emerged: these petitions had to be properly addressed, passed to the Navy Board through the office of the resident commissioner and signed by those responsible for their

---

[1] BL Add. MS 41,400, 1 June 1818.
[2] Ibid.
[3] During periods of mobilisation in both 1739 and 1775 the workforce had successfully resorted to strike action. See B. Raft, 'Labour Relations in the Royal Dockyards in 1739', *Mariner's Mirror*, 47 (1961), 281–91; M. Haas, 'The Introduction of Task Work in the Royal Dockyards, 1775', *Journal of British Studies*, 8 (1969), 60. In 1793, concern existed as to a possible strike by the rope makers of Chatham yard; see NMM CHA/E/48, April 1793. A further strike at Chatham did take place at Chatham in 1795; see NMM CHA/E/48, Jan.–Feb. 1795.

submission. Failure to adhere to protocol, particularly regarding the signatures, resulted in the petition being returned unread [280].

Petitions, in themselves, might originate from an individual, from a small group or from all the workers employed in one or more trades. Those from individuals and small groups [276, 279, 285, 289] or individual trades [270, 310] were diverse in their concerns but one common issue of anxiety was skill demotion. This had come about as the result of a scheme to retain skilled workers in the yard. Shipwrights, caulkers and others with high-level skills could remain in the yard at a reduced wage by carrying on the work of artificers who possessed skills of a lower order [281, 285]. As for petitions from an entire trade, or combination of trades, these were usually concerned with core workforce demands. For the great mass of artificers, the most pressing matter was the subject of wage levels, the reduction of overtime having had a considerable impact upon standards of living [277]. In addition, from the late 1830s, a series of petitions emanated from a group of temporary workers known as hired men [324], requesting that, while employed at the yard, they should receive perquisites similar to those enjoyed by permanent employees [309, 328]. After 1834, the concern of trade groups dramatically altered, the result of the widely hated scheme of classification introduced that year [298, 300]. This placed the most efficient workers in the highest or first class, with higher levels of remuneration than other members of the same trade in the second or third classes. The scheme was supposed to encourage higher rates of work output [298, 305] and replace payment by the day and piecework. Hitherto, day pay had been determined only by hours of attendance while piece rates had depended upon a measured amount of output. For those working around the docks and building slips, piece rates might be paid either under the denomination of 'task', when work directly involved construction of a new ship, or of 'job', when connected with a ship under repair.[1]

Workforce opposition to classification was total and unremitting. Using the petition as its chief weapon, the entire dockyard community was drawn into a major political campaign. Signs of orchestration began to appear in 1835 when a series of petitions emanated from a variety of trade groups employed in all the naval dockyards [306]. The failure of these petitions to move the Admiralty forced the leaders of the campaign to rethink their strategy. Following considerable contact between the various yards, public meetings were held in Chatham, Woolwich, Portsmouth and Devonport [307]. Each of these meetings resulted in lengthy petitions being signed

---

[1]For background information on the use of piece rates within naval dockyards see J. Haas, *A Management Odyssey: The Royal Dockyards, 1714–1914* (Lanham, Md, 1993), esp. pp. 34–7.

by many thousands of local inhabitants [308]. Over the next three years, petitions against classification were submitted to the Admiralty on a regular basis. In addition, Members of Parliament became involved. They often attended meetings and accompanied delegations of workmen to express their views to the Admiralty in London [311].

This pressure, combined with the increasing difficulty of recruiting skilled workers [312], resulted in the Admiralty reviewing the issue of classification. In April 1840, it was announced that the hated third class would be abolished; then, in September 1840, the Admiralty further announced the abolition of the first class, so bringing a complete end to the scheme [313]. The men returned to being paid by the day, the rates adjusted for certain groups [314]. Only in wartime or emergencies were piece rates reintroduced; for example, at the time of the Russian War (1854–56) and brought to an end in 1858 [321].

Another Whig reform bitterly opposed by the workforce was the ending in 1833 of superannuation payments to artificers who had served thirty years or been incapacitated by injury while in employment. Shipwrights and caulkers had been entitled to £25 per annum, while other trades such as joiners, sail makers and riggers received £20, £15, and £10 respectively [315].[1] This, in the eighteenth century, had represented 60 per cent of their standard day wage, but, with no increases, the value of these pensions had declined considerably [279, 289] and by 1833 had fallen to about 30 per cent of the current day wage.[2] However, following another petitioning campaign [279], superannuation was reintroduced in 1839 and the rate at which it was paid was subsequently increased [315]. Not all workers of the yard could claim this benefit, so that some old, infirm or injured workers still had to be retained in the yard performing light duties [293]. Hired workers were also excluded. These exclusions would be separately addressed in March 1864 [329]. Besides superannuation, a further benefit of dockyard employment was medical care: entitlement included admission to naval hospital facilities in the event of injury caused through dockyard service [273, 286].

A new apprenticeship scheme, introduced by the Whigs in 1833, was a further cause of grievance [302]. Under it, all apprentices entering the yards were bound to the government whereas previously they had been bound to officers. However, selected deserving workers, termed instructors, carried out actual instruction. It was they, rather than the officers, who received, as their reward, part of the pay earned by an apprentice. This had become a highly prized perquisite, as both parents and instructors

[1]NMM, CHA/E/27, 24 Oct. 1771.
[2]PRO, ADM1/5511, 4 June 1841.

gained [310]. Yet, owing to the limited number of apprentices engaged, only a small number of artificers benefited. As for the means by which apprentices were selected, this initially depended upon luck and influence as an assessment was rarely made of a candidate's ability [303]. Since the early years of the nineteenth century evening classes for the instruction of apprentices had existed[1] [274] and in 1843 Chatham became the first of the dockyards to establish an apprentice school [316, 317]. Inspection of these schools was instituted in 1846 [318].

The achievement by petitioning of a much sought after pay increase in 1857 [319] contrasted sharply with an Admiralty dismissal of ironsmiths following their stoppage of work in 1862 [325]. To replace them, volunteer shipwrights were moved to No. 2 dock where they received training from dockyard engine smiths and the small number of ironsmiths who had remained outside the dispute. These newly transferred shipwrights, eventually reaching 500 in number, were employed in plating *Achilles* with iron. Yard labourers performed drilling and riveting. The latter were granted a higher rate of pay and became known as 'skilled labourers'. Many of the shipwrights who transferred to *Achilles* were on the verge of redundancy, for the Admiralty was about to replace them with a larger number of ironsmiths. With the laying-down of iron battleships such as *Achilles*, shipwrights' work was transformed [327].

The improvement of workplace conditions was the most important object of artificer organisation. Yet collective activities did not stop at that point. In cases of individual distress, collections of money were often undertaken, with injured workers most frequently the recipients.[2] Sometimes, trade groups formed their own friendly societies, with each man paying a weekly amount.[3] In addition, the yard workforce organised itself for recreational purposes. The anchor smiths of the yard celebrated their patron, St Clement, with an annual parade on 23 November, although this ceased to receive Admiralty support after 1833 [299]. To coincide with the officially recognised dockyard holidays, the rope makers and others organised recreational activities for themselves and their families: for instance, an annual summer festival [330]. However, one activity in which the workforce refused to become involved was the dockyard chaplain's chapel choir [288].

---

[1]Morriss gives 1802 as the year in which a school was first established at Chatham. Established by the Commissioner and yard officers, it taught reading, writing and arithmetic. See Roger Morriss, *The Royal Dockyards during the Revolutionary and Napoleonic Wars* (Leicester, 1983), 112.

[2]TNA, ADM 1/5881, 22 Jan. 1864; *Chatham News* 13 Feb. 1864, 4; Mavis Waters, 'The Dockyard Workforce: A Picture of Chatham Dockyard *c*.1860', *Archaeologia Cantiana* 97, 92–3; *Chatham News*, 11 Nov. 1865, 4.

[3]Waters, *op. cit.*, 93. *Chatham News*, 11 Nov. 1865, 4.

267. *Admiralty to Commissioner Barlow: dismissals*

[NMM, CHA/F/29]   9 March 1816

The Lords Commissioners of the Admiralty having been pleased, by order bearing this date, to signify their approval of a recommendation from us, that each of the artificers and workmen who are ordered to be immediately discharged from His Majesty's dockyards, and many of whom, it is probable, will be in great distress from want of money before they can obtain any employment, should have a sum of money, equal to a week's day pay of the class to which he belongs. We desire that you will give directions for every person so discharged to be paid the sum authorised by their Lordships, in addition to the wages, which may be due to him at the time of his discharge.

268. *Navy Board to Commissioner Barlow: overtime*

[NMM, CHA/F/29]   6 July 1816

We desire you will cause the women who are employed in making signal colours to work from five o'clock in the morning until eight o'clock in the evening, until the whole of the signal colours wanted are completed.

269. *Navy Board to Commissioner Barlow: overtime*

[NMM, CHA/F/29]   10 July 1816

Commissioner Cunningham having suggested that in consideration of the number of hours which the women are to be employed in making colours, they should not come into the yard until six o'clock in the morning instead of five as desired by your letter of the 6th instant, and that the tailors may attend the same time to cut out and superintend the work. We acquaint you that we approve of this suggestion and therefore desire that you will cause it to be adopted at Chatham. The women are to be paid two pence per hour for the additional time.

270. *Navy Board to Commissioner Barlow: petition*

[NMM, CHA/F/29]   13 September 1816

Having received a petition from the house carpenters belonging to your yard, who are employed in repairing the lower part of the steps, docks and wharfs, praying to be granted an allowance on account of the water boots, which they are obliged to find. We desire you will acquaint them that their request cannot be complied with.

271. *Commissioner Barlow to Navy Board: reduction of sail makers*

[TNA, ADM106/1815]   17 October 1816

Owing to the additional work which the making and repairing sails for the revenue vessels has occasioned in the sail makers department of this yard (and which was not calculated on the reduction of the six men that took place, proposed by the officers on the 10th and ordered by your letter of the 11th January last), the present number employed, 16 sail makers and 7 apprentices, is not sufficient to enable the Master Attendant to keep pace with the Master Shipwright, by providing sails for ships in good condition and bringing forward, agreeable to the 39th article of the printed instructions.

I therefore recommend the temporary employing in the sail loft of three sail makers who were discharged in January last and are now serving as yard labourers.

272. *Navy Board to Commissioner Barlow: reduced hours*

[NMM, CHA/F/30]   13 February 1817

It being considered expedient to reduce the quantity of work obtained under the existing limitations of the yard hours, we have thought it right, in order to give effect to the directions of the Lords Commissioners of the Admiralty, with the least possible inconvenience to the several classes of workmen, to act on the principle which before induced us to prefer a curtailment of the time of labour, other than order an extensive discharge of men at a moment when it is so difficult to procure employment elsewhere. We have therefore submitted to the Lords Commissioners of the Admiralty a proposition to the above effect. With their Lordships' concurrence we have to desire that you will give orders to the officers to carry into execution the following regulations as to the working hours and the limitation of earnings of the several classes of artificers (which are to commence on Monday next the 17th inst).

The men are to come into the yard at eight o'clock (summer and winter) so as to be called and at work by half past eight.

The dining time to be two hours and a quarter in summer and an hour and a half in winter: the men to quit the yard at five o'clock in summer and four o'clock in winter.

The earnings to be limited [as shown in the enclosed paper].

And whereas it appears that there are several descriptions of workmen for whom work cannot be found even on the reduced hours, the following persons are to be discharged from their several employments allowing the rope makers to fall back into the place of rope makers labourers, so far as the establishment of the latter class will admit. The remainder of the rope makers and their labourers are to be included in the number to be discharged. The sail makers are to have the option of becoming scavelmen and labourers, letting scavelmen fall back into the place of labourers, discharging such a number of labourers as may be necessary to give effect to this arrangement. Such of the bricklayers also as may have served their apprenticeships in the yard are to have the option of a single indulgence.[1]

The men discharged are to have a week's wages as heretofore, and the discharge is to take place gradually – so many in the week – so as to be accomplished in three weeks, taking care that strict attention be paid to character.

[*Numbers to be discharged*]

Rope makers' spinners	22
Labourers	9
House boys	12
Bricklayers	5
Sail makers	none

[*Limitations of earnings*]

Sail makers	3s 5d per diem

Shipwrights	
Mast makers	
Top and Capstan makers	
Boat builders	4s 0d per diem
Caulkers	
Oar & treenail makers	
Pump makers	
Screw cutters and turners	

---

[1] Bricklayers who had not served an apprenticeship in the yard were to be the first to be dismissed.

Masons Joiners Wheelwrights	3s 7d per diem
Smiths when employed on anchors above 20 cwt	4s 0d per diem
Smiths on other works House carpenters Bricklayers Top men Sawyers	3s 5d per diem
Pitmen Sawyers	2s 10d per diem
Scavelmen	2s 8d per diem
Bricklayers Labourers Yard labourers	2s 4d per diem
Oakum boys	1s 0d per diem
Yard spinners Line and twine spinners Hemp dressers	3s 5d per diem
Rope makers' labourers	2s 10d per diem
House boys	1s 0d per diem
Wheel boys'	11d per diem

All exclusive of chip money where it is allowed.

273.   *Commissioner Barlow to Navy Board: injured labourer*

[TNA, ADM106/1815]   4 August 1817

I have to acquaint you in reference to your letter of 20th April 1815, for the information of the Lords Commissioners of the Admiralty, that under the extreme case of hurt of Jeremiah Mahoney, a labourer in this yard, stated in the enclosed representation from the Master Shipwright and the surgeon, it has been judged expedient to send him to the naval hospital ship for cure, which I trust meets their Lordships approbation.

274. Voluntary Apprenticeship School

[Dupin, *Two Excursions*, p. 65[1]]   1818

For several years past the officers of Chatham dockyard have subscribed to form at their own expense a school where the young apprentices are received during the winter evenings. They are taught reading, writing and arithmetic, and even, as I understand, the first elements of geometry. They are admitted without charge and free of all expenses but dismissed on the first serious fault they commit, or merely if they cease to be punctual.

275. Admiralty to Commissioner Barlow: working hours

[TNA, ADM1/3462]   8 March 1822

General Instructions to the officers of His Majesty's dockyards, 19th Article.

The common working hours, both of the yard and ordinary, being from 6 in the morning until 6 in the evening, the bell will ring at those hours when the workmen are to repair to or leave the yard. This rule is to be observed as long as day light will admit; at all seasons, the workmen are to be governed in their attendance by the ringing of the bell. The common allowance of time for breakfast shall be from eight o'clock in the morning to half past eight and for dinner from twelve to half past one during the summer months. During the winter months, that is, from the 9th of November until the 1st February, both days included, it is desirable that all workmen should breakfast before they enter the yard; in which case they shall appear as early as to have been mustered and be at their work by eight o'clock every morning. Their allowance of time for dinner, during the above period, shall be one hour only.

276. Petition: skill demotion

[TNA, ADM1/5132]   26 September 1822

That your petitioners acknowledge with the greatest thankfulness your Lordships past favour's to the trade in general, which has been a means of your petitioners being look'd upon as a respectable class of mechinicks [*sic*], and from their respectability have all without exception paid their

---

[1]Charles Dupin, *Two Excursions to the Ports of England, Scotland and Ireland in 1816, 1817 and 1818* (London, 1818).

quota of the assess'd taxes. But from your petitioners having been recently order'd to be employ'd as sawyers and scavelmen, their wages are so reduc'd, which entirely renders them incapable of paying taxes and puts many of them to the greatest strait to maintain their numerous families. Your petitioners with all humility beg to state that they have always been found ready to serve their country as shipwrights in any clime or country, where your Lordships were pleased to send them, or the cause of their country requir'd their services. Your petitioners, therefore, mostly humbly pray that your Lordships will be pleased to take their case into your kind consideration and grant that your petitioners may not be sent to work, either as sawyers, scavelmen or labourers, and your most humble petitioners shall as in duty bound, ever pray.

[*Appended note*]
Send this to Navy Board. Their Lordships having understood that the shipwrights volunteered to take this employment rather than be discharged.

277. *Petition: earnings*

[TNA, ADM106/1827] 6 December 1823

The petition of Thomas Wilkins, William Wood, John Rockcliffe, William Champness, Joseph Wells and William Greenfield, labourers born as scavelmen and employed in the boats of the foremen afloat and measurer most humbly sheweth.

That your petitioners have not been paid equal to the class of men to which they belong, having at this season of the year been 11 shillings and eight pence, when the scavelmen, with whom your petitioners are borne, are at this time earning by task seventeen shillings per week. Your petitioners most humbly pray that you will be pleased to take their case into consideration and grant them some additions to their pay and your petitioners as in duty bound for ever pray.

[*Appended note*]
Acquaint the commissioner that we cannot authorize an addition to the pay of any labourers herein mentioned.

278.　Order-in-Council: calculation of superannuation

[TNA, PC2/205]　　　　　　　　　　　　　　　　19 January 1824

May it please your Majesty, having recently had under our consideration the case of the class of workmen called riggers employed in your Majesty's dockyards, we beg leave, with all humility, to represent to your Majesty that it having been deemed expedient for the benefit of your Majesty's service to give a preference in the selection of such persons to men who have previously served at sea, being better qualified for the employment. By the regulations established by His late Majesty's order in council of the 16th December 1814, we are prevented granting pensions to the workmen and artificers of the dockyard who may be discharged from causes not dependent on themselves, unless they shall have completed thirty years of service in a dockyard (exclusive of apprenticeship time). Upon the recent reductions, which have taken place in the several dockyards, some riggers have been discharged, whose service therein, independent of their sea services is not sufficient to entitle them to the benefit of superannuation. We think it reasonable under the circumstances above set forth, that these persons ought not to lose the benefit of their previous service at sea. We do with all humility beg leave to recommend to your Majesty, that your Majesty will be graciously pleased to authorise us in granting superannuation to such persons employed as riggers in your dockyards.

279.　Petition of Superannuated Artificers of Chatham, Deptford and Sheerness Yards

[TNA, ADM1/5133]　　　　　　　　　　　　　　　12 June 1824

That your Lordships petitioners, feeling grateful for the interest your Lordships have at all times taken in their situation, and urged by a consideration of the condescending liberality which has been extended to every other superannuated branch of his Majesty's service, have ventured most humbly to pray that your Lordships will be pleased to consider the inadequate proportion of every article in life from the time your pensions first being settled by King and Council, and at this present time, and be pleased to make such addition to their superannuated allowance as the nature of their services and the merits of their case may deem them to deserve. Your Lordships petitioners beg most humbly to state that many of them have been employed in His Majesty's Dockyards fifty years and upwards, that the constitutions of your petitioners have greatly suffered, owing to the laborious character of the services in which they have been engaged and that the superannuated allowances in no case exceeds £24 per annum. That your petitioners, from injuries received in the service are prevented from adding thereto by any great exertions, and that many are reduced to such a state of distress, with their families, as to be under the necessity of receiving parochial relief. Under these circumstances your petitioners are induced, in a humble and dutiful manner, to obtrude this prayer upon the gracious and compassionate feelings of your Lordships, trusting you will be pleased to afford to their case that humane consideration and relief, of which they stand in so much need. Your most humble petitioners as in duty bound, will ever pray.

280. *Navy Comptroller to Secretary of Navy Board: unsigned petition*

[TNA, ADM106/1829] 17 November 1824

I return the petitions from the mechanics of Chatham, Woolwich and Deptford yards, evidently the result of communication and concert, and originating at the former yard.

The petitions are without signature, and may have been fabricated by any two or three men at each yard, but whether this is an objection to receiving them, the Board will decide, according to what may be the general practice.

Supposing the petitions to be considered unobjectionable, the difficulty is to know how to dispose of them; we have not the power to accede to the prayer, even if it were thought to be reasonable. To tell the men that they must apply to the Admiralty would be to tell them that which we should consider offensive; and no doubt it is right that every dockyard matter should come direct to the Navy Board.

To return the petition and say that we did not think proper to forward them would be forever to deprive the men of a chance of redressing what they consider a grievance and in the event of any public discussion upon the subject the Admiralty might complain that they had been kept in ignorance of any such application.

That the Admiralty will not be pleased with such petitions, I can readily believe; but as you ask my opinion with respect to the mode of disposing of them, I state that I know not how in duty, and in fairness, we can do otherwise than forward them to the Admiralty, *if the* Board admits that such unauthenticated documents are proper to be received.

This subject requires the serious consideration of the Board so that they may not be taken by surprise when it is brought under discussion I wish you would give the Committee of Correspondence and Sir Robert Seppings an opportunity of talking it over.

P.S. You may use this letter as you please within the Board room.

281. *Admiralty Response to Petition*

[TNA, ADM3/206] 18 December 1824

Acquaint the Navy Board that, in consequence of their representation of the dissatisfaction expressed by the mechanics generally in His Majesty's Dock Yards of Plymouth, Chatham, Woolwich and Deptford (as appears by their petitions) at having to perform inferior work; which arrangement was resorted to with a view to their benefit (by preventing their being discharged from the said yards when the reduction of work in their respective trades rendered it proper to diminish the number of persons employed on such description) but which it now appears by the petition before alluded to has not proved satisfactory to those who it was intended to benefit, their Lordships desire that the Navy Board will forthwith instruct the several resident commissioners at the aforesaid yards to select about 370 (which we understand to be about the number employed at those yards as smiths, scavelmen and labourers) belonging to those yards who they may deem more proper to discharge, taking care to select for discharge those of indifferent character and inferior abilities and to report to the Navy Board as early as may be convenient the names and other particulars of the persons so selected for discharge. The commissioners are to be given to understand that it is not the intention to discharge on this occasion persons entitled to pensions unless based on the age or disability of any individual.

Their Lordships have excluded Portsmouth yard from this arrangement as no complaining petition has been submitted from that yard. The Navy Board to enter such proportion of labourers as to supply the places of mechanics discharged in pursuance of the order herewith as they may deem necessary.

282. *Commissioner Cunningham to Navy Board: discharges*

[TNA, ADM106/1830] 8 January 1825

With reference to your letter of the 22nd ult., and 6th instant, to discharge shipwrights and caulkers, I request to be informed whether the persons who may be discharged in pursuance thereof, are to have the same indulgence as was allowed the workmen who were reduced in the year 1822, of one week's wages of the first class day pay over and above what may be due at the time of their discharge, agreeable to your letter of the 8th July 1822.

[*Appended note*]
The men directed to be discharged by order of the 6th are to be allowed a week's pay in the same manner as those discharged at the previous reduction.

283. *Commissioner Cunningham to Navy Board: help for discharged artificers*

[TNA, ADM106/1830]   13 January 1825

Several of the artificers who were lately discharged from this yard on reduction, have applied to me for some pecuniary assistance to enable them to remove their families to different parts in the North of England, they being unable, in many instances, to pay for a conveyance of such a distance, without greatly distressing themselves. A peculiarly hard case occurred yesterday to William Pierson, one of the shipwrights so circumstanced, who was compelled to sell his furniture in order to procure a passage to Hull in a trading vessel, for himself, his wife and three children. After having so done, he declares he shall possess but one shilling when he arrives there.

I therefore beg to suggest that some relief may be granted to such as the artificers who have been, or may be discharged in the reduction, and wish to leave this place, to enable them to proceed to their native places.

[*Appended note*]
The Board can do nothing because they have obtained a week's pay.

284. *Commissioner Cunningham to Navy Board: discharged artificers*

[TNA, ADM106/1830]   24 January 1825

With reference to your letter of the 17th instant, desiring that passages might be procured for such men, and their families, as have been discharged, and are going to the North Country, in empty sea colliers and authorising the sum of twenty shillings being paid to each man, upon his actual embarkation. I beg to observe that there are several of the discharged artificers who have been waiting for an opportunity to return by some vessel from this river, and are in daily attendance at my office in expectation of a passage being obtained for them to Hull and other places in the North Country. As there appears to be very little prospect of procuring a passage for them in vessels sailing hence for Hull &c., I suggest to the Board whether it would not be advisable to pay the twenty shillings to each of the individuals so circumstanced in order that may procure themselves with a conveyance from the London river, whence vessels are sailing almost every day for the aforementioned places.

And with regard to those with whom a stipulation was made when they were engaged I have to state, that the following men, in addition to those to whom you have authorised 20s being paid, have also applied for the same sum, stating that they were engaged under similar conditions. As there are not any documents in my office here to guide us as to whether the statement is correct or not, I request to be informed whether they are to be considered entitled to the same indulgence, and allowed the sum of 20s each to enable them to return home. I have to add that an early decision hereon is desirable, as the people appear to remain in this neighbourhood under great disadvantage and in some instances are much distressed.

[*Appended note*]
The Board cannot authorise payment in the way he suggests but must leave him to take such measures as the letter he has already used as he may judge to be necessary as they think it will be a very bad precedent.

285.   *Riggers' Petition*

[TNA, ADM106/1830]   21 April 1825

Your petitioners being informed that there is a want of sawyers to work in the pits in His Majesty's Yard at Chatham and your petitioners being healthy and strong men and having reason to believe, that their earnings will enable them better to support their families at sawing than remaining as riggers (as the price of provisions is at this time very high) your petitioners most humbly pray your honourable board will be pleased to direct that your petitioners may be entered as sawyers in His Majesty's Yard at Chatham. Your most humble petitioners will as in duty bound ever pray.

[*Appended note*]
Recommended for the consideration of the Board as we see no objection thereto. R.S.[1]

[1] Robert Seppings.

286. *Commissioner Cunningham to Navy Board: injured workman*

[TNA, ADM106/1830] 22 July 1825

With reference to your letter of 20 April 1815 I acquaint you for the information of the Lords Commissioners of the Admiralty that under the extreme case of hurt of Isaac Bristow, shipwright, as stated in the enclosed letter from the officers, it has been judged expedient to send him to the naval hospital ship for cure.

[*Enclosed letter to Cunningham from Rowlands*]
We beg to acquaint you that Isaac Bristow, shipwright, while in the execution of his duty, fell from the stern stage of the *Hogue* (about forty-five feet in height) into the dock at three o'clock this afternoon and received a dangerous wound of the skull and general contusion of whole body endangering his life; which has rendered it expedient to send him on board the *Argonaut* Hospital Ship.

287. *Commissioner Cunningham to Navy Board: holiday*

[TNA, ADM106/1832] 8 May 1826

His Majesty's birthday falling on a Sunday this year, I did not think it proper to allow the workmen of the yard the usual half-day's holiday on the Monday; but they having stated in a petition to me, that the workmen of Deptford and Woolwich yards were granted the indulgence on that day; and have requested that they may be allowed the same; I beg to be informed whether their statements relative to the workmen of the above yards is correct and if so whether the like indulgence is to be now granted to those belonging to this yard.

[*Appended note*]
See the minutes in which the general directions of 20th April 1820 are given.

16 May 1826. The officers of Woolwich were wrong in allowing the holiday and extra pay under the general order of 20th April 1820, which informed the indulgence was not to be allowed. The Board does not think it proper to allow the indulgence at Chatham. P.S. There has been no holiday at Deptford.

288.   *Commissioner Cunningham to Navy Board: chapel choir*

[TNA, ADM106/1832]   18 May 1826

Attempts have been made without affect to establish a choir of singers, with musical instruments, to assist in conducting the service at the chapel of this yard; there being consequently a great deficiency in that part of sacred worship. I beg to suggest that a suitable organ may be provided for the use of the chapel, as I understand has been done at Plymouth.

[Appended note]
Acquaint the Commissioner that his application is under consideration.

289.   *Petition: pensions*

[TNA, ADM1/5133]   27 September 1827

That your humble petitioners pray to be admitted to lay before your Royal Highness their deplorable situation they are now placed in from the low pensions they now receive, as not to procure the common necessaries of life for themselves, and family's [*sic*] now our worn out frames require more nourishment, as many of us have been employed in His Majesty services, upwards of forty years (during long wars and arduous services) and many have received such injury's [*sic*] as not to be able to help support themselves, and family's in the least, without any remuneration, let them be ever so numerous or severe.

   We trust your Royal Highness will be pleased to perceive, that our long and arduous, (and hazardous) services, has been so essential, as to raise the British navy to an undisputed Empire, so that the country has reached a degree of security, prosperity, and renown, not to be equalled by any other nation, to which we have ministered (in common) with the other branches of His Majesty's service. We beg to state after witnessing the particular attention that have, and is paid to the different departments under your Royal Highness inspection, we feel it rather hard, as our utmost exertions and orderly conduct have merited the high honour (several times) of the Right Honourable Board of Admiralty, thanks, and now may it please your Royal Highness, (we believe) we are the only ones who are situated inside such a distressful situation.

   We beg to state that our pensions (at first) granted in the year 1764 the highest rate of pension for a mechanic was £20 a year two-thirds of our daily pay, at that time and now our highest rate of pension is £24 a year.

Let our service be ever so long, and every article of necessaries of life (and house rent) now is double (or more) the price it was then.

We pray further to state that by an Honourable Board of Revision, some year's [*sic*] back, we were to have been pensioned with a more ample provision. As well as for every other department, in His Majesty service, we are sorry to say the working party only had not been paid agreeable thereto, clerks of His Majesty Dock yard who before received £30 a year pension, can now receive £200 or £300 a year, and our late quartermen who then received from £24 to £28 a year can now receive up to £80 a year pension, for their longest servitude.

290. *Commissioner Cunningham to Navy Board: teams*

[TNA, ADM106/1836] 24 January 1828

Received your letter of the 27th ultimo acquainting me that it is intended to discontinue as much as possible the use of teams in His Majesty's dockyards by the substitution of convicts. You therefore wish arrangements made for carrying this plan into execution when the present contract for teams terminates, according to the notice given to contractors on the 21st of last month.

In reply to which I beg to observe that I have caused various trials to be made with a view to ascertaining if possible to what services the convicts could be applied, instead of horses and, where it was applicable, how many would be required to supply the place of one team. The result has proved that in the removal of timber and heavy articles of stone, forty convicts were only equal to one team of horses. There are many services, where it would be impossible that labour and men could be supplied for that of horses: drawing the timber from the wharf to the pickling pond (a distance of at least half a mile) and from thence, after being immersed, to the pits for conversion; removing the larger pieces (such as beams, stems, stern posts, keels &c) to the docks and slips and other heavy stores from place to place (such as lead, chain cables, mooring chains, anchors &c &c.). Likewise tarring of yarn.

When the great length of this yard and its hilly nature is considered, in connection with the foregoing services which are daily carrying on, it must appear that manual labour cannot be applied here so successfully as in other yards where the operations are more contiguous to each other. Under all these circumstances, I do not consider that the service of the yard, with all the aid derived from the convicts, can be carried on with a less number than ten teams. Even with that number, I am fearful that some works will unavoidably fall into arrears, especially if the building and repair of large ships continues to be carried on to the extent they now are in this yard.

291. *Admiralty to Commissioner Cunningham: termination of chip money*

[NMM, CHA/E/151]   13 January 1830

In pursuance of an Order from the Lords Commissioners of the Admiralty, dated 9th inst., I am commanded by the Commissioners of the Navy to direct that payment of chip money to the workmen will cease on 1st of next month.

In communicating to the Board these directions, their Lordships have been pleased to state that there was no other alternative than that of immediately dismissing one-sixth of the workmen to offset the necessary retrenchments. Their Lordships are led to hope, and believe, the mode adopted is that which is likely to produce the least individual distress, which you are, accordingly, to make known to the workmen. If, however, there be any of them who may not be desirous of continuing in the yard after the reduction of the chip money, such persons are to be discharged forthwith.

Their Lordships further desire that it be most distinctly understood that the regulation against the removing of chips or any other article whatsoever are to be kept in full force. Any person offending against them is to be immediately expelled and never again received into His Majesty's service. It is also strictly enjoined that the orders should continue in force, which forbid the entering of any more men or apprentices in the yards (except appointed in lieu of others dying, or discharged before the expiration of their time) until the total number be reduced to a scale to be hereafter made known to you.

The Board is to be informed of any vacancies, which may occur among the apprentices from the causes above mentioned.

292. *Commissioner Cunningham to Navy Board: services upon which convicts were employed during the week ending 9 July 1831*[1]

[TNA ADM106/1841]   12 July 1831

Loading and unloading mud barges	51
Excavating and driving piles at engine house (well)	8

[1] Figures refer to days worked.

Getting materials into and clearing out ships	30
Filling in earth &c at culvert drain to docks	19
Assisting riggers on works in Master Attendant's department afloat	47
Excavating for burying masts in mud	15
Excavating at mast pond	10
Boathouse storing boats, gear &c	16
Carting and clearing timber for survey	11
Clearing docks and slips	21
Mast houses storing gear &c	7
Shipping, landing, weighing and housing stores	22
Stowing, spreading, fitting, carting &c timber	213
Beating hemp	6
Sweeping, weeding and clearing the yard	30
Stacking old timber for monthly sale	6
Sorting chips from rubbish	12
Picking oakum	7
Picking nails from dirt rubbish	7
	538

293.   *Chatham Yard Officers to Navy Board: infirm rope makers*

[TNA, ADM106/1841]   15 December 1831

In obedience to your directions of yesterday's date we beg to report that the rope makers named in the margin are the only persons employed in the ropery who, from age or infirmity, are incapable of performing a day's work. These men were so reported to your honourable board in January last, in the quarterly returns No 125, but it was ordered by your secretary's letter of the 31st of that month, that they should continue to be employed in the yard, on such light works as they were able to perform; their periods of service not being sufficiently long to entitle them to superannuation.

294.   *Plight of Dockyard Artisans*

[*Rochester Gazette*]   18 September 1832

The late extensive reductions in the civil naval establishment of this country have created the greatest surprise amongst those most conversant with the subject, and who very naturally enquire, what can be the object the ministers have in view? Is it that our navy is less than it has been in former times – or is it intended that it shall be so reduced? – So far from the former being the case, it will be found on comparison that we have four times the number of ships that we had ninety years ago; and viewing the present efficient state of the navies of other countries, it must be admitted that we have occasion for them at least in four-fold degree. Yet, with these facts staring us in the face, it will scarcely be credited that the establishment of Chatham dockyard is now so reduced as to give employment to 600 mechanics less than it did ninety years since. What must be the result of this misplaced economy may readily be conceived. When our ships require to be repaired and fitted for sea, the effective men now discharged and who are wandering the country to seek subsistence, will either have emigrated to other lands or be found to have prematurely died in consequence of being deprived of that employment which they had hitherto been led to believe was of permanent duration. Every enlightened man admits that a Navy is necessary for the protection of this country. It is also considered indispensable that each ship should be provided with masts, anchors and all the material necessary to her equipment; but of what can these avail, if they have not the skilful hand of the mechanic to fix and support them? Are not then, we would ask, these animated appendages of ten-fold more value than the equipments? And be it remembered that while the latter make no return on the capital expended on them (and that a sinking one) the mechanic must positively earn his five shillings before he can receive it. We trust that those who at present hold the helm of our naval affairs may yet be induced to put the ship about ere they find the water too shallow to float her.

295.   *Chatham Yard Officers to Superintendent Gordon: anchor smiths*

[TNA ADM1/3386]   9 November 1832

In obedience to your direction of the 2nd instant to report on the propriety of allowing the smiths to go out of the yard to dine and to state fully our objections. We beg to submit that we think the practice objectionable for the following reasons:

1st   When on anchor work it frequently occurs that the heat requires the men, between the hours of twelve and two, and also when the *Hercules* is used, to obtain the assistance of other men not employed on the anchors.

2nd   Most of the men reside at a considerable distance from the yard and there will be some time lost in washing themselves and changing their clothes before going out. In summer time they will be exhausted on their arrival at home, will not readily partake in their dinner and returning in haste, with a stomach loaded, it will operate much to the injury of their health.

The smiths are differently circumstanced to the rest of the workmen. When detained their dinnertime in the yard they [the rest] cannot without any interruption to the service put their dinner in a kettle on the fire, which will be in a state of preparation against the time appointed to dine. Again, such men, whose habits are not quite correct, will be exposed to the temptation to take some spirits on the way home under the notion of producing a better appetite and, on their return, repeat the principle under the idea of promoting digestion. We apprehend an additional expenditure of coals especially in the large fires. Another objection is that it frequently happens that at 12 o'clock a demand is made for ironwork afloat (and otherwise) which, by the time the workmen return, such work will be prepared and the service will be expedited.

296. *Admiralty to Superintendent Gordon: reduced working hours*

[NMM, CHA/H/5]   3 January 1833

Notwithstanding the order of the late Navy Board of June 1822, 'to employ artificers upon ships in commission, fitting or repairing six days in the week' I am commanded by My Lords Commissioners of the Admiralty to signify their directions here to consider that part of the said order cancelled. You are to direct them to work only the usual time upon such ships without special order from their Lordships.

297. *Superintendent Gordon to Admiralty: hours of employment*

[TNA, ADM1/3391]   23 May 1833

			Morning		Afternoon
October	9	[*From*]	6 o'clock	[*until*]	¾ past 5
	15		6 o'clock		½ past 5
	22		6 o'clock		¼ past 5
	29		¼ past 6		5 o'clock
November	9		½ past 6		¾ past 4
	21		¾ past 6		½ past 4
	27		7 o'clock		¼ past 4
January	9		7 o'clock		½ past 4

	18	¾ past 6	¾ past 4
	29	¾ past 6	5 o'clock
February	8	½ past 6	¼ past 5
	16	¼ past 6	½ past 5
	24	6 o'clock	¾ past 5
March	1	6 o'clock	6 o'clock

Times for Breakfast and Dinner

	Breakfast	Dinner
From the 2nd February to the 8th November inclusive.	In the yard from 8 to ½ past.	One hour and a half from 12 to ½ past 1.
From the 9th February to the 1st February. In which case are to appear so early as to be mustered and appear at their work by 8 o'clock.	Before they come into the yard.	One hour.

298. *Admiralty to Dockyard Commissioners: ending of task work*

[TNA, ADM1/3480]   22 June 1833

The reductions of the establishment of artificers, labourers and tradesmen in HM Dock Yards to 6,000 men being now completed (and their Lordships having now carefully considered the opinion and propositions of the several superintending and professional officers submitted to them in consequence of my circular letter of the 18th of April last) I am directed to signify to you the decision they have come to on this important subject. It appears to be a general opinion in which their Lordships entirely concur that the system of task work as carried out in the dockyards is wholly inapplicable to the number of workmen still borne on the yards as compared with the quantity of work to be done. Instead of it being what task work implies, a means of enabling a man to earn additional pay beyond what ordinary day work would give him, task work in the dockyards prohibits a man from earning beyond a fixed maximum which being little if anything more than a common day's work is without any extraordinary exertion obtained by all, or which amounts to the same thing, is paid to all with very few exceptions. Yet, in order to ascertain whether the workmen exceed or fall short of this maximum, or perhaps more correctly speaking to square the earnings of all precisely to it, not fewer than 40 measurers are employed with very high salaries. Such a fallacious and nugatory system as this in time of peace, especially when at least 10,000 men are kept in the yards, more than absolutely necessary ought not to be suffered any longer to continue in operation. Their Lordships have therefore decided that for the present all task work shall cease. That in lieu thereof, a moderate rate of day pay (to be the same in the summer and winter) shall be established for the several descriptions of artificers and labourers in the yard. [The artificers and labourers] shall, for the present, be classed and arranged in such a manner as their Lordships trust will ensure to each man the fruits of his good conduct, skill and industry [and] excite a spirit of emulation by the encouragement it holds out to the good and efficient workmen. At the same time it will place in a lower scale the less efficient, idle and indifferent, preparatory to the introduction of the new scheme of work about to be explained.

Their Lordships' commands are to signify to you their directions that you forthwith make such arrangements as maybe necessary for measuring up and settling all the accounts to the 30th of the present month so as to enable to commence working on day pay on the first of July next. It ought to be mentioned that if at any future period it should be found expedient on an emergency again to have recourse to task work, their Lordships reserve to themselves to judge of the nature of the work to be performed and the class and number of men to be employed as the occasion may appear to be required.

The scheme which their Lordships have proposed for putting the whole of the workmen in the dockyard under your control on a system of day pay will be at once explained by taking that class of men which are the most numerous and important, the shipwrights, caulkers and joiners employed under the Master Shipwright. This officer has the general superintendence of all the artificers and labourers of this extensive department, but the artificers above mentioned may be considered as more immediately in charge of his assistants who in those yards where there are two may divide between them in equal proportions or nearly so the superintendence over the said artificers and labourers. They are also in like manner to divide and take under their charge the foreman of the yard, a new class of officers to be named inspectors and the leading men. The shipwrights, caulkers and joiners (including apprentices) are to be classed into divisions of sixty men each, subdivided into companies of 30 and again into gangs of 15 men each.

Over a division of 60 is to be placed one foreman, over a company of 30 one inspector, of 15 one leading man [who will] work with his gang.

299.   *Admiralty to Superintendent Gordon: St Clements's Day*

[NMM, CHA/H/7]   12 July 1833

I am commanded by My Lords Commissioners of the Admiralty to signify their direction to you to give notice to the smiths that the absurd custom observed on St. Clements's Day is to be discontinued. If they wish to cease working for a half a day they must also cease to be paid for it.

300.   *Superintendent Gordon to Admiralty: classification scheme*

[TNA, ADM1/3394]   30 July 1833

In obedience to the commands of My Lords Commissioners of the Admiralty communicated in Mr Barrow's circular letter of the 21st ultimo and 20th inst. I beg leave to transmit enclosed a scheme for the proposed classification of the artificers and workmen of this yard. I beg you will assure their lordships that I have taken every means in my power, which my observations and the assistance of the officers have obtained, for me to render impartial justice to all.

In order that their lordships may be enabled to judge better of my proceedings in this very important matter I have to state that as regards the three principal divisions of shipwrights, caulkers and joiners I first caused each foreman to deliver to me a list of the men who were in their opinion best fitted to the respective classes. I then assembled all the shipwright officers from the Master Shipwright to the inspectors and put every man's qualifications to the vote, causing the inspectors to make a show of hands in each instance previously to and distinct from the other officers in order that they might not be influenced by the votes of their superiors. After every man's abilities and merits had been thus canvassed I selected the names of those who had the most votes for promotion into the first class. I find on examining the papers that some of the men whom the foremen had previously recommended for the first class had scarcely any votes from the inspectors. This leads me to infer that the choice made by the latter was wholly uninfluenced and unbiased by the former. I have paid more attention to the inspectors from their having actually worked with the men and thus had more means of knowing them thoroughly than to the votes of the other officers.

In selecting sail makers for the first class I made choice of 4 men who, in addition to being good workmen, volunteered to serve in Canada, Malta and Bermuda at periods when their service was much required.

Although it may appear there is one inspector borne to the shipwrights beyond the number authorised, yet – the whole number of inspectors to the three classes of shipwrights, caulkers and joiners is as nearly as possible the proportion allowed.

In conclusion, I beg to remark that, for many years past there has been no general entry of workmen, but on the contrary, there have been frequent and extensive reductions. On these occasions I am informed by the officers, the idle and worthless have been discharged. I trust this will satisfactorily account to their Lordships for so few men having been placed in the third class on the present occasion.

[*Enclosure*]

Scheme of the classification of the workmen of this yard as arranged by the Captain Superintendent per Admiralty orders of 21st ultimo and 20th inst.

Shipwrights.
Number
borne this day   484

Inspectors	16
Single station men	
1st class	11
2nd class	7
Leading men of gangs	30
1st class men	60
2nd class men	345
3rd class men	8
Apprentices	7
Total	484

Block makers	2	
2nd class		1
3rd class		1

Treenail
and coke makers   4
         All in the 3rd class

Oar makers   1
         In the 2nd class

Caulkers   30

Inspectors	1
Leading men of gangs	2
1st class men	4
2nd class men	23
Total	30

Joiners   71

Inspectors	2
Single station men	3
Leading men of gangs	5
1st class men	10
2nd class men	51
Total	71

Turner   1
      In the 2nd class.

Wheelwrights   2
      1 in the 1st class for servitude and the other in the 2nd.

Coopers   2
      In the 2nd class

Smiths   103

Leading men	7
1st class men	14
2nd class men	72
Apprentices	10
Total	103

When employed on anchors above twenty hundredweight have 4/6d a day.

Sawyers. Top men.   37

In the 1st class	4
In the 2nd class	33

Six top men are necessarily employed in sharpening saws at the saw mill.

Sawyers. Pitmen   29

In the 1st class   4
In the 2nd class   25

Bricklayers   6
   1 leading man in charge of stores and acting as master.
   3 in the 2nd class
   2 in the 3rd class

Paviours   2
   In the 1st class for yard labourers

Masons   1
   In the 2nd class

Painters and Glaziers   13
Grinders   1
   Leading men   1
   In the 1st class   2
   In the 2nd class   8
   In the 3rd class   3
        Total   14

Braziers and tin men   3
Plumbers   4
   In the 1st class   1
   In the 2nd class   6
        Total   7

Steam engine keepers   3
   All in the 2nd class

Locksmiths   2
   Both in 3rd class

Millwrights   5
   In the 1st class   1
   In the 2nd class   4

Oakum boys   5
   At 10d a day

Yard labourers   76

Single station men	22
Assistant Boatswain of Yard	1
Leading men of gangs	3
In 1st class	7
In 2nd class	43
Total	76

Sail makers   25

Leading men	2
In 1st class	4
In 2nd class	18
Apprentices	1
Total	25

Riggers   40

Single station men	4
Leading men of gangs	3
1st class	6
2nd class	17
3rd class	10
Total	40

Rope makers   127

Layers		3
Leading men		4
1st class		16
2nd class	Varying from day to day and	
3rd class	according to work in hand.	122

Those employed as labourers paid as 3rd class men

Houseboys	18	paid at 1s per day

Storehouse men   17

Single station men in loan tool shed	1
Leading men	3
1st class men	2
2nd class men	11

Taylor   1
    At 3s per day

Messengers   7
    At 3s per day

Total
    1st class   171
    2nd class   700
    3rd class   251
Total borne this day   1122[1]

301. *Admiralty to Superintendent Gordon: holidays*

[NMM, CHA/H/7]   13 September 1833

I am commanded by My Lords Commissioners of the Admiralty to acquaint you that when the holidays authorised by the new general instructions fall on a Sunday they are to be observed on the following day.

302. *Admiralty to Dockyard Superintendents: apprentices*

[TNA, ADM222/3]   5 November 1833

Their Lordships having decided that all apprentices admitted in future into the dockyards shall be bound to the Master Shipwright, Master Attendant or foreman of the trades that they may respectively belong as apprentices to the government; and that the above mentioned officers shall be held responsible, with inspectors and leading men. The said apprentices shall be properly instructed and fully qualified on the expiration of their apprenticeships [and] to be entered into the establishment of the yards as efficient workmen. To ensure which, the officers shall be required to produce to the superintendent, quarterly certificates of their ability and good conduct during the progress of their servitude.

    Their Lordships having further decided that for the present the entry of apprentices shall be confined to the Master Shipwright's department, and that 130 shipwright apprentices shall be considered as the number to be allowed for the purpose of keeping up a succession of these valuable artificers of which number it appears the yard under your superintendence requires 18.[2] You are, therefore, directed to select and propose the names of 18 candidates for the approval of their Lordships before the expiration of the present month. In doing [this] you are to give the preference to the sons of meritorious artificers and to those who have generally been well educated. In sending them up for their Lordships' approval you are to

---

[1]All figures are as given in the original document.
[2]This number varied between yards: Pembroke 9, Devonport 23, Woolwich 2, Sheerness 10 and Portsmouth 24. TNA, ADM 222/3, 30 Oct. 1833.

accompany them with a certificate from the surgeon conformable with the ninth article of his instructions.

The scale of pay to be allowed to apprentices is as follows:

1st year	1/-d per day
2nd year	1/6d per day
3rd year	2/0d per day
4th year	2/6d per day
5th year	3/0d per day
6th year	3/6d per day
7th year	Eligible for entry into the 2nd class if in all respects fit, but not in preference to the rest in that class equally fit.

You are clearly to understand and the parents or guardians of the boys, they are definitely to be told that no other allowance, whatever, will be granted either for instruction or maintenance.

With regard to the apprentices now belonging to the yards, they will be continued under the existing regulations during the remainder of their apprenticeship, except that in the event of the promotion or removal of their present instructors they will then become government apprentices and no other instructors are to be appointed.

303. *George Hammond, Retired Inspector of Shipwrights, in Conversation with a Local Newspaper Reporter*

[*Chatham News,* 10 July 1897]

'And when did you enter the yard?'

'It was in the year 1834 that I went in as a shipwright apprentice, and it might be interesting to note the difference of entry then and now. Captain Sir James Gordon was the captain-superintendent at the time, and my father who was employed in the yard, went to see him with a view to getting me into the dockyard. The captain told him to let me write a letter. I did so and took it to his office. The captain, who had lost a leg, was resting his wooden stump on a chair, and when I presented my letter he read it and then roared out "Who wrote this?" "I did, Sir James," I replied. "And who edited it?" he enquired. To which I again replied, "I did, Sir James." "Don't tell any lies," he said. Calling to his clerk for a pen and paper, he made me write my name, and also gave me a sum to work out. And what do you think it consisted of? Simply two sums of figures to add up. When I finished he caught hold of my hair and thundered out, "why the h — don't you get your hair cut?" Swearing was very rife in those days. That was the only examination I had to pass, but things are very different now.'

304. *Admiralty to Dockyard Superintendents: working hours*

[NMM, CHA/H/35]   11 June 1834

I am commanded by My Lords Commissioners of the Admiralty to send to you a copy of a proposal for fixing the hours of work in the several yards. I am to signify their Lordships directions to you in concurrence with the Master Shipwright to report your opinion thereof for their information.

Proposals for Dock Yard Hours as follows:

First
The bell to ring at 6.45 for ten minutes in the morning.
Call to commence at 7 o'clock in the summer months.

Second
At 11.50 the bell to toll to break off work and return cabin stores and tools and then to ring out at 12 o'clock.

Third
At 1.15 the bell to ring for ten minutes. Muster to begin at 1.30 and the yard gates to close at that time.

Fourth
At 5.15 the bell to toll for breaking off work and to return stores and tools & then to ring out at 6 o'clock, completing a day of nine and a half hours work including muster.

By this mode of proceeding I am of the opinion that the dockyard people will be employed 9 hours per day (Summer months).
    It appears that the great difference in the hours of each yard amounts to time lost only by mustering &c – All these points will be rectified by the superintendent as the localities of each dockyard will dictate and it will not exceed 30 minutes in a day's work, and not interfere with the general hours of the yard here laid down.
    In all cases when the steam engines and forges are worked, the man should be employed dinner hours and paid at the rate of 6d per day for

such or permitted to go out of the yard one hour sooner at night. This matter [absence during dinner time] is very objectionable and of great inconvenience to the other workers of the yard who frequently experience delay in completion of a particular piece of work by the smith or engineer being out of the way. With respect to shipwrights, caulkers and joiners when employed afloat in the equipment of ships for sea, they being employed their dinner hour and having their time in the evenings is also a great inconvenience to the riggers and fitting out by the ships company. In all cases, if on ships in commission, they should be paid for the hour but when in ordinary then only at that time should this be attended to. It would be highly beneficial not only to the facility of equipment but a great saving as to expenditure of material and labour, which is unquestionably lost by the delay of getting up fires and steam at a rate of about 25% in the half day.

305. *Admiralty Memorandum: classification*

[TNA, ADM1/3484] 15 November 1834

My Lord Commissioners of the Admiralty, having had under their consideration, on their return from the late visitation to the dockyards, the recent mode of distinguishing the shipwrights and other artificers, where their number will admit of it into three classes. [They are also] persuaded that this mode of classification, if duly carried into practice, is equally calculated for the good of His Majesty's service and for the benefit and encouragement of good workmen. As a sure road to promotion whenever vacancies occur, [they] have been pleased, as a further encouragement to able and meritorious workmen, to direct that one additional first class man shall be promoted in each gang of 15 where the gangs are complete.

Their lordships having understood that in some of the yards, the selection of men to be promoted from one class to another, differs from the manner in which it is made in others. Being of opinion that one fixed rule ought to be observed in all, their lordships have been pleased to direct that, from and after the receipt of this order, that upon a vacancy occurring of a leading man of any of the gangs, or of a first class man, the selection is to be made on the principle of seniority and merit: where a zealous exertion has been manifested and no objection exists to either on the score of inability or good conduct on the part of the man to be so selected. If the senior workman be considered by the Master Shipwright and shipwright officers, or by the heads of these departments in which the vacancies may occur, as disqualified to fill the situation, a report of his unfitness is to be made to the Surveyor of the Navy (stating the grounds thereof). [He] is to represent the same for their lordships. The second in seniority is then to be appointed as above-mentioned. In this manner is to be selected the third first class man now ordered to be promoted in each gang. My lords further desire that you be present at the examination of the persons reported to be as unfit.

On the same principle of rewarding gangs for meritorious work their lordships are equally desirous that the idle, the negligent and undeserving, either from inability or misconduct, should be punished by disrating and placing them in the third class, provided such an inability and misconduct be not of the degree which will merit their discharge from the yard altogether.

The third class is also to be considered, conformably with the original intention, as the proper class for the probation of new men, whose abilities have not been ascertained.

306. *Admiralty to Dockyard Superintendents: reaction to petitions*

[TNA, ADM1/3486]   21 July 1835

My Lords have under their consideration a petition from several workmen of the royal dockyard at Devonport as well as the representations which have been made to them from other yards the purport of which is an augmentation of wages, for the abolition of the present system of classification, and for such relief as may otherwise be afforded to the grievances of which they complain.

My Lords command me to assure you that it is their anxious desire that all who are employed in the yards under the direction of the Board of Admiralty shall receive a fair remuneration for their labour. Having given their best attention to the rate of wages as at present regulated they are satisfied that it was fixed after the most mature consideration by the Board of 1833 and after the most careful enquiry into the rate of wages in merchant yards.

From all the information which they have been able to obtain, they have no doubt that the rate of pay in the yards paid to men in the second class according to the present system, independent of other advantages, is at least equal to the earnings which can be gained from year end to year end in merchant yards even in the River Thames. They cannot but feel that if they were to raise the wages of artificers in the dockyards it would give greater force to the representations made to them of the advantage on the grounds of economy of work done by contract and which might consequently lead to the reduction of the dockyard establishment.

While therefore my lords lament that in some instances the necessity of the men, particularly those with large families, should press too closely upon their earnings, they cannot feel themselves justified in the view they take in their present duty in holding out to them expectation of an increase in wages.

307. *Report of a Speech Given by William Evenden, a Dockyard Joiner of the Second Class, at the Sun Tavern*

[*Rochester Gazette*] 13 December 1836

Mr Evenden said he was convinced that all his fellow countrymen would agree that there was not any body of mechanics so grievously oppressed and so ungratefully treated as those employed in His Majesty's dockyards. When it was considered that they were the men who built their ships and framed the bulwarks of their country, it was hard that they should be called on to suffer so many privations. They had a claim on their country for their exertions at a time when those exertions were most needed. When had there ever been since the peace a cry raised throughout the country of the necessity for retrenchment, in which the dockyards had not suffered most severely. Various had been those retrenchments; they had suffered in their time, in their pay, and in their perquisites; and such being the case, they must of necessity suffer a retrenchment in their comforts.

Previous to the conclusion of the war they continued on what was termed 'task work', when the lowest pay was 5s a day, and that being the case they were not allowed to earn more. This continued for a short time, when a further reduction was made. In 1822 a still further reduction was imposed upon them. At that time the necessities of life were very cheap. If his recollection failed him not, bread was 8d. per gallon, whereas they were now called to labour under a further reduction of wages to £1 and 17s per week, with an increased price as respects bread; &c, which rendered their wages quite inadequate to their support.

When some of them with large families had taken a portion of their wages for rent, rates, and other necessary expenses, what did the meeting suppose they had left? Why, nothing more than 2¼d a head per day! Was this right? Were those men, who had contributed so largely by their labour in forming the bulwarks of their country, to be called upon to suffer every privation, and to feed upon bread and salt?

Quite willing were they to bear their proportion of the burden, but they were overloaded. After all the retrenchments that had been made, after all they had suffered, they thought they had endured the worst; but then was introduced that degrading and humiliating system of classification. (Cheers).

They had thought that the blessings of peace would surely bestow upon them some privileges of which they had now a taste; but no, sunk as they were almost to the earth by hardships, yet there was introduced this system. Some perhaps present did not understand what the system was. The advocates for it stated that it was a stimulus for exertion, and he would ask the meeting what necessity there was for this, at a time when they had received a vote of thanks from the Admiralty for their exertions. It was a useless thing – it was an oppressive system – inasmuch as it deprived a man and his family of many of those comforts of which they had before been partaking. He had said it was a degrading system, and it certainly was so.

He would appeal to any present, supposing they had been in the yard 20 years, and were put in the second class – how would they like to see a young man, who had been probably the apprentice, placed in the first class? Would it not be naturally supposed that the aged workman had done something whereby he had disgraced himself? The number of first class men was limited to 3 and 15 …

308.   *Public Petition: classification*

[Rochester Gazette]   13 December 1836

That your memorialists believe the system of classification adopted in His Majesty's dockyards was introduced with the earnest desire to reward merit and encourage industry, but are fully assured from observation and the testimony of the workmen, that it has signally failed to accomplish this object. They believe that it has created most invidious distinctions amongst the workmen where no difference exists in merit. So much so as to cause in many instances the promotion to be deprecated rather than desired; that it is the cause of continual discord and jealousy, and tends to destroy that unity and good feeling which should at all times subsist between fellow-workmen, and that no beneficial effect has resulted, or can result there from, to the service of His Majesty.

Your memorialists are also respectfully to represent to your lordships that the evils of classification under which our fellow townsmen are borne down and disheartened, are much aggravated by their low wages, especially with the present advanced prices of nearly all kinds of provisions. At the same time, the wages of operatives in private yards, are steadily on the advance. In London and Liverpool, where there is constant employment, the rate of pay is considerably higher than in the dockyard.

Your memorialists respectfully beg to draw your lordships attention to the foregoing statement, and venture with entire confidence to appeal to your lordships on behalf of our fellow-townsmen, entirely to abolish the system of classification, and so to advance the wages of the men in His Majesty's dockyard in this place that they may be enabled to educate and bring up their families in as respectful and comfortable manner as the operatives in private yards and prevent the secession of valuable young men from the service of His Majesty.

309.   *Petition of Hired Rope Makers*

[TNA, ADM1/5137]   5 January 1839

Your Lordships have been pleased to establish and recognise certain holidays for the workmen of Her Majesty's dockyards. Your petitioners, when engaged by the master, were promised their pay on these occasions, and equal privilege with the regular workmen. Your petitioners beg to state that they were deprived of their wages for Christmas Day. As most of your petitioners have families dependent upon them for support, as their wages are barely sufficient, with the present high price of provisions, to procure the necessaries of life. Such deprivation most seriously affects them and increases their present indigent circumstances. Your petitioners respectfully state, that they entrusted to the superintendent of this yard a humble petition to your Lordships, soliciting of your Lordships the favour to order them to be paid for the day of the late King's funeral, as the hired rope makers of Portsmouth yard were allowed their pay upon that occasion. To their humble request your petitioners received no answer.

Your petitioners, in case of injury in the service, receive neither medical assistance, nor other relief, to which the regular workmen are entitled. They, therefore, consider this circumstance a strong argument in promotion of the claim upon your Lordships' favour. Your petitioners also beg leave to mention, that, as they perform the same description of work as the regular workmen (but with less wages per week) it appears to them an additional motive in support of the claim they lay before your lordships.

Your petitioners, under these circumstances, are induced most humbly to solicit your lordships to take their case into your favourable consideration, and that you will be pleased to grant to your petitioners their wages for all the established holidays. Your petitioners for such favour will be most grateful, and are in duty bound, will ever pray.

310. *Petition of Anchor Smiths*

[TNA, ADM1/5137]   12 January 1839

Your lordships petitioners have been many years in Her Majesty's service, during which they trust their conduct has been such as to merit the approbation of their officers.

Your Lordships' petitioners have families dependent on them, and each a son who is of the proper age, and qualified for entry as apprentices in the dockyard. As your Lordships' petitioners are precluded the advantage of having them entered as apprentices to shipwrights, caulkers &c in consequence of the men belonging to those branches having sons eligible for entry, who have of course a prior claim to the sons of your petitioners, they therefore most humbly beg your Lordships will be graciously pleased to take their case into your consideration and grant them the indulgence of having their sons entered as apprentices to smiths in this dockyard. For which your Lordships' petitioners will as in duty bound ever pray.

311. *Deputation of Shipwrights to Admiralty*

[*Rochester Gazette*]   2 June 1840

A deputation of two of the shipwrights from Chatham dockyard, with a like number from each of the other yards, and accompanied by thirteen Members of Parliament, had last week an interview with the Lords of the Admiralty, relative to the extremely low rate of their wages. Amongst the members who accompanied them were the Hon. G.S. Byng, Mr Bernal and Mr Barnard, the members for Greenwich. The deputation having stated the object of their visit, Lord Minto observed that the shipwrights in Her Majesty's dockyards had privileges, which were equivalent to 7s per week; and the deputation inquired in what those privileges consisted? His Lordship named superannuation as one of them. To this it was answered, that only one in nineteen on an average lived to be entitled to it, and that if they received a proper remuneration for their labour, they were willing to contribute to a fund for that purpose. Another advantage, his Lordship considered, was that of having a medical man to attend them. To this the deputation replied, that it was only in cases of being hurt in the service that his assistance was called for and that most master builders in private yards under such circumstances, allowed the whole wages to be continued to their servants, while government only allowed half their pay. The system of classification also came under discussion, the deputation strongly protesting against its continuance. In this they were ably supported by Mr Bernal. It was also stated that while the shipwrights employed in one of the docks at Woolwich yard, repairing a ship for government received 4s per day, those employed on the Thames in the next dock, fitting her by contract for a convict ship, were receiving 6s 6d per day.

312. *Admiralty to Superintendent of Pembroke Yard: shipwright recruitment*

[NMM, CHA/H/36]   3 September 1840

With reference to your letter of the 2nd Inst., I am to signify their directions to you that you are to send Mr Blessley to Ireland to enter 40 shipwrights for HM dockyards, at Chatham and Sheerness, allowing the men to select the Yard they may prefer. You are to refer him to his former instructions and to the printed advertisement, for his guidance, worded to avoid all complaints on the part of the men. He must make clear our agreement with them in writing.

With regard to the information required by Mr Blessley, as reported in your letter, you are to acquaint him that a week's wages will be allowed from the day of embarkation for the time lost in the passage. If the time so employed should exceed a week, no more shall be allowed. Subsistence of 1/4d per diem is to be allowed as in his former instructions, to be deducted from the week's wages.

The men are at liberty to embark their wives and families at the Irish port and if approved at Pembroke they will proceed to Chatham and Sheerness. If rejected they will be sent back to Ireland without any claim to the balance of the week's wages beyond the sum of 1/4d per diem advanced for subsistence.

If any man should embark for Pembroke, and having passed, return to Ireland for their wives and families, they will not be allowed the time so lost. Nor will they receive more than one week's wages in subsistence.

Their regular pay will begin from the day they commence work in the dockyard, and whenever there is a naval surgeon he will be directed to examine the men.

My Lords desire that you will order Mr Blessley to proceed to such ports as he thinks will furnish the best men, and to report his proceeding at each point to the Surveyor of the Navy, taking care to give timely notice for a steam vessel to take the men over.

313. Mechanics' Grievances

[*Rochester Gazette*] 15 September 1840

Messrs Buchan, Rowe, Nichols, Simpson and Sampson, deputation from the mechanics of the dockyard, had an interview with the Lords Commissioners of the Admiralty at the Superintendent's office on Thursday se'nnight, for the purpose of hearing the opinion of their Lordships respecting the petition setting forth a statement of grievances recently forwarded to the board. The deputation was most courteously received, and their Lordships stated, that with respect to classification, they should accede to the wishes of the workmen. As vacancies occurred, in what is now called the first class, they would not be filled up. Those now receiving the pay would continue to do so. Promotion would take place, too, without regard to the distinction. Their Lordships further said that no increase of pay could be granted.

314. Order-in-Council: revision of pay rates

[TNA, ADM1/5502] 10 November 1840

Having had occasion to revise the table of pay authorised by His Late Majesty's order in council of 18 July 1833 for the civil artificers of Your Majesty's dockyards so far as relates to the pay of Smiths employed in heavy anchor work and being humbly of opinion that the pay therein sanctioned is insufficient and having moreover ascertained that a different pay has prevailed in the eastern and western dockyards from a misconstruction of the aforesaid order we beg leave most humbly to represent to your Majesty that we are of opinion that it would be beneficial to your Majesty's service that the higher rate which has prevailed in the yards first mentioned were generally adopted as the pay of smiths when employed on anchors above 20 hundredweight. [This] shall be fixed at 4/6d a day in all classes with an additional allowance of 6d a day for beer instead of 4d a day as was the intention of the order in council above mentioned.

We further beg leave most humbly to represent to Your Majesty that at the various great changes made with regard to the pay and situation of the dockyard artificers by the said order in council of the 18th July 1833 (and our arrangements considered thereon) a few instances have occurred of our having granted an increase of 6d and in some cases a shilling a day to certain artificers the amount of whose pay did not appear to be sufficiently considered at the time without having received the authority of Your Majesty's Order in Council with such deviations from the established Pay Table. We humbly adjoin a list of such deviations in the hopes that Your Majesty will be pleased to sanction the same and we beg leave to most humbly state that the Lords of Your Majesty's Treasurer have signified their concurrence.

315.　*Order-in-Council: superannuation*

[TNA, ADM1/5511]　　　　　　　　　　　　　　　　11 August 1842

We beg leave to most humbly to bring under your Majesty's consideration the situation as regards the superannuation of the rope makers employed at Your Majesty's dockyards.

Under the authority of an order in council dated 20 September 1809 these men are classed with carpenters, bricklayers and others and are granted pensions varying from £15 to £20 a year according to their length of service, character. Under the authority of the same order in council caulkers, joiners and others are allowed pensions varying from £20 to £24 a year.

Noting this, the rope makers are thus placed upon an inferior scale in regard to their pensions. It appears that the duties that they have to perform are not only of a more laborious nature than those generally performed by many of the first class artificers of the yards but are also in their effects more detrimental to their constitution and tend to impair their strength and to shorten the duration of their lives. To this may also be added the great difficulty of obtaining good workmen of this class. In all of which circumstances we are humbly of opinion that they are fairly entitled to be favourably considered as regards their superannuation allowances.

We do therefore most humbly submit that Your Majesty will be graciously pleased by your order in council to authorise us to grant for the future to the rope makers employed in Your Majesty's yards pensions varying from £20 to £24 a year, as is now granted to first class artificers.

316.　*Admiralty to Superintendent of Chatham Dockyard:*
apprenticeship school

[Chatham Dockyard Library, November 1842]　　　28 November 1842

My lords having taken into their consideration the measures, which have already been taken for the distribution, employment and control of the apprentices in H.M. dockyards, are of opinion that schools should be established to secure to them the benefits of a religious and professional education.

As to the nature and extent of such professional and general instruction, it is important not to keep the average too high, particularly at first, but eventually to give opportunities for carrying it higher where greatness, aptness or talent displays itself in particular boys.

If the general average of instruction be too high there is a danger of giving to the apprentice an officer's rather than a workman's education, and he will afterwards find a better market for his abilities than the dockyards can afford. Thus the Public would have been educating him not for their own service but the advantage of others, and all return for the expenses of this education would be lost. Before proceeding to the plan on which My Lords desire that the schools may be established, it appears to their Lordships that much elementary teaching will be got rid of, by making it in future an indispensable requisite for the admission of an apprentice, that he should be able in some degree to read and write and that he should be acquainted with the first three rules of Arithmetic, the parents being in receipt of such wages as makes the neglect of such instruction inexcusable.

A school will be forthwith established and a schoolmaster appointed upon whom the apprentices of whatever trade shall attend every afternoon for three hours, commencing an hour and a half previous to that at which the yard closes.

The school to be divided into five classes:

The three lowest classes (namely, the third, fourth and fifth) into which all the apprentices in the first instance will be placed according to their attainments and without reference to their age, will occupy the first three years of their apprenticeship, the promotion from class to class being made by an annual examination. Bad conduct or non-attendance is to be punished by loss of time towards the annual increase of pay and in extreme cases by cancelling of indentures and expulsion. In these classes they may learn such elementary matters as reading, writing, common and decimal arithmetic, scripture, English, history and geography.

At the end of the third year an examination should take place and a selection be made from among the shipwright apprentices of those whose ability may entitle them to a two years' course of higher instruction in the second class. Those who are rejected as unfit remaining however, on a similar course of education to that of the third class, for the sake of forming in them regular and industrious habits.

Those promoted to the second class should, in addition to their general instruction, be shown the method used in taking an account of work, in trimming timbers and in forming, combining, fastening the different parts of the structure in a systematic manner.

This would end the general and regular education with the exception of the two or three best who would be selected as the first class to enter the mould loft to learn the laying off of ships, the leading principles of construction and, as far as it is necessary for that purpose, mechanics, hydrostatics and mathematics.

During the last years of their apprenticeship some might be allowed to go on board H.M. ships to learn what is necessary to make a ship complete in hulls, masts, yards, &c.

My Lords would leave the arrangement of details to a commission in each dockyard consisting of the superintendent, the Master Shipwright, the chaplain, and any intelligent person connected with the service whom they recommend. The chaplain should at some convenient time on Sundays give religious instruction in the school and exercise a general supervision on other days on this most important part of their education.

All detailed regulations or instructions drawn up by the commissioners are to be submitted to their Lordships for approval.

With regard to the schoolmaster, you will see by the foregoing plan what will be required of him, and what qualifications will be necessary. He should if possible, be capable of lecturing as well as of the usual modes of teaching and My Lords desire that you will state whether you are acquainted with any person whom you consider adequate to the discharge of the duties which would be required of him.

The salary would be £70, with an allowance of fuel and candles if living within the dockyard, which would be desirable.

My Lords desire you will report how far this would be practicable and also what room or building exists in your dockyard, which could be converted to the purpose of a school.

317.   *Order-in-Council: schoolmaster*

[TNA, ADM1/5537]   1 February 1843

We beg leave to represent most humbly to Your Majesty that the system of taking apprentices in the dockyards being proved most advantageous to Your Majesty's service, both as to efficiency and economy. And the regular entry of apprentices which takes place every year in the yards, amounting now to nearly 700 boys, who have no means of religious or other instruction provided for them, we deem it proper that evening schools should be established for them in which they may acquire a scientific knowledge of their profession, from which we anticipate the greatest advantage. We therefore propose that should Your Majesty be graciously pleased to authorise the same, that we may be empowered to appoint schoolmasters to Your Majesty's several dockyards, with salaries varying from seventy to one hundred pounds a year, according to the amount of any other emolument which the person selected to perform the duty may receive from any other appointment he may hold in the dockyard.

318. *Admiralty to Superintendent Shirreff: inspection of schools*

[Chatham Dockyard Library, June 1846]   27 June 1846

With the object of promoting greater emulation amongst those attending the school and also for the better regulation of the latter, it has been decided to establish a system of reward and punishment. The Inspector of Greenwich Royal Hospital Schools has been directed to make an annual inspection and examination of the dockyard schools, report on their condition, and after consultation with the school committees recommend apprentices who were considered deserving of reward for their progress and conduct at school. The superintendents of the yards, acting on reports of the school committees, are authorized to fine any apprentice guilty of misconduct or repeated neglect and disobedience while at school, a sum up to a month's pay (or as an alternative direct them to work extra time without pay). Any apprentice who, notwithstanding punishment by fine and extra work, proves incorrigible is to be reported to the Admiralty who will decide whether his discharge would not be for the general good of the service.

319. *Admiralty to Dockyard Superintendents: wages*

[TNA, ADM89/2]   29 June 1857

My Lords, having had under their consideration the wages of the labourers in HM dock and victualling yards at home, have decided that from and after the 30th instant, the present wages of all the labourers who are in receipt of twelve shillings a week may be increased at the rate of two pence per diem. By command of their Lordships.

320. *Chatham Yard Officers to Admiralty: sawyers*

[TNA, ADM89/2]   8 November 1857

In reference to your minute of the 4th instant, directing us to report the necessity of increasing the number of sawyers at the yard. We beg to state that for several years past (although the number of hired sawyers has been very considerable, so as to make the aggregate number of sawyers approach nearly to that now stated to be desirable) we have constantly had the utmost difficulty in keeping up with the shipwrights, so that these might be adequate if advantageously employed. As the sawyers work by task, there is no want of exertion on their part [while] the sawmills [are] all kept in full activity. Notwithstanding, our programme, embracing so a large a proportion of new work, the demand for timber materials has been such, that little provision is made for the *Atlas* 90, none for the *Bulwark* 90, and none for the *Orpheus* 22, all to be converted this financial year.

We would also respectfully refer to our former report on the subject dated 28 February last, in which we mentioned the great advantage, which would accrue from being enabled to get the conversion in advance. Not only would the shipwrights be more economically employed, but also the necessity avoided of using unseasoned materials, wet from the saw, [to] the undesirability of which we need only refer.

321.   *Board to Surveyor of Navy: ending of payment by task and job*

[TNA, ADM89/3]   17 August 1858

With reference to your letter of the 13th instant, their Lordships have signified their directions to the superintendents of the several dockyards, that the system of employing and paying the men by task and job is to be brought to a close on the 28th instant. Also the practice of allowing extra exertion money to certain classes and that the officers and men placed in acting appointments when the task work came into operation are to fall back to their proper positions.

322.   *Board to Surveyor of Navy: additional shipwrights*

[TNA, ADM89/3]   29 April 1859

My Lords desire me to instruct you, to take immediate steps to enter 850 shipwrights and the necessary proportion of other trades and labourers at the several dockyards.

323.   Procedure for Payments of Wages

[Hobbes, *Reminiscences and Notes*, p. 207]   *c.*1860

The wages for each man having been made up in the books by Wednesday night were laid out on Thursday in receptacles numbered to correspond with the muster-tickets, and occupying three long tables in the pay-room. By Thursday night all was ready for the payment, which was made on Friday at noon. At a quarter to twelve on Friday a bell was rung by the police, which summoned the men from their work to the pay office. Meanwhile, two clerks had stationed themselves at each table, one of which was to receive each man's ticket, and call out its number, and the other to pay. The accountant and his chief clerk took up position in the centre, with the wages books, to enable them to answer any inquiries or complaints of the men; and the Captain Superintendent came to supervise the payment, as directed by the Admiralty. At the ringing of another bell, the men, who had by that time arrived at the pay office, and arranged themselves, began to enter at the several doors in distinct streams, and in numerical succession; and each gave up his ticket, as he entered, to the calling clerk, received his wages from the paying clerk, and made his exit through a door at the end. If not satisfied, however, of the correctness of his wages, he came to the centre, where his statement was investigated and settled. Men who through sickness, etc, could not attend, sent wages orders, printed forms for which were supplied on application at any time. In this way all were paid in the short space of about fifteen minutes.

324.   Admiralty to Superintendent Goldsmith: hired men

[NMM, CHA/H/105]   23 January 1861

Hemp spinners	134
Labourers	15
House boys	43
Saw mill	5
Caulkers	1
Joiners	8
Sawyers	24
Smiths	9
Millwrights shop	24
Painters	15
Plumbers, Braziers and tin men	10
ditto labourers	9

Metal mills boys   4
Oakum boys   3

325. *Strike by Ironsmiths*

[*Chatham News,* 13 May 1893]   3 July 1862

A complete transformation took place at Chatham dockyard from wood to iron. The Admiralty selected Chatham as the first yard to commence iron shipbuilding. The first to be constructed was the present armour clad *Achilles*.

A large staff of ironworkers was employed, they being gathered from the Thames and elsewhere. The authorities soon found these men very unsteady. None of the yard shipwrights were to be employed on the ship with the exception of a few for mould making. When they had got to the first floor-heads however, they made a sad mistake, and a scene which I shall never forget, as taking place in one of H.M.'s dockyards was the following.

After dinner every man and boy turned out on strike, and the scene was indescribable. The Captain Superintendent, noticing an unusual gathering of the ironworkers after the dinner hour in front of his office, despatched a messenger to the Chief Constructor for his immediate attendance. On arrival he was asked the meaning of that large concourse of ironworkers there. The chief said it was a great surprise to him to hear them state that they would do no more work until they got an advance of money, on what was originally agreed upon. This naval captain was moved with indignation at the course the men had adopted, for which there was no precedent but the great mutiny at the Nore and Spithead on April 28th, 1789 [*sic*]. He said, 'I cannot find language strong enough to condemn the means employed by these men.' My orders are, 'Give them fifteen minutes to decide whether they will leave the yard or return to their duty; failing this, call on the whole force of police to be in readiness to drive the whole of them out of the gate, which they shall never enter again. Should there be any resistance, call to your aid the armed military guard.' The chief, on putting in his appearance, replied to the men. He said he had but one request to make, 'that they were all to return to their duty at once.' Furthermore, he could give them no assurance whatever that their grievances would be considered. They would have fifteen minutes given to them to leave. Those who were disposed to return to duty at once could do so, and those who declined would be removed by force.

Conceive, my readers, what a consternation this must have caused throughout the dissatisfied ranks. One quarter of an hour to decide a question that might affect them the whole of their lives. Eyes were fixed upon the large clock just where they stood, until it chimed the quarter. The chief of the police at once emerged from the rear of the office at the head of a strong and powerful force. 'Forward,' was the order given in a loud tone of voice. There were but two only who had the moral courage at once to return to duty, Bill Morgan and Welsh Bob, both powerful men; these men have ever since been cared for by the authorities. The gate being reached, many went there for the last time with a sad heart. Many lessons may be learned from this for the consideration of our workmen.

The question may be asked: Did the ironwork remain at a standstill? Oh dear, no. The Admiralty wired, 'try and get your own shipwrights to take the entire ship in hand.' No sooner was this known throughout the yard, than immense numbers of volunteers came forward, and with a little instruction from the two men named, they succeeded. Riveting and plating was taken up by the shipwrights, while the drilling was kept exclusively for the labourers, who were then styled for the first time 'skilled labourers.' The work went on with amazing rapidity. So great was the change that their Lordships on their visitation frequently alluded with delight to the shipwrights in Chatham yard so nobly responding to their call.

326.   *Allowed Time for Visiting the Great Exhibition*

[*Chatham News and North Kent Spectator*]   2 August 1862

The employees of the Royal Dockyard were fortunate today in having splendid weather for their holiday. The Lords of the Admiralty some time since announced that the persons employed in the dockyard should have two days holiday to visit the International Exhibition – today and tomorrow. As work closes in the dockyards at four o'clock on Saturday, those employees who wished to make rather long excursions were, thanks to the facilities of locomotion, enabled to do so; and some left Chatham on Saturday evening. On Monday morning, great numbers of dockyard people, with their wives, families, and friends, departed by the railways in various directions, the greater number, however, proceeding to London to visit the Exhibition. An immense train departed from Chatham station; and great numbers of excursionists went by way of the North Kent Railway – the early boats to Strood pier were crowded.

327. *Building* Achilles

[Dickens, *The Uncommercial Traveller*[1]]   1863

Ding, Clash, Dong, Bang, Boom, Rattle, Clash, BANG, Clink, BANG, Dong, BANG, Clatter, BANG, BANG, BANG! What an earth is this. This is, or soon will be, the *Achilles*, iron armour-plated ship. Twelve hundred men are working at her now; twelve hundred men working on stages over her sides, over her bows, over her sterns, under her keel, between her decks, down in her hold, within her and without, crawling and creeping into the finest curves of her lines wherever it is possible for men to twist. Twelve hundred hammerers, measurers, caulkers, armourers, forgers, smiths, shipwrights; twelve hundred dingers, clashers, dongers, rattlers, clinkers, bangers, bangers, bangers!

328. *Meeting of Hired Men*

[*Chatham News and North Kent Spectator*]   13 February 1864

Last night there was a meeting of 300 hired shipwrights in Chatham dockyard, to discuss the question of the disadvantage under which they are at present placed in relation to the established workmen, and deciding on some action with a view to bettering their position. The meeting was held in Providence Chapel, Brook. It had been called at the Mitre Hotel, but the chief room there was not capacious enough for holding so large a meeting. There are now 500 hired workmen employed in the shipwrights' department at this establishment, and the grievance of which they complain is, that while the establishment hands are, after a certain time of servitude, entitled to a superannuation allowance, a similar boon is not extended to themselves, although the rate of pay they receive is the same, namely 4/6d per day. The meeting decided upon drawing up a petition to the Lords of the Admiralty, and to request Captain-Superintendent Stewart, C.B., to forward the same, praying their Lordships to take the matter into their consideration, and if possible to grant an augmentation of the present wages of hired hands. In the event of the Captain-Superintendent refusing to comply with the request of the petitioners it was arranged to send a deputation of their body to the Admiralty. A similar petition has already been forwarded by the hired shipwrights employed at Woolwich and it is expected a like step will be taken by the same class of workmen in the other royal yards.

---

[1]Charles Dickens, *The Uncommercial Traveller* (London, 1865), ch. 26.

329.   *Controller of the Navy: memorandum on increase of pay for
hired men*

[TNA, ADM1/5889]   5 March 1864

The hired shipwrights at Chatham, who have been taught iron shipbuilding
in the dockyard, are beginning to leave in large numbers, as they state that
they can obtain higher wages elsewhere. There appears to be only two
courses to pursue, either to raise the pay of the hired artificers, or to obtain
an order in council for the increase of the present establishment. The latter
course is I believe one the Board would be most reluctant to adopt, and
the surest way of dealing with the question would be to increase their
pay.

The amount to be taken in the navy estimates for the wages of hired
artificers for the year 1864–5 is £324,979. This sum would be the wages
of 5,678 at the present rate. If the men were granted 6^d per diem additional,
the number to be hired would only amount to 5,065, and if 1^s/- a day were
thought necessary only 4,453 could be hired.

Fearing, as I do, that the prospect of hiring the whole number required
is not favourable (and looking to the various petitions which the artificers
have recently presented) I am disposed to suggest that in order to obtain
the services of such men as we may require, it will be necessary to make
the retirement from the establishment at the age of 60 imperative and to
grant to all classes of hired men an addition of 6^d per day to their pay.

330.   *Rope Makers' Holiday*

[*Chatham News and North Kent Spectator*]   3 September 1864

On Saturday last, by the aid of the indefatigable Mr. George Payne, a large
number of the rope makers employed in Her Majesty's dockyard set a
splendid example of the much-coveted half holiday, by turning out on the
'Lines'. The spot selected was the Napier Arms Hotel, where a large booth
and three marquees were erected. At half-past one o'clock wickets were
pitched, and two elevens commenced an exciting match of cricket, in the
presence of hundreds of excited spectators. Other games also took place
– good humour and hilarity prevailing – until at length the bell sounded
for a magnificent supper, provided in Mr. and Mrs. Saxton's best style at
the Napier Arms. The tables were laid out precisely as they were for the
officers of the garrison and members of the Star Club on the previous day.
Ample justice having been done to the viands placed before them,
ourselves, our host and hostess, success to the half holiday movement,

and thanks to Mr. Payne having been duly honoured, the tables were cleared. Mr. D. Holloway was called to the chair, and Mr. J.J. Jones to the vice-chair. Songs and recitations followed and a pleasant evening closed the rope makers' holiday.

331. *Admiralty Printed Circular: superannuation*

[TNA, ADM1/5889]   30 September 1864

With reference to the order of my Lords Commissioners of the Admiralty, dated the 18th of March last, directing, with a view to the increased efficiency of the service of Her Majesty's dock and victualling yards, hospitals, and other civil establishments, that all inferior officers and workmen above 60 years of age, who are not in every respect efficient, shall be superannuated and that all such officers and workmen shall, under any circumstances, be retired on superannuation at the age of 65 years. I am commanded by their Lordships to furnish you with the following instructions for your future information and guidance in carrying out the above order:

When any inferior officer or workmen belonging to the establishment under your superintendence arrives at the age of 60, a statement of his services and salary (in duplicate) is to be transmitted on the usual treasury return, care being taken that the form relating to 'cause of retirement,' is duly filled up, either with the words 'at his own request,' or with the word 'age,' or 'age and infirmity,' as the case may require. This order is to extend also to hired men and factory men, *who have reached 60 years of age and completed 20 years or upwards of continuous service.*

6

LOCAL MANAGEMENT

Of paramount concern during the immediate post-war period was the necessity of bringing a greater degree of managerial efficiency to the dockyards [333]. A fundamental weakness was the position of the resident Commissioner. Working as a member of the Navy Board, it was the Commissioner's task to provide a link between the subordinate board and the dockyard. All correspondence between the boards in London and the respective officers of the yard passed unsealed through his office [342]. Aware of any Navy Board instructions, it was the Commissioner's task to report upon any shortcomings in the subsequent performance of the principal officers. However, should chastisement appear necessary, this would emanate entirely from the Navy Office [337, 340]. While Sir Thomas Byam Martin felt that this was sufficient for effective management [343], the Board of Admiralty disagreed and believed the authority of the Commissioner should be strengthened [341].

A further structural weakness identified by the Board of Admiralty during one of their post-war inspections was the number of post holders who had either overlapping authority or sub-divided duties. Between them, the Master Shipwright and Master Attendant were responsible for all the artisans and labourers employed in the yard. The former had authority over those directly employed on ships building and repairing, while the Master Attendant controlled similar groups employed on vessels moored in the harbour [332]. The Storekeeper, Clerk of the Survey and Clerk of the Check were responsible for overseeing the delivery of stores. Additionally, the Storekeeper was charged with the safekeeping and distribution of these stores; the Clerk of the Survey kept accounts of the quantities arriving and held in stock; and the Clerk of the Check examined the Storekeeper's accounts [332]. The Clerk of the Check was also responsible for keeping the pay and muster books. It was his office that inspected the indentures of all new artificers and kept a record of workers employed and discharged [332]. The ropeyard was regarded as a completely separate entity. The Clerk of the Ropeyard took responsibility for stores while the Master Rope-maker [337] was responsible for the direction of the workforce [341].

It was not only at principal officer level that there was an apparent excess of managers. The same was true at 'inferior officer' level. Here was a diverse group, which included some eligible for a dockyard house with others paid only slightly more than the ordinary yard artisan. They included, at the highest level, assistant master shipwrights, assistant master attendants, foremen of the yard and numerous trade masters. In addition, there were a vast number of measurers, foremen of trades and quarter men [332, 333]. Many of these were deemed superfluous by the Admiralty. It noted that the lowest ranking of these, the quarter men, in at least one situation, were found to be performing the work of the two officers senior to them, the foreman and trade master [341]. As with the general work force, officers were eligible for a superannuation allowance [338, 340, 347].

To remedy the structural weaknesses of the managerial system, the Board of Admiralty determined upon a number of fundamental changes. The first of these was communicated to the Navy Board in December 1821 [342]. Although Byam Martin, the Comptroller, challenged many of the conclusions reached by the Admiralty, he was ultimately overruled and the dockyard commissioners were informed of the new scheme in the summer of 1822. Ultimately, these changes did little to strengthen the authority of the Commissioner, other than having correspondence addressed to him rather than the principal officers. Admittedly, his office now played a greater role in the checking the Storekeeper's accounts, a result of the abolition of the office of Clerk of the Survey [342]. A further reduction in the number of principal officers was achieved by ending the separate distinction given to the ropery; the duties of Clerk of the Ropeyard were assumed by the Storekeeper and the management of the ropeyard by the Master Attendant.

Commissioner Cunningham, writing some eighteen months later, thought these changes did little to alter the situation that had existed prior to 1822 [346]. However, the reforms of 1822 did result in the abolition of a number of trade masters together with foremen of trades and quarter men [342]. For the individuals concerned, this proved a particularly grievous blow [344]. Quartermen had been attached to gangs of twenty working shipwrights and had been responsible for ensuring the quality of work performed [333]. They had taken their instructions from one of the foremen of the yard [333]. To undertake the duties formerly undertaken by quartermen, a new set of junior officers was created, officially known as leading men [342].[1] They differed from quartermen in respect of being raised workmen who carried out the same tasks as those overseen. At the

---

[1]Morriss notes that the use of the term 'leadingman' pre-dates the 1822 reforms and was applied as an occasional and unofficial alternative designation for 'quartermen'. See Roger Morriss, *The Royal Dockyards during the Revolutionary and Napoleonic Wars* (Leicester, 1983), p. 139.

same time, the number of yard foremen was increased, these officers being relieved of clerical duties that they might be more proactive in the inspection of working gangs [341]. These arrangements were confirmed in general instructions issued in 1833 [356]. Both the removal of quarter-men and the introduction of leading men proved controversial, not least from one outspoken anonymous critic, possibly a clerk employed at Chatham dockyard, who forwarded a printed volume of his views to the Board of Admiralty [345]. He was in august company, for Byam Martin also saw abolition of quartermen as a backward move [343, 349]. Concern was expressed for the reduction in the number of principal officers (particularly with regard to the receipt of stores) and the limited practical experience of newly appointed clerical officers [345], which contrasted sharply with the wealth of experience of operative officers prior to their arrival at the yard [338, 347, 358].

The dockyards were subjected to further extensive reforms. The first of these was in 1827 when the Timber Master, responsible for the reception, storage and conversion of timber, was replaced by a Timber Receiver [348] and a Timber Converter, the latter having charge of all sawyers and others connected with the conversion of timber. Ironically there was a reversion to the original system of a single Timber Master in 1847. In 1829, the office of Clerk of the Check was abolished, most of his duties being transferred to the Storekeeper. Recognising that this would leave an inadequate number of officers available for the receipt of stores, especially as the Storekeeper was to be exempted from 'out door duties', a new post was established. This was the Receiver of Stores who, in attending the arrival of stores, was to be assisted by an appropriate trade master and a clerk from the Storekeeper's office. In contrast to the Storekeeper, the Master Shipwright was designated a 'superintending out door officer' and was to direct himself entirely to the task of inspecting works in progress and the performance of the workforce [350].

It was the reforms of 1829 that saw the abolition of all remaining trade masters and their replacement by foremen [350]. Despite these changes, there were still some who felt that the yards were overburdened with managers [352]. The years 1832–34 witnessed a further series of reforms that tackled the central weakness of dockyard management, the limited authority of the Commissioner. Under a Parliamentary Act of 1832 the commissioners were replaced by superintendents, with the Act suggesting that these new officers would perform the same duties as their predecessors [353]. But this was not the case. The subsequent general instructions, empowered by an order-in-council of 18 July 1833, made it clear that the Superintendent had full authority over all his yard officers. Furthermore, all future correspondence would not just pass through his office; instead it was to be directly addressed to him, with any returning correspondence, whether from the officers or workmen, subject to his approval [356, 359]. The introduction of the new title also meant that those styled Commissioner would now cease to hold office, so that the Whig administration was able to make its own appointments. At Chatham, the newly appointed Superintendent was Sir James Alexander Gordon [355].

Totally omitted from the Act, and resulting from an 1831 policy document, was the recommendation that appointed superintendents retain naval rank [351]. Like the former commissioners, they were to be drawn from serving naval officers, but unlike commissioners they were not to lose their seniority. For this, there were sound reasons. Those who had been appointed had frequently found their authority undermined when working with those of naval rank, the latter sometimes countermanding their instructions. To legalise this particular point, and to establish the amount of the salaries to be paid to the officers, an application was made by the Admiralty to the King in council [354].

With regard to the reforms of 1833–34, a backward step concerned the reading of instructions to the officers. Prior to 1833, the principal officers of the yard had gathered together, listened to the Commissioner reading the instructions from the boards in London and had then jointly discussed how these duties might be performed [356]. From July 1833, those meetings were to cease. Instead, the superintendents were merely to read the orders of the day, the officers being immediately despatched to their duties. Unable to share their problems with each other, they were forced to approach the Superintendent as individuals, communicating with him in private. As was noted by Bromley, a senior clerk of the Admiralty who eventually rose to become Accountant-General, and who was appointed by Lord Auckland to examine the workings of the dockyards, this situation not only prevented the superior officers from working in concert but created 'petty jealousies' [360]. A further retrograde step created by the instructions of 1833 was the ending of the daily meetings that once took place between the superior and inferior officers.

Subject to the Master Shipwright, the department of the Master Measurer was responsible for calculating amounts of work performed and consequently precise levels of payment made to those artificers working by the piece. However, each measuring task was approached as if unique, with measurers repeatedly undertaking new sets of minute and detailed calculations. The 1821 Board of Admiralty inspection of the dockyard highlighted this point, leading to a new scheme of prices for task work by shipwrights in 1825 [361]. A further criticism of measurers was that, upon the introduction of restricted earnings as a post-war economy, they devoted much time to adjusting their measurements to ensure that each artisan still received that exact maximum [339]. In 1822 it was ordered that measurers should also take responsibility for inspecting the quality of work [341, 342]. The ending of piece rates in 1833, and its replacement by classification, resulted in a temporary abolition of measurers, with responsibility for ensuring quality given to new inspectors [357]. Upon the return to piece rates in 1842, inspectors were also given responsibility for measuring. However, the measurers department was revived in 1847 with their former zeal softened by the judicious application of occasional measurements, which were usually applied to those gangs or companies whose own calculations were viewed as suspect [361]. On occasions, the measurers themselves came under review. Nevertheless, their necessity was grudgingly accepted and they survived several potential reductions [363, 364, 365, 366].

In his report of 1847, J.S. Bromley concluded that there was a need for better supervision and accountancy [360]. A committee of revision (with Bromley among the appointed members) reaffirmed many of the earlier findings, noting that each of the yards should be treated as a single unit, not a collection of separate parts. As a result, the daily consultative meetings of the officers were reinstituted [361, 362]. In 1855, a dockyard accountant was appointed to check earnings [363].

Concern over the efficiency of the Royal Dockyards during the Crimean War resulted in the appointment of a Royal Commission of Inquiry that presented its report in 1860. Although much of the commission's attention was directed to the constitution of the Board of Admiralty together with measures for the improvement of centralised management [404], a number of references were made to the quality of local management. In particular, a number of dockyard officers were viewed as either incompetent or indifferent while measurement by check and the numerous (and often outdated) regulations of the yard came under criticism. To bring about improvements a number of minor revisions were undertaken [367] and check measurement was abandoned.

332.   *Instructions for the Principal Officers of the Dockyards*

[1st Report, Commissioners for Revising the Civil Affairs of the
Navy]   1806

[Instructions for the Masters Attendants at His Majesty's Dock Yards,
Article 4]
You are to consider yourself answerable for the general care and
management of the ships in ordinary at your port, and to see that the several
warrant officers do keep their ships clean, and otherwise strictly perform
their duty; that in the proper season, the awnings be spread, and the wind
sails duly made use of; that they be in all respects kept well aired and dry;
and that no ladders be affixed to the stern-ports, but that all persons entering
into or going out of the ships shall do so at the usual place only. You are
also to take care that no men or servants shall be employed on private
concerns, and that no articles belonging to government be embezzled or
carried on shore; and you are to pay the most strict attention to the due
execution of all instructions and orders which relate to this branch of the
public service, the persons therein being under your immediate control.

[Instructions for the Master Shipwrights at His Majesty's Dock Yards,
Article 5]
You are to be constant in your personal attendance at the launching,
docking, undocking, grounding, and graving of all ships, and diligently
to apply yourself to the execution and dispatch of all works carrying on
in your department, whether in building or repairing ships; taking care to
divide the immediate superintendence of all such works between your
assistants, foremen, and other subordinate officers, in such manner,
according to their several abilities, as you may judge that the most
advantage may probably be derived from their respective services. You
are also to take care that all the shipwrights and other workmen belonging
to your department be advantageously disposed of, ashore and afloat, so
that each particular work may be completed as expeditiously, and with as
little expense as possible, consistently with the circumstances of the case,
and the orders which you may have received.

[Instructions for the Storekeepers at His Majesty's Dock Yards, Article
5]
You are by warrant from this Board [the Navy Board], to receive into your
charge, all stores of every description, as well manufactured articles as
raw materials, that may be delivered for the use of the dockyard, whether
by contractors or otherwise, and to deposit them in suitable places of

safety, according to their respective natures, so that they may not decay, nor be wasted or embezzled; observing however, that all timber and wood of every denomination, whether rough or converted, new or old, although to be considered in your charge, is to be stowed in such places, and in such manner, as the Master Shipwright, or the assistant who may be appointed to act as Timber Master shall think fit. The arrival of all ships with foreign stores is to be reported to you by this office, agreeably to the form annexed.

[*Instructions for the Clerks of the Survey at His Majesty's Dock Yards, Article 4*]
You are, with the Clerk of the Check, Storekeeper, or Clerk of the Rope-yard, and the other respective officers and masters of trades, carefully to inspect the quality and dimensions of all stores, articles, and materials of all kind, which may be delivered into store, as well as of all works performed by contract. You are to join with those officers in rejecting all articles which may not be in every respect agreeable to contract, or in fixing abatements in the price proportionate to any defects which may have been discovered, reporting to us the actual state of all such articles, as the same shall appear in comparing them with the patterns delivered, or with the descriptions given of them in the several warrants and contracts under which they may have been supplied. If it should appear to you and the other officers, that the prices charged for any articles are too high, you are to report the same to us. For this purpose it is highly necessary that you should make yourself conversant with the signs and qualities of hemp, and all other articles usually purchased for the service of the yard.

[*Instructions for the Clerk of the Survey at His Majesty's Dock Yards, Article 15*]
You are once in every month, or more frequently if you should judge it necessary, to take a survey of the remains of stores issued for the current service of the yard. The issues of expenses from the store-cabins shall be examined by the Master Attendant and Master Shipwright, at least once in every week, and after their approval of the same, each relating to his department, you are to make an abstract thereof, together with the supplies, and the former remains, so as to be enabled to judge how far the accounts may have been fairly kept.

[*Instructions for the Clerk of the Check at His Majesty's Dock Yards, Article 9*]
All artificers and workmen of every description employed in the yard are to be mustered by you or your clerks, every time they may come into the

yard to work, and also upon their leaving it at night ... After every muster, correct lists are to be made out of all persons who may not have answered to their names, and those lists are to be immediately sent to the Commissioner, who will cause the muster books to be checked thereby, previous to the pay books being made out; and no check is to be taken off without his authority.

333. *Instructions for the Foremen of the Yard, Trade Masters and Quartermen*

[1st Report, Commissioners for Revising the Civil Affairs of the
Navy]   1806

[*Instructions for the Foremen of the Yard at His Majesty's Dock Yards, Article 4*]
When the workmen intended to be employed under you shall have been mustered upon coming into the yard, you are to cause them to proceed, without delay, to the works which may be allotted to them respectively, taking care that all the quartermen pay constant and unremitting attention to their duty; and you are to allot to each quarterman the particular work upon which his company is to be employed; and to keep an account of such allotment, in order that you may make each answerable for the due execution of the work entrusted to him.

[*Instructions for the Master Mast-maker at His Majesty's Dock Yards, Article 2*]
You are, every evening, to attend the Master Shipwright for the purpose of receiving his instructions relative to the work to be done on the following day. You are to take particular care, that all works under your superintendence be performed in a good and workmanlike manner, and with as much expedition and economy as the nature of the service may possibly admit; observing that you will be answerable for the conduct of all persons employed under you, therefore if any of them should misbehave, or improperly perform their duty, you are, without delay, to report the circumstance to the Master Shipwright.

[*Instructions for the Quartermen of Shipwrights at His Majesty's Dock Yards, Article 4*]
You are to employ your company upon such works as the foreman, or other your superior officer may direct; and you are to take care, as far as it may depend on you, that by the time one piece of work shall be finished, every thing be prepared for the men to begin another, so that they may

always be fully employed. You are also to take particular care, that all works performing by your company be in all respects executed in a substantial workmanlike manner, and with as much expedition and economy as the nature of the service will admit, observing that you will be answerable for all such works, as well as for the conduct of all the persons employed under you. You are, therefore, always to dispose of your men to the best advantage, and, when necessary, you are to allot to each individual the particular stint which he is to perform, keeping an account of the part of a ship on which each man may be employed, especially in the cases of driving copper bolts and treenails, and coppering of ships, in order that any defects, when discovered, may be traced to the parties concerned, and that those who may have improperly performed their work may be mulcted or discharged, as the case may require. And for this purpose you are also, upon the completion of each piece of work, to deliver to the foreman a certificate, to be lodged in the Master Shipwright's office, of the copper bolts driven by each person under your inspection.

334. *Navy Board to Commissioner, Chatham: report on duties of officers*

[NMM, CHA/F/30]   24 May 1817

We desire that you will examine very minutely into the duties of each office in the dockyard for the purpose of reporting your opinion of the advantage and good effect of the present system of keeping accounts and particularly whether the checks on the issue and receipt of stores are not more multiplied than is necessary. After consulting with the officers, you will state to us your opinion what offices or duty of offices might be dispensed without injury to the service.

In making this examination you will keep in view the duty of the Timber Master and the Master Measurer, for the purpose of pointing out any reduction or alteration which you will consider practical and advantageous.

335. *Navy Board to Clerk of the Rope Yard: duties*

[NMM, CHA/F/31]   22 July 1818

[*Question*]
If the office of Clerk of the Ropeyard did not exist do you think that the attendance of a Master Attendant or one of his assistants would be sufficient on the receipt of hemp? Could the other duties appertaining to

your department be discharged to advantage by the Clerk of the Check for muster and making out task notes and by the Clerk of the Survey and Storekeeper as to the other points of duty?

[*Response*]
I do not think the attendance of a Master Attendant, from his other duties could be sufficient on the receipt of hemp, where a constant personal attendance is required the whole working hours of the yard (in time of war) for a period of three months in the year. An Assistant Master Attendant might probably be spared for constant attendance. If the stores were placed in charge of the Storekeeper how is he to be made responsible for the stores received by his Assistant Master Attendant? I am of opinion the other duties of my office, might be discharged by the Clerk of the Check for musters and making out task notes &c and the other points of duties by the Storekeeper and Clerk of the Survey without any disadvantage to the service.

336.   *Master Attendant to Commissioner, Chatham: appointment of Master Sail Maker*

[TNA, ADM106/1816]   23 August 1818

The Lords Commissioners of the Admiralty have been pleased to allow Mr William Beare, Master Sail-maker, superannuation.

We beg leave, agreeably to the 7th Article of the General Instructions, to recommend to you, Mr Thomas Rencher, now foreman to succeed to the situation of Master Sail-maker. He has been in this yard twenty-seven years independent of his apprenticeship and his conduct and exertion merit every commendation from us.

We further beg to recommend William Pike leading man; to become foreman; provided Mr Rencher is promoted; he having been fifteen years in this yard, and is also a very deserving officer.

Mr. Lash, sail-maker who has been in this yard seventeen years, and is a most deserving man, we would also recommend to the appointment of leading man, in the place of Mr Pike.

337. *Commissioner Barlow to Navy Board: complaint against*
ropeyard officers

[TNA, ADM106/1816]   15 December 1818

I have received your letter of the 11th instant, enclosing, for my information, a letter which you have received from William Merrells, late a rope-maker in this yard, complaining of ill treatment and misconduct on the part of the Clerk of the Rope Yard and Master Rope-maker; and desiring that I will enquire and report to you as to the allegations therein contained.

In reply, I have to acquaint you, that I have attentively examined into all the charges preferred against the Clerk of the Ropeyard and against the Master Rope-maker of this yard by the said William Merrells. The result is a firm persuasion that the charges of tyrannical treatment of the rope-makers; of improper conduct in the receipt of hemp; of an unauthorized mode of paying the workmen and of improper delays at the call office; are wholly unfounded and malicious. They arose out of the circumstance of the Master Rope-maker having sharply, though very properly, reproved William Merrells for neglect of duty and not making due exertion, when employed at the crane unloading a hemp ship. On this occasion the said William Merrells behaved in so insolent a manner, as to induce me, at the suggestion of the ropeyard officers, to suspend him from duty: to which in a few days he would probably have been restored.

With respect to the charge of employing men in their houses, and in their private concerns; I find that two of the elderly men, Seth Petfield and William Snooks (whose general duty has been of late to clean out the tar cellars) have, about once in a fortnight, washed out the court yard of the Clerk of the Ropeyard's House. [Also, they] have been in the habit of cleaning the windows of his house, during part of the working hours of the ropeyard. [Further] before the morning call, and after the afternoon call (in what he considers his own time) Seth Petfield has watered the Clerk of the Ropeyard's garden and collected dung for the same.

It also appears that Joseph Lambert, a houseboy, has been permitted to go almost daily to the house of the Clerk of the Ropeyard, after morning call, and to stay there an hour or two, if not particularly wanted in the loft. He frequently gathers chips for the Clerk of the Ropeyard's house, occasionally goes on messages, and assists to wash the court yard and to clean the windows of the house.

338. *Surgeon of the Yard to Navy Board: memorial*

[TNA, ADM1/3376] 22 July 1819

That your memorialist first gave his service to his country in 1778, when there existed great want of medical assistance in the Navy, and a time when the first Grand Fleet was hastily fitted to meet the enemy; then from that period to the present moment he has been constantly in the public employ unremittingly giving up to it, upwards of 41 years of the prime and most active part of his life,

That in the performance of his duty on board His Majesty's ship the *Chatham* cruising in the North Sea, by falling down a hatch while returning from the sick bay he fractured both bones of his leg, so badly that the preservation of that limb, under the best advice, was for a considerable time doubtful and leaving it ever since, extremely weak with unsightly deformity. That by the same fall, he contused and wounded his right arm and elbow so seriously as to occasion painful exfoliations at the end of the bones of that joint producing an autolysis or stiffness painfully detrimental and inconvenient to him (even on common occasions) more particularly in the exercise of his profession as surgeon.

That when hastening to an accident in the yard he got jammed between a team of horses and some logs of timber, which brought on a pain in his chest, a cough and spitting of blood, increasing in severity every winter.

That in assisting the sick of the ordinary under his care, going on board the *Majestic*, a light ship high out of the water, in blowing weather, in want of strength in his arm (from the before stated injuries) to support himself he fell back on to a boat alongside, by which he got ruptured. In consequence [he is] suffering under a distressing affliction, which is dangerous (in its consequence) even in youth, but more especially to a person in his advanced time of life.

Thus hurt, injured and nearly worn out in the service of that country from which no offer from foreign powers (though some were made) could lure him, he ventures to bring his long and he trusts useful service, not only to his own country but to her allies under the view and consideration of your Lordships, unaided by any other interest or recommendation.[1]

[1]Dr White was seeking superannuation for a claimed twenty years of service. Commissioner Barlow, in an accompanying letter, fully supported Dr White's memorial and request. However, Barlow had submitted this direct to the Board of Admiralty, without the memorial having been first passed to the Navy Board. This was seized upon, with the inferior board pointing out that the computed years of service claimed by the memorialist were incorrect and that Dr White was three months short of twenty years' service in the yard and, for this reason, was not entitled to a pension equivalent to three-fourths of his annual wage.

339. *Commissioner Barlow to Navy Board: earnings of workmen*

[TNA, ADM106/1817]   21 June 1820

I have received your letter of the 7th instant, acquainting me that Mr Manclark, the Master Measurer of the yard, having, by your directions, attended you, to account for the uniform earnings of the workmen of this yard, you find his explanation very unsatisfactory.

That he states, that since the earnings have been limited, it has been the practice of the sub-measurers to calculate the amount of the value of the works performed previous to closing their accounts for the week. [Should] the works then entered in their books not produce to the workmen the limited earnings per day now established, they consult with the quartermen as to what other works it may be necessary to bring to account to make up the earnings to the limited sum. In some instances they have been allowed sums for works as finished, which were not completed until the following week. On the other hand, if the works which had been performed and entered, were sufficient in amount to cover the limited earnings, they closed their accounts and sought for no other works. Such as were in hand, or finished, were included in the following week's accounts.

340. *Navy Board to Commissioner Barlow: chastisement of Master Measurer*

[NMM, CHA/F/34]   7 September 1820

We have under serious consideration the report made by the committee of this Board, which lately visited Chatham yard, on the conduct of the officers, and others belonging to that yard, to whom the business of measuring the works in the shipwrights' department belongs. We have also weighed the several explanations made by the parties concerned; and we have now to desire that you will make known to the Master Shipwright our strongest displeasure at his conduct in permitting so unwarrantable a system of deviation from established regulations; as that which was disclosed in the course of the examination of Chatham.

All the circumstances connected with this case have been communicated to the Lords Commissioners of the Admiralty, and Mr Croker has, in consequence, been commanded to express their Lordships request that the officers connected should have been found so extremely blamable [*sic*], and more particularly the Master Shipwright, whose station and respectability ought to have secured a peculiar degree of attention from him.

In respect to the Master Measurer, their Lordships have been pleased to order (in conformity with our regulation) he should forfeit all pay during the time he has been under suspension, and be removed to the status of Master Measurer at Sheerness. That the Master Measurer of that yard be removed to Chatham. Furthermore, that the sub-measurer be enjoined not to depart in future from their instructions without an order in writing in all cases in which a deviation there from may be thought necessary: We have therefore to desire that you will apprise the officers of their Lordships sentiments and directions on this occasion and order Mr Manclark to prepare for removal to Sheerness as his warrant may be expected immediately.

We shall have occasion to make a communication shortly to all the yards arising out of the irregularities at Chatham, and shall at the same time transmit to the officers of that yard some observations for their guidance in reference to the duties of the Master Measurer's branch.

341. *Admiralty Report: management of yards*

[TNA, ADM1/3462]   8 December 1821

[I]t is evident that in order to put His Majesty's dockyards on some uniform, regular and efficient footing, a general revision ought to be made of the present complicated system of management and a new code of instruction prepared for carrying it into effect. In the arrangement of which it should be kept in mind (what seems unaccountably to have escaped the Commissioners of Naval Revision) that the very best instructions will be of little avail, without the establishment of some great controlling power, some active and efficient superintendence, which shall pervade, and be felt by, all the subordinate departments. That it was intended, by the present instructions to invest this power in the resident commissioner, would naturally be inferred from the first article of his particular instructions where it is stated that he 'shall have full authority over all officers and other persons whatsoever, employed in the dockyard and ordinary, and is to control every part of the business carried on therein, and to exercise the power vested in him, as often as he may see occasion, for the purpose of enforcing obedience to all orders and regulations issued by this Board (Navy Board) or himself.'

Yet this officer, in point of fact, has not, under the present system, any real authority over any one class of artificers, or any means of knowing how they are distributed or employed. Although nominally invested with complete authority, it is evident that he actually possesses none, as far as active or personal duties are concerned. His interference is therefore very rare and limited to a few trifling points, his superintendence very limited and superficial, and his responsibility, out of his immediate department, considered by him to be equally so.

Such an example set by the head officer of the establishment must necessarily have a bad effect on the principal officers of the several departments; and accordingly their Lordships remarked with concern that very little personal attention was directed by these officers on their respective duties, that generally every thing [was] left to be transacted and managed by their clerks. This delegation of duty was observed to be remarkably the case in the two instances of the Storekeeper and the Clerk of the Check, the former being unable to answer any questions respecting the mode of keeping his accounts, and the vouchers requested from him to obtain his discharge, without a direct application to his first clerk, and the latter exhibiting an instance of unconcern and inattention on a point wherein his personal interest was deeply involved. Their Lordships found that this officer had in the course of the present year, public monies passing through his hands to the amount of £60,000, and in possession of a balance of about £7,000 for which he was solely responsible. Yet his chief clerk was entrusted with keeping his cash account, and also with the custody of the above-mentioned balance, which, impudently enough, he declared to be deposited in an iron chest pointed out by him in [the] presence of his messenger, while the principal stood by, in apparent unconcern.

If, then, these two public accountants, personally responsible to a very large amount for the cash and stores in their charge, are thus found actually to entrust the whole management of their offices to their chief clerks, and to be unable, without immediate reference to them, to answer almost a single question, with regard to the details of their respective duties, it is not likely that a closer attention will be met with, in the less important departments of the dockyards. In point of fact their Lordships' enquiries enable them to state that the same system of devolving all the labour and responsibility on some subordinate appeared to pervade every department. From the latter only could be collected the real mode in which the business of the establishments was conducted. Thus the checks, which were unquestionably intended to be entrusted to the superior officers, really and solely, depend on the honesty of persons holding the most inferior situations.

[*Marginal note:* 'The principal officers of Portsmouth yard were generally found to be somewhat better informed of the duties of their respective stations than at Chatham but took no efficient part in them beyond superintendence.']

Another instance of this improper delegation of the duties of a superior to the inferior of his department occurred in that of the Timber Master. [He] has the sole charge of this important article of store, until it shall be converted for its proper purpose. This officer affirmed strongly that he surveyed and measured every stick of timber that came into the yard, in company with his assistant and two clerks, and has two converters and a quarterman assisting him. Whereas, on further investigation, it appeared that a principal part of the measuring of the timber was entrusted to his assistant and by his assistant to [that of] common shipwrights. Instead of two converters and a quarterman only, he had actually no less than thirty employed in measuring, chipping and preparing the timber which had been appropriated by the Master Shipwright, but of which appropriation the Commissioner was wholly ignorant. Nor was it quite clear that the builder himself knew of it, until he consulted the entry of distribution, in consequence of a return to that effect being called for by their Lordships.

Thus was this important branch of the dockyard duty (for the superintendence and control of which such high salaries are paid) for want of a proper and efficient system of control, actually carried on (in the main points of it) by the individuals of the lowest class in the yard, to save trouble to the salaried officers, charged by their instructions with its execution. And this was by no means the only case, when the shipwrights appeared to be working, as they judged right, with little or no control, from the many salaried officers appointed and paid for overlooking them.

From the many instances of this kind, their Lordships feel themselves compelled to declare, as far as they were enabled to judge from a minute investigation, that the greater number of the officers, receiving high salaries in the several departments, appeared to them an unnecessary and useless encumbrance, tending rather to afford a sanction to idleness than of any use in keeping the artificers to their labour. Indeed, it appeared that in proportion to the number of salaried officers in any department, was the quantity of useful labour diminished. The number of such officers amounts at present in Chatham Dockyard to 155, exclusive of the commissioner to superintend and take account of the labour of 1977 artificers, being on average about 13 working men to one officer who does nothing. As the amount of the salaries of the officers exceeds £32,000 a year, the expense of superintendence alone is about £16 per man. Such an expense under any system of management [w]ould be enormous. When it is considered the task and job scheme is almost universally adopted, and that the average number of men employed on day pay in this yard does not exceed 350 (when by this scheme the artificers cannot or ought not to receive any wages beyond the work actually performed) and that the attention of the overseers is principally confined to the quality rather than to the quantity of work performed, this establishment appears to their Lordships to be quite indefensible, and to require a complete revision. It would be quite preposterous to admit for a moment that a mere superintendence of common artificers and labourers should in any case require to be paid one fourth part of the value of the labour of those they are appointed to overlook.

That such a superintendence is not necessary in the dockyards was exemplified by the fact of one quarterman found performing the duties of the Master, the foreman and the quarterman of the mast-house, and as it appeared, having very little to do, although the whole duties of the three officers were combined in him. Indeed, it was admitted by the Master Measurer, a shrewd and intelligent man (in speaking of the number of foremen, measurers and quartermen, scattered over the works of the yard) that no private concern, to use his own words, could stand it. He had himself inspected the building of four or five ships alone at the same time in different parts of the river.

The masters of other trades besides that of mast making, together with their foremen, appeared to their Lordships, wholly superfluous, with the two exceptions of the master and foreman of Smiths and the timber master who is an assistant of the Master Shipwright. It cannot indeed be supposed that 19 bricklayers should require a Master and Foreman: yet they have them (one with a salary of £250, and the other £140 per annum). The same observation will apply to the Master and Foreman of Painters, whose numbers amount to 15 or 16, occasionally assisted by a few labourers. In short, there appears to be no necessity, whatever, for that enormous disproportion which prevails in all the departments between those who labour and those who are supposed to oversee that labour.

The system of task and job, or of paying the workmen according to the quantity and quality of the work performed, is unquestionably a good one, but it may be carried too far. This will probably be found to be the case in His Majesty's dockyards, more especially in those where the principal part of the work consists in building new ships; for in such work every portion of every class of ship must have its precise value ascertained without going through the process of minute measurement and of the detailed calculations made afterwards by the clerks in the master measurers department. Besides, nine-tenths of the workmen perform daily an excess of work beyond the value of the limit of their daily earnings (which is four shillings) so that the public gets a full share of work for the money paid for it, which is the only object of the task and job scheme. And when it is considered that the master builder and his assistant, the foremen and quartermen, all of them inspect the new works in progress and considering also how very slowly the various parts of a ship's hull proceeds, this accumulated inspection can scarcely be deemed necessary, especially that of the quartermen. Indeed, as all the sub-measurers have been selected from the quartermen, and must necessarily be well acquainted with their duties, there seems to be no reason why the ten sub-measurers should not inspect the work at the same time that they measure it, and thus perform the only duty which the quartermen have to do. On putting the question to the Master Measurer, he admitted that he saw no reason why the duties of the sub-measurers and the quartermen should not be united in the same person. It being, in fact, stated by him that the sub-measurer did not take the work off the men's hands when it was properly performed. It is therefore quite clear that these men are perfectly competent to perform the quarter men's duty. To the inspection was added that of the superior officers, who should be required to give their personal attention to the arrangement and execution of the works more than they now do. Their Lordships are of the opinion that the whole of the quartermen might be struck off, by which, in Chatham yard alone, would be effected an annual saving of about £5,000.

It could not fail to strike their Lordships that, as the shipwrights can earn with ease twenty shillings in five days by working six hours in each day, the Task and Job scheme must be fixed too high. Instead of making Saturday a whole holiday, it might be more advisable to make them work on Saturdays for the same sum per week, by which the task and job scheme would be reduced one-sixth, and the public would gain one-sixth more labour for the same money.

The same efficient and active controlling power is not less required in the direction of the receipt and expenditure of stores, than in the economical distribution of labour. A great parade appears on the face of the instructions with regard to the attendance of the principal officers and their clerks on receipt of stores from the contractor, but the only effect produced by it appearing to be an unnecessary number of useless vouchers. The only person who does not attend is the resident commissioner who, of all officers, ought to be the principal officer present on such an important occasion. [Instead] he is required [only] to put his initials to the certificates of stores received, not as any proof that such certificates are correct, but as is expressed in his instructions 'as a proof that they (the certificates) have undergone his inspection.' He is also directed to withhold his signature 'if he should perceive any inaccuracy in the said certificate'. But this can never happen, as he is utterly ignorant of the quantity and quality of the stores said to be received (as well as of the price described in the certificate) and is consequently unable to detect any inaccuracies.

The stores when received are delivered into the charge of the Storekeeper. An account of them [is] taken by the Clerk of the Check, who also sees that, the Storekeeper charges himself with the proper quantity. The only check that at present exists upon the Storekeeper's issues is vested in one of the clerks of the Clerk of the Survey. His signature to the Storekeeper's daybook of issues is the only voucher to the Navy Board that the stores under the charge of the Storekeeper have been properly expended. None of the original vouchers, the only authentic ones, are transmitted to the Navy Office to enable the clerks there to check the Storekeeper's issues. The only examination therefore which the Storekeeper's accounts undergo at Somerset House is that of merely checking the posting of his Ledger from his day book, and the totalling of the pages; and the initials of the name of a clerk in the Clerk of the Survey's office to the daily sections of the Storekeeper's Issue Book, with a certificate at the end signed by the Clerk of the Survey that this examination has actually taken place (though they have neither been checked nor examined by himself) is the only voucher at present required by the Navy Board for the correctness of the Storekeeper's accounts; this Board (as before mentioned) having dispensed with the quarterly transmission of all the vouchers required by the 26th Article of the storekeeper's instructions, contained in the First Report of the Commissioners of Naval Revision.

A very considerable portion of the stores received into the yard is issued by the Storekeeper to the cabin keepers, on their demand monthly, being signed by the proper officers. This issue to the cabin keepers, as at present conducted appears to be highly objectionable were it for no other reason than that of entrusting labouring men and artificers of a very low description with very large quantities of valuable stores, while their receipts serve to clear the Storekeeper's charge without any further enquiry on his part as to how they are expended.

The several quartermen make their demands on these cabin keepers and their receipts clear the cabin-keepers charge, but here ends all trace of the stores thus delivered to the quarterman. He expends them on the work he is appointed to superintend, or otherwise, just as he pleases, as he does not give in any account whatever of the manner in which they have been disposed. Therefore, if disposed to be dishonest they have the power of making improper uses of them.

The Clerk of the Rope Yard stands alone, and is left wholly without any check on the issues. He transmits no document to the Navy Board to show in what manner the valuable stores of hemp and tar have been discharged from his account. He is directed by his instructions to be a check on the rope-makers, but appears to be left without any officer's check on himself. The cordage when manufactured is delivered over to the Storekeeper and a duplicate of the rough issue note delivered over to the Clerk of the Survey. [He] sends one of his clerks to see that the storekeeper has entered the proper quantities in his day book, as a charge against himself, and certifies accordingly – but whether the Clerk of the Ropeyard has delivered over a proper quantity or not, neither the Storekeeper nor the Clerk of the Survey knows or enquires.

It is quite obvious therefore, that there is not at present any efficient check on the expenditure of stores. Indeed, it was frankly avowed, both by the Storekeeper and the Clerk of the Survey, that the checks were merely nominal. The Storekeeper might make up his balance of remains to be as much more or as much less than his actual remains as he thought fit, without the possibility of detection, unless by an actual survey of his remains in the storehouses.

But according to the present system of delivering large quantities of stores to the cabin keepers, the balances in the Storekeeper's ledgers, afford no clue to the quantity of the stores in the yard. Yet it is from those nominal balances that the supply of stores is regulated. It would be necessary, in order to obtain the true quantity; to add the remains of every cabin-keeper to the remains on the Storekeeper's ledger. The quantity of these remains in the cabins may partly be conceived when it is stated that it requires two clerks from the survey office to be employed wholly in keeping the accounts of these cabin keepers – one having 12 and the other 8 under his charge. In taking the monthly remains, it requires each of these clerks to attend the cabins for 7 or 8 days – a proof of the loose manner in which the monthly demands for stores are made.

From these general observations on the present defective system of management in the dockyards, it will be manifest that a complete revision of the instructions is extremely desirable with some new arrangement to be adopted which shall secure a more economical distribution of labour and [provide] a more satisfactory check on the receipt and issue of stores.

342.   *Admiralty Minute: reform of yard management*

[TNA, ADM1/3462]   24 December 1821

From various visitations of the several dockyards and more particularly from a recent investigation into the manner in which the business of the respective departments in those of Chatham and Portsmouth is conducted, the Lords Commissioners of the Admiralty are satisfied of the expediency of causing certain alterations to be made in the present system of management which prevails in all the dockyards (more especially as it regards the distribution of the strength of the yards, and the receipt and expenditure of stores) by the introduction of a more simple, efficient and economical arrangement than that which at present is in practice.

The Resident Commissioner

In the first place, then, their Lordships consider it absolutely necessary that the commissioners should be required to exercise duties more in keeping with the first article of the General Instructions than appear to have hitherto been the practice. Keeping this leading principle in view, they would propose: that all correspondence from the Navy Board with the several dockyards and ordinaries, on whatever subject, should be addressed solely to the Resident Commissioner (where there is one) and that he should be required to issue his directions thereafter, to the respective officers of the yard. That all reports and orders, of and for all the officers of the yard should be transmitted through the commissioner, who alone should correspond with the commissioners of the Navy.

Secondly. That the distribution of the labour of the yard should be regulated by the Commissioner for which purpose the respective officers, at the close of each day's work, should be directed to receive his orders for the distribution of the strength of the yard for the succeeding day.

Thirdly. The Commissioner should become an additional check on the receipt and expenditure of stores and also on the contingent cash account of the yards. For this purpose it is proposed that a clerk from his office should be required to attend all receipt of stores that are brought into the yard, a Clerk of the Storekeeper, and a Clerk from the Check office, being present, together with the proper officers whose duty it may be to survey and examine the quality of the same. The clerk of the commissioner should deliver to his principal, the same evening, the rough receipt book in which his entries have been made. On the following morning, the Clerk of the Check, and the Storekeeper should send to the commissioner, under sealed cover, the respective accounts of the receipts as taken by their clerk the preceding day. That if these two accounts, when compared by the commissioner with that of his clerk, should be found to agree, he is to return this to the parties, with his initials, as a proof of this having undergone his examination. If they do not agree, he should call before him the officer and the two clerks who attended the receipt of the stores, in order that the cause of the error may be discovered and rectified, and such steps taken, as may appear to him best adopted, for preventing the re-occurrence of similar errors.

At all times he must be acquainted with the quantities of the various kinds of stores expended, with the quantities received into the yard and to see that the Storekeeper's remains correspond with the balance of stores on the face of the ledger. The Storekeeper should record the earnings of each day, sent to him under sealed cover, the total amount of each species of store, which may have been issued in the course of that day.

And finally, it is proposed that the commissioner should have the ordering of all surveys of old stores and of all other arrangements and operations of the yard after consultation with the proper officers to whose duties they may respectively relate.

Where there is no resident commissioner, or where he may be absent, the officer next in rank should be charged with the execution of all the duties of his department except such as are placed under the captain superintending the ordinary.

The Master Attendant

Their Lordships have no material alterations to propose in the duties of the Master Attendant, except that he shall take his orders directly from the Resident Commissioner and that, in addition to the Master Sail-maker, the Master Rigger, boatswain of the sheer hulk, the Master Rope-maker should also be placed under his directions; but for reasons hereafter assigned, the duties of the Foreman of Riggers, the Foreman of Rope-makers, and the Foreman of the Sail-makers may be dispensed with, and these offices abolished.

The Master Shipwright

The Master Shipwright upon whom has hitherto devolved the general distribution of the labour of the yard, will be required by the proposed alterations to receive his orders daily from the Resident Commissioner and conformably with those orders to make arrangements with his assistants, foremen and boatswain of the yard, for the due execution of them.

The great number of superintending officers, in all the branches of this extensive department of the yard, could not fail to attract their Lordships' particular attention. It was quite evident that, in consequence thereof, much of the inspection, care and responsibility, which were instituted, and ought to be, vested in the higher superintending officers, were but too frequently transferred by them to their respective subordinates. In many instances the common workmen were left without any superintendence at all.

To remedy the serious evils arising out of this accumulation of inefficient superintendence, their Lordships would propose that, instead of the present system (which requires a number of superintending officers to be especially attached to the various classes of artificers) a certain limited number of foremen should be appointed, to have a general superintendence of all the artificers under the Master Shipwright and his assistants. Instead of the distinctions which now exist among this class of officer, as Foreman of the Yard, Foreman Afloat, Foreman of New Works &c, the whole should be named 'foremen of the yard', and that such particular duties should from time to time be assigned to each of them, by the Master Shipwright, as instances might require. To give a general view of what occurs to their Lordships as to this additional number of foremen, they consider that four additional officers of this description to each of the great yards would enable the commissioner to place one to overlook the mast and boathouses, another to superintend the house carpenters, joiners and other trades, and leave him two others disposable to superintend all other works, where they may be required.

By this new arrangement, their Lordships have no hesitation in stating, as their opinion, that the following masters & foremen of trades, would no longer be necessary and might be consequently discharged.

The Master and Foreman of Mast Makers
The Master and Foreman of Boat Builders
The Master and Foreman of House Carpenters
The Master and Foreman of Joiners
The Master and Foreman of Bricklayers
Foreman of Painters
Foreman of Caulkers
Foreman of Scavelmen
Foreman of Yard Labourers
Foreman of Teams
Quarterman of Shipwrights
Quarterman of Caulkers
Quarterman of Mast makers
Quarterman of Boat Builders

Their Lordships' opinion that the employment of the masters of trades above mentioned would no longer be necessary, under the new system of superintendence by the Foremen of the Yard, as now proposed, is founded on the great similarity of most of the works superintended by these masters, with those produced by the shipwrights, and on the small numbers of workmen employed under the rest of them. [Also], that the place of the foremen would be supplied with advantage by the appointment of an intelligent and trustworthy working man to each class of trades. He should continue to be a working man, to be called the 'Leading Man', and to be allowed a small addition to his weekly earnings so long as he shall hold the situation.

In like manner, a Leading Man with a very small addition to his weekly earnings may, with the assistance of the additional foremen proposed, supply advantageously the place of the present quartermen; and it is a question for consideration whether it might not prove convenient, under the regulations proposed, if the present gangs of shipwrights were reduced or divided, so as to have two or three of these working Leading Men in each, or one to every ten artificers.

The Clerk of the Check and the Storekeeper

By the proposed arrangement which gives to the Commissioner a perfect knowledge of whatever stores are received into and issued from the yard, and by some few alterations which it is proposed to make in the present instructions to the Clerk of the Check and the Storekeeper, their Lordships are purposed to state, that, in their opinion, the whole establishment of the Clerk of the Survey and the Clerk of the Ropeyard, would seem superfluous, and both of them might consequently be abolished. At present the Clerk of the Survey is an imperfect check on the Storekeeper and rendered unnecessary by the arrangement now proposed; and the small remaining part of the duties of his office may be transferred advantageously, by the proposed new regulations, to the Clerk of the Check, who would then, in addition to his present duties, become an efficient check on the Storekeeper's issues, as he is now on his Receipts.

With this view, all the demands for Stores, whether for the use of the yard, or of ships in commission, after being signed by the proper officers, should be carried to the Clerk of the Check, who should be required to deliver a note for the issue of the same to the Storekeeper who should take care that those demanded for the ships, whether in commission or in ordinary, do not exceed the proper establishment.

With regard to the present mode of keeping accounts of stores received and issued, and posting them into a ledger under their several heads, their Lordships do not consider any alterations in the system to be necessary; but they would recommend that the original vouchers of the issues should be transmitted quarterly, with the ledgers, in addition to the day books now sent to the Navy Office, to be there examined, in lieu of the examination they at present undergo by the clerks in the dockyard, and of the Certificate of the Clerk of the Survey that such examination had taken place.

As it is proposed to abolish the establishment of the Clerk of the Ropeyard, the Storekeeper should be required to take charge of all the duties heretofore attached to that establishment.

The Store Cabins

The system of having numerous store cabins, as at present, established in various parts of the several dockyards, for supplying stores for the current service, appeared to their Lordships objectionable, not only on account of the expense and the frequent employment it causes to clerks in taking an account of their monthly remains, but also from its liability to fraud, and the facility with which the Quartermen obtain whatever they please from these cabins, without rendering any account of the expenditure of the articles they may have thus taken.

Their Lordships are not however prepared to say that these cabins can at once be wholly dispensed with, but they would propose that the several commissioners should have their attention called to the subject, and be directed to reduce gradually, and with as little delay as may be found practicable without injury to the current service, the number of these store cabins. They further recommend that after due investigation and consideration of the subject, each commissioner should be directed to state, whether, in his opinion, by establishing two or three 'present use storehouses', in different parts of each yard, these very objectionable store cabins, as now managed, might not be altogether got rid of. In the meantime stores should only be taken from these cabins by the authority of the Foremen, under their signatures, as at present by the Quartermen, who should render an account of the application of them daily into the Master Shipwright's office.

The Present Use Stores

Their Lordships deem it proper to add, as connected with this subject that, in their opinion, the large storehouses which exist in each of the dockyards with the name of 'present use storehouse' should be made that which the name implies: a store in which articles of every different description should be placed (as far at least as may be practicable). The issues of the day should be made as much as possible from this store only, it being replenished from time to time as might be necessary from the other storehouses, which would then only be required to be opened for the purpose of delivering out of them these occasional supplies for the 'present use store'. If this regulation was put in practice, a Storekeeper's clerk attending at this store to regulate and take an account of the issues from it, would be quite sufficient for the purpose. At present it is necessary to employ Storekeeper's clerks in several different storehouses at the same time throughout each day (and other clerks for the special purpose of issuing some particular species of stores). Thus, at Portsmouth Dockyard, if canvas should be required to be issued from the 'present use store', where one of the Storekeeper's clerks attends all day, the attending clerk could not issue it. [Instead] another clerk is obliged to go from the office to the store, because the latter is the clerk charged with issuing canvas and colours.

According to the general outline of the arrangements proposed, the principal officers of a dockyard establishment will consist of

The Resident Commissioner
The Master Attendant
The Master Shipwright
The Clerk of the Check and
The Storekeeper

whose several instructions will necessarily be required to be revised and altered conformably with the new system which is now proposed.

The Clerks of the Dockyards

When this system shall be ordered to be carried into effect, their Lordships are of opinion that it will be highly expedient, and of great advantage to the public service, that all the clerks of the several departments of the dockyards should be placed on a new footing. Instead of being, as at present, nominated by their immediate superiors in each office (as belonging to such office only) at various rates of salary and rising in regular succession from desk to desk, they should in future be appointed as clerks of each dockyard generally. [They should] be classed, paid and considered on a similar plan to that established for the second and third classes of clerks in the Navy Office, or on a modification of that system. All first appointments of clerks to any of the dockyards should be vested in the Admiralty. Their promotion from one class to another, or their removal from one department of the yard to another, should be regulated by the Navy Board, at the recommendation of the respective commissioners according to the individual ability and attentions to duty of each clerk, and not by seniority alone. They should all be considered eligible to rise to the higher situations of Storekeeper and Clerk of the Check, whenever their abilities and good conduct may be so marked, as to induce the Lords Commissioners of the Admiralty to select any of their number for direct advancement. [However], it is by no means implied that, by their having such advancement open to them, the two principal officers above mentioned, should be invariably selected from among the clerks of the yard.

343.   *Comptroller to Admiralty: observations*

[TNA, ADM1/3462]   11 June 1822

Foremen

The proposed establishment of Foremen will I think be found inadequate
to the discharge of the duty expected of them in one of the large yards. I
do not see how the Foreman of one particular trade can judge of the works
of another to which he has not been bred. I do not think a Master Foreman
is necessary in all the yards.

With respect to the caulkers, a very important duty, it must be borne in
mind that there is no master, and I therefore think a foreman indisputably
necessary.

The distinction of foremen according to their particular trades, where
any are allowed, is convenient, and attaches a responsibility of the
individual, and acting in their different departments, they are a check upon
any wasteful expenditure.

Quartermen

It is certainly not very material whether the persons having charge of a
company of artificers are called Quartermen, or Leading men, so that they
are totally independent of the workingmen, and have an acknowledged
authority & distinct salary.

It must be borne in mind that the men working by task or job will
accomplish as much work as possible, no matter to them whether well or
ill done, the object is to swell the amount of their earnings, and as a
portion of their work is often closed in before the measurer arrives to take
account of it, the quantity done must in many instances be rendered by
the man, if not under the superintendence and constant observation of
some responsible person whose pay is totally distinct from the earnings
of the people; and I believe it may be fairly said that a quarterman will
well earn the reduced salary suggested by the late committee of the Navy
Board, namely £156 per annum if he sees to the perfect execution of the
work of thirty men.

If bolts are not driven, and the work upon important parts of a ship
should be slighted for want of a sufficient superintendence, the evil may
not be discovered immediately, but when the ships are brought into
service, lamentable & fatal instances of feebleness may occur, calculated
to prove that the present system, with all the extravagance inflicted to it,
is that which is the most safe and economical.

A reference to the complaints made of the condition of the *Achilles*, *Sterling Castle*, *Ajax* &c on their first going to sea, will show how necessary it is to watch over the works of every shipwright.

Leading Men

The substitution of leading men for quartermen and paying them as proposed, is, I fear likely to break down all the securities arising out of the deep investigation of the Commissioners for Inquiring into Fees and Gratuities, the Commissioners of Naval Enquiry, and the Commissioners of Naval Revision. It is exposing the public to all the abuses which formerly prevailed both as to workmanship and wages.

In proposing that the Leading Man shall have a small allowance in addition to his earnings, it is of course to be understood that he is to work in order to acquire earnings, and as the amount must depend upon his exertions, and the time he is employed, it is not very likely that he will part with his tools to look after the men. Consequently the work will be hurried on by the men, on the principle that 'the more done the more pay' and if this observation is correct the public money will be spent in building unsafe ships.

But suppose the Leading Man does quit his tools in order that he may act the part of a Quarterman, by giving strict attention to the works. In that case he personally can have no earnings. But as the earnings of the company are divided between them, he must share in the labour of others, who will have first cause to complain of such an arrangement.

The person charged with the superintendence of a gang of shipwrights has a very considerable responsibility attached to him. All the materials required from the store cabin and from the Timber Master, are issued upon his demand. He is responsible for the right application of those materials, and accountable for any that may not be used. He also renders an account of the timber expended.

He is to see the fastenings properly placed, and the workmanship substantially performed. In order to guard against a reoccurrence of those abuses to which I have before alluded, the Quarterman is obliged to take an account of the names of the persons who drive each bolt in the lower part of the ship, that in case the work is improperly executed it may at once be traced to the individual. This has the best effect in securing the most perfect workmanship. But a leading workingman cannot do this, as he will be busy about his own earnings.

If a Leading Man who is to share in the earnings of the people, and who would have a direct interest in endeavouring to swell the earnings to the greatest amount, by allowing them to slight their work, and by giving exaggerated statements of the work closed in, is to take the place of a Quarterman, whose wages are totally distinct from the earnings of the people, I cannot but think the worst consequences will result from such a measure.

344. *Petition of Quartermen*

[TNA, ADM1/5132]   July 1822

The memorial and humble petition of the quartermen belonging to His Majesty's Yard at Chatham sheweth, that your memorialists, attained the situations they now hold, either as a reward for faithful service, or as a step towards future promotions in the line of shipwright officers. That many of your memorialists acquired these appointments for having fulfilled the arduous and responsible duties as overseers of ships building or repairing, which they undertook sometimes with loss and inconvenience to themselves & their families, with a view to the ultimate benefit of being quartermen for life, or at least until they were past service. That others of your Lordships memorialists had hoped, by great assiduity and attention to their duties & by professional skill and ability, to get further advanced as officers. But this recourse, having been cut off by the appointment of young men educated at the Naval College, the only hope left them was that of holding their present appointment and income which, when their Services were required by day and by night as well as on Sundays, they were told (in answer to an application for some extra allowance on this account) that their salaries were fixed for peace & war. Therefore, what they lost in one they would gain in the other. These views being again frustrated by the reductions that your Lordships feel necessary to make in the dockyards, your memorialists are under apprehension that themselves, and families will be exposed to distress and that at a time of life when your memorialists cannot seek any other line of support, unless your Lordships be pleased to make an adequate compensation for their loss. They therefore most humbly lay their cases before your Lordships and respectfully and earnestly entreat you will be pleased to consider their uncomfortable and uncertain prospects, and grant them such compensation as shall best make up for the loss of their situation & salaries.

345. *Views of an Anonymous Writer*

[*Observations on the Recent Abolition of Certain Situations,* ... (1824)[1]]

[*On the Abolition of the Offices of Clerk of the Check and Clerk of the Rope Yard, p. 4*]
I would ask when stores are to be received at *one* or *more* parts of the yard; lots to be delivered at another; and the measurement of works performed by contract at another; *who is to superintend?* This is not an improper question, nor is the statement by any means exaggerated. *All those duties* are *frequently* to be *performed* at the *same time.* Who then is to superintend? How are they to be attended to? Are the merchants, the clerks, the workmen, the horses, &c. to *wait* at one part of the yard, until the officer be disengaged from some other service to attend to them? If so, the expense of paying so many persons and horses for standing idle should be considered. As well as, whether the merchant will be satisfied with the delay, or whether he will not in anticipation thereof, require *additional prices* in his *future contracts,* to compensate for the same. If so, who can calculate the consequent loss to the Public?

[*On the Limited Practical Experience of Clerical Officers Appointed to the Dockyards, p. 21*]
With respect to the appointment of the clerks of the Check and the Storekeeper, the same omission of previous practical experience is observable, as that in the civil commissioners of the Navy Board; those officers being frequently appointed from secretaries to admirals, pursers in the Royal Navy, and officers and clerks from other departments of the Navy. Now, whatever may be the general utilities of those gentlemen, they can have but little, if any, knowledge of dockyard duty previously to their appointment as responsible dockyard officers. Such previous knowledge would be so advantageous to the public service, and the want of it must operate in an inverse ratio.

[*On the Abolition of Quartermen, pp. 11–13*]
[It is] with extreme concern that I find so respectable and useful a body of officers abolished; and the places supplied by an inferior class, denominated *leading men.* Each [Leading Man] has charge of *ten* working men; whose *workmanship* he must superintend the due *execution* of; the stores for whose use he must *draw* (that is *obtain officially* from the

[1]Anon., *Observations on the Recent Abolition of Certain Situations, including Quartermen and the New Arrangement of the Clerks in His Majesty's Dockyard* (London, 1824).

storehouses) and have the charge of; as also of whatever *conversions* of *materials* may be required for him to attend to (so that no wasteful expenditure of the *one*, nor *improper conversions* of the other may take place). At the *same time*, that all these *important duties*, are *required from him* (for which additional duty he is allowed only *six pence per diem* extra) he is to *perform* the *same quantity of work*, as *each* of his *men*, or otherwise, will be *paid as much less*, as his work may fall short thereof.

Let us here compare the expense of the two systems. The salary of a Quarterman of the 1st Class was £180 per ann.; that of the 2nd class £160 per ann.; each of whom had charge of a company of working shipwrights, the average number of which has been before stated to be twenty men. *Two* leading men have now the charge of the *same number of men*, for which duty they are allowed sixpence per diem extra *each*. Allowing 313 working days to the year, [this] will amount to £15. 13s. per annum, by which a saving appears to the public of £164. 7s. per annum for each company; reckoning the Quarterman to be of the 1st class. This saving, however, can *only really* be the case in the event of each Leading Man being able to discharge *every part* of his duty, with the *same correctness*, as a Quarterman. Should he, from *want of time fail to attend* to the *expenditure* of the *stores* used by his party, and they in consequence should *waste*, or *improperly expend stores*, to the *amount only* of sixpence per diem *each man* (which cannot be considered an extravagant calculation, when the nature and *value* of the articles used in shipbuilding are considered), annual loss to the public would be £156. 10s. per diem for each company.

346. Commissioner Cunningham to Navy Board: duties of commissioner

[TNA, ADM106/1828] 29 January 1824

I have received your letter of the 12th instant, adverting to the several warrants issued by you on the subject of the preservation of timbers and masts; and admonishing me, that under the new system of conducting the dockyard duties, I must feel it rests with me to see that nothing is left undone which can tend to secure to the public the advantage to be expected from a due attention to this important matter.

Upon which I am induced to remark that as far as the short time I have been here, has enabled me to discover, the officers appear to have attended strictly to the several instructions contained in the said warrant for the preservation of timber and masts as much as the local situation of the yard will admit.

With regard to the allusion that under the new system, <u>more responsibility</u> rests upon me than before, I conceive it to be only in terms, and not in fact. It has always been impressed on my mind that the commissioner was, in a degree, responsible for the arrangement and duty of the business of the dockyard, notwithstanding the former mode of conducting it, differing from the present. Upon [this] principle I have invariably acted, keeping in view every possible measure that would tend to economy, or conduct to the good order and safety of the King's stores in general (as well as to the preservation of timber and masts in particular). Being fully aware of the importance and necessity of a due attention to this matter, to secure to the public, the advantage that would naturally be expected to arise there from.

I therefore regret that the Board should have considered it necessary thus to enforce upon me a particular point of duty which has uniformly occupied my unremitting attention, and I trust has not, by omitting anything that could be effected either at this yard (or at those over which I have before had the control), given the least occasion for such a caution, which in my view implies a censure for the want of due attention to this part of the important duty entrusted to my care.

As everything that can be done to accompany the object the Board have in view, in preserving timber and masts, has been attended to here, I have not any suggestions to offer at present on the subject.

347. *Master Attendant to Navy Board: memorial of Charles Duncan*

[TNA, ADM106/1832]   September 1826

Your memorialist is now in the seventy-fifth year of his life. He entered merchant sea service in the year 1768 and continued serving therein in the Baltic, Mediterranean, North America and West Indies until the 20th August 1779 when he entered into His Majesty's service on board the *Princess Royal* (being the flag of Admiral Byron in the West Indies). On the 7th September following [he] received a warrant from Admiral Parker (whose flag was then on board the ship) appointing him Master of the *Conqueror* of 74 guns commanded by Captain Walter Griffiths who was killed in action with three French line of battle ships in Fort Royal Bay, Martinique. Your memorialist has hence forth continued in His Majesty's Service up to the present time (with the exception of three years in which he commanded a vessel on a voyage round the world and three years in the service of the Honourable Hudson Bay Company on a voyage of discovery), in times of peace and with leave from the Honourable Navy Board.

Your memorialist has served forty years in active service, in which time he has commanded three of His Majesty's Store ships viz. the *Serapis*, *William* and *Prevoyante*, with valuable cargoes in the Mediterranean in time of war. He has served in three of His Majesty's dockyards viz. one year and upwards as warden of Woolwich yard, five years as Master Attendant of Sheerness yard and upwards of seventeen years in the latter capacity at Chatham yard, making altogether twenty-three years of civil service. [In] all these services of trust and responsibility your memorialist has had the satisfaction of meeting the approbation of every Admiral, Captain and Commissioner under whom he has served, at home and abroad, three of which Captains have become Deputy Controllers at the Navy viz. Commissioners Harwood, Martell and Shield. Your memorialist herewith encloses a certificate from the surgeon of Chatham Dockyard where he is now serving.

Your memorialist on the 25th August 1817 had the misfortune to fall on board His Majesty's Ship *Poictiers* while in the execution of his duty whereby he received a serious hurt in the left thigh, which confined him at home for six weeks. He was also about five years since knocked over the wharf into the water by the shipping of horses, while he was superintending one of His Majesty's cutters, and must on that occasion have been drowned but for the timely assistance of one of the walking wardens.

Your memorialist in consequence of his age and infirmity feels that he can no longer carry on his duty with that energy that he wishes and to which he has been accustomed; and therefore thinks he may be allowed to retire from His Majesty's service with such remuneration as he may be thought deserving and your memorialist will as in duty bound ever pray ...

[*Appended note*]
The facts stated by the Memorialist relates to the hurts received in the Yard are perfectly correct. I personally attended him on the last occasion and considered it a serious one. P. Roland, Surgeon.

[*Enclosed certificate*]
These are to certify that Mr Charles Duncan was born on the books of His Majesty's ships above mentioned the time and qualities expressed:

Woolwich Yard	2nd August 1801 to 16 August 1802
Sheerness Yard	13 September 1804 to 13 November 1809
Chatham Yard	14 September 1809 to 27th September 1826

348.   *Yard Officers to Commissioner Cunningham: timber receiver*

[TNA, ADM106/1834]   21 April 1827

Proposal
The duty of Timber Receiver is to consist in receiving all timber brought to the yard under the same regulations and in the same manner as is now done by the Timber Master.

Observation
It is presumed that the Timber Receiver will have from time to time as many Shipwrights as may be necessary to prepare the timber for his inspection and survey, prior to its measurement and receipt by him and a Clerk from the Check Office. Also that he will be allowed a Clerk from the Storekeeper's Office to write the Storekeeper's section of the receipt, as is now the custom for one to attend from the Timber Master's office.

   Whenever it may occur that any article of timber shall be found by the Timber Receiver not agreeable to the contract under which the same has been delivered, yet would be useful in His Majesty's Service, is [*sic*] the Storekeeper, in conjunction with the Timber Receiver and Master Shipwright, to report the same to the Board and propose terms for its receipt, as is now the practice in the office of Timber Master.

Proposal
The duty of the Timber Converter is to consist in taking charge of the timber when passed by the Receiver, and in directing and regulating its conversion.

Observation
It is inferred that the charge hereby intended will consist in the proper stowage and preservation of the timber previous to its conversion so that the Converter may at all times know where to find that timber which is best adapted for any particular purpose.

Proposal
The Timber Receiver and the Timber Converter are to keep memoranda of what they do in the execution of the said duties, as may be deemed most advisable. Such notes or memoranda to be delivered into the office of the Storekeeper when the people leave the yard for dinner and when they quit at night – by which means it is considered that these two officers will check on each other.

Observation

The daily sections of the receipt of timber will be the only memoranda taken in the presence of the Timber Receiver, which, under his signature, with that of the clerks named in the first remark, will constitute the authority for charging the Storekeeper with the received articles and will enable him to keep his unconverted store as well as the state of contracts. Moreover, we do not perceive that any memoranda this office could keep would prove a check upon the transactions of the Timber Converter.

To enable the Timber Converter to keep an account of what he does in the execution of his duty, he must be allowed the same assistance as the Timber Master has at present: that is a shipwright to take an account of the timber brought to the saw pits and another at the saw mill for conversion and [to] compare its distinguishing or marked contents with the received contents entered in the Storekeeper's ledger and after its conversion to measure and bring to account on form No. 324, the particulars of the several articles that arise from the conversion of each piece of timber thick stuff or plank: which memoranda (under the signature of the Timber Converter) will be the only memoranda that can be kept, from which the Storekeeper can discharge his unconverted store and charge himself with the converted articles. With due deference to the Board we would propose that these memoranda should be returned once only in the course of the day instead of twice, as is directed.

Proposal

Instead of the work being measured daily and paid for weekly, such proportion as may be deemed proper of the estimated earnings are to be paid weekly only.

Observation

We consider that four shillings per diem would be a proper advance on account to shipwrights and a proportionate sum to the other branches of workmen. [This] advance would not be likely to exceed the earnings of the men during the month. In taking account of the works performed by each gang, the several measurers should have two books. Form No. 315, to make their entries therein, alternately week and week, as the works are completed and likely to be closed in or hid from view, or otherwise removed from the place of execution. [This] measure will afford the Clerk of the Check an opportunity of valuing the work, so as to close the account of earnings of each gang at the end of the month (which we presume will always terminate on the last Saturday) and pay the balance on the subsequent week.

Proposal

The afore going arrangement will save much labour, the measurers in addition to the measuring which will be required under the system will be able to render efficient, assistance to the Foreman, to whom they may respectively be attached, and who will exercise over them the same superintendence respecting the measurement duty as was heretofore done by the Master Measurer.

Observation

We do not perceive that the afore [*sic*] going arrangement will relieve the measurers from so great a proportion of duty as appears to be contemplated, nor that they will be able to afford efficient assistance to the Foremen to whom they may be attached.

The duty of the Measurer is greater and of more consequence than is generally conceived – and although the present number of measurers do perform the duty, we are by no means satisfied that it would not be an advantage to the service to augment their number, rather than heap additional duties upon those now employed.

In consequence of the constantly varying number of workmen employed under the Foremen's superintendence the measurer will not be able to be attached to any particular Foreman, they must follow the men from time to time, so as to keep an equal distribution of their services. From the constant intercourse that the Foreman will have with the Measurer while directing the execution of the works, they will have frequent opportunities of witnessing the measurement of works. In all such cases we would propose that the Foreman shall sign the measurements thus taken, as well as the general account of works performed. [This] will operate as a check upon the measurements, and cause a more vigilant superintendence of both the Foreman and Measurers than might otherwise be given and that the measurers do attend the muster and working hours of the yard, with the workmen.

349. *Comptroller of the Navy Board: minute on quartermen*

[BL, Add Ms 41,367, f271]   No date, *c.* 1829

It was an anxious desire to effect reduction of expenditure that led the Admiralty, in my opinion, to the hasty abolition of the description of petty officers, called quartermen, and I think without sufficient consideration of the importance of their duty as regards the superintendence of the shipwright workmen.

I did at the time state my objection to this measure, both verbally and in writing. [I] suggested as a preferable mode of reduction, that the measurers (as a distinct branch of business) should be discontinued; and that each quarterman (having the superintendence of thirty men) should also be charged with the measurement of their work, thus uniting the duties of superintendence and measurer. Taking care at the same time to provide for a suitable superintendence in the event of a portion of the 30 men being employed by and in immediate reach of the quartermen.

350. *Admiralty to Navy Board: proposed reforms*

[TNA, ADM1/3470]   27 November 1829

The Storekeeper is to take receipts from all the stores he issues either to the Masters of His Majesty's Ships, the Foremen of the Yard or other duly authorized persons to whom he may deliver them, the form of these receipts, to be arranged as the Navy Board think proper. These receipts are to be considered sufficient vouchers to clear the storekeeper of the stores mentioned in them, when he passes his accounts, provided the persons who have signed the said receipts were duly authorized to demand and receive the said stores upon which point it is to be the duty of the Storekeeper in future to be informed. To meet this object he is to have the several documents transferred to him, which have hitherto enabled the Clerk of the Cheque to ascertain the propriety and correctness of demands for Stores and likewise their value.

The Storekeeper is also in future to have in his office and under his superintendence the several clerks and other persons employed in valuing the work performed in the yard and costing the pay of the workmen or as many of them as may be undertaking the duty.

All the salaries of the officers and the large and regular payments of the yard will hereafter be made by the Treasurer's Clerks. The Storekeeper must make such of allotment, pensions &c as are directed by Acts of Parliament to be paid by clerks of the check and to satisfy the said Acts. The Storekeeper is to be designated as 'Clerk of the Check and Storekeeper' until the contemplated Act for consolidating and amending the several Acts relating to the Navy shall legally transfer the payments in question to the Treasurer's Clerks resident in the yards, after which the title 'Clerk of the Check' will be wholly abolished.

The Storekeeper is to receive all small payments hitherto received by the Clerk of the Check and all their fees for commissions &c. delivered in the yard. To facilitate which latter object, the Commissioner is to send to the Storekeeper all the commissions, or other documents, upon which fees are payable, sent to him for delivery to the parties on the spot. On the parties calling upon him for them, he is to direct them to proceed to the Storekeeper's Office to receive them and pay the Fees. The Store-keeper's account current for these receipts and disbursements is to be balanced weekly and to be certified as to its correctness by the commissioners. Whatever sum appears to be in his hands beyond what the Navy Board shall deem necessary for the current service under the intended arrangement, is to be paid over to the Treasurer's Clerk. Through whom he shall receive what the Commissioner may at any time certify to the Navy Board to be necessary to enable him to make the payments required of him, should, the fees and other small payments received by him fall short of that amount.

The better to enable the Storekeeper to perform with perfect correctness the several very important duties with which he is thus charged, he is to be wholly exempted for the future from the various out door duties performed by the other officers of the yards. [This is] so that his undivided attention may be given to the stores, keeping correct accounts of their disposal, with the value of those issued, and giving a really efficient superintendence of all the persons under him in his office and department.

The other duties of the Clerk of the Check are to be disposed of as follows: all the receipts and payments of money are to be paid to the Treasurer's clerk resident in the yard under such arrangement, as may be settled between the Navy Board and the Treasurer for this object.

The duty of mustering ships afloat, which has hitherto been performed by the Clerk of the Yard (or another subordinate officer from his office), is for the future to be performed by the Master Attendant or one of his assistant masters (as is now done with regard to the ordinary). For the purpose of transmitting the muster books, the clerks now in the Check Office for this particular duty (or such as them as may be deemed necessary) are to be transferred to the office of the Master Attendant. The mustering of the people into and out of the yard may be likewise performed by a clerk of the Master Attendant's office, instead of by one as hitherto from the Check Office.

The situation of Clerk of the Check of the dockyard will thus be abolished, but an officer of the same pay and qualification is to be established as 'Receiver of Stores'. [His duty will be] to examine strictly all stores supplied to the yard; to receive only such as he finds to be according to contract and fit for the service, and to reject such as are not so. The better to enable him to execute this duty perfectly, he is to be attended while receiving stores, by the foreman of the trade or business to which such stores appertain. That is, if iron is to be received, he is to be attended by the Master Smith or a foreman of smiths; if hemp, by the Master Rope-maker or foreman of rope-makers and so on. When timber is to be received he is to be attended by one of the assistants of the Master

Shipwright or by a foreman of the yard, but the former always in preference, when the duties of the yard can admit of it without material inconvenience.

The Store Receiver will also be attended by a clerk of the Storekeeper's Office to check on the part of the Storekeeper the quantities received. The stores, on being passed by the Store Receiver, are to be immediately charged to the Storekeeper and to be disposed of by him, subject however to being re-examined, either as to quantity or quality, by such officers as the Commissioner may direct, in the event of the Storekeeper seeing reason to demand it. Previous to placing any of the said articles in his storehouses, the Store Receiver is to send daily to the Navy Board a correct account, of the quantity and description of all the stores he has received and passed to the charge of the Storekeeper in the course of the day. He is to enter in books to be kept by him correct copies of the said daily returns made by him to the Navy Board. [The keeping of these] books, and noting the quantities and description of stores whilst examining and passing them, will be the only clerical duties to be executed under him. It is supposed that two or three clerks at most will prove as many as he will require but this point may be left to the discretion of the Commissioner to report upon after a short experience of the quantity of clerical labours required in the efficient execution of the duty now described.

When more than one delivery of stores shall be going forward at the same time, the Commissioner, on being requested to do so by the Store Receiver, is to direct his secretary, or such other first class officers of the yard that he may think proper (excepting always the Storekeeper), to inspect and receive one of such deliveries for the Receiver. The officer so appointed to assist the Receiver is to deliver to him immediately afterwards a statement signed by such officer, of the quantity and description of stores received and packed by him, that the Store Receiver may include the same in his daily return to the Navy Board.

Thus the Navy Board will have a perfect and constant check on the Storekeeper, as to all new stores delivered to him, from which he can only clear himself by producing receipts of their delivery to persons duly authorized to demand and receive them from him.

When old stores are returned to the dockyard from His Majesty's Ships, or from other quarters, the Storekeeper is to give receipts for them to the parties returning them, copies of which receipts are to be sent to the Navy Board at the earliest opportunity by the Storekeeper, and the originals to be transmitted with the accounts of the party who returned the stores.

The Commissioner's Secretary and the Store Receiver will be expected to take their turn of all the out door duties required of the first class officers of the yard such as attending the gates after work, the sales of old stores etc. etc. It [is] intended that the Storekeeper [will] be the only officer exempted from them, and confined to the store and clerical duties.

The Master Shipwright is to be considered almost entirely as a superintending outdoor officer. The only clerical duty to be performed under his direction being to mark out the progress of works performed and performing for transmission to the Admiralty and Navy Board and to prepare for the Commissioner's consideration the daily scheme for the distribution of the officers and workmen of the yard. It is supposed that one clerk will be quite sufficient to attach to him for such duty and to answer any reference, which may be made to him. It [is] understood that as the Commissioner's order book to him, and all letters addressed to him individually, are left with him, it is quite unnecessary for him to have them copied into other books, nor in short to have any writing going forward in his office, beyond that which has been above specified.

351. *First Lord to Prime Minister, Earl Grey: discussion paper*

[Cumbria R.O., D/GN/3/1/9]   6 December 1831

It will be necessary to make an alteration in the nature of the appointment of the officers now styled commissioners of the dockyards and victualling establishments at the out ports and abroad. Instead of being commissioners by patent, they must be superintendents of their respective stations under warrant from the Admiralty. In making these appointments, the practice has generally been to send the officers selected first to a foreign yard, and then, after a long probation abroad, to place them either in the Navy Office or in one of the yards at home. The consequence of this is that when they arrive at the most important stations that require the utmost energy and activity, they are generally worn out with age and infirmity and too frequently consider their appointment in the light only of an honourable retirement. This course is altogether inconsistent with the interests of the public service and it is most desirable to select young able and intelligent naval officers, in the full vigour of life, who alone are fit for filling situations of this high responsibility, where active exertions are required. They should have a commission from the Admiralty, giving them authority afloat, according to their rank as on full pay. [This will prevent] the improper interference of junior officers in commission, of which the civil servants of the dockyard have too frequent reason to complain. Their rank should not be stopped, but they should proceed by seniority to their flag, as if serving at sea. When from age, infirmity, or any other cause, it may be necessary to remove them from their civil appointments, they should fall back to their place on the list and be entitled to the half pay of the rank which they may have attained. If fit for service, they may at any time be allowed to volunteer for employment afloat, to which their acceptance of the civil office should not be considered a bar. The present system of granting superannuation on retirement, in addition to the half pay of the Rear Admiral, frequently together amounting to £800 or £1000 a year ought, on no account, any longer to be permitted. The civil pay and emoluments of the Superintendents, while actively employed in the civil service, should remain the same as those now enjoyed by the commissioners.

352. *Excess of Yard Officers*

[Wade (ed.), *The Extraordinary Black Book*, p. 376[1]]   1832

The expenditure in the Royal Dockyards and arsenals is most lavish in storekeepers, clerks, chaplains, surgeons, measurers, master-attendant, master shipwright and others, many of whom are apparently kept up for mutual superintendence, and forming a gradation of office and multi-plication of expense wholly unnecessary. Not a single trade is carried out without a master; there is a master-smith, bricklayer, sail-maker, rigger, rope-maker, painter, and others. They have each £250 a year, and many of them have not above four or five men under their superintendence. How differently private and public business is conducted was strikingly shown in the evidence of Mr Barrow. There is a private builder who employs 250 shipwrights: he has one foreman, one measurer, two clerks and ten labourers. In Woolwich yard, which comes nearest to it, there are 248 shipwrights, eighteen clerks, six masters of trades, eight foremen, eight measurers, eleven cabin-keepers; besides surgeons, boatswain, wardens and other people.

353. *Abolition of Resident Commissioners*

[Act of Parliament, 2 William IV c.40 Ch X]   1832

... such superintendents from time to time to be appointed, shall have full power and authority to do, execute, and perform all duties, matters and things which by any Act or Acts of Parliament now in force any

---

[1]John Wade (ed.), *The Extraordinary Black Book: An Exposition of Abuses in Church and State* ... (London, 1832).

commissioner of the navy or victualling, resident at any naval or victualling yard or establishment, or at any naval hospital, at home or abroad, is authorised or required to do.

354.   *Order-in-Council: retention of naval rank by dockyard superintendents*

[TNA, ADM1/3477]   9 June 1832

And whereas the Act, above mentioned, provides that the duties hitherto performed by commissioners for the several dockyards and other naval victualling and medical establishments at home and abroad, shall in future be executed by principal officers to be called Superintendents.

We would humbly suggest that Your Majesty would be graciously pleased by Your Majesty's order in council to nominate and appoint such superintendents to all those naval victualling and medical establishments at home and abroad at which commissioners of the navy or victualling have been heretofore resident, which we may find that each superintendent may be advantageously placed for the benefit of Your Majesty's naval service. That it may be further authorised to assign to each of the said superintendents such duties, and to give them such instructions, as the service over which they are respectively appointed, may appear to us to require. And as it appears that it may be conducive to the better discipline and management of Your Majesty's dockyards, and other naval establishments, if the said superintendents, or such of them as may desire it to be expedient, were put in commission, by which they would be able to exercise a more extended and complete authority. We would humbly submit to Your Majesty that Your Majesty would be pleased to authorise us to place in commission accordingly such as the said superintendents, more especially of Your Majesty's dockyards, as we may think will enable them to execute their duties in better effect for the public advantage.

And that all of them, whether in commission or not, should be allowed the time which they may pass in the discharge of their civil duties to be reckoned as so much sea time past afloat, and their rank may regularly go in the service, without intervention, so long as they shall continue in their respective civil capacities. That upon retirement, instead of being granted any superannuation allowance, they shall fall back on half pay according to the rank they may then respectively have obtained. That if fit for active service afloat they may be considered eligible for commissions corresponding with their rank in the same manner as if they had not served in the civil departments of the Navy.

355. *Warrant: appointment of Superintendent Gordon*

[NMM, CHA/H/1] 9 June 1832

By the Commissioners for executing the office of Lord High Admiral of Great Britain and Ireland to Sir James Alexander Gordon, KCB, a Captain in His Majesty's Navy, hereby appointed Captain Superintendent of His Majesty's Dock Yards at Chatham and Sheerness by virtue of the power and authority to us given we do hereby constitute and appoint you Captain Superintendent of His Majesty's dockyards at Chatham and Sheerness to be employed in conducting the business of the said dockyards during our pleasure willing and requiring you to take upon you the charge and duties of Captain Superintendent of the said dockyards accordingly and to obey all such instructions as you may from time to time receive from us for your guidance in the execution of the said duties strictly charging and commanding all persons employed as subordinates to you to behave themselves jointly and severally with all respect and obedience unto you as their Captain Superintendent and for your care and trouble in the execution of the duties of your office you will be entitled to receive a salary of £1,000 per annum until further orders and for so doing, this shall be your warrant.

356. *General Instructions for Principal Officers*

[TNA, ADM1/3480] 18 July 1833

Article 1
The resident Admiral or Captain Superintendent shall have full authority over all officers and other persons whatsoever employed in the dockyard and ordinary and shall control every part of the business carried on therein. He is to exercise the power vested in him, as often as he may see occasion, for the purpose of enforcing obedience to all orders and regulations issued by us, or by himself, to the end that every person may discharge the duties of his office with zeal, alacrity, and fidelity. To ensure which, he has the power of suspending any officer, clerk, or other person belonging to the dockyard, reporting to us the cause and circumstances thereof, in order that the case may be dealt with, as it may appear to require.

Article 2
All orders, warrants, and letters from this Board [the Admiralty] will be addressed to the Superintendent; from whom the Principal Officers will receive such instructions on the several points contained in the said orders,

letters and warrants, as may concern their respective departments, immediately after the receipt thereof, or as speedily as the same can be done. All reports from the officers of the yard shall be made to, and transmitted when necessary by, the Superintendent to our secretary for our information and directions.

Article 3
> The Master Attendant,
> Master Shipwright,
> Storekeeper,
> Store Receiver,
> Surgeon and
> Chaplain,

are to be considered as the principal officers of the yard. In case of the absence of the Superintendent, the Master Attendant shall be charged with his duties, with the exception of those belonging to the ordinary, which are to devolve upon the Captain or Senior Officer. In the absence of the Master Attendant, the Master Shipwright is to be charged with the Superintendent's duties, care being taken that not more than one of these officers be absent at the same time, if it can possibly be avoided. Generally, in the absence of any of the respective officers, the next in rank in his department shall be charged with the duties thereof.

Article 4
The several officers shall reside in the houses allotted for their use by the establishment of the yard and shall enjoy the gardens and offices respectively attached to them. They shall not have the power of letting them, in whole or in part, to any person whatever. No expense in repairs or alterations is to be incurred in any of them without our express authority. No artificer or labourer is to be privately employed for domestic purposes, either within doors or without, upon any pretence whatsoever.

Article 5
The principal officers are to consider themselves responsible for the correct discharge of the duties of their respective departments, and for any neglect in those who are placed immediately under them. They are also generally to prevent (whether in their own department or any other) the artificers, labourers, and others, from loitering away their time, committing embezzlement or waste, or misbehaving in any manner to the prejudice of the service. They are to report all instances of misconduct to the Superintendent.

Article 6

When any vacancy occasioned by promotion or otherwise shall occur, the Superintendent, after consulting the officer in whose department such vacancy may happen (except in the case of first appointment of clerks), shall forward to the Admiralty the name of the person who may appear the most fit for the situation, provided it be absolutely necessary to fill it up. No person whatever shall be entered on the establishment of the yard without previous concurrence.

357. *General Instructions for Foremen and Inspectors*

[TNA, ADM1/3480] 18 July 1833

[Foreman of the Yard, Article 4]

When the workmen intended to be employed under you shall have been mustered, upon coming into the yard, you are to cause them to proceed, without delay, to the works which may be allotted to them respectively (taking care that all the Inspectors and Leading Men pay constant and unremitting attention to their duty). You are to allot to each of these officers the particular work upon which his company is to be employed.

[Inspectors, Article 4]

You are to employ your company upon such work as the Foreman, or other your superior officer, may direct. You are to take care, as far as it may depend on you, that by the time one piece of work shall be finished, everything be prepared for the men to begin another, so that they may always be fully employed. You are also to take particular care that all works under performance by your gangs [of twenty shipwrights] or companies [two gangs of shipwrights working together] be in all respects executed in a substantial and workmanlike manner, and with as much expedition and economy as the nature of the service will admit; observing, that you will be answerable for all such works, as well as for the conduct of all the persons employed under you. You are, therefore, always to dispose of your men to the best advantage, and, when necessary, you are to allot to each individual the particular stint which he is to perform. [You are to keep] an account of the part of the ship on which each man may be employed, especially in the cases of driving copper bolts, and coppering of ships, in order that any defects, when discovered, may be traced to the parties concerned, and that those who may have improperly performed their work, may be mulcted, or discharged, as the case may require. For this purpose, you are also, upon the completion of each piece of work, to deliver to the Foreman, a certificate to be lodged in the Master

Shipwright's office, of the copper bolts driven by each person under your inspection.

358.   *Superintendent Gordon to Admiralty: retirement of Master Attendant*

[TNA, ADM1/3403]   9 July 1836

In Obedience to the commands of My Lords Commissioners of the Admiralty, signified in your circular of the 7th instant, I beg leave to report that I consider Mr William Payne, the Master Attendant of this yard, to be incapable, from age and infirmity, of performing his duty in an efficient and proper manner; but that his Assistant, Mr Alexander Southern, though no longer a young man, has sufficient energy and activity to enable him to do all that can be required of him; and he still is as zealous an officer, as he proved himself to be, in the whole period he served at sea under my command.

359.   *Admiralty to Superintendent of Chatham Dockyard: workforce correspondence*

[TNA, ADM222/11]   16 March 1841

I am commanded by my Lord Commissioners of the Admiralty to acquaint you that numerous letters are daily addressed to their Lordships by the artificers and workmen in the dockyards, which their Lordships consider highly irregular and improper. It is their direction that you do acquaint the various persons under your control that my Lords will not entertain any application for the future which are not previously approved, and transmitted by you for their consideration.

360.   *J.S. Bromley to First Lord: recommendations for dockyard management*

[Report of Inquiry into the Management of H.M. Naval Yards, 1860]   1847

[Meeting of Shipwright Officers, p. 487]
I would submit the propriety of the Master Shipwright assembling around him every morning all his assistants and foremen, to read the orders of the day, and to receive from them reports, and to discuss the state of the works in progress, and advise together on all points connected with their

joint duties. There must be many points upon which the concurrent judgment of the executive officers would prove of great value in carrying on the duties of the shipwright department. According to the system at present pursued at some yards, the foremen do not see the Master shipwright for days together, but receive their instructions from him on slips of paper.

[Meeting of Superior Officers, p. 488]
It is generally admitted that at almost all the yards, with the exception of Pembroke, there is an absence of that cordial communication between the superior officers, and co-operation in their duties, which the interest of the public service demands. To remedy this, the officers generally are of opinion that the practice pursued at the time when the yards were presided over by commissioners of the navy should be resorted to: that all the superior officers of the yard should meet the superintendent at a certain hour every day, to hear the orders read, and *consult* together upon the orders of the day. The officers should be required to bring forward every matter affecting their departments at these open meetings, instead of reserving their communications for a private consultation with the superintendent when no other superior officer is present to advise him.

[Printed Instructions, p. 489]
It is generally admitted at the yards that the printed instructions should be divided, so that each officer might be furnished with that part of them which relates to his own particular duties. As many corrections in them might be made; I would suggest, before they are reprinted, the superior officers of each yard should be called upon for any remarks they may consider necessary to make upon their respective instructions: the most practical of which should be embodied in the revised instructions.

[Task Work and Day Pay, p. 487]
With reference to the great question of task work and day pay, I have not failed to gather the opinion of professional officers upon it. They all seem to favour task work as the best means of obtaining quantity, but prefer a system of day pay for the quality of the work performed. The difference of quantity is stated to be about one-fifth more by task than by day pay. I am assured, however, that if a more marked line should be drawn between the inspecting officer and the men, and a higher degree of control and responsibility attached to his position, a decided improvement would take place. The establishment of schools will be the means of providing hereafter a better educated class of inspecting officers, whose superior qualifications may give them greater influence

over the men, and lead to a very efficient superintendence of dockyard labour.

[Pay Books and Establishments, p. 490]
In the four dockyards, Chatham, Sheerness, Portsmouth and Plymouth, a very imperfect check has existed for years upon the computation of wages and payment of yard workmen.

361. *Minutes of the Committee of Dockyard Revision: measurers*

[TNA, ADM1/5591]   November 1848

In all the yards that we have visited, we have examined the measurers, personally, and collected the opinions of others as to the workings of the system. The value of 'measurements', as a check, is universally recognised. In one instance, (and in one only) a question was raised as to the propriety of confiding this duty to a distinct class of officers, instead of calling upon the inspectors to make a weekly return of the work of the gangs under them. The general opinion, in which we entirely concur, was in favour of a separate independent, measurement.

For, though the Inspectors would not now have the same interest that the old Quartermasters had, in exaggerating the earnings of their gangs, because they gain nothing from increasing them, there would be a natural inclination to swell the amount of work done, in order to enhance the merits of their own superintendence. Besides, an Inspector, if he watches vigilantly the 60 men for whom he is answerable, and keeps his 'Day Book' and his weekly 'Expense Sheet' properly, has quite enough office work to do already. Nor have we found any trace of that jealousy of interference on the part of the Measurers, upon which the argument for making Measurers of the Inspectors was founded. On the contrary, the Inspectors generally have had the good sense to see that the tendency of the new system is to increase their authority, by enabling them to threaten their gangs with having their work measured, when its progress is not satisfactory. The only thing wanting, to give weight to this threat, is that in all cases where idleness is proved the power of mulcting the men should be used firmly by the Master Shipwright.

For the principle of the present system is this: not to measure all work done in the dockyards (which would require ten times the present strength in the measuring office) but that all work, while doing, should be measured occasionally. The Measurers are an instrument, of which the Superintendent, or the Master Shipwright is to avail himself whenever he is dissatisfied with the work of a particular gang and wishes to ascertain whether the men are earning their money. For this purpose, a scale, or Scheme of Prices, has been prepared for each department (based upon an estimate of which a fair day's work ought to produce, or has produced, according to past experience) and the Measurers, founding their calculations upon this scheme, work the results out in money. [This] shows, in any given time, the excess or deficiency of the earnings. There is a 'Scheme of Prices' for labourers' work; another for smiths; another for caulkers; another for shipwrights. Great merit is due to Mr Fincham, the Master Shipwright of Portsmouth Yard, for the care and attention with which they have been compiled. Of course, the accuracy of the result depends upon that of the Schemes of Prices. If too high, they are unfair upon the crown. If too low, they are unfair upon the men, whose labour is estimated by them. In some branches, the present schemes are avowedly deficient, the prices for shipwrights' work being founded upon the old scheme, of 1825, corrected in 1829, which makes no provision for the new works, and works connected with the steam navy. But every day's experience is furnishing additional data, and enabling the Measurers to correct errors and supply deficiencies. The returns ordered by the Board from all the yards, at the end of the first months, some of which have been transmitted already, will suggest valuable alterations. We have no doubt that at the close of the year a general revision of the schemes by a committee of Master Shipwrights and Measurers will supply all that is wanting.

In the meantime we recommend a steady adherence to the system which, even in its present incipient state, is most valuable, as a check upon the men and is furnishing the superintendents and Master Shipwrights with the means of estimating, by accurate data the exertions of all under them. The practice of occasional measurement, judiciously applied, and the certainty that the results will come under the eye of the superintendent at stated intervals – as they ought to do – and will materially guide him in his recommendations for promotion will furnish a great incitement to industry. We recommend the Board of Admiralty to include a monthly inspection of the measurer's book amongst the new duties, with which the Superintendents are charged, and to satisfy themselves at their own annual inspections that this order has not shared the fate of the many excellent rules, which have been allowed to fall into oblivion in the dockyards.

362.   *Committee of Dockyard Revision: dockyard superintendents*

[TNA, ADM1/5591]   14 December 1848

But the system [for administering the royal dockyards] is undeniably defective in some of its most important parts. There is a want of unity about it, and of real responsibility, which generate laxity, and must lead ultimately to abuse. The rules laid down in the dockyard instructions for the guidance of the principal officers are admirable, but their efficacy depends more upon the spirit in which they are carried out as a whole than upon a rigid adherence by particular offices to particular parts. For instance, the Storekeeper and the Store Receiver may conduct their departments in perfect conformity with their respective Instructions, and yet there may be a very lavish expenditure of stores. The Master Shipwright may be careful with expenditure of stores, and yet the public will gain little if the arrangements connected with the landing, stowage and preservation of timber be made without proper forethought and economy (or, if what is technically termed the 'Receipt' of stores, be conducted in a negligent or slovenly manner).

Each dockyard, therefore, must be dealt with as a whole – a machine, the working of which depends upon the systematic action of all its parts. A great manufacturing establishment, to be conducted without the aid of that enlightened self-interest, which regulates and animates, private establishments of a similar kind; and when the only safeguard for the public is to be found in the vigilance and ability of the superintendence substituted for the master's eye.

We entirely concur in the observations contained in the report of the committee on Navy, Army and Ordnance Estimates, upon this point and cannot express our own opinions better than by repeating theirs.

'Whether the Establishment shall perform its work with the diligence and economy depends in great measure upon the vigilance, and assiduity, of the Superintendent. Unless he asserts himself to protect the interest of the public, innumerable expenses from misapplication of labour and materials, [will] pass unregarded and the cost of useful works [will be] enhanced by changes, which should never have been incurred.

The correspondence of the Superintendent affords the only channel through which the Board of Admiralty are made acquainted with the daily transactions of the dockyard. A relaxation of vigilance on his part, or an inaptitude for the complicated duties of his office, must seriously injure the interests of the Navy and render comparatively useless the money granted by Parliament for the maintenance of their establishments.

A public establishment naturally labours under this great disadvantage: no motives of private interest stimulate the officers to enforce the performance of the full amount of work which can be produced, laxity on their part, appears kindness to the workmen; additional hands are readily obtained for work that additional industry that might easily have accomplished.

The officers who superintend the dockyards should not, in the opinion of your committee, be conferred an honorary retirement for past services, however meritorious. It requires activity, habits of command, and methodical arrangement. The order and efficiency of each dockyard will be found principally to depend on the fitness of the Superintendent for the peculiar duties which he is selected to perform'.

We are bound to express our belief that the apprehensions of the committee have been realized in more than one of Her Majesty's Dock Yards. Whether from the shortness of the period, over which their services were likely to extend, or from the difficulty of mastering the details of the system, which they had to administer, or from mistaken kindness towards those under them ... discipline *has* been relaxed – additional labour *has* been employed to do that which additional industry might have accomplished. There has not been that vigorous, and well combined, scheme of direction on the part of the superintendent, which is the only preventative against abuse.

We recommend therefore a division of the rules by which these appointments are now determined. Active habits and vigorous intellect are more essential in such a situation than long familiarity with command; and when men of this stamp can be found, the public has a right to require that there shall be more encouragement to exertion than the present system affords, and a greater security against those frequent changes which, in some of the dockyards, have rendered the adoption of any permanent system impracticable.

For change in itself is a most serious evil. No Superintendent can make himself master of the varied and complicated duties attaching to his office in less than six months; and if he once acquires the habit of regarding them as a matter of routine his power and utility are at an end. By his instructions, he is everything; but, unless he comprehends their full scope and intention, in attempting to execute them literally, he becomes the mere organ of the permanent officers of the dockyard, who assume ascendancy from their familiarity with official details. His signature is appended, mechanically, to their statements and his ideas of responsibility satisfied by their assurance that the instructions throw upon them the responsibility of their several departments, with which it is neither necessary nor desirable for him to interfere.

The Admiralty itself has, to a certain extent, tolerated this view, by not imposing upon the Superintendent duties, the execution of which would bring him periodically into contact with all the branches of the service under him, and force him to regard himself as responsible for their harmonious working; and we shall consequently begin by recommending a change in this respect, which upon mature consideration we regard as calculated to produce an affable practical result.

[Recommendations]
We recommend that a rule should be laid down for all the dockyards, which will bring the Superintendent into daily contact with his officers, and make him the medium of checking more effectually the expenditure both in wages and stores, over which he exercises at present, very little control. We have found almost universal concurrence in the dockyards as to the advantage of reviving the old custom of a morning meeting of the officers to hear the orders of the Admiralty read.

It has been represented to us with singular unanimity that these meetings, when held punctually at a convenient hour by the Superintendent, facilitated business by enabling the heads of the different branches at once to make the necessary arrangements amongst themselves and by placing them more immediately in communication with the superintendent, and giving them the opportunity of making personally and publicly any suggestions, which they may think necessary for the better conducting of their departments, or the more prompt execution of the particular duty assigned to them, which, under the present system, they can only do by a written communication passing through the Superintendent's clerk.

We recommend therefore that a meeting be held at half past nine a.m. precisely in each Dock Yard, at which: the orders for the day are to be read in the presence of the Superintendent, or the officer next to him in rank, and which all the Principal Officers will be expected to attend; and, as this is part, and part only, of a system from which we anticipate important economical changes, we trust that the Board of Admiralty will impress upon the Superintendents, generally, the necessity of strict punctuality in the discharge of a duty, in which their own regularity will be the measure of that yard.

We recommend, further, that a quarterly meeting of all the principal officers be held, at which the Superintendent will preside, to settle the demand for stores for the ensuing quarter.

We feel satisfied that greater economy in the use of stores will best be enforced by greater difficulty in obtaining them. At present nothing can be looser than the system, or less satisfactory than the result. There is no proper check in the Board of Admiralty, and no proper responsibility in the yards. The Superintendents have no accurate knowledge of what is asked, and do not consider it a part of their duty to ascertain whether the stores demanded are really required for the service of the yard, or whether there may not be, on hand, repairable articles, fit to supply their places. The matter is decided between the Storekeeper General, and the Storekeeper of the dockyard, who receives from the professional officers at the commencement of every quarter, the demands for their respective departments, and calculates his own by the quantities in store of the principal articles required. Over the statement thus prepared, the Storekeeper General exercises a large, and useful, discretionary power, but the Superintendent takes no cognizance of [the] original demand, or of the reductions made in it at Somerset House, and holds himself in no way responsible either for the insufficiency or the superabundance of the supply.

We propose to remedy this by directing that the professional officers shall make their demand upon the Storekeeper in writing on the fifth day of the first month of each quarter, and that on the seventh, or the following day, if the seventh be a Sunday, the Superintendent should hold an estimate board in which the demands of each department shall be discussed and settled.

363. *Surveyor of the Navy to Board: dockyard accountant*

[TNA, ADM89/1] 26 October 1855

With reference to the enclosed documents respecting a proposal for the appointment of dockyard accountants and for checking of yard wages, I beg to state that after a careful consideration of the latter subject it appears to me very desirable that the earnings of the workmen employed by task and job, and the large amount of wages now expended in the dockyards should be subjected to efficient and proper control. As the task & job system which was re-introduced in January 1854, was only instituted as a temporary measure, it does not seem to me necessary that a large staff of measurers should be created to carry out the proposed check. If however it should be found requisite to continue the system of task and job for any lengthened period, it may then be considered advisable to adopt a more extended plan for the measurement of work performed.

The system formerly in practice of measuring the work to regulate earnings of the men on task & job was partially re-established in 1847 to check the earnings of the people who were then paid day pay, and a portion only of the work was measured weekly by four measurers in each of the large yards and two in the smaller. [At that time it had become] necessary, in order to meet the pressure of work at a time when it was very difficult to obtain more men, to pay the men by task & job to stimulate them to the utmost exertion and to give them an increase of wages to meet the high prices of all the necessities of life. A large increase had to be made to the number of measurers and measurers' writers to enable the whole of the work performed by the mechanics to be measured and valued.

Previous to this, in the year 1852, *new* schemes of prices were devised for the yards by a committee of Master Shipwrights, after many months labour, upon a greatly condensed and improved principle, and although there may be discrepancies in these schemes, still it is believed that the government got a full amount of work for the sums paid. When these schemes were promulgated for calculating the earnings of the workmen employed by task & job, the officers were directed to report from time to time any alterations which experience might point out as necessary. These schemes were subsequently revised in this department with such changes as were therein considered advisable to render them as far as possible efficient before being printed in May 1854. Arrangements are in operation for further revisions to adapt them to variations and improvements, which may arise from time to time in the execution of workmanship. It may be observed that when the men in the dockyards were on day pay, a large proportion of time of both Inspectors and Leading Men was occupied in seeing that the work was sufficiently and properly executed. Now (the Men employed by Task & Job and the Leading Men sharing with them in the amount of their earnings) it is more important that the Inspectors should give their undivided attention to the superintendence and execution of the work. I was therefore of opinion that it is not advisable to adopt that position of the Accountant General's proposal for the Inspectors to perform the responsible duty of measuring the work for payment in addition to that of carefully and vigilantly inspecting its performance. A large proportion of the Inspectors being elderly men and unaccustomed to keeping accounts, it is considered that they would be found incompetent for this duty which, with their sixty men frequently widely dispersed, would under such circumstances prove a most arduous task.

It is desirable, however, that the Inspectors should be occasionally directed, as is now the case, to re-measure the work of a gang so as to afford a check upon the measurements as rendered by the Measurers. The attention of the Superintendents of the dockyards was especially directed to this point by my submission of the 17th October 1854, in order to ensure the most complete and full supervision of this duty by the Master Shipwright, his assistants and foremen.

If it should be found expedient to continue the system of task & job work, it will no doubt ultimately be necessary to increase the number of Measurers. It appears to me very desirable that one of the Measurers in each of the yards should be appointed 'Superintending Measurer', at a small increase of Salary, with a view to control the others and to distribute and change their duties from time to time as he may think fit in order to prevent ever the suspicion of collusion between the measurers and the workmen.

364.   *Chatham Yard Officers to Admiralty: measurement of works*

[TNA, ADM89/1]   12 January 1856

In reference to your minute of the 8th inst. respecting the extent of measurement by the Measurers, of work done by task and job, we beg to state that the works of the following classes viz.

shipwrights
caulkers
joiners
oar makers
painters
white washers
labourers (when scraping pitch &tc)

are taken by the measurers. Smiths work is abstracted from the Forge Book Per Admiralty Order 23rd October 1854 by the measurers. Size work is returned by the 'Reducers' rated and valued by the measurers per manufacturing accounts of March 1853. Page 9.

With respect to the number of measurers: we beg to say that the staff is not sufficient to do justice to the duty with the increased number of men, quantity of work done &c. The Measurers are excessively driven, and hurried, to get through their work in time; and in some cases of great pressure, and much minutiae, are obliged to accept the Leading Man's measurement, though this is avoided except on extraordinary occasions.

It will require two more Measurers, and an additional Writer to perform the duty satisfactorily.

With regard to the contract of the Measurement: on any occasion on which the Measurer requires information or check, he receives the assistance of the Inspector or Foreman. In cases of doubt, of the Master Shipwright and his assistant.

As to the valuation of the work done: after the work is entered, and the rate set by the Measurer, this rate is checked by the Writer, who also sets off the value in pencil. Another writer then checks this and inks in the amount.

The account is finally examined by the Measurer and forwarded.

The only other check is that of the totals, in the Captain Superintendent's office.

365.   Chatham Yard Officers to Admiralty: task and job

[TNA, ADM89/1]   19 February 1856

Your report of the 9th inst. on the task and job system of work in the dockyards has been under the consideration of the Board.

My Lords are not prepared to adopt any permanent scheme for establishing more Measurers in the various dockyards but they desire that persons may be appointed temporarily to discharge the duties pointed out by you; and they will sanction such an experiment for a period of six months and grant allowances in the pensions to the persons so employed at the rate proposed by you.

366.   Isaac Watson to Admiralty: reducers

[TNA, ADM89/2]   13 November 1857

With reference to the Chatham officers' letter of the 11th inst. on the Reducers being employed extra hours during the winter months to insure the sawyers' earnings being valued and brought to account in time for the weekly payment. I beg most respectively to observe that when these men were employed from November 1855 to March 1856 as per Admiralty order of the 14th November 1855, they had to refer the account of sawyers work to the Measurers office to be valued and brought to account. As the men were on task work and the length of the day was much reduced, this additional time was found to be necessary. But when the Measurers department was revised and temporarily enlarged in April 1856, and instructions given for the guidance of the Measurers, it was instructed that 'the workman (smiths excepted) employed on task and job is to be actually measured by the Measurer'. The Reducers therefore discontinued this duty from March 1856 till the workmen returned to day pay in April 1857 when they again resumed this duty, as per draft of instructions for the guidance of the Measurers when the Workmen are on Day Pay, 5 March 1857.

The Surveyors of Chatham Yard have however, been confined on task work up to the present time, and are paid to the full extent of their earnings. Their work should therefore have been measured by the Measurer and not by the Reducers, as it was intended that the Reducers should only return the account of size work when they were on day pay, it being considered that when the payments of the men depend upon the measurements taken, the Reducers as single station men only, do not hold that position in the service and which is required for performing this responsible duty.

367.   *Comptroller to Board: supervision of labour*

[TNA, ADM1/5931]   20 August 1864

I beg leave to forward herewith the reports from all the dockyards on the new arrangements for the supervision of labour ordered by their Lordships on 5th March last, and to observe as follows:

The officers are unanimous in their opinion that the degree of trustworthiness and intelligence necessary for satisfactorily drawing a great number of stores are hardly to be expected in a man whose pay amounts only to 13/6^d per week. They think it also bad policy to entrust valuable stores to a man whose very low pay renders him particularly open to temptation.

Some of the officers also state that skilled knowledge is sometimes necessary to the proper selection of stores, especially timber. In some cases one labourer is not sufficient to fetch all the stores for all the men who may be employed under one foreman.

I consider these opinions to be well founded, and I recommend that the foremen and masters of trades be authorised occasionally to detach other persons for fetching stores, when excess of quantity or special knowledge as to kind or quality may render it in their opinion desirable to do so. I submit for their Lordships favourable consideration whether it would not be advisable under all the circumstances to give the labourers, who are permanently employed on this service, the position of single station men and the pay of 3/- per diem.

7

CENTRAL MANAGEMENT

At the pinnacle of naval administration was the Board of Admiralty, its pre-eminent position empowering it to decide all matters relative to the navy and its departments and expressed in these terms in 1787 by the Commission for inquiring into Fees. It was a description that was equally valid for the period 1815 to 1865. Encompassed within the Admiralty's area of authority were the dockyards, the Board able to give directions on all matters relating to management, construction and design of ships, the nature and quality of materials produced, wage and salary levels and the conditions under which the workforce was employed [368].

Situated between the Admiralty and the dockyards was an intermediate body, the Navy Board. Created to take instructions from the Admiralty and offer advice when called upon, the commissioners of the Navy Board, over nearly two centuries of continuous existence, had gradually become a semi-autonomous body. This independence arose partly from the means by which commissioners on this board were appointed. While those who made up the Admiralty were political appointees who held office no longer than any government, the commissioners of the Navy Board had semi-permanent tenure arising from appointment by letters patent from the sovereign. This gave the inferior Board an authority based on experience, which gave rise occasionally to apparent resentment at being told what to do by Admiralty 'amateurs' whose term of office was uncertain [385].

By 1816, the Navy Board consisted of four principal officers and seven commissioners. The principal officers (the Comptroller and three Surveyors) had duties that brought them into direct contact with the dockyard at Chatham. In addition, the seven commissioners frequently shared in decisions relating to the yard at Chatham, the result of each being a member of one of three committees that were responsible for executing board business. Introduced by an order-in-council of 1796 [369], the establishment of these committees resulted from a recommendation by the Commission on Fees that followed an investigation of the Navy Office in 1786–87. It was the intention that these committees should help reduce the amount of work placed before full meetings of the board. One outcome was that each individual member, through attendance at committee and board meetings, had little time to oversee the department for which he was responsible.

The three committees formed in 1796 were those for Correspondence, Accounts and Stores. Most important for the dockyard at Chatham was the Committee of Correspondence, consisting of the senior Surveyor and two commissioners. The latter were required to have had naval experience. The Committee of Correspondence [370] was the body responsible for overseeing the work of the yard through correspondence with the resident Commissioner and, through him, the Master Shipwright and Master Attendant. George Smith, Secretary to the Navy Board from 1820 to 1832, considered that a large proportion of this correspondence was unnecessary [377, 378]. The Committee of Stores also had responsibility for managing aspects of the yard at Chatham [370]. Membership of this committee consisted of the junior Surveyor and two commissioners; one of the commissioners had naval experience, the other an administrative background. Responsible for ensuring that all stores delivered to Chatham were used in a proper manner, they would frequently engage in correspondence with the Storekeeper at Chatham. This committee also oversaw two departments within the Navy Office, the Office for Stores and the Office for Examining Storekeepers' Accounts [369, 370]. The third committee – for Accounts – was composed of three commissioners, one always a former naval officer, the other two both civilian administrators. It was the role of this committee to supervise the various accounting offices at the Navy Office, including the Office for Bills and Accounts (through which all accounts were eventually passed) and the Office for Seamen's Wages within which payments of both seamen and dockyard personnel were determined and agreed.

The most senior member of the Navy Board was the Comptroller, a post that was held between February 1816 and November 1831 by Sir Thomas Byam Martin. It was an office only available to a former sea-going naval officer of senior rank. The Commission on Fees had recommended that the Comptroller have a 'general superintending and directing power' over the work of the entire Board. To achieve this, he was to preside at general meetings of the Board, through which passed more important items of business, while also chairing each committee. Not surprisingly, the latter proved an impossible task, and in 1806 the Commissioners for Revising and Digesting the Civil Affairs of the Navy lightened him of this particular duty. Instead, each committee was to call upon him for advice when required, the Comptroller retaining the right to attend committee meetings and have access to financial accounts [370]. As to the office of Navy Surveyor, it was unusual that in 1816 there were three separate post holders. Throughout much of the eighteenth century there had most frequently been two Surveyors, the third appointment being made in 1813 [371]. The tasks to which they gave attention were those of overseeing the running of the yards and designing warships [370]. Because of their close connection with the yards, the Surveyors were always drawn from the ranks of the Master Shipwrights; Robert Seppings, formerly of Chatham dockyard, held the post of third Surveyor, as a result of the appointment in 1813.

The committee system as a means of transacting Board business was itself abolished in 1829 and replaced by a system that was outwardly similar to that in force prior to 1796. A particular shortcoming of the committee system, highlighted by George Smith [374], was its inability to identify individual responsibility. Under the new system, introduced by the order-in-council of 30 January 1829 [380], individual commissioners became entirely responsible for clearly defined areas of business [379, 385]. Each, once again, was expected to attend a daily meeting of the Board during which all non-routine incoming correspondence was considered [381].

In addition to correspondence, Chatham yard was subject to inspection, or visitation, by a committee of the Navy Board that normally consisted of the Comptroller and junior Surveyor with, occasionally, a commissioner of naval experience. Between 1818 and 1823, these visitations occurred annually, but thereafter there was only one further inspection, this attended by the Duke of Clarence (later King William IV) in his capacity as Lord High Admiral (1827–28). During such an inspection the workforce would be mustered, any new building works viewed, and most of the more important stores and centres of manufacture inspected [373].

Relations between the Admiralty and Navy Board during the period 1816 to 1832, despite a potential for animosity, was one of relative tranquillity. In part, this was a result of the extraordinary longevity of the Tory administration under Lord Liverpool with Robert Dundas, second Viscount Melville, the longest serving First Lord. Having taken office in February 1812 Melville had, by 1816, not only appointed the Comptroller, Sir Thomas Byam Martin, but the majority of those who made up the Navy Board. Through a number of careful selections, Melville created a politically allied body that made the system work. Nevertheless, members of the Navy Board were still intent upon upholding their own professional opinions. In particular, differences occurred over the extent to which the dockyards should economise following the conclusion of the war with Napoleon. Melville proposed that the workforce should receive a wage cut and work longer hours. Among those who gave Melville their support was Robert Barlow of Chatham. However, Martin was quick to refute the opinion of the newly appointed resident Commissioner [372]. In his efforts to maintain artificer numbers within the dockyards, the numbers that he considered adequate for the works to be performed, the Tory Martin appears to have received the support of the Whig Earl of St Vincent [376], a man who had revealed an intense dislike of the civilian administrators of the Navy Board. In general, Martin was highly critical of those who called for excessive economies [382] and supported measures that protected the most skilled workers from dismissal [375].

The ability of the Admiralty and Navy boards to work in harmony during the years that followed the Napoleonic Wars did not extend to the administration of the Whig-led coalition that entered power in November 1830. Having experienced, while First Lord between February and September 1806, the difficulties that could result from a hostile inferior board, the new Prime Minister, the second Earl Grey, was intent upon abolishing the Navy Board. Shortly after his accession to office, the new First Lord of the Admiralty, Sir James Graham, with the help of John Barrow, put together a discussion document that outlined the reasons for abolishing the board and indicated how it was to be replaced [385]. Instead of two inferior boards, five principal officers were to be appointed, these carrying out the tasks performed by the Navy and Victualling boards. These officers were neither to act in concert nor have any form of executive authority. Instead, a naval lord was to be placed in immediate authority over each of them, with each principal officer having only the power to refer matters to his directing naval lord for discussion by the Board of Admiralty. It was upon the terms of this discussion paper, with but a few amendments, that the Naval Civil Departments Act reached the statute books on 9 June 1832 [391]. In that original discussion document, much had been made of the advantage of bringing the two departments under one roof at Whitehall [385]. In the event, inadequate space forced those responsible for conducting the civil departments to remain at Somerset House. Barrow subsequently attempted to justify this arrangement [393], but in reality it was far from advantageous [400].

For many, the reforms imposed upon the Admiralty during this period, were seen as beyond criticism. Admittedly, John Croker and Sir Thomas Byam Martin had given the Civil Departments Act a rough ride through Parliament [390], but this was only to have been expected. In paving the way for the introduction of the reforms, Graham had been highly critical of the earlier administration, suggesting that Croker and Martin were responsible for some of the failings [387, 388]. In particular, they were among those accused of having misled Parliament through the presentation of estimates that deliberately deflated the cost of certain projects, with amounts subsequently transferred to other under-spending projects [383,

384, 387, 397]. On the other hand, the changes brought about by the Act [392] were supported by mainstream moderates as well as by members of a vocal radical wing led by Joseph Hume.

Outside of Parliament some naval administrators also maintained the reforms had proved successful. Both John Barrow and John Henry Briggs, in separately published memoirs, declared their approval for the reforms [399, 407]. Neither was impartial in this matter: many of Barrow's own ideas had been incorporated [395]. However, by the latter part of the century, the system as laid down by Graham appeared badly flawed [398, 399]. At the time of the Russian War (1854–56), the Admiralty commissioners had been unable to devote sufficient time to strategy and the individual departments were clearly overworked. Reference to Croker's attack upon the Civil Department's Bill, during its second reading, makes it clear that he, for one, would not have been surprised at such a problem [390]. However, the years following the Russian War saw little effort to improve matters. Admittedly, a limited degree of rationalisation took place, but this would not really have helped in the event of a future war. Primarily, these changes resulted in greater powers for both the Surveyor General and the Accountant General, and the establishment of a separate contracts and purchasing branch [404]. But these changes did not reduce the main problem, the concentration of a mass of detail upon the Board of Admiralty. It was for this reason that, in 1832, members of the opposition had favoured a scheme for one civil board that would have been completely subservient to the Board of Admiralty [387, 389].

A major problem for the newly reformed system was the general expansion of dockyard business and a consequent growth in correspondence directed to the Admiralty [396, 398, 399]. According to Barrow, there was a 33 per cent growth in letters received and despatched from the Admiralty during the period 1827 to 1833 [399]. Graham had believed the opposite would take place [385]. In 1836, John Barrow indicated that the Admiralty was potentially overburdened [395]. A reference to the Admiralty minute books confirms this: one entry [394] indicates that the principal officers were not to oversee the accounts without these being examined on a quarterly basis by members of the Admiralty Board – even though that board had no understanding of accountancy matters. Incoming correspondence for February 1837 also demonstrates the range of business laid before the Admiralty [396]. In 1841, Earl Minto, upon retiring from the office of First Lord, maintained that the Admiralty commissioners were generally incapable of performing all the business expected of them [398]. Thus, in 1847, J.S. Bromley suggested the adoption of a committee system, whereby the principal officers would meet two or three times a week, these meetings chaired by a member of the Board of Admiralty [400].

It was under the pressures of war that the system was expected to collapse. However, it was not until the Crimean War (1854–56) that these pressures were exerted. By that time few people were able to draw a comparison with what had gone before. As a result, although the system proved inadequate, and came under considerable criticism [401, 402, 406], the system was only modified [400, 403]. Frequent criticism in Parliament resulted in the setting up of a commission to inquire into the control and management of the dockyards. Reporting in 1860, this confirmed both constitutional and organisational failings, its main recommendation was that a Minister for the Navy should be appointed and that a Controller-General, appointed by the minister, should be responsible for managing the dockyards [404]. However, these proposals were not acted upon. Instead, the Surveyor was given increased powers to manage the dockyards by an order-in-council of January 1860 [405].

368. *Responsibilities of the Board of Admiralty*

[3rd Report, Commissioners appointed to enquire into Fees, 1]
December 1787

The business of the Board of Admiralty is to consider and determine upon all matters relative to Your Majesty's Navy and departments thereunto belonging. To give direction for the performance of all services, all orders necessary for carrying their directions into execution; and generally to superintend and direct the whole naval and marine establishment of Great Britain.

369. *Establishment of Committee System*

[TNA, PC2/146]   8 June 1796

We humbly conceive that the business in general would be carried on with more effect if the commissioners instead of presiding over distinct departments were formed into committees and the business to be so divided as to admit of competent officers in each branch possessing time and opportunity to examine, digest and conduct the business allotted to them, subject ultimately however to the opinion of the Board at large.

Under this idea we propose that the Board shall be divided into the following committees: a committee of correspondence, a committee of accounts and a committee of stores.

The Comptroller to belong to and preside at every committee. The Committee of Correspondence to consist of the Deputy Comptroller, one Surveyor, the present Clerk of the Acts and the Secretary.

The Committee of Accounts to consist of the present Comptroller of Treasurer's Accounts, the present Comptroller of Victualling Accounts, one Commissioner and Secretary (to be the Comptroller's first clerk for the time being).

The Committee of Stores to consist of one Surveyor or sea officer, the present Comptroller of Storekeeper's Accounts, the present Sea Commissioner and Secretary (to be the Chief Clerk and Accountant of Stores for the time being).

The several duties attached to the various committees are to be as follows. Committee of Correspondence: to conduct the correspondence of the Board. The Committee of Accounts: to superintend, examine and pass all accounts; subject however to the approbation of the Board at large. Committee of Stores: to consider the proper quantity of stores necessary to be provided for the service in general, to direct their distribution and to take cognizance of the receipt, issue, remains and return of stores of every kind and every service depending on this branch.

370. *Duties of the Navy Board*

[4th Report, Commission for Naval Revision]   1806

[The Duties of the Navy Board, p. 4.]
The duties of the Board at large, under the direction of the Lords Commissioners of the Admiralty: to consult and advise together how to transact to the best advantage all affairs tending to the well-being and regulation of the civil establishment of His Majesty's Navy, and all the subordinate instruments thereof (wherein they are to proceed by common council and agreement of most voices; to make contracts for naval stores of every kind, and attend to the proper distribution thereof); to prepare all Estimates of the expense of the Navy; to direct all monies for Naval services into the Treasurer's hands; to examine and certify his accounts for the expenditure thereof.

[The Duties of the Committee of Correspondence, p. 6]
The general duty of the Committee of Correspondence is, by His Majesty's Order in Council, bearing date 8th June 1796, to conduct the correspondence of the Board, and all such other business as may not especially fall under the direction of the two other committees. In the execution of this duty, all such letters as do not obviously relate to the business of the other committees are read to, and are considered and answered by the Committee of Correspondence, except in cases of importance, in which the committee think proper to refer them to the consideration of the Board at large.

[The Duties of the Committee of Account, p. 4]
[C]onsist in the examination of, and carrying on a very extensive correspondence relative to accounts and certificates for payment of stores supplied to His Majesty's Dock Yards; of accounts of Commanders in Chief and Consuls abroad; of officers employed upon the sea fencible, impress, and signal service in Great Britain and Ireland; of officers commanding His Majesty's Ships, for stores purchased by them of agents employed to purchase naval stores; and a variety of contingent accounts from different offices in the naval department.

[The Duties of the Committee of Stores, p. 5]
The general duty of this Committee, as prescribed by His Majesty's Order in Council of 8th June 1796, is to consider the proper quantities of stores

necessary to be provided for the service in general; to direct their distribution, and to take cognizance of the receipt, issue, remains and returns of stores of every description, dependent on this branch, and to transact the current business relative thereto …

[*Duties of the Comptroller of the Navy Board, pp. 7–8*]
To preside at the Navy Board; to submit to the consideration of the Board any improvements in the mode of conducting the business which may appear to him to be likely to prove advantageous to the public service, and, with the other members thereof, to superintend, direct and control all the departments and business of the Navy Office, and the expenses in every branch thereof, having in all cases, when the voices of the members of the Board shall be equal, a second vote; to be a member of each of the committees of Correspondence, of Accounts, and of Stores; and when present to preside therein; to visit Deptford and Woolwich yards occasionally, and more distant yards when necessary; to attend the Treasury, Admiralty, and the great offices of state when required; to perform all secret services, and to enter into contracts as may be necessary for the execution thereof; and after the secret service shall have been performed, to communicate his orders and proceedings in consequence to the Board for their concurrence.

[*Duties of the Surveyor of the Navy, pp. 9–10*]
The senior surveyor, besides the ordinary duty of his office in the Committee of Correspondence is to direct the preparing (in conjunction with the junior surveyor) of drawings for ships and vessels ordered to be built for His Majesty's service, either in the king's or merchants yards and to determine the dimensions and scantlings of their frames and masts and yards; also the dimensions of the masts and yards of such ships as may be purchased for the service, or taken from the enemy; to examine and approve all notes from the yards for task and job work; to propose prices to be allowed to workmen, not already established (as also any alteration of extra); to consider of any alteration which may be proposed to be made in the hulls, masts and yards of ships, or in their equipment, jointly with the junior Surveyor; to examine and consider the annual estimates from the several dockyards, out-ports and foreign yards, and to correspond with the officers of the yards, &c thereon respecting the propriety of them, and for an explanation of such parts thereof as do not appear clearly stated, and to make such alterations and additions therein as he may see necessary in order to lay them before the Board for their approbation, prior to their being laid before Parliament; and in doing thereof to consider of the proper ships and works of the yard which it may be most consistent with

the good of the service to give preference to, and regulate the estimates accordingly; to consider the prices proposed by the officers of the yards for all works performed by contractors upon valuation; to attend the sale of old stores, and cause the several lots to be put up at such a high price that there is no reason to expect any person will bid for them at the first named price, and to stop the sale of any lot where the price is dropped so low that it is not right to part with it at a lower rate, and to do the same on the sale of any of His Majesty's ships or vessels; to correspond with the officers of the dockyards on particular points respecting the works carried out; to consider in conjunction with the junior Surveyor, of the proposition made to the Board from time to time by the officers of the several dockyards, of such things as fall under the Surveyor's line of duty, and to make minutes for grounding orders on, as answers thereto, as well as to consider, in common with the other members of the Board, of such correspondence as may relate to his department; to correspond with the proper dockyard officers of the propriety of performing any particular work which the Board may have in contemplation to carry out; and to visit the several dockyards, but particularly Deptford yard, and jointly with the junior Surveyor to inspect the buildings or repairs of king's ships in merchant yards, as often as he may feel necessary; to examine the reports of all surveys taken of the hulls, masts and yards of His Majesty's ships at the several ports, and to consider of the propriety of the officer's proposals for either repairing, selling or taking them to pieces, as the circumstances of the condition of the ship, &c. may appear to require, and to give his opinion to the Board thereon, and to cause reports to be made to the Admiralty accordingly; to examine the progresses from the dockyards, jointly with the junior Surveyor; to examine the progresses of the foreign yards, and compare them with the several works carried on in the yards, and to ships and vessels under repair, and to report any irregularity or impropriety therein to the Board; also to notice if any extra artificers or labourers appear to have been unnecessarily hired.

371. *Introduction of Third Surveyor*

[TNA, PC2/194]   3 June 1813

Sir William Rule the senior Surveyor of the Navy, is on account of his age and infirmities about to retire from that office. It is now provided by His Majesty's Order in Council of the 28th October 1807 establishing the regulations proposed in the fourth report of the Board of Revision, that when a vacancy occurs in the place of senior Surveyor, the junior Surveyor should succeed thereto (under the title of First Surveyor) and that a second not a joint Surveyor should be appointed in the place of junior Surveyor. The latter should assist the former and be considered as his deputy in his capacity of Surveyor, in the same manner as the Deputy Comptroller acts under the Comptroller, which arrangement, in the opinion of the Commissioners of Revision, would forward the peculiar duties of the Surveyors without those difficulties which are liable to arise among persons engaged in the same pursuit vested with equal powers.

We are of opinion that the object recommended by the Board of Revision would be most satisfactorily obtained and that other great and important advantages would result to the public service if instead of a Surveyor of the Navy and a Deputy Surveyor as proposed in the said report, there should be three Surveyors who should compose a committee of the Navy Board for the transaction of the business of the surveyors department.

We therefore most humbly propose that your Royal Highness will be graciously pleased to order and direct that in consideration of the great and growing extent of the navy and the increase in duties of the department of the surveyor, there be appointed three surveyors of His Majesty's Navy with the same privileges and emoluments as the joint surveyors of the navy now enjoy.

That these three surveyors shall be members of the Navy Board and shall form a distinct committee for the transaction of the peculiar business of the surveyors' department; that the senior Surveyor shall be chairman of the said committee and that questions, wherein there is a difference of opinion, shall be determined by the majority.

That besides the duties now considered as exclusively belonging to the Surveyors all questions relating to civil and naval architecture, mechanic and other branches of science, or to the general economy, system and arrangement of the dockyards shall be referred in the first instance to this committee.

That one of the surveyors shall in addition to these duties be charged with the execution of those other and distinct duties which His Majesty's Order in Council appropriated to the senior Surveyor.

That another of the surveyors shall, in addition to these duties, be charged with the execution of those other and distinct duties which His Majesty's Order in Council appropriated to the junior Surveyor.

That another of the surveyors shall be charged with the duty of visiting under our directions His Majesty's several dockyards for the most necessary and important purpose of exercising a constant control and frequent personal superintendence over the several dockyard departments and of introducing and maintaining one settled and uniform system of labour, arrangement and economy throughout the naval arsenals of the country.

In addition to the last mentioned duties and his attendance on the surveyors' committee, we humbly propose that this Surveyor should, when in Town, and not otherwise employed, assist in the Committee of Correspondence and exercise a more immediate and strict control over the surveyors' department, than the individual allocation of the other surveyors may enable them to do.

We further most humbly propose and request that Your Royal Highness would be graciously pleased to authorize us to assign to the several surveyors such departments of the aforementioned duties as they individually may seem the best calculated to execute with advantage to His Majesty's service and that your Royal Highness will further authorize us to prepare and establish such detailed instructions and directions as may be necessary for the due execution of the new duties which we thus propose to commit to the surveyors of His Majesty's Navy.

372.   *Navy Board Comptroller to First Lord: opposition to an increase in yard working hours*

[BL, Add Ms 41,400]   1 June 1818

Our friend Barlow seems to think that if we have the right to keep the men in the yard ten hours we have an equal right to demand ten hours active hard labour or a scheme of task, when the very commissioners of Naval Revision admits that the extension of the men working by task shall entitle them to earn half as much again, and in the merchant yards double.

373.   *Minutes: Navy Board visitation*

[TNA, ADM106/3233]   30 September 1819

Chatham. Thursday 30 September 1819. Present Sir Thomas Byam Martin and Robert Seppings.

The committee arrived here this morning and having reported their arrival to the Commissioner proceeded to inspect the several works of the yard.

They first visited the new dock constructing and found everything going on well, that the number of workmen were now sufficient and that there was no want of stone or other material for proceeding with the works.

Mr Rennie was here present. The subject of draining the dock and providing the new gates, which will be wanted in January next having been discussed, the mode of draining was approved. Mr Richards the clerk of the works was directed to inspect the models for the gates intended for the tunnel to the mast pond in Sheerness yard and to provide models for the dock at Chatham. The committee were of opinion that it would be most desirable to advertise for a contract for the whole of the gates wanted at both yards, which was considered of sufficient magnitude to induce the masters of the first respectability to offer tenders.

The Committee having observed that it was intended to let additional altars on the broad altars now forming in the dock, which were attended with very considerable expense without producing any adequate advantage, and having consulted Mr Rennie on the subject, who concurred in opinion with the committee that they might be dispensed with, it was determined that direction should be given to the officers for that purpose.

The Committee inspected the lead mill and painters' shop, now constructing and found them in a considerable state of forwardness, the mill for rolling lead being complete and at work. It was suggested, and appeared necessary to the committee, that a separate building should be appropriated for melting the lead to divest it of its impurities previous to it being carried to the mills to be cast into cakes for rolling. A small building adjoining, which is now used as a lot house seemed from its situation to be well calculated [for this purpose]. In the event of the north hemp house being raised as is in contemplation a part of it may be appropriated to supply the place of the lot house before mentioned.

It was noticed, that there are at present 1,827 tons of hemp and 100 tons of hemp yarn in store. [The committee] considered it advisable that it should be removed as soon as possible after the contract with Messrs Bush & Co and Mr. Maberly is expired.

On proceeding round the yard it was perceived that there were 15 of the mooring blocks on Mr Hemman's principle, weighing from 7 to 9 tons each, remaining on the anchor wharf and several more to come on shore. They are now unserviceable, and the officers are not aware of any purpose to which they can be applied, nor how they can be disposed of unless they are broken up and disposed of as old iron.

The committee viewed the saw mills and machinery appertaining thereto for stacking timber and were much satisfied with works going on there, the same being well executed. Seven of the sawing machines were at work and the whole eight may be worked.

The Master of the Mill was directed to prepare an account of the full particulars of the quantity of work that may be executed.

The *Trafalgar* and *Prince Regent*, building in this yard, were inspected, particularly with regard to the formation of their sterns. Some observations were made with regard to the angles, which may be formed in pointing the guns in the after part of both ships, and the advantages of those in the ship with the round stern were very manifest. The ships appeared in excellent condition and the timbers well seasoned.

It was stated by the Master Shipwright that timber was much wanted in this dockyard, particularly for the line of battleships building. He was instructed, in all cases, to give timely notice that supplies may be hastened.

It was noticed that none of the timber, which has been received from the Stratfield Saye Estate, has been found fit to be cut into thick stuff, being too small but that the timber is good.

The officers here were detailed to report whether they can suggest any improvement which might be adopted in the construction of the several offices for the officers of a dockyard and whether they are of opinion it would be more advisable to have them all together, or separate. Their answer was decidedly in favour of the offices being near together.

374. *Review of the Committee System undertaken by Secretary of Navy Board*

[TNA, ADM1/3571]   1 June 1821

The Navy Board should be so constituted that every individual member of it should have a responsibility attached to him; whereas under the present formation of the Board into Committees, individual responsibility is entirely withdrawn! Responsibility placed in a committee of members collectively is misplaced. It amounts to nothing, because under a specious appearance, it is calculated only to deceive!

I have already submitted papers in which I have ventured to give an opinion that the business of the Board is not dispatched as it ought to be or as it might be with more correctness as well as dispatch even under the present regulations.

Every individual member ought I conceive to take up and follow up a branch of business as his own exclusively. He should consult his colleagues in committee on points that he may consider not within the compass of his own authority to decide on. If after this the committee may differ, or not feel competent to decide or determine, then a case should be made for it to be submitted to the Board. This coming to the Board for authority or decision on matters on which it may be necessary to consult the Board naturally imposes upon the Commissioner, the necessity of explaining matters, which they can only be enabled to do by having a perfect knowledge of the business themselves. Under the present system, the business generally speaking is done at a deliberation collectively at a public reading of papers and statements drawn up by the Secretary or Clerk attending at the committee table. The information acquired thus cannot be so satisfactory and complete as that acquired by personal application, labour, personal inspection and examination of papers.

According to my opinion, the committee should be composed of members under certain denominations. I hold it essential that every one should have a peculiar designation by which it may be inferred what may be their particular duties – for example:

The Comptroller of the Navy, as his designation imparts (being a naval officer), is the principal and supervisor of the whole and belongs to all the committees. There should be a Deputy Comptroller and he should be a civilian, and chairman of the Committee of Correspondence.

The Comptroller of Accounts, a civilian and chairman of the Committee of Accounts.

The Comptroller of Stores, a naval officer and chairman of the Committee of Stores.

A commissioner of transport service, a naval officer to be a member of the Committee of Correspondence.

The Surveyor of the Navy, to be also a member of the Committee of Correspondence.

A civilian commissioner superintending the store accounts to be a member of the Committee of Stores.

In war: a naval officer superintending sea store accounts to be a member of the Committee of Stores; a naval officer superintending sea pay and wages to be a member of the Committee of Accounts.

Under these ten denominations every branch of business will be comprised and the chairmen as well as the Comptroller should have salaries in amount higher than the others for obvious and good reason.

I hope never again to see joint surveyors, or two surveyors at the Board: the controversies which their opinions on professional subjects lead to, are not conducive to the well conducting of business. When the Board is called on to decide between them, responsibility on the individual is at an end, as any measures arising out of such a decision becomes the measure of the Board, and not of the individual.

375.   *Secretary of Navy Board to Commissioners: memorandum on*
retention of skilled labour

[TNA, ADM1/3571]   [undated, *c*.1822]

Contemplating the necessity for reducing the naval establishment of the
country, it occurred to me sometime since [the ending of the war] to
suggest that in order to retain the most useful set of artificers in our
dockyards, it would be a very beneficial and political measure to begin
by discharging such description of workmen as were not so essentially
necessary and conducive to the maintaining of the navy in the building
and repairing of ships, as shipwrights and caulkers. From having a larger
number of shipwrights and caulkers at the conclusion of the war, than it
might be necessary to retain during peace, to allow these men (as it
became necessary from time to time to lessen numbers) to fall back upon
other and what are considered inferior trades, as compared with
shipwrights and caulkers. [This would allow a reduction in] the
establishments by getting rid of a description of men who could more
readily find employment out of a dockyard, namely house carpenters,
joiners & etc. [while] retaining a large proportion of more useful workmen
at reduced prices (such as shipwrights and caulkers who in their respective
calling should be kept as it were, by retaining wages) that their services
might be available on any moment of emergency. If this system had been
adopted at the conclusion of the war, and continued on a gradual scale,
the object might by this time have been gradually accomplished, which
it is at length become necessary to effect by an overwhelming discharge
of men from the dockyards. I am aware however that it was not considered
right to reduce the establishment of the dockyards until the fleet had been
brought into an efficient and permanent state of good repair! As a general
principle, everybody must concur in the wisdom of this measure. The
inconvenience arising out of the circumstance of delaying the discharge
of the workmen progressively and the consequent reduction of them at
this period in large numbers are more seriously felt in being brought into
operation at the present moment of agricultural distress.

Another difficulty arises, I conceive out of the unlimited or sweeping
kind of orders which have been given to allow the shipwrights & caulkers
to fall back upon other occupations generally and not confining the
principle of falling back to the occupation of house carpenters and joiners
and others in their own line, until the reduction in numbers shall have
been brought to its intended limit. By retaining all our shipwrights, some
of them are necessarily put to work to which they may not in all cases be
competent, only to get old in the service and to be of no use as shipwrights

when their services, as such, may be called for. On the other hand, if all the house carpenters and joiners had been discharged (these can always find employment in the country while shipwrights and caulkers could not find it) and shipwrights and caulkers employed instead of them, the best hands would have been retained, who would always have been ready to review their business as shipwrights and caulkers as vacancies occurred. The principle of allowing the superior artificers to fall back upon inferior trades, to retain active and good shipwrights and caulkers is excellent but like many other good plans, it has, I fear in its extended operation not produced the benefit which was expected. I am apprehensive that the dockyards will soon become filled with old men, and now that the admission of apprentices is forbidden the measure will be worse and worse.

According to my notion on the subject, the changing of the workmen periodically from one trade to another, which is a part of the system adopted, is not correct! I fear it has already produced and still will produce mischief and inconvenience.

I submit to those who are better judges than myself on these points whether a man can efficiently perform work at two different trades employed alternately on each periodically. Is it not more probable that he will produce both indifferently than excel in either? In short, is it not to be expected that a shipwright or caulker can do as much work in the capacity of a scavelman or labourer, as a man who has always been accustomed to such business? I think not! What then are you doing? Is it not evident that you are paying more wages for scavelmen and labourers work than you ought to pay? If they get no more than they can earn by task, the work they perform is not adequate to a labourer's work! The application of any given number of shipwrights to employment upon that work which would otherwise be performed by labourers in the same given time and numbers, is a misapplication! They cannot produce an equal quantity of work! What I consider to be still worse economy is the changing of the performance of the shipwrights and the sawyers' duty. The sawyer's duty or profession, if I may call it so, is almost as peculiar a duty or business, as that of a shipwright's. If a shipwright, when employed as a sawyer, cannot earn a sawyer's wages, it is obvious that his employment as such is not economical to the public! According to my opinion therefore, in no case should this principle of employing shipwrights and caulkers on other trades or works, be applied, when they are not competent to the duty and able to earn as much as the people whom they may be appointed to displace! Still less then will they be able to do this, if they be changed in their occupation periodically.

376. *St Vincent to Benjamin Tucker: dockyard administrators*

[Tucker, *Memoirs of St Vincent* II, p. 425[1]]   11 September 1822

I agree with you *in toto* as to the rapid ruin of the British Navy. Instead of discharging valuable and experienced men, of all descriptions from the dockyards, the commissioners and secretaries of all the boards ought to be reduced to the lowest number they ever stood at and the old system resorted to. One of the projectors of the present diabolical measures should be gibbeted opposite to the Deptford yard and the other opposite the Woolwich yard, on the Isle of Sad Dogs.

377. *Secretary of Navy Board to Commissioners: referral to dockyards for information*

[TNA, ADM1/3571]   May 1828

I feel it to be my duty to call the Board's attention to the practice, which prevails too generally in this office, of referring to the dockyards for information, which ought to be had from the books and papers belonging to the office. I have on many occasions brought this circumstance to notice, and have endeavoured in other instances without appealing to the Board for its authority to bring about a change in our system of doing business here, but without effect.

We have numerous periodical returns and accounts from the dockyards which it is practicable in my opinion to reduce, and many of which might be discontinued.

The circumstance, which induces me to bring this to the notice of the Board now, is the disruption which has taken place in regard to the means of answering a precept from the Select Committee on Public Income and Expenditure.

The precept called for an account of sums paid for the construction of docks, wharfs, storehouses, architectural buildings &c., since the year 1805 to the present time.

All monies voted for services of this kind, have been shown on the extra estimate, and in order to show the expenditure on the head of extra, the annual return No 87 is sent up from the yards. Why then should the yard officers be called upon to furnish this amount, which it appears to me is, or ought to be, already prepared in the office? Perhaps it may be said, that the return No. 87 is not of sufficiently long standing to afford information

[1]J.S. Tucker, *Memoirs of the Right Honble The Earl of St Vincent*, Vol. II (London, 1844).

from 1805. On the other hand there ought to be other documents to give the same information, or else it must be implied that the Board has never known what has been expended under the head of extra.

In order however that there should be no delay unnecessarily created in answering the precept, I have been obliged to write to the yards for the information required. I take this opportunity of suggesting to the Board that some steps should be taken to alter the present system of doing business in this office.

5 June 1828. An instance occurred this day, which marks very thoroughly the constant habit which prevails here, of applying to the yards unnecessarily for information which might be obtained in our own office: namely, the report of iron deliveries and quantity not delivered and what remains due on contract from Messrs. Crawshay & Co. All this information we have in office.

378.   *Secretary of Navy Board to Commissioners: memorandum on*
returns and accounts

[TNA, ADM1/3571]   July 1828

I am of opinion that there are too many returns and accounts and that they occasion unnecessary trouble. They certainly may be reduced and consequently a reduction of business will follow.

Many attempts have been made to reduce them in number. I, myself, have more than once attempted it, and have at this time proposals before the Board to annul some of them but in carrying a measure of this kind, difficulties have always occurred and stood in the way.

In the first place the doing away with returns and accounts militated against the instructions under which the officers of the dockyards act and consequently it will be necessary in such cases to make corresponding alterations in those instructions which originate in the authority of order in council and can only be altered by the Admiralty! The system of conducting the dockyard duties, having lately undergone many changes, and still liable to more, under recent orders, makes it difficult to undertake (to say the least of it) any material alterations either in regard to the number or nature of the returns now required. The only effectual way of accomplishing such an object will be, by revising the instructions to the officers of the dockyards and, in doing so, to establish a new code of returns, to meet the views of any improved system of management which it may be considered right to introduce into the service.

379.   *Comptroller's Notes of a Meeting with the First Lord:*
constitution of Navy Board

[BL, Add Ms 41,368]   24 January 1829

Having been sent for by Lord Melville, a short conversation took place respecting certain alterations to be made in the navy estimates and his Lordship presently said, 'by the way let me tell you that when we were discussing the estimates on Thursday at the Duke of Wellington's, a good deal passed about reducing the number of commissioners of the Navy, and as it was thought decidedly better to give to an individual commissioner the charge of each separate branch of business (this is the case at the Ordnance and the system approved by the Duke) and a Comptroller and Deputy Comptroller for the general direction and management of the affairs of the office: one surveyor, one commissioner under the denomination of Storekeeper-General, one commissioner for accounts, one for transport, one for stores, making a comptroller and five commissioners'.

380.   *Order-in-Council: constitution of Navy Board*

[TNA, PC2/210]   30 January 1829

His Late Majesty was graciously pleased by his Order-in-Council of the 8th June 1796 to make considerable changes in the constitution of the Navy Board and to direct that the number of commissioners in the Navy should be increased from seven to ten and should be divided in three committees with a corresponding distribution of business. The number of commissioners and the distribution of business among the several committees have been varied, and modified by several subsequent orders in council. It appears to us, from a due consideration of all the before mentioned Orders in Council, from the experience we have had from the mode of executing the public service in the department and from the inquiries that we have made into the actual state and distribution of business amongst the several commissioners, that a considerable saving of expense to the public (combined with a more efficient execution of the duties) might be made by a reduction in the existing number of commissioners (without departing in any real degree from the principal establishment in the aforesaid orders in councils).

We therefore beg most humbly, that Your Majesty may be graciously pleased by your order in council, that in future the said Board may be constituted as follows (with the salaries under-mentioned being the same already established for the Comptroller, Deputy Controller and Commissioners of the Navy residing in London). That is to say a Comptroller with a salary of £1,200; a Surveyor with a salary of £1,000; an Accountant-General with a salary of £1,000; a Surveyor General with a Salary of £1,000; a Superintendent of Transports with a salary of £1,000.

That the Board so constituted be denominated as heretofore the 'Principal Officers and Commissioners of Your Majesty's Navy' to have and to execute all powers and duties hereto vested in the principal officers and commissioners of Your Majesty's Navy; and that as for the particular distribution of the business in the said department, the Comptroller and Deputy Comptroller should be especially charged with, and responsible for, the execution of all duties heretofore allotted to those offices respectively, and in addition thereunto all the duties now belonging to the Committee of Correspondence.

That the Surveyor shall be charged with all the duties and responsibilities of the Surveyors of the Navy but shall only visit the dockyards or give any orders with the concurrence and by direction of the Board at large.

The Accountant-General shall be charged with all the duties and responsibilities now belonging to the Committee of Accounts and the Surveyor-General and Superintendent of Transports with all those belonging to the Committee of Stores and Transport respectively.

We further humbly propose that although the said offices shall be in the first degree charged with and held responsible for the respective duties before mentioned, yet the united Board shall not thereby be relieved from its general contract and collective responsibility. On the contrary, every matter of importance shall in the first instance be brought before the Board. The respective officers shall meet every morning for the dispatch of general business, and especially that all contracts and purchases [shall] be decided upon by the Board at large [while] the other business being afterwards distributed for detailed consideration or execution agreeably to the established distribution of business or to any special direction of the Board. Everything done by the aforesaid respective officers [shall] be reported to the collected Board for its sanction at least twice a week. In order to provide for the occasional absence by sickness or otherwise of any of the aforesaid officers, we propose that the Comptroller or Deputy Comptroller, who will be, by their general superintendence, acquainted with every branch of the business, shall carry on the duties of any officers during such occasional absence ...

381. *First Secretary to Comptroller: duties of Comptroller*

[TNA, ADM1/3470]   14 July 1829

The Comptroller of His Majesty's Navy having expressed a wish to receive some further information as to the views of my Lords Commissioners of the Admiralty as to the mode of conducting the business at your office under the late new arrangements, and my Lords being desirous of guarding against any doubt or misconception as to the duties of the members of your board collectively and separately, I have their Lords' commands to observe to you that the fourth report of the Commissioners of Naval Revision provided the Comptroller should be a member of each of the committees and, when present, should preside therein. Their Lordships' late order did not in any respect interfere with the general duties and powers of the Comptroller and Deputy Comptroller but instituted one commissioner to superintend the business of each branch instead of a Committee. It was their Lordships' intention, when the Comptroller should see fit or occasion might require him, to assist and advise with the members charged with each particular branch of business. He should, on such occasions, be considered as the principal presiding person, according to the sense in which he was so, on each of the committees as they formerly existed. Again, when the Comptroller is executing the duties of his station [and] finds it necessary to call for information from any quarter but especially from a clerk in the office, it ought not to be considered necessary for such clerk to delay furnishing the information required until he has obtained from his superintending commissioner or other superior person to answer the controller's question. The latter is head of the whole office and his functions and duties in that respect are in no degree altered by their Lordships late order. Any such previous reference, if required as a regulation, would not only be productive of delay and inconvenience but would be inconsistent with, and subversive of the due authority inherent in these situations. Each commissioner is personally to superintend the due execution of the business of his department but the general superintending functions consequently authorized of the Comptroller and Deputy Comptroller and of the Board collectively remain unaltered and unimpaired.

382. *Comptroller to Admiral Malcolm: opinion on excessive economisers*

[BL, Add Ms 41,398]   1 June 1830

We yield much too easily to a set of noisy ignorant blockheads who make no discrimination between foolish and needless extravagance and objects of vital importance to the interest and credit of the country: but the thing of all others, to me the most annoying is that they seem to forget that the safety and glory of England depends upon her naval strength and her constant and ample state of naval preparation. We shall perhaps (at no distant time) rue the day that such opinions prevailed. I shall, however, have the consolation to know that I am no party to such views or measures.

383. *Admiralty to Navy Board: naval estimates*

[TNA, ADM1/3473]   21 January 1831

It is most desirable that the estimate should approximate to the actual expenditure, as nearly as varying circumstances will admit. In all events it is highly proper that their Lordships and the public should be made acquainted with the different branches of the expenditure. You are, therefore, in addition to the quarterly and annual returns of the state of the money, as drawn from the exchequer and expended under the several heads of charge on the estimates to furnish their Lordships, at the end of every year, with a full and accurate statement of the surplus and deficiencies as the case may be under each head of charge in the said estimates exhibiting thus a balance sheet to be laid before Parliament at the commencement of every succeeding session.

384. *First Lord to Comptroller: naval estimates*

[BL, Add Mss 41,368]   22 January 1831

I must confess to you that I should have felt less anxiety than I do with respect to the state of the Fleet and the supply of stores ready for immediate use, if I had no reason to know that the entire sum voted annually by Parliament has been considered as a gross sum applicable to purposes not contemplated in the estimates. That in some items, more, and in others, less, has been expended, than the precise sum allotted to each service under the appropriation act.

385. *First Lord to Prime Minister: consolidation of naval departments*

[Cumbria R.O., D/GN/3/1/9]   6 December 1831

Having endeavoured, by the strictest inquiry, and by a careful inspection of every department connected with the Board, to acquire a competent knowledge of the great interests committed to our care, I have formed a very decided opinion that all the concerns of the naval department, both civil and military, should be placed under the direction and superintendence of one superior and undivided authority. This authority should be vested in the Lords Commissioners for executing the office of Lord High Admiral, responsible to the crown and to the public for the due exercise of the powers entrusted to them. The system, which has hitherto been pursued, although sanctioned by long usage, is in direct contradiction to the principle of individual responsibility. The whole history of the civil concerns of the navy, from the first establishment of the dockyards to the present time, exhibits the fatal effects of clashing interests and rival powers. The consequence has been, inattention to the public welfare; gross neglect of important duties; a systematic counteraction of the supreme powers of the Board of Admiralty; an extravagant expenditure of stores; group peculation in a variety of instances and all those evils, which have been brought to light in the various reports of the Commissions of Naval Enquiry and Naval Revision.

Many salutary reforms have within the last few years been successfully introduced. Checks on the expenditure of public money have been rendered more efficient and all the more flagrant abuses of the ancient system have disappeared. Still the evils resulting from the imperfect control of the Admiralty over the Navy and Victualling boards are apparent. The supreme power of the Board [of Admiralty] is reluctantly acknowledged and their orders in consequence are still more reluctantly obeyed: in some cases silently disregarded, in others openly counteracted. On the whole, while the Lords of the Admiralty alone are really responsible, the Commissioners of the Navy divide the powers.

Great inconvenience, moreover, has been experienced from the Comptroller of the Navy and the Chairman of the Victualling Board, on a change of administration, not sharing the fate of their political friends and leaving office together with them. It is their duty to communicate confidentially with the First Lord of the Admiralty and to obey his directions. On a change of government, it frequently happens that they are his political opponents, are actuated by the warm passions of party and, entertaining adverse opinions, are tempted to thwart and to frustrate measures, which the duty of obedience in their situations should lead them only to execute. Whereas they now, too often, deliberate and sometimes even disobey.

The appointment of the commissioners of the subordinate Boards by patent is also another principal cause of disobedience and dissension. The commissioners of the Navy and Victualling boards in London have, at times, avowed that they considered their situations independent of the Lords Commissioners of the Admiralty. The commissioners of the out ports have even arrogated an authority independent of their respective boards, because their names being inserted in the same patent, they held themselves entitled to coequal powers.

It would be in vain, amidst such a conflict of passions and of interests, to expect that degree of zeal and assiduity in the discharge of public duties, which can only be obtained from the servants of the crown, when acting in due subordination. They are directed by one supreme authority, which regulates their appointment and controls their conduct.

In order therefore, to render the administration of naval affairs more consistent with the principles of good government, more efficient in execution and more economical in result, it cannot be denied that the consolidation of departments will have a direct tendency to effect these objects. The Board of Admiralty, which now only exercises immediate control over the military operations of the Fleet, would then also have under its constant view the actual state of all the civil establishments connected with the navy: the number of artificers, the quantity of stores, the condition of the ships in ordinary, the progress of work on ships being built or under repair. All these various considerations being brought to one point, the whole would be well and easily regulated with an enlarged view of the demands of the public service and economical arrangements would be the necessary consequence. It cannot be denied that the establishment of such a system would be beneficial; it remains to be shown that, by certain arrangements, it is feasible.

The first and indefinable condition appears to be that all the three consolidated departments should be brought under one roof, so that ready and easy communication may at all times take place between the Board and the different branches into which the offices must be divided. The present position of the Admiralty, in the immediate vicinity of Downing Street and the Horse Guards is most advantageous: and there are grave objections to the removal of the whole establishment to Somerset House. The First Secretary's house and the houses of the four naval Lords are easily convertible into commodious offices and will afford ample accommodation for the consolidated department. Houses, under the proposed arrangement, will be vacated in Somerset Place, to which the

Lords of the Admiralty may remove (or an increase in salary may be given to each in lieu of a house provided at the public expense).

The patents appointing commissioners of the Navy and Victualling must be resolved. Henceforth, no commissioner in the naval service, excepting the commissioners of the Board of Admiralty, should bear this title. They would continue to exercise all their present functions with the addition of all the duties now vested in the Navy and Victualling boards. It will be asked; how can the Board of Admiralty, already so much occupied, efficiently discharge, more especially in time of war, duties so multifarious as those, which, tho' hitherto subdivided, it is now proposed to accumulate? The answer, in the first place, is, that a large portion of business of each of the boards consists in correspondence with the others. This interchange of correspondence has been ascertained to amount to one eighth of the whole. With the division of labour arises also a clashing of authority, which the union would effectually remove and business, now transacted with difficulty, would flow smoothly without the jar of opposing interests.

It must be admitted however, that the success of the consolidation depends on a judicious arrangement of the business; and after much consideration and consultation with those, who from long experience are most competent to advise, I propose to divide the whole consolidated business into five departments, under the immediate superintendence and control of the Board, with the two secretaries who will, of course, conduct the entire correspondence.

1st the Department of the Surveyor of the Navy.
2nd the Department of the Accountant for Cash
3rd the Department of the Accountant for Stores
4th the Department of the Accountant for Slops & Pursers' Accounts
5th the Medical Department

At the head of each of these departments to be placed a responsible officer without a seat at the Board. Each of them to be superintended by one Lord of the Admiralty who will daily report to the Board such matters arising in his department as he shall deem proper to be brought before it. An additional Lord Commissioner of the Admiralty will be absolutely necessary to fulfil this arrangement. To secure to the Board full cognizance of all that is transacted in the five departments, there must be a Lord Commissioner superintending each and I would suggest that a lay Lord be appointed, to whose superintendence the Branch of the Accountant for Cash should be committed. The division of labour would then stand thus,

1st Naval Lord – Surveyor's Department
New Lay Lord – Accountant's Department
2nd Naval Lord – Storekeeper's Department
3rd Naval Lord – Purser's Department
4th Naval Lord – Medical Department.

The Transport Department, as now conducted at the Navy Board, would easily be distributed between the branches of the two Accountants and Storekeeper and the Ticket and Wages Branch, now conducted by a 1st clerk of intelligence and experience, would be superintended by one of the junior naval lords. The Commissioners of the Admiralty and perhaps the 1st Secretary would of course be removed with each change of administration. They alone would be removed. The heads of the departments would be continued during good behaviour and thus the general routine of the business would never be interrupted. The directing control would follow the change of administration, and be naturally guided, as it ought to be imperceptibly, by the general policy of the government. The Board must meet daily, holidays excepted, to read the correspondence; to receive and consider the various reports from the five departments; to give their orders and to sign all such documents as may be required. Although the Accountant General for cash should have the power of drawing money, yet his draft should in no case be valid, unless approved by two commissioners, signed by the secretary and countersigned by the superintendent of the branch of service under which the claim arises.

It is evident that a great addition of labour will devolve, under this arrangement, on the several members of the Board. A constant and regular attendance will be indispensable for the due execution of such heavy additional duties. But, when it is remembered, how large a portion of the present business of the Board of Admiralty arises from references made to them by the Navy and Victualling Boards, the consolidation, while it adds new duties, will remove the impediment of much needless delay and unnecessary correspondence, and counterbalance by increased dispatch any increase of business to be transacted. I am quite convinced that punctual attendance and daily Boards would, even in war, with a slight addition to the establishment, be equal to the prompt dispatch of the whole business of the naval service.

With respect to the economy of this new arrangement, it is only necessary to state that there are at the present moment employed in the Navy Board 108 clerks, and in the Victualling Board 68 clerks, besides a very large number of messengers and watchmen and a heavy annual charge for taxes and contingencies in each department. The aggregate of the salaries of the clerks in each department amounts to:

Navy Board	£36,000
Victualling Board	£26,100
	£62,100

Experience alone can safely prove to what extent this establishment of clerks, and the consequent annual expense, may be reduced by the proposed consolidation of officers. One fifth of the whole, which is the present strength of the secretary's department in the two subordinate boards, may from the very commencement be spared without difficulty; and this will be equivalent to a saving of £13,000 a year. I am disposed to hope that, upon trial, after the adjustment of the new duties, and with some further new arrangements, a still greater reduction may be effected.

With respect to high-salaried officers, the following reductions would take place immediately:

Comptroller	£2,000 per annum
Deputy Comptroller	1,000
Chairman of Victualling Board	1,200
Accountant of Victualling Board	800
Purser	800
Secretary Navy Board	1,200
Secretary Victualling Board	1,000
	£8,000

Thus abolishing seven high salaried officers, and saving £8,000 per annum, and adding only, for the present at least, one Lord Commissioner of the Admiralty, with a salary of £1,000 per annum. To this must be added the saving of clerks, as above, £13,000: making the entire saving annually £20,000.

But there is annually paid for contingencies, travelling expenses, messengers &c.

at the Navy Board	£6,500
at the Victualling Board	£4,000
	£10,500
add savings, as above	£20,000
Total Annual Saving	£30,500

In addition to which, the large offices at Somerset House will be vacated and rendered available for other departments of the public service. Neither will it be necessary that this new arrangement should be tainted by the appearance of a large exercise of patronage, for I would propose that only one new appointment should take place. The Comptroller of the

Navy having been removed, his vacancy is not filled up; the present Deputy Comptroller should be appointed Accountant of Stores; the present Surveyor: Sir R Seppings; the present Storekeeper: Captain Middleton; the present Accountant of the Navy: Mr. J. Thomson who, on retiring, [are] well entitled to some mark of the King's favour, should be superannuated; General Stapylton, Chairman of the Victualling Board, and Mr Edgecombe, one of the Purser Commissioners, should retire on a superannuation allowance. The appointments would then stand thus:

Mr Dundas, the present Deputy Comptroller, to be Accountant for Stores.

Mr. Briggs, the present Accountant for Victualling, (whose skill as an Accountant I think superior to the Accountant for Cash).

Mr. Meek, the present Purser Commissioner, to be Accountant for Purser's Slops and Accounts.

Sir William Burnett, present Medical Commissioner, to be Head of Medical Department.

And a new appointment, the only one, in room of Sir R. Seppings, Captain Symonds to be Surveyor General.

386. *Graham as First Lord*

[Wade, *The Extraordinary Black Book*, p. 537]   February 1832

Sir James [Graham] by improvements in the civil administration of the navy, and reductions in the estimates nearly to the amount of a million, has almost silenced Mr. Hume, and set a splendid example to the heads of departments.

387. *Melville to Sir George Clerk:*[1] *uniting the civil departments*

[SRO GD/2/3335]   8 February 1832

In 1828 when the Duke of Clarence was at the Admiralty with every prospect of his remaining there, I drew up at Goulbourn's request a project for the uniting the Navy and Victualling boards, and conducting the business of the Navy on the same principles as the Ordnance Board which Board was then the favourite hobby horse of the House of Commons, or

---

[1]Sir George Clerk had been a Commissioner on the Board of Admiralty, serving under Melville from 1819 to 1827 and 1828 to 1830.

at least the Finance Committee. The success of the scheme must depend materially on its details; but I have no idea that it is either impracticable or difficult, even in war, and certainly not in peace. If it shall be found practicable, it will unexpectedly simplify by concentrating the business of the Navy. It will of course cut off at once the voluminous correspondence between the several boards, and bring the whole concern more immediately under the eye and cognizance of the Admiralty.

If the same operation could be performed in regard to the Treasury and the several revenue boards, but which I consider to be wholly impracticable on account of the extent of their business, the same results would follow. The reason why I think it practicable in the Navy is because it appears to me that their affairs are not on so an extensive a scale as to prevent their being so managed and superseded. Cockburn[1] used to think that the whole might be brought into one board under the Admiralty by uniting together the Navy and Victualling Boards.

388.   *First Lord addressing House of Commons: misapplication of estimates*

[*Hansard's Parliamentary Debates*, X, p. 353]   14 February 1832

First Reading of the Navy Civil Departments Bill

When his present Majesty, then Duke of Clarence, presided at the Admiralty, he referred to a very salutary order made by Lord Sandwich in the year 1776, which made it imperative that not less than two years' consumption of timber in reserve should be provided for ship-building at the different naval establishments. The right hon. Gentleman (Mr. Croker) wrote to the Navy Board to make an inquiry upon this subject; and he held in his hand the answer to that inquiry. It was signed by the gallant officer (Sir Byam Martin), and two other Commissioners of the Navy. That letter contained this passage. 'We beg to acquaint you, for the information of His Royal Highness the Duke of Clarence, that when the Comptroller of the Navy submitted the draft estimates to the Admiralty, the sum required was stated at £180,000. We also beg to inform you, that the excess of expenditure in 1826 and 1827, beyond the grants of Parliament, would make it indispensably necessary to refrain, as much as possible, from the purchase of stores, chiefly timber, so as, under a limited grant, to obtain a sufficient surplus to last up to the meeting of Parliament

---

[1] Sir George Cockburn, a naval officer of substantial experience, had served on the Board of Admiralty under Melville from 1818 to 1827 and 1828 to 1830.

in 1829'. Having stated to the House the excess of outlay under the head of building, from the year 1826 to the year 1830, beyond the votes of Parliament, he would state to the House how that outlay was met during those four years. In the year 1827, the sum voted by Parliament for the purchase of timber and stores was £1,060,000; the sum expended was £876,000, leaving a balance of £184,000 unaccounted for. In the year 1828, the sum expended less than that voted was £42,000; in 1829, it was £230,000; in 1830, £195,000. Under the head of timber and materials, there was expended in four years £1,029,000 less than Parliament had voted.

389. *First Lord addressing House of Commons: overriding of Admiralty authority*

[*Hansard's Parliamentary Debates*, X, p. 354]   14 February 1832

First Reading of the Navy Civil Departments Bill

Two regulations which, had they been strictly followed up, would have been found extremely useful, were introduced by the right hon. Baronet (Sir George Cockburn) when he was in the Admiralty. The first of those regulations had reference to the establishment of a check on the issue and receipt of public stores in the dockyards; and it was supposed that, by keeping a ledger at each of the out ports, and a counter-ledger at the Navy Board, no fraud could be committed as long as the two books corresponded in their items. A more judicious regulation, if carried into effect, could not have been devised; but it unfortunately happened that, up to the present moment, it was impossible to obtain any information whatever from the ledger kept at the Navy Office. It was so much in arrears, that to attempt to complete it must be abandoned as hopeless. The other regulation had reference to the reduction in the number of labourers in the different dockyards. It had been made by the Admiralty and was signed by Lord Melville. The principle, laid down in that regulation, was most explicit, containing, at the same time, a positive direction that the number should be reduced. The instructions were, that no more men should be entered until the number was reduced to 6,000; and that when the number was reduced to 7,000, the men should be allowed to work on Wednesdays; and when to 6,000 on every day of the week. The regulation was issued about a year before the late government quitted office; and at that time the number employed was 7,716; the number employed on 31st of January last amounted to 7,439; so that the reduction, in all that time had not amounted to more than 200 men [*sic*]. He stated these facts to prove there was an insufficient control on the part of the Board of Admiralty, and an imperfect obedience on the part of the other boards.

390. *Croker[1] addressing House of Commons: consolidation of civil departments*

[*Hansard's Parliamentary Debates*, X, pp. 800–801]   27 February 1832

Second Reading of the Navy Civil Departments Bill

If the right hon. Baronet [Sir James Graham] would constitute these inferior officers [the proposed principal officers] a Board of five, the whole would equally come under the general superintendence and control of the Board of Admiralty. This proposition would make no alteration to the right hon. Baronet's plan, except the placing the responsibility where it should really lie … And so far from his plan offering any diminution to the superior control of the Board of Admiralty, it would, in his opinion, increase it; for instead of having five Lords of the Admiralty, worn down by the fatigue of details, so as to be unable to look after the higher duties of their station, all those details would fall to the share of the subordinate board, and the Board of Admiralty would constitute a complete and effective check upon their actions, instead of being, as by the proposed plan they would be, puzzled and embarrassed between absolute authority, semi-responsibility, and complete ignorance.

391. *First Secretary addressing House of Commons: consolidation of civil departments*

[*Hansard's Parliamentary Debates*, X, pp. 800–801]   27 February 1832

Second Reading of the Navy Civil Departments Bill

When he looked at the manner in which the right hon. Baronet [Sir James Graham] had argued the propriety of making this change, it appeared to him as if he had entirely overlooked what was the great object of the country for which the Board of Admiralty had been constituted. What according to this plan, was to become of all the military transactions connected with the naval service? What was to become of the natural occupation of these naval officers? They would be wearied with the details

[1] John William Croker had served on the Board of Admiralty from 1809 to 1830.

of duties they could not understand, and incapacitated by fatigue and confusion for those they did. For his part, he did not think they could adequately perform those various duties, even on their recent introduction to office, when the proverb would be on their side, that 'new brooms sweep clean.' He would ask the hon. Baronet himself, whether he and his colleagues had, since they had been in office, found the labour so light, or that they had so little to do, as to justify the surcharging of them with additional duties? For his own part, he did not think it possible that more duties could be adequately executed, though he saw, without admiring, the boldness with which more were undertaken: and he said, that, even in time of peace, we ought to take care how we overload the public servants, lest, when the real time of difficulty arrived, it should be found that they broke down under the weight imposed upon them, and at that very moment when it would prove most pernicious to the interests of the country.

392.   *Civil Departments Act: abolition of Navy Board*

[Act of Parliament, 2 William IV, Cap XL]   1 June 1832

It has been deemed expedient that the number of officers in the civil departments of the Navy should be reduced. To that end the offices or departments of the principal officers and Commissioners of His Majesty's Navy, and of the Commissioners for Victualling His Majesty's Navy, and for the Care of Sick and Wounded Seamen, should be abolished. And whereas various duties of the said commissioners being established and regulated by divers Acts of Parliament, it is requisite that such Acts should, in some cases be altered, and new provisions made for the due execution of the said duties. Be it therefore enacted by the King's most Excellent Majesty, by and with the advice and consent of the Lords Spiritual and Temporal, and Commons, in this present Parliament assembled, and by the authority of the same, that in case His Majesty shall be leased to cancel and revoke the said Letters Patent by which the said several persons were respectively constituted and appointed Principal Officers and Commissioners of the Navy, and Commissioners for Victualling His Majesty's Navy, and for the Care of Sick and Wounded Seamen, as aforesaid, all the interests, titles, authorities, powers, and duties vested in the said respective commissioners by any Act or Acts of Parliament, and every matter relating to them and their respective offices, shall from and after such revocation be and the same are hereby declared to be transferred to the commissioners for executing the Office of Lord High Admiral of the United Kingdom …

393.	*Second Secretary Barrow[1] to Board of Admiralty: memorandum on naval department offices*

[TNA, ADM1/3478]					11 September 1832

In turning over in my mind whether any and what changes or modifications might with benefit to His Majesty's service be introduced in conducting the civil affairs of the Navy in consequence of the Act of 2nd William IV, I was strongly impressed with the conviction that it would be wholly unnecessary to have recourse to a measure at that time appeared to be almost indispensable. When the consolidation of the several civil departments of the navy under one board was first contemplated and indeed until the measure was brought into operation, it was a very general opinion, in which I participated, that it would not only be expedient, but absolutely necessary, to consolidate and conduct the united duties under one and the same roof. That either the establishment of the Admiralty should be removed to Somerset House, or the department of the navy and victualling establishments at the latter place, transfer to Wallingford House. The best consideration I could then give to the subject inclined me to participate in that opinion.

The experience of three months practice however, and they are as good as three years, have satisfactorily proved to me, that neither the one nor the other is at all necessary, or even expedient. On the contrary, any change in the local situation of the departments would be attended with much inconvenience, and embarrass the public service. Nothing indeed can be more regular, nothing more easy and expedient, than the mode in which the Civil Affairs of the navy are now administered, while the respective localities of the Board of Admiralty and its subordinate department maintain their places, and the arrangement as to the several offices left undisturbed, and preserved nearly as they stood previous to the change. Nothing has occurred since the plan was introduced, nor likely to occur, to give the slightest interruption to the regular chain of official routine, to impede the increased despatch, which was anticipated, to create the least delay, or to diminish the promised economy of labour and expense.

---

[1]John Barrow served an unbroken term as Second Secretary from 1807 to 1845 and so was well placed to comment upon the workings of both the old and new systems.

394. *Draft of a circular issued to the Surveyor-General and Accountant for Stores*

[TNA, ADM1/3479]   14 January 1833

You are to lay before the Lords of the Admiralty superintending the departments under your control the quarterly accounts of expenditure from the heads of the establishments both at home and abroad in order that those items of contingencies and incidental expenses and extra charges may be examined with a view of ascertaining that they have been incurred by proper authority either from the Board of Admiralty or by discretionary powers given in the instructions of the several superintendents and the heads of the several establishments and to report to their Lordships any irregularities that may appear therein and if correct to certify and sign them accordingly.

395. *Second Secretary Barrow addressing committee of inquiry: civil departments*

[Commission to Inquire into the Civil
Administration of the Army]   18 February 1836

[*Outline of the Manner in which the Consolidation of the Different Civil Departments of the Navy Was Carried Out, p. 1*]
When Sir James Graham first came into office, he told me it was Lord Grey's desire, and indeed it was his full intention, that the Navy Board, the Victualling Board, and the Transport Board, should be dissolved; that their patents should be revoked. As the whole of Sir James's Board were new, and the secretary also, he said that he must depend upon me to lay down some plan for the purpose. I asked him what was intended to be the general outline: he said that Lord Grey's wish was, that the principle should be individual responsibility and a vigilant superintendence. Those were to be the principles upon which I was to proceed. I drew up two or three sketches of plans for his consideration, and in a very short space of time we worked out the plan that was finally adopted.

[*Duties of the Surveyor and the Overseeing of His Department, p. 2*]
As the name implies, he has the whole charge of building and repairing ships, but has no power either to build, or to repair, or to dock a ship, except by the order of Board of Admiralty. It was thought proper that the whole and sole power should rest there. The surveyor divides and portions out the artificers and workmen into their different stations for the week. He sees, through the proper officers, and by himself, as well as can be

done, the nature of the timber to be used, the quantities in hand, and the quantities that may be wanting. This is done in communication with the Storekeeper-general, who keeps an account of the receipt and expenditure of all the timber, and all other stores.

Sir Charles Adam superintends the Surveyor of the Navy. He of course sees that the proper returns are made of the state of the Navy and when a ship is ordered to be fitted-out for a particular service. Sir Charles Adam has the charge of seeing that she is properly fitted. He consults with the Surveyor of the Navy how ships shall be distributed to the different ports, or in the different docks, and how the artificers shall be distributed upon them, in order to bring them forward in succession, or simultaneously, just as they may be wanted. Sir Charles arranges with the Surveyor the mode in which the ships shall be stowed, what quantity of powder they shall take, what guns they shall carry, and how ships shall be stowed as to their holds, and fitted and stored as to their provisions, &c.,

[Duties of the Storekeeper-General, p. 3]
The Storekeeper, of course, as his name implies, is charged with keeping up a proper quantity of stores, seeing that they are kept up, and also the manner in which they are expended. He has very accurate accounts sent up to him from his several storekeepers in the dockyards. They come up all regularly signed and vouched to him and from these weekly details he makes up his books at Somerset House, so as to know at any moment the state of all kinds of stores, which are very numerous.

396.   *Items of Business Submitted to the Board of Admiralty*

February 1837

(a) [TNA, ADM1/3404, 20 February 1837]
[Covering letter from Sir Robert Barlow, Superintendent of Chatham dockyard, together with an enclosure signed by the principal officers of the yard, giving reasons for the employment of two millwrights.]

The enclosed I beg leave to submit for the consideration of My Lords Commissioners of the Admiralty a letter from the officers of this yard proposing that assistance be rendered to Boulton & Watt in fixing the spare boiler of the fourteen horse engine at the ropery, stating that the millwrights are so fully occupied that one can not be spared for the purpose. I beg leave to add that although their Lordships were pleased to sanction on the 4th of November last the employment of two extra millwrights the officers have only been able to introduce the services of one man.

[*Enclosure*]

The spare boiler of the fourteen horse engine at the ropery requiring several holes to be stopped up and others must connect the various parts before the boiler can be fixed. As is proposed that the fixing of the boiler should be carried on at the same time as the engine is being fixed it is necessary to afford Messrs. Boulton & Watt the assistance of a millwright or engineer. We beg to acquaint you that the works at the ropery fully employ the millwrights so that we cannot afford one for that purpose.

(b) [TNA, ADM1/3404, 20 February 1837]

[*Detailed statement, provided by William Payne, Master Attendant of Chatham Dockyard, outlining the breakfast arrangements for those employed in the rigging house, ropery and sail loft. This was one of three similar reports from Chatham yard made in response to an Admiralty circular sent out to all of the yards on 13 February 1837.*]

In reply to Admiralty order of 13th inst. I beg leave to report that the workmen in the rigging house, ropery and sail loft used to formerly come into the yard at 6 o'clock in the Summer and had half an hour for their breakfast which interfered with their duties, particularly with the riggers when called afloat as much depended on the tides. With respect to the ropeyard, there are disadvantages as from the men breaking off from their work at any fixed time, for should they be laying a rope when partly made, that rope having as much twist as it would bear, remaining in that state for the time allowed for breakfast would be injurious to it, with various other disadvantages in the spinning department. The practice was in time of war not to stop until the rope was made and the men then had their breakfast taken to them in whatever part of the building they were employed. As to the sail makers, when once a man is seated to work in his sail form for sewing it will be attended with delay and disadvantage in breaking off and returning to it again. I therefore consider the present system works with much greater advantage to the service than would be than should they be allowed to breakfast in the yard. With respect to embezzlement should any alternative take place it would be advisable for them to bring their breakfast with them.

(c) [TNA, ADM1/3404, 27 February 1837]

[*Report of the Master Attendant at Chatham yard following an Admiralty request to Sir Robert Barlow for information on the employment of sail makers.*]

In reply to Admiralty order of the 20th inst. directing the sail makers to be employed six days in the week and to report whether the work in that branch may be best increased by employing the men extra hours or adding additional hands. I most respectfully request that as the people are now at day work it would be preferable to adopt the latter mode by entering three or four additional men. I consider each man does as much work within the working hours of the yard as can be done by an efficient workman, that the service would not benefit by increasing the hours of labour as by a limited entry of an additional number of men in the ordinary working hours of the yard.

397.   *First Secretary of the Admiralty to the Committee of Supply: naval estimates*

[*Hansard's Parliamentary Debates*, XIV, p. 655]   1 March 1841

Previous to the enactment of the 1 and 2 William 4th, cap. 40, the un-expended balances at the end of each financial year remained in the Exchequer to the credit of the naval service and were expended by the Admiralty either to meet an excess on any particular year or for any other purpose deemed beneficial to the public service. Out of these accumulated balances the extensive victualling facilities at Weevil and Cremill were erected without the knowledge or sanction of Parliament. This was deemed to be a great abuse, and was strongly commented upon by the right hon. Baronet, the Member for Pembroke who, when he became First Lord of the Admiralty, announced his intention of introducing an act to put an end to this and other abuses in the civil administration of the Navy. By the 30th section of that act the Board of Admiralty were required to lay a statement of their expenditure, with vouchers, before the Board of audit in the month of November of each year and the auditors were required to make such observations as they might deem fit, so as to call attention of Parliament to any unauthorised expenditure.

No. 8.   Wages to Artificers at home; the increase is considerable: it amounts to £46,784; £11,000 will be applicable to the full establishment of shipwrights, which was completed in the course of the year …

No. 10.   The vote for stores for the service of the navy; the increase is considerable, amounting to £242,527. When it is recollected that this head of expenditure covers everything used in the building and furnishing of ships … and the materials for all the repairs in the dockyards … the committee will not consider the sum too large … At Chatham the sum of £4,000 will be spent on groins to prevent the accumulation of mud in the river, and £4,000 on the improvement of the smitheries, and the erection of anchor fires.

398. *Gilbert 2nd Earl of Minto: Memorandum on workload of Admiralty commissioners*

[NMM, ELL/239]   1841

The labour at present required from the Lords to enable them to conduct the business satisfactorily is very greatly beyond the degree of exertion to be generally found or expected

399. *Increase of Business*

[Barrow, *Autobiographical Memoir*, pp. 418–19][1]   1847

With the increase of individually responsible officers must necessarily have arisen an increase of the whole correspondence which now passes through the Board of Admiralty and which, before the change, was conducted through the Boards, generally. This, of course has multiplied to a great extent the number of letters and the quantity of writing within the Admiralty office at Whitehall. At the end of six years an account was taken of what the number of letters received, and what the number of pages of entry, consisted, at the two periods of 1827 and 1833:–

In 1827.	Letters received		25,428
1833.	Ditto		31,330
		Annual increase	5,902
1827.	Dispatched		25,402
1833.	Ditto		47,886
		Increase	22,484
1827.	Pages of entry		20,783
1833.	Ditto		39,162
	Increase		18,379

Yet, with all this addition to the correspondence, the establishment of the office was only increased by three or four junior clerks; but during the first two or three years *my* labours were at least doubled. It was not found

[1] J. Barrow, *Autobiographical Memoir* (London, 1847).

necessary to add to the members of the Board, and they remain at five, with the First Lord.

400.   *J.S. Bromley: report on dockyard administration*

[Report of Inquiry into the Management of H.M. Naval Yards, appendix 16, pp. 485–90]   1847

[Control of Workmen]
It is not the duty of any one of the principal officers at Somerset House to control specially this great and important body of men, or the wages paid to them; hence I find the practice at one yard differing from that of another, upon innumerable points of the utmost moment to the proper working of the establishment and the 'economy of labour and expense.' The several yards differ in their working hours; in their system of muster and of payment; in the size of the gangs; in the manner of shoaling the shipwrights; in the employment on extra and on task work; in checking wages due; and in the construction put on orders relative to the employment and wages of workmen. This diversity of practice exhibits the want of some central officer to control this important branch of the naval expenditure.

[Admiralty Superintendence and Control]
It is most desirable that in any arrangement that may be made for controlling the authority of the principal officers at Somerset House, and for maintaining the full authority of the Board, care should be taken not to press too heavily upon the collective duties of the Board; and, moreover, not to lay down a fixed course of proceeding which shall not be equally useful and practicable in time of war as in time of peace.

In the event of war, it is more than probable that the Board of Admiralty would, as formerly, be compelled to hold its sittings daily, to provide for the pressing political wants of the service, leaving all executive and detail matters to the consideration of some subordinate authority.

After much consideration as to the best mode which the Board could adopt, of delegating their authority in certain matters of detail without weakening their control, I have arrived at the conviction that the best practical course will be to form a committee of the principal officers at Somerset House, to be presided over by a Lord of the Admiralty or the political Secretary, that the committee should meet once or twice a week, or as often as might be necessary, for the purpose of discussing all matters arising out of their duties beyond their defined powers as separate officers.

Under an arrangement of this kind a desirable communication would be established between the principal officers which does not now exist, and every officer would bring to the consideration of general practical questions his previous knowledge and experience, much to his own improvement and to the benefit of the public service. The superintending Board officer would decide with more confidence, and in cases of doubt he would be supported by the practical opinion of the committee, in his reference to any point for the consideration of the Board at large.

[*The Need of Having the Departments under One Roof*]
Even now, in time of peace, the inconvenience arising from one portion of the office being so far detached from the other, must be felt by every member of the Board who has to seek information on questions of detail. In time of war a rapid execution of orders will become indispensable, and I fear that much difficulty and confusion will ensue. I am quite certain that not an objection, which can deserve consideration, can be raised against this consolidation. The cost, whatever it may be, of providing accommodation for the whole of the Admiralty department at Whitehall would be but small in comparison with the advantages to be derived from the whole being more immediately under the eye of the Board.

401. *Earl of Ellenborough[1] addressing the House of Lords: reformed system*

[*Hansard's Parliamentary Debates*, CXXXII, pp. 656–7]   7 April 1854

I confess, my Lords, that I am adverse to all boards. They appear to me to be but an excuse for want of responsibility. The only real security for good conduct on the part of a public officer is the sense of entire and sole responsibility for everything that is done; but if you impose upon him – as I think you should for the public benefit – that feeling of entire and sole responsibility, it is but just that you should give him also full and complete power to carry his wishes into effect; otherwise you treat him ill, and place him in a position in which he cannot carry out what he believes to be necessary for the benefit and welfare of the country. My experience of the Admiralty was extremely short, and it was experience obtained under the most adverse circumstances, for I only entered upon the administration of that department as the representative of an expiring Government – a position in which no one who has had the misfortune to be placed would

[1]Edward 1st Earl of Ellenborough held the office of First Lord from January to July 1846.

ever desire to stand again. But, I must say, from the short experience which I did have, that it is, without exception, the most inefficient, and the most utterly incapable of doing good service to the public which at any time has come under my notice ... and I recollect very well when the Act [Civil Departments Act, 1832] to which the noble Earl [Grey] alluded, which was passed at the suggestion of the present First Lord of the Admiralty [Graham], was carried through Parliament, hearing the opinion of persons who were then thoroughly acquainted with the practical administration of the Admiralty, that it might do very well in time of peace, but that it would be found to break down in time of war. Our experience, as yet has not been sufficient to enable us to come to any judgment on that subject.

402. *Admiral Arthur Duncombe, former Naval Lord, Addressing the House of Commons: reformed system*

[*Hansard's Parliamentary Debates*, CXL, p. 300]   12 June 1860

In 1832 the right hon. Gentleman, the Member for Carlisle [Sir James Graham], when First Lord of the Admiralty, abolished the Navy Board. Great evils had admittedly arisen from the conflict of authority, and he did not question either the policy or the ability of the Right Hon. Gentleman. Affairs had gone on smoothly for a number of years, as long as there was no pressure on the department; but during the last six or eight years, when the reconstruction of the navy, and the difficulty of manning the fleet, had forced themselves upon our attention; and when the novelties which modern science had introduced into every department, entailed the necessity of increased supervision and expense, it became evident that the machinery of the Board of Admiralty must undergo extension and adaptation to the altered circumstances. It was with the object of discovering what improvements or modifications were required, and with a view of accommodating the system to the sentiments of the nation in the present day, that he brought forward this motion.

The noble Lord might say he had no right to make objections, without being able to show that what he proposed would be an improvement. If his opinion had any weight in the committee, he thought the suggestions he should be disposed to make would be improvements of the present system. He would recommend that the First Lord of the Admiralty should be a Minister of Marine, and be placed on the same footing as the Minister of War. Of course, he would have a seat on the Cabinet, and would conduct the political and diplomatic part of the business connected with that office. The Board of Admiralty should be entirely a Navy Board. He said this without any disparagement of the present civilians on it. He knew from experience that many points came before them for decision, on which decision was very difficult, without some knowledge of naval matters. He would also make it a *sine qua non* that the Comptroller of the Navy should have a seat at the Board of Admiralty and be the immediate means of communication between his own department and the Board. It should be borne in mind that the largest expenditure took place in the Comptroller's department. Ships were ordered to be built, and great outlay might be incurred without the Board, as a Board, knowing anything about it. He ventured to say that it frequently happened that the first knowledge which the Lords of the Admiralty obtained of a certain ship, the *Algiers*, for instance, being launched, or the *Princess Royal*, being laid down on the same slips [*sic*] the next day, was from seeing the announcement in the newspapers a few days afterwards. That was not as it ought to be. It could not occur if the Comptroller had a seat on the Board and laid the business of his department regularly before it. All matters relating to building ships, and their steam machinery, should be brought immediately under the notice of the Board and all representations of the Comptroller could be directly considered by it. As the Comptroller was at present overworked, he should have under him a Board of Construction, composed of three individuals, thoroughly competent to superintend the building of ships, who might prevent an enormous expenditure upon certain vessels, and their inefficiency after being lengthened and altered.

403. *Constitution of Board of Admiralty*

[Report, Commissioners on Managing H.M. Dockyards, p. vi]   1860

The Board of Admiralty consists of a First Lord, who is a Cabinet minister, four naval lords, and a civilian, who is a Member of the House of Commons. There are two secretaries; one of whom is permanent; the other is political, and the organ of the Admiralty in the House of Commons. Any two Lords constitute a Board, and an order signed by any two Lords is of equal validity as if signed by the whole Board.

404. *Deficiencies in Dockyard Management: general recommendations*

[Report, Commissioners on Managing H.M. Dockyards, pp. v–vi] 1860

2.   We regret to state that in our opinion the control and management of the dockyards is inefficient.

3. We are of opinion that the inefficiency may be attributed to the following causes:–

    1st. The constitution of the Board of Admiralty.
    2nd. The defective organization of the subordinate departments.
    3rd. The want of clear and well-defined responsibility.
    4th. The absence of any means, both now and in times past, of effectually checking expenditure, from the want of accurate accounts.

8. The fluctuating character of the Board of Admiralty has been brought under our notice as being incompatible with effective and economical management of the dockyards. The late Controller, Sir Baldwin Walker, states that he has seen six or seven changes in the thirteen years that he has been in office, every change causing different arrangements and alterations. Sir Richard Bromley, the Accountant-General, states that there have been 15 First Lords, 65 other Lords, and 17 Secretaries of the Admiralty since 1829, making a total of 97 changes within that period. There have been six Civil Lords in succession over his Department since he became Accountant-General in 1854. Colonel Greene, the Director of Works, states that in eleven years he has acted under six superintending Lords.

10. With a view of rendering the control and management more efficient, we humbly offer the following suggestions:

    1st. That a minister for the navy department should be appointed, and should be held entirely responsible for the control and management of the dockyards.
    2nd. That the dockyards should be looked upon as large manufacturing establishments for the purpose of building and repairing the ships of Your Majesty's Navy.
    3rd. That the Minister of the Navy should have the power of appointing a Controller-General acquainted with and qualified to manage such establishments.
    4th. That the Controller-General should have the power (subject to the approval of the Minister), of selecting the superintendents of the different dockyards, as these officers are the instruments for carrying out his instructions.
    14th. That all the departments of the Admiralty connected with the dockyards should be brought under one roof.

405.   *Order-in-Council: Comptroller of the Navy*

[TNA, PC2/251]   23 January 1860

[The Surveyor] should be in future called the Comptroller of the Navy, a name which would be more in accordance with his duties and we beg leave to also submit, with reference to the regulations established by the said Order-in-Council [12 October 1832] and more particularly with reference to the 11th and 12th clauses of the same, that the Comptroller of the Navy be authorised to correspond direct with the respective officers of the dockyards and to issue such orders as he may deem necessary for the proper conduct of the works to the several superintendents.

The Comptroller of the Navy will, however, as heretofore, consult with the superintending lord upon all matters connected with the preparation of ships for commission, the repair of ships in commission, with the state of works in the dockyards, and generally with the business of his office.

And whereas the superintendents of Your Majesty's Dockyards are ordered by the instructions issued under the authority of Your Majesty's Order-in-Council of 1 June, 1844, 'to correspond with our secretary, acquainting him with the transactions of the dockyards &c.' we humbly submit that those officers be now instructed to correspond with the Comptroller of the Navy and to follow such orders as may be connected with the works that relate to his department.

406.   *Baillie Hamilton addressing the House of Commons: reformed system*

[*Hansard's Parliamentary Debates*, CL, p. 300]   28 February 1861

Previous to the year 1832 these duties [those of the Surveyor of the Navy] were performed by a Board called the Navy Board, consisting of the Comptroller and two Surveyors, sometimes three. The duty of the second Surveyor was to attend the department of construction; the junior Surveyor had the exclusive superintendence of the dockyards. In 1832 the right hon. Baronet the member for Carlisle [Sir James Graham] was First Lord of the Admiralty, and a change was made as to the Navy Board. There was no man to whose opinion he would yield greater respect on this subject, or any other, than to the right hon. Baronet, who he regretted was not in his place. But when he made this change he was only at the beginning of his brilliant ministerial career, and the change was avowedly made as an experiment.

407.   *John Briggs: reformed system of 1833*

[Briggs, *Naval Administrations*, p. 32[1]]

Each Lord of the Admiralty had assigned to him certain specific duties, and each member at the meeting of the Board was to bring under its consideration such matters of importance, connected with his own department, as he deemed necessary for the collective decision of their lordships.

This division of duty was established on so sound a basis that, after sixty years, it still remains in full force, though of course certain additions have been made consequent upon the altered requirements of the service, attributable to the introduction of steam and the general expansion of the navy together with the placing of the transport service under Admiralty control, etc. The system laid down by Sir James Graham has proved to be not only sound in theory, but to have worked successfully when put to the test of practical experience. By this arrangement the whole business of the Admiralty was brought under the immediate eye of the First Lord, as well as the cognizance of every member of the Board: each individual being thus afforded an opportunity of giving expression to his opinion on any subject in which he may feel either a personal, departmental, or professional interest. By this procedure every subject was well considered, and promptness and uniformity of action secured. In the event of any details being required the principal officer was always near at hand to give the necessary explanations.

---

[1]H.J. Briggs, *Naval Administrations 1827–1892* (London, 1897).

Appendix 1

SHIPS AND OTHER VESSELS BUILT AT CHATHAM ROYAL DOCKYARD, 1815–1865

Sailing Ships

Launch Date	Name	No. of Guns	
28 March 1815	*Howe*	120	1st rate
25 April 1815	*Defence*	74	3rd rate
5 September 1815	*Hercules*	74	3rd rate
16 January 1816	*Diamond*	38	5th rate
15 April 1816	*Minotaur*	74	3rd rate
3 May 1817	*Starling*	10	cutter
12 December 1818	*Bustard*	10	brig-sloop
10 February 1819	*Brisk*	10	brig-sloop
25 June 1819	*Blanche*	46	5th rate
26 July 1820	*Trafalgar*	106	1st rate
16 June 1821	*Latona*	46	5th rate
8 January 1822	*Diana*	46	5th rate
26 March 1822	*Rattlesnake*	28	6th rate
26 March 1822	*Weazle*	10	brig-sloop
7 May 1822	*Basilisk*	10	cutter
21 June 1822	*Procris*	10	brig-sloop
12 April 1823	*Prince Regent*	120	1st rate
21 August 1823	*Thames*	46	5th rate
20 November 1823	*Rainbow*	28	6th rate
30 March 1824	*Unicorn*	46	5th rate
14 May 1824	*Aetna*	12	bomb
22 October 1824	*Hearty*	10	brig-sloop
20 February 1825	*Lapwing*	10	brig-sloop
19 May 1825	*Formidable*	84	2nd rate
16 July 1825	*Harpy*	10	brig-sloop
30 July 1825	*Mermaid*	46	5th rate
28 October 1825	*Crocodile*	28	6th rate
26 January 1826	*Sulphur*	12	bomb
25 April 1826	*Fairy*	10	brig-sloop
9 May 1826	*Espoir*	10	brig-sloop
21 June 1826	*Powerful*	84	2nd rate

19 August 1826	*Calypso*	10	brig-sloop
16 November 1826	*Acorn*	18	sloop
16 November 1826	*Mercury*	46	5th rate
23 August 1827	*Childers*	18	brig-sloop
22 September 1827	*Royal George*	120	1st rate
20 December 1827	*Africaine*	46	5th rate
19 January 1828	*Cruizer*	18	brig-sloop
19 February 1829	*Eurotas*	46	5th rate
1 August 1829	*Algerine*	10	brig-sloop
13 August 1829	*Penelope*	46	5th rate
27 November 1829	*Delight*	10	brig-sloop
12 January 1830	*Thalia*	46	5th rate
23 June 1830	*Lark*	4	cutter
4 August 1830	*Jackdaw*	4	cutter
24 August 1831	*Hornet*	6	schooner
22 November 1831	*Seagull*	6	schooner
2 February 1832	*Conway*	28	6th rate
2 May 1832	*Castor*	36	5th rate
15 June 1832	*Scout*	18	sloop
17 July 1832	*Rover*	18	sloop
28 August 1832	*Forrester*	10	brig-sloop
11 September 1832	*Griffon*	10	brig-sloop
18 December 1832	*Monarch*	80	2nd rate
18 June 1833	*Waterloo*	120	1st rate
10 July 1835	*Wanderer*	16	brig-sloop
23 September 1835	*Spider*	6	schooner
13 October 1836	*Wolverine*	16	brig-sloop
30 May 1839	*Fantome*	16	brig-sloop
5 May 1840	*Maeander*	46	5th rate
28 September 1840	*London*	92	2nd rate
25 July 1842	*Goliath*	80	3rd rate
21 October 1842	*Cumberland*	70	3rd rate
20 April 1844	*Espiegle*	12	brig-sloop
20 April 1844	*Mutine*	12	brig-sloop
8 May 1845	*Raleigh*	50	4th rate
8 May 1845	*Calypso*	20	6th rate
19 July 1845	*Active*	36	5th rate
31 March 1847	*Arab*	16	brig-sloop
27 September 1847	*Elk*	16	brig-sloop
27 September 1847	*Heron*	16	brig-sloop
1 July 1848	*Mars*	80	3rd rate
25 November 1851	*Despatch*	16	brig-sloop

| 31 August 1852 | *Kangaroo* | 16 | brig-sloop |
| 24 January 1856 | *Severn* | 50 | 4th rate. Last sailing warship built at Chatham. |

Wood-hulled Steam Vessels and Warships

Launch Date	Name	Type of Vessel
25 September 1832	*Phoenix*	Wooden paddle sloop. First steam vessel built at Chatham
30 September 1833	*Gulnare*	Post Office steam packet
May 1834	*Blazer*	Paddle Vessel
12 September 1837	*Widgeon*	Small paddle packet
5 December 1837	*Dasher*	Small paddle packet
13 June 1838	*Hydra*	Paddle sloop
14 January 1839	*Hecla*	Paddle sloop
30 March 1839	*Hecate*	Paddle sloop
7 September 1839	*Alecto*	Paddle sloop
28 September 1840	*Polyphemus*	Paddle sloop
12 February 1831	*Ardent*	Paddle sloop
20 July 1841	*Growler*	Paddle sloop
28 February 1842	*Bee*	Paddle/screw tender
25 July 1842	*Virago*	Paddle sloop
5 April 1843	*Penelope*	22-gun first class paddle frigate
6 February 1844	*Janus*	Paddle sloop
2 July 1844	*Retribution*	22-gun first class paddle frigate
2 October 1845	*Bulldog*	Paddle sloop
25 June 1846	*Teazer*	22-gun second class screw gun vessel
7 February 1848	*Vivid*	Paddle packet
8 February 1849	*Elfin*	Paddle dispatch boat
1 December 1849	*Tiger*	16-gun second class paddle frigate
17 June 1850	*Horatio*	Screw frigate (converted from 5th rate)
2 June 1851	*Brisk*	Screw sloop
21 July 1853	*Cressy*	80-gun screw ship
5 October 1853	*Euryalus*	51-gun screw frigate
1 December 1853	*Majestic*	80-gun screw ship
6 November 1854	*Orion*	91-gun screw ship
20 March 1855	*Hawke*	60-gun screw ship
27 September 1855	*Chesapeake*	51-gun screw frigate

23 November 1855	*Mars*	80-gun screw ship (converted from 3rd rate)
20 May 1856	*Cadmus*	21-gun screw corvette
28 March 1857	*Renown*	91-gun screw ship
25 April 1857	*Racoon*	21-gun screw corvette
30 November 1857	*Goliath*	80-gun screw ship
15 April 1858	*Hero*	91-gun screw ship
13 August 1858	*Mersey*	40-gun screw corvette
21 March 1859	*Trafalgar*	89-gun screw ship (converted from 1st rate)
4 May 1859	*Hood*	91-gun screw ship
13 June 1859	*Charybdis*	21-gun screw corvette
27 October 1859	*Irresistible*	81-gun screw ship (conversion from 3rd rate)
23 June 1860	*Orpheus*	21-gun screw corvette
21 July 1860	*Atlas*	91-gun screw ship
1 January 1861	*Undaunted*	51-gun screw frigate
25 May 1861	*Bombay*	80-gun screw ship
9 July 1861	*Rattlesnake*	21-gun screw corvette
9 August 1861	*Arethusa*	51-gun screw frigate (conversion from 4th rate)
19 May 1863	*Salamis*	Paddle despatch vessel

Wood-hulled Steam Vessels and Warships

Launch Date	Name	Type of Vessel
10 September 1862	*Royal Oak*	32-gun iron clad frigate
23 December 1863	*Achilles*	26-gun screw armoured iron frigate
26 April 1865	*Bellerophon*	Screw central battery ironclad ship. First to be designed from outset as an ironclad
27 May 1865	*Lord Warden*	20-gun wooden hulled ironclad frigate

Miscellaneous Dockyard Working Craft

Launch Date	Name
1818	Mud Boat 3
1818	Mud Boat 4
1820	Open Barge No.1

1820	Tank Schooner No. 2	
1821	Dockyard Barge No. 2	
1824	*Van*	Barge
1825	*Fly*	Barge
1825	Dockyard Barge No. 3	
1828	*Dove*	Lighter
1833 (April)	Mud Barge No. 8	
1833 (April)	Mud Barge No. 9	
1835 (24 September)	*Devon*	
1836 (4 April)	*Bat*	Hoy
1836 (4 April)	Mooring Lighter No. 1	
1836 (5 April)	Mooring Lighter No. 2	
1837 (7 February)	*Mercury*	Tender
1837 (19 May)	Tank Vessel	Built for Malta dockyard
1838 (30 November)	*Aid*	Store carrier

Appendix 2

POST HOLDERS, 1815–1865

Admiralty

Lord High Admiral

2 May 1827–19 September 1828	William Henry 1st Duke of Clarence

First Lord of the Admiralty

25 March 1812–2 May 1827	Robert Dundas, 2nd Viscount Melville
19 September 1828–25 November 1830	Robert Dundas, 2nd Viscount Melville
25 November 1830–11 June 1834	Sir James Graham
11 June 1834–23 December 1834	George 2nd Lord Auckland
23 December 1834–25 April 1835	Thomas 2nd Earl de Grey
25 April 1835–19 September 1835	George 2nd Lord Auckland
19 September 1835–8 September 1841	Gilbert 2nd Earl of Minto
8 September 1841–13 January 1846	Thomas 9th Earl of Haddington
13 January 1846–13 July 1846	Edward 1st Earl of Ellenborough
13 July 1846–1 January 1849	George 2nd Lord Auckland
18 January 1849–2 March 1852	Sir Francis Baring
2 March 1852–5 January 1853	Algernon 4th Duke of Northumberland
5 January 1853–8 March 1855	Sir James Graham
8 March 1855–8 March 1858	Charles Wood
8 March 1858–28 June 1859	Sir John Pakington
28 June 1859–13 July 1866	Edward 12th Duke of Somerset

First Secretary

12 October 1809–29 November 1830	John William Croker
29 November 1830–24 December 1834	Hon. G. Elliot
24 December 1834–27 April 1835	G.R. Dawson

27 April 1835–4 October 1839	C. Wood
4 October 1839–9 June 1841	R. More O'Ferrall
9 June 1841–10 September 1841	J. Parker
10 September 1841–13 February 1845	Hon. S. Herbert
13 February 1845–13 July 1846	Hon. H.T. Lowry Corry
13 July 1846–21 May 1849	H.G. Ward
21 May 1849–3 March 1852	J. Parker
3 March 1852–6 January 1853	S.A. O'Brien Stafford
6 January 1853–9 March 1858	R.B. Osborne
9 March 1858–30 June 1859	Hon. H.T. Lowry Corry
30 June 1859–30 April 1866	Lord C.E. Paget

Second Secretary

9 April 1807–28 January 1845	John Barrow
28 January 1845–22 May 1855	William A. Baillie Hamilton
22 May 1855–7 May 1857	Thomas Phinn
7 May 1857–29 June 1869	William Romaine

Surveyor General

11 June 1832–1848	Capt. William Symonds
1848–1860	Sir Baldwin Walker

Controller of the Navy

1860–January 1861	Sir Baldwin Walker
7 February 1861–February 1871	Rear-Admiral Robert Spencer Robinson

Storekeeper General

11 June 1832–	Hon. Robert Dundas

Accountant General of the Navy

11 June 1832–February 1854	John Thomas Briggs

Chief Engineer and Inspector of Steam Machinery

1850–1869	Thomas Lloyd

Director of Engineering and Architectural Works

1842–7 November 1846	Capt. Brandreth
7 November 1846–December 1849	Lieut Col. Archibald Irvine
December 1849–1864	Col. Godfrey Thomas Greene
1864–c.1890	Andrew Clarke

Chief Assistant to Director of Engineering and Architectural Works
1845–April 1852   William Scamp

Deputy Director of Engineering and Architectural Works
April 1852–1867   William Scamp

Navy Board

Comptroller
24 February 1816–2 November 1831   Sir Thomas Byam Martin
2 November 1831–9 June 1832   Hon. George H.L. Dundas

Surveyors
20 June 1806–25 February 1822   Henry Peake
14 June 1813–1 March 1831   Joseph Tucker
14 June 1813–11 June 1832   Robert Seppings

Secretary
31 August 1796–19 September 1820   Richard Alexander Nelson
29 September 1820–11 June 1832   George Smith

Surveyor of Buildings
28 November 1812–2 November 1823   Edward Holl
3 February 1824–11 June 1832   George Ledwell Taylor

Chatham Dockyard

Resident Commissioners
October 1808   Capt. Sir Robert Barlow,
                                         KCB
January 1823   Capt. Charles Cunningham
December 1831   Capt. Charles Bullen, CB

Captain Superintendents
June 1832   Capt. Sir James Alexander
                                         Gordon, KCB
7 April 1837   Capt. John Clavell
4 August 1841   Capt. William Henry Shirreff
September 1846   Capt. Sir Thomas Bourchier,
                                         KCB
5 May 1849   Capt. Sir Peter Richards,
                                         KCB

June 1854	Capt. Christopher Wyvill
March 1856	Capt. George Goldsmith, CB
April 1861	Capt. Edward Gennys Fanshawe, CB
November 1863	Capt. William Howston Stewart, CB

Master Shipwrights

10 June 1813	George Parkin
4 February 1830	William Stone
6 April 1839	John Fincham
2 October 1844	Francis J. Laire
4 October 1858	Oliver Laing
22 January 1844	Philip Thornton

Assistant Master Shipwrights

2 October 1844	Oliver W. Laing
16 June 1849	John Fincham
16 June 1849	Inwood Fincham
13 July 1853	William Henwood
11 March 1859	Alexander Moore
8 June 1860	William Hutchens

Master Attendants

1809	Charles Duncan
25 October 1828	William Payne
9 February 1837	William Purdo
21 August 1840	F.W.R. Sadler
27 June 1846	Alex Karley
15 May 1849	Thomas Laen
5 November 1853	Charles Pope
11 March 1859	Alexander Southern
7 January 1864	Richard Stokes

Assistant Master Attendants

27 September 1833	Richard Easto
9 February 1837	James Henderson
21 August 1840	Alexander Karley
21 July 1843	Henry Peacock
27 June 1846	G.J. Northcote

Clerk of the Check

15 September 1822   William Proctor Smith

Storekeeper

3 May 1816   John William Lloyd
20 July 1839   Matthew Bowan Mends
7 November 1831   William Proctor Smith
17 June 1846   John Miller
11 May 1854   Robert Law

Store Receivers

1 May 1837   Thomas Baldock
9 May 1849   George Chiles
16 January 1854   Edmund J. Brietzke
8 June 1859   Benjamin H. Churchwood

Timber and Store Receivers

7 November 1831   Thomas Irving

Chief Engineer

30 June 1846   Alexander Lawrie
11 November 1856   Thomas Baker

Wardens

23 September 1822   Lt William Cockcroft

Director of Police

11 January 1834   Lt Francis Gray
23 November 1835   Lt William Hubbard
7 September 1841   John Wise

Surgeons

1 January 1824   David Rowlands
9 May 1838   George Johnstone
21 June 1842   William Warden
27 April 1849   Peter Suther

Chaplain

25 September 1806   Revd Alexander Brown
3 March 1832   Revd Robert Whitehead
2 March 1844   Revd Edward Pettman
17 September 1851   Revd Allen Fielding

DOCUMENTS AND SOURCES

The documents in this volume come from collections of eighteenth-century naval and political materials in the British Library, London; Chatham Dockyard Library; the Cumbria Record Office; the National Archives of the United Kingdom (Kew); the National Maritime Museum (Greenwich); Rochester Bridge Trust; the Royal Naval Museum (Portsmouth); and the Scottish Record Office (Edinburgh).

British Library

Add Ms 41,367–8   Minutes and correspondence of Sir
                   Thomas Byam Martin
Add Ms 41,398–400 Official Letter Books of Sir
                   Thomas Byam Martin as
                   Comptroller of the Navy, 1816–31

Chatham Dockyard Library

November 1842; June 1846   Uncatalogued: Apprenticeship
                            Schools[1]

Cumbria Record Office

                   Graham Papers: Consolidation of
                   the Navy and Victualling Boards

D/GN/3/1/9   Graham Papers: Correspondence
                   with Earl Grey, 1830–32

The National Archives of the United Kingdom

ADM1/3376   Navy Board In-letters from
                   Dockyards
ADM 1/3376, 3391–99 Letters from Commissioners of
                   Dockyards

---

[1]These papers were viewed prior to the closure of Chatham dockyard and the establishment of a library of records by the Chatham Dockyard Historic Trust.

377

ADM1/3403–4, 3411, 3502	Letters from Superintendents of Dockyards
ADM1/3462, 3473, 3480–81, 3484, 3486	Internal Admiralty Correspondence
ADM1/3469	Admiralty: Miscellaneous
ADM1/3477	Papers relating to the Reorganisation of the Navy Board
ADM1/3479	Correspondence of Principal Officers
ADM1/3502, 5521, 5939	Letters from the Surveyor of Buildings (later Admiralty Architect)
ADM1/3571	Suggested Reforms Submitted to the Navy Board by George Smith, 1830–32
ADM1/5132–7	Petitions submitted to Admiralty.
ADM1/5591	Report on Committee of Revision: Dockyards
ADM1/5502, 5511, 5537, 5913	Orders in Council respecting Admiralty
ADM1/5660	Report of a Committee of Enquiry into the Office of Secretary
ADM3/206	Admiralty Rough Minutes
ADM85/1, 7	Surveyor's Department: Steam branch
ADM87/77, ADM89/1–3, ADM222/1, 2, 3, 4, 6	Records of the Surveyor of the Navy
ADM106/1815–41	Navy Board In-letters from Chatham Commissioner and Officers
ADM106/	Navy Board Minutes, 1830–32
ADM106/3233–4–39	Visitation of yards
ADM106/2267, 2281, 2287, 2289	Navy Board Out-letters to Admiralty
ADM106/3375	Yards Letter Books
ADM114/40	Records of Victualling Departments
ADM116/3453	Evidence Presented to 1861 Select Committee
ADM135/2	Ships' Books: *Achilles*
ADM222/1, 3, 4, 6	Submissions by Surveyor to Admiralty
MEPO1/58	Metropolitan Police: dockyards general correspondence
PC2/146,194, 205, 210, 251	Privy Council Office: Registers

National Maritime Museum

ADM/BP/376	Letters to Admiralty from the Navy Board

CHA/E/126, 140, 151	Chatham Dockyard: In-letters from the Navy Board
CHA/F/27–33	Chatham Dockyard: Letters from Navy Board to Commissioner
CHA/H/1, 3, 5–10, 35–40, 104–5	Chatham Dockyard: Letters from Admiralty to Captain Superintendent
ELL/239	Papers of Gilbert Elliot, 2nd Earl of Minto
L67/277	Printed Instructions for Constables Appointed to the Dockyard Police Force, 1834
POR/G/5	Portsmouth Dockyard: In-letters

Rochester Bridge Trust

Ms. 214	Rochester Bridge Wardens: In-letters, 1818

Royal Naval Museum

Mss 286 (previously Da 0126)	Deputy Director of Works: Report on Manufacturing Departments

Scottish Record Office

GD51/2/335, 1017, 993/1–2	Private correspondence of Robert, 2nd Viscount Melville

Printed Sources

Acts of Parliament

An Act to Amend the Laws relating to the Business of the Civil Departments of the Navy, and to make other regulations for more effectually carrying on the Duties of the said Departments. 1 June 1832, 2 William IV c.40 Ch X

An Act to enable the Admiralty to acquire property for the Enlargement of Her Majesty's Dockyard at Chatham in the County of Kent, and to embank part of the River Medway (1861), 24 & 25 Victoria XLI, 351

Parliamentary Papers

3rd report of the Commissioners appointed to inquire into fees, gratuities, perquisites and emoluments which are, or have been lately, received in the several public offices, 1787, Commons Reports 1806 (309), VII

1st and 2nd reports of the Commissioners for revising and digesting the civil affairs of His Majesty's Navy, Commons Reports 1806 (312), V

Report of the Commissioners appointed to inquire into the Practability and Expediency of consolidating the different departments connected with the civil administration of the army, presented to both Houses of Parliament, Command Papers, reports of commissions 1837 (78), XXXIV

Report of the Commissioners appointed to inquire into the Control and Management of Her Majesty's Naval Dockyards, reports of commissions 1861 (2790), XXVI

Appendix 16 of the last report comprises the *Report upon the Dockyards made by Mr Bromley for Lord Auckland, First Lord of the Admiralty, 13 February 1847*

Books

Anonymous, *Observations on the Recent Abolition of Certain Situations, including Quartermen and the New Arrangement of Clerks in his Majesty's Dockyards* (London, 1824)

Barrow, J., *Autobiographical Memoir* (London, 1847)

Briggs, H.J., *Naval Administrations 1827–1892* (London, 1897)

Dickens, Charles, *The Uncommercial Traveller* (London, 1865)

Dupin, Charles, *'Two Excursions to the Ports of England, Scotland and Ireland in 1816, 1817 and 1818* (London, 1818)

Hobbes, R.G., *Reminiscences and Notes of Seventy Years,* Vol. II, *Civil Service and Royal Dockyards* (London, 1895)

Rennie, John, *Treatise on Harbours* (London, ?1851)

Tucker, J.S., *Memoirs of the Right Honble The Earl of St Vincent* (London, 1844) Vol II

Wade, John (ed.), *The Extraordinary Black Book: An exposition of Abuses in Church and State* ... (Effingham Wilson, London, 1832)

Wildash, W.T., *The History and Antiquities of Rochester* (Rochester, 1817), 73

Wright, I.G., *Topography of Rochester, Chatham, Strood, Brompton &c* (Chatham Hill, 1838)

Newspapers and Periodicals

Chatham News and North Kent Spectator
Chatham News
Illustrated London News
Kentish Gazette
Rochester Gazette
Saturday Magazine, The
The Times (London)

Numerical list of the documents in this volume

Chapter 1: Towards Achilles: *Shipbuilding and Repair*

1	To Admiralty: ship construction	28 June 1815	TNA, ADM106/2267
2	To Commissioner: ship surveys	16 May 1816	NMM, CHA/F/29
3	To Commissioner: estimate	24 May 1816	NMM, CHA/F/29
4	To Commissioner: ship design.	27 June 1816	NMM, CHA/E/126
5	To Navy Board: prices	13 May 1818	TNA, ADM106/1824
6	To Navy Board: caulkers	26 Nov 1818	TNA, ADM106/1816
7	To Yard Officers: mast construction.	21 Dec 1818	NMM, CHA/F/32
8	To Commissioner: ordinary	27 Mar 1819	NMM, CHA/F/33
9	Committee of Visitation: report	30 Sept 1819	TNA, ADM106/3233
10	Committee of Visitation: minute	25 July 1820	TNA, ADM106/3234
11	To Navy Board: circular sterns	2 Mar 1824	TNA, ADM106/1828
12	To Navy Board: docking	27 July 1824	TNA, ADM106/1829
13	To Navy Board: sheer hulk	29 July 1824	TNA, ADM106/1829
14	To Navy Board: launch	21 Feb 1825	TNA, ADM106/1830
15	To Navy Board: ship breaking	2 July 1825	TNA, ADM106/1831
16	To Navy Board: repairs	26 Aug 1825	TNA, ADM106/1831
17	To Board of Admiralty: new construction	13 Oct 1825	TNA, ADM106/2289
18	To Navy Board: completion	21 Dec 1825	TNA, ADM106/1831
19	To Navy Board: caulking	16 Jan 1826	TNA, ADM106/1832
20	From Yard Officers: caulking	16 Jan 1826	TNA, ADM106/1832
21	To Navy Board: docking	15 Mar 1826	TNA, ADM106/1832
22	To Navy Board: docking of guard ships	27 April 1826	TNA, ADM106/1832
23	To Navy Board: launch	10 July 1826	TNA, ADM106/1833
24	To Navy Board: *Prince Regent* grounding	18 Jan 1827	TNA, ADM106/1834
25	To Navy Board: corrosion	25 Jan 1827	TNA, ADM106/1834
26	To Navy Board: copper sheathing	18 May 1827	TNA, ADM106/1834
27	To Navy Board: ship roofing	13 Oct 1827	TNA, ADM106/1835
28	To Navy Board: docking	1 Nov 1827	TNA, ADM106/1835
29	To Navy Board: ship fitting	29 Nov 1827	TNA, ADM106/1835
30	To Navy Board: quarter galleries	2 Jan 1829	TNA, ADM106/1838
31	Thomson to First Lord: yard specialisation	25 Jan 1829	SRO, GD51/2/1017
32	To Navy Board: ships' galleries	18 May 1829	TNA, ADM106/1838
33	To Navy Board: ship alterations	23 Aug 1829	TNA, ADM106/1838
34	To Navy Board: capsizing of convict hulk	16 Oct 1829	TNA, ADM106/1839
35	To Navy Board: capsizing of convict hulk	16 Oct 1829	TNA, ADM106/1839
36	To Navy Board: report on convict hulk	19 Oct 1829	TNA, ADM106/1839
37	To Navy Board: coppering	6 Nov 1829	TNA, ADM106/1839
38	To Navy Board: mode of launching ships	19 Nov 1829	TNA, ADM106/1839

39	To Navy Board: ship dimensions	27 Nov 1829	TNA, ADM106/1839
40	To Chatham Yard Officers: power capstans	29 Mar 1830	NMM, CHA/H/1
41	From Yard Officers: embezzlement	19 Oct 1830	TNA, ADM106/1840
42	From Yard Officers: fitting of hospital ship	28 May 1831	TNA, ADM106/1841
43	From Yard Officers to Navy Board: docking	8 June 1831	TNA, ADM106/1841
44	To Superintendent: preservation of ships	20 Sept 1832	TNA, ADM222/1
45	Minute: employment of model maker	25 Sept 1832	TNA, ADM222/1
46	Minute: roofing of ships in ordinary	27 Oct 1832	TNA, ADM222/1
47	Minute: ship model	30 Oct 1832	TNA, ADM222/1
48	To Board of Admiralty: undocking problem	5 May 1833	TNA, ADM1/3392
49	To Superintendent: protection of decks	6 May 1833	NMM, CHA/H/6
50	To Superintendent: construction of packet.	30 May 1833	NMM, CHA/H/6
51	To Superintendent Gordon: Post Office packet	12 June 1833	NMM, CHA/H/6
52	To Admiralty: launching	18 June 1833	TNA, ADM1/3393
53	To Admiralty: prices	22 June 1833	TNA, ADM1/3393
54	To Admiralty: observations on a proposal	25 June 1833	TNA, ADM1/3393
55	To Superintendent: new mould loft floor 1	12 Sept 1833	TNA, ADM1/3396
56	Admiralty Minute: new ship construction	2 Oct 1833	TNA, ADM222/3
57	Admiralty Minute: new ship construction	7 Oct 1833	TNA, ADM222/3
58	Surveyor General's Minute: lax workmanship	22 Jan 1834	TNA, ADM222/4
59	Description of Launch	8 Feb 1834	*The Saturday Magazine*
60	To Superintendent Gordon: use of spike iron	19 May 1834	NMM, CHA/H/10
61	To Board of Admiralty: poor workmanship	11 Feb 1835	TNA, ADM222/6
62	To Admiralty: employment of shipwrights	24 May 1838	TNA, ADM1/3411
63	To Superintendent: icing of river	9 Feb 1841	NMM, CHA/H/38
64	To Superintendent: boiler linings	5 April 1841	NMM, CHA/H/39
65	To Superintendent: frames for paddle steamers	6 April 1841	NMM, CHA/H/39
66	To Superintendent: ship breaking	12 April 1841	NMM, CHA/H/39
67	To Superintendent: engine gear	13 April 1841	NMM, CHA/H/39

68	To Steam Department: trial of machinery	26 Jan 1851	TNA, ADM85/7
69	To Superintendent: machinery alterations	10 Feb 1852	TNA, ADM85/7
70	To Superintendent: millwrights	10 Feb 1852	TNA, ADM85/7
71	Fitting Out of Frigate	25 Feb 1854	*Illustrated London News*
72	To Master Shipwright: request	9 Jan 1856	TNA, ADM89/1
73	To Superintendent: drawings	10 Nov 1860	NMM, CHA/H/40
74	Progress on *Achilles*	1 Feb 1862	*Chatham News*
75	Progress in the Construction of *Achilles*	26 April 1862	*Illustrated London News*
76	Bending of Armour Plates	24 May 1862	*Chatham News*
77	Alterations to *Royal Oak*	7 June 1862	*Chatham News*
78	Iron for *Achilles*	28 Feb 1863	*Chatham News*
79	Construction of New Ironclad Ordered	10 Oct 1863	*Chatham News*
80	Commencement of New Ironclad	7 Nov 1863	*Chatham News*
81	Floating of *Achilles*	23 Dec 1863	Hobbes, *Reminiscences and Notes* p. 308
82	Construction delays	6 Aug 1864	*The Times*
83	To Admiralty: *Achilles* corrosion	16 Jan 1865	TNA, ADM135/2]

Chapter 2: Improving the facilities

84	From John Rennie: defects of yard	27 Aug 1814	Rennie, *Treatise on Harbours*, pp. 46–8
85	To Admiralty: land purchase	22 Feb 1815	TNA, ADM106/1815
86	To Admiralty: dock and slip roofs	12 June 1815	NMM, CHA/F/27
87	From John Rennie: sea wall	19 July 1815	TNA, ADM106/3138
88	From John Rennie: estimate for new dock	29 Aug 1815	TNA, ADM106/3138
89	To Commissioner: dredging	29 Jan 1816	NMM, CHA/F/29
90	To Usborne Benson & Co: land purchase	2 Sept 1816	TNA, ADM106/3138
91	To Admiralty: purchase of land	25 June 1817	TNA, ADM106/2273
92	To Admiralty: covering of docks and slips	25 Oct 1817	NMM, ADM/BP/376
93	Minute: navigation of Medway.	Nov 1817	BL Add Ms 41,367
94	To Commissioner: docks and slip covers	5 Nov 1817	NMM, CHA/F/30
95	To Bridge Wardens: navigation of Medway	10 Jan 1818	NMM, CHA/F/31
96	To Bridge Wardens: navigation of Medway	20 Jan 1818	Rochester Bridge Trust Ms. 214
97	From John Rennie: construction of stone dock	21 Mar 1818	TNA, ADM106/3138
98	Laying of First Stone of New Dock	31 Mar 1818	*Kentish Gazette*
99	Description of New Bridge	19 May 1818	*Kentish Gazette*

100	Committee of Visitation: stone dock	30 Sept 1819	TNA, ADM 106/3233
101	To Commissioner: employment of convicts	7 Dec 1819	NMM, CHA/F/33
102	Abstract of Correspondence: stone dock	21 Mar 1818	TNA, ADM 106/3138
103	To Admiralty: purchase of marshlands	24 May 1821	TNA, ADM106/2281
104	To Admiralty: dock entrance	25 May 1821	TNA, ADM106/2281
105	From John Rennie: proposals	1 Sept 1821	Rennie, *Treatise on Harbours*, pp. 48–50
106	To Navy Board: escalating costs	18 Mar 1824	TNA, ADM 106/2287
107	To Navy Board: construction of caisson	18 Dec 1824	TNA, ADM 106/1829
108	To Navy Board: mud shoals	10 Feb 1825	TNA, ADM 106/1830
109	To Navy Board: progress of works	12 July 1825	TNA, ADM 106/1830
110	From Usborne Benson & Co.: problems encountered	28 Mar 1826	TNA, ADM106/1832
111	To Navy Board: land for depositing of mud	20 Nov 1826	TNA, ADM 106/1833
112	To Navy Board: dredging expenses	26 June 1828	TNA, ADM 106/1836
113	From Chatham Yard Officers: estimates	17 Oct 1828	TNA, ADM 106/1837
114	To Navy Board: dock roof	22 Nov 1828	TNA, ADM 106/1837
115	From Commissioner Cunningham: steam pump	23 April 1829	TNA, ADM 106/1838
116	From Master Attendant: steam vessels	8 Nov 1832	TNA, ADM 1/3386
117	To Civil Architect of the Navy: No. 4 dock	22 Dec 1834	TNA, ADM 1/3502
118	From Master Attendant: proposed landing place	3 May 1837	TNA, ADM 1/3404
119	From Architects' department: dredging river	1842	TNA, ADM 1/5521
120	Report: proposed extension	8 Jan 1857	RNM, Mss 286
121	From Director of Works: convicts	6 July 1858	TNA, ADM1/5703
122	Re-opening of No. 2 dock	13 Nov 1858	*Illustrated London News*
123	Controller of the Navy: building sheds	5 Oct 1860	NMM, CHA/H/104
124	Controller of the Navy: building sheds	10 Oct 1860	NMM, CHA/H/104
125	Surveyor of the Navy: building sheds	23 Oct 1860	TNA, ADM 92/21

126	Controller of the Navy: building sheds	6 Nov 1860	NMM, CHA/H/104
127	Planned Dockyard Extension	10 Nov 1860	*Chatham News*
128	Director of Engineering and Architectural Works: building sheds	3 Dec 1860	NMM, CHA/H/104
129	To Superintendent: building sheds	13 Dec 1860	NMM, CHA/H/104
130	To Superintendent: smithery roof	11 Feb 1861	NMM, CHA/H/105
131	To Admiralty: slotting machine	12 Feb 1861	NMM, CHA/H/105
132	To Superintendent: roof over smithery	14 Mar 1861	NMM, CHA/H/105
133	From G.T. Greene: estimated costs	6 May 1861	TNA, ADM1/5838
134	Enlargement of Chatham Dockyard	22 July 1861	24 & 25 Victoria XLI, 351
135	Sheds for Metalworking Machinery	15 Feb 1862	*Chatham News*
136	Improvements to dockyard facilities	22 Feb 1862	*Chatham News*
137	Construction of Tramway	26 April 1862	*Chatham News*
138	Inspection of New Works	10 Dec 1864	*Chatham News*
139	Description of Proposed Extension	21 Mar 1865	TNA, ADM1/5913
140	Estimate of Expenses for Extension	29 Mar 1865	TNA, ADM1/5913
141	Appointment of Superintending Officer	12 July 1865	TNA, ADM1/5939

Chapter 3: Manufacturing and the Move to Steam Power

142	Block-making Machinery	20 Dec 1815	NMM, CHA/F/27
143	Block-making Machinery	29 Dec 1815	TNA, ADM106/1815
144	Appointment of Sawmill Master	30 Jan 1816	TNA, PC2/197
145	Royal Visit	12 Mar 1816	*Kentish Gazette*
146	Dismissal of Sawmill Superintendent	23 April 1816	NMM, CHA/F/29
147	Dismissal of Sawmill Superintendent	9 May 1816	NMM, CHA/F/29
148	From Marc Brunel: objection to dismissal	23 May 1816	NMM CHA/F/29
149	Retention of Sawmill Superintendent	30 May 1816	NMM, CHA/F/29
150	Description of the Sawmill	1817	Wildash, *Antiquities of Rochester*, p. 73
151	To Commissioner Barlow: rope making	1 Jan 1817	NMM, CHA/F/30
152	From Marc Brunel: timber for other yards	15 Jan 1817	TNA, ADM106/2272
153	From yard officers: new painters' shop	15 Jan 1817	TNA, ADM106/2272

154	From Navy Board: experiments in rope making	29 Jan 1817	NMM, CHA/F/30
155	From Navy Board: sawmill expenses	17 Feb 1817	NMM, CHA/F/30
156	From Leading Man of Plumbers: milling of lead	24 Feb 1817	TNA, ADM106/1815
157	From Marc Brunel: objection to use of mill for storage	30 Mar 1817	NMM, CHA/F/30
158	To Commissioner: milling of lead	20 April 1817	TNA, ADM106/1815
159	To Commissioner: milling of lead	31 May 1817	NMM, CHA/F/30
160	To Master Shipwright: milling of lead	5 June 1817	TNA, ADM106/1815
161	To Commissioner: treenail mooting machinery	25 June 1817	NMM, CHA/E/126
162	To Admiralty: milling of lead	27 June 1817	TNA, ADM106/2273
163	Committee of Visitation: lead mill and paint shop	30 Sept 1819	TNA, ADM106/3233
164	Committee of Visitation: sawmill	30 Sept 1819	TNA, ADM106/3233
165	To Navy Board: millwrights	1 Aug 1823	TNA, ADM106/1827
166	Committee of Visitation: rope manufacture	4 Nov 1823	TNA, ADM106/3237
167	From Commissioner: commentary on submitted sawyers' petition.	10 Mar 1824	TNA, ADM106/1828
168	From Commissioner: steam machinery problems	19 Jan 1826	TNA, ADM106/1832
169	From Architect: employment of saw mill engine	16 Mar 1827	TNA, ADM114/40
170	Committee of Visitation: quality of cordage	25 Sept 1827	TNA, ADM106/3239
171	To Navy Board: increased demand upon sawmill	11 Oct 1827	TNA, ADM106/1833
172	To Navy Board: employment of saw mill	5 Mar 1829	TNA, ADM106/1838
173	To First Lord: chain cable	19 Jan 1831	BL, Add Ms 41,399
174	To Superintendent: milled lead	26 Nov 1832	NMM, CHA/H/4
175	To Superintendent: boiler repair	4 Dec 1832	NMM, CHA/H/4
176	To Superintendent: tarring machine	20 May 1833	NMM, CHA/H/6
177	To Admiralty: manufacture of cordage	22 Aug 1833	TNA, ADM1/3395
178	To Admiralty: inferior cordage	4 Oct 1833	TNA, ADM1/3396
179	Report: French rope manufactory	8 Oct 1833	NMM, CHA/H/8
180	To Admiralty: powering of turning lathe	22 Jan 1834	TNA, ADM222/4
181	To Superintendent: powering of turning lathe	24 Mar 1834	NMM, CHA/H/9
182	From Architect: engine house for ropery	2 Mar 1836	TNA, ADM1/3502

183	To Admiralty: engine house for ropery	20 Feb 1837	TNA, ADM1/3404
184	Description of the Sawmill	1838	Wright, *Topography*, p. 73
185	To Superintendent: millwrights	8 June 1840	NMM, CHA/H/35
186	To Superintendent: chain power	14 Aug 1840	NMM, CHA/H/35
187	To Superintendent: hauling off yarn.	6 Jan 1841	NMM, CHA/H/38
188	To Superintendent Shirreff: tilt hammer	24 Feb 1841	NMM, CHA/H/38
189	From Architect to Admiralty: estimate	1842	TNA ADM1/5521
190	Description of the Rolling Mill	*c.*1849	Hobbes, *Reminiscences and Notes*, pp. 120–21
191	Description of the Manufacturing Departments	*c.*1849	Hobbes, *Reminiscences and Notes*, pp. 143–8
192	From Chief Engineer: steam machinery	5 June 1850	TNA, ADM85/1
193	From Chief Engineer: new machinery	7 June 1850	TNA, ADM85/1
194	From Chief Engineer: smiths and joiners	9 June 1850	TNA, ADM85/1
195	Deputy Director of Works: report on manufacturing departments	8 Jan 1857	RNM, Mss 286
196	From Chief Engineer: artisans and labourers	3 Dec 1857	TNA, ADM89/3
197	From Chief Engineer: increased demands	3 Dec 1857	TNA, ADM89/3
198	To Storekeeper General: apprentices	24 June 1858	TNA, ADM89/3
199	Controller to Admiralty: manufactured items for *Achilles* and *Black Prince*.	15 Feb 1863	ADM1/5840
200	Steam Spinning Jennies	3 Sept 1864	*Chatham News*
201	Inspection of Ropery	10 Dec 1864	*Chatham News*

Chapter 4: Storage, Security and Materials

202	*Annual Report on the State of the Navy*: immersion of timber	16 Jan 1817	TNA, ADM106/2272
203	To Commissioner: economies	23 Jan 1817	NMM, CHA/F/30
204	To Navy Board: reductions of storehouse labourers.	23 May 1817	NMM, CHA/F/30
205	To Commissioner: preservation of rope	26 June 1817	NMM, CHA/F/30
206	Visitation to Ropeyard Officers	22 July 1818	NMM, CHA/F/31
207	Committee of Visitation: storage of cordage	23 July 1818	TNA, ADM106/3232

208	To Commissioner: overheating of yarn	5 Jan 1819	NMM, CHA/F/33
209	To Commissioner: oil dressing of hemp	3 Feb 1819	NMM, CHA/F/33
210	Committee of Visitation: old sails	29 July 1820	TNA, ADM106/3234
211	To Dockyard Commissioners: storehouses	15 June 1822	NMM, POR/G/5
212	Report on Chatham and Portsmouth ropeyards	4 Nov 1823	TNA, ADM106/3237
213	From Commissioner: hemp storage	30 Dec 1823	TNA, ADM106/1827
214	From Commissioner: hemp house	2 Dec 1824	TNA, ADM106/1829
215	From Commissioner: present use storehouse	27 Dec 1824	TNA, ADM106/1829
216	From Commissioner: rigging house	4 June 1825	TNA, ADM106/1830
217	From Commissioner: linseed oil	6 Feb 1827	TNA, ADM106/1834
218	To Storekeeper: accounting procedures	3 Feb 1832	NMM, CHA/H/4
219	To Master Shipwright: saturation of timbers	21 Mar 1833	NMM, CHA/H/5
220	To Superintendent: timber storage	29 Mar 1833	NMM, CHA/H/5
221	From Superintendent: repairs to mast house	5 Nov 1833	TNA, ADM1/3399
222	From Surveyor of Navy: storage of timbers	16 Aug 1834	TNA, ADM222/4
223	To Superintendent: store men	7 Dec 1859	TNA, ADM89/4
224	From Commissioner: warders and watchmen	29 April 1815	TNA, ADM106/3375
225	From Commissioner: theft	29 April 1815	TNA, ADM106/3375
226	To Admiralty: withdrawal of military guard	1 May 1815	TNA, ADM106/3375
227	To Navy Board: theft from yard	18 Dec 1815	TNA, ADM106/1815
228	Admiralty to Commissioner: mustering	1 Feb 1816	NMM, CHA/F/29
229	Commissioner to Admiralty: mustering	3 Feb 1816	NMM, CHA/F/29
230	Confession of John Ayres	12 Mar 1816	TNA, ADM106/1815
231	Navy Board to Commissioner: inspection of buildings	28 Oct 1816	NMM, CHA/F/29
232	Navy Board to Commissioner: inspection of buildings	17 Dec 1816	NMM, CHA/F/29
233	Theft of Copper Bolts	31 Mar 1818	*Kentish Gazette*
234	Comptroller to First Lord: dockyard police force	6 Aug 1820	SRO, GD51/2/993/1–2
235	Commissioner Cunningham to Navy Board: military guard	3 April 1824	TNA, ADM106/1828
236	Commissioner Cunningham to Navy Board: King's mark	29 April 1824	TNA, ADM106/1828

237	Master Attendant to Navy Board: theft of copper nails	23 July 1827	TNA ADM106/1835
238	Commissioner Cunningham to Navy Board: reduction of watchmen	2 Oct 1827	TNA, ADM106/1835
239	Admiralty to Superintendent: specialised security force	29 Mar 1833	NMM, CHA/H/5
240	Secretary, Metropolitan Police to Admiralty: dockyard police	2 July 1833	NMM, CHA/H/6
241	Admiralty to Superintendent: police oath	20 July 1833	NMM, CHA/H/7
242	Superintendent to Admiralty: policing	11 Aug 1833	TNA, ADM1/3395
243	Superintendent to Admiralty: new policing arrangement	17 Sept 1833	TNA, ADM1/3396
244	Comparative numbers of watchmen and wardens	8 Oct 1833	TNA, ADM1/3481
245	Commissioner's *Code of Instruction* for Dockyard Police	17 Oct 1833	TNA, ADM1/3398
246	Commissioner to Admiralty: dockyard police	1 Nov 1833	TNA, ADM1/3399
247	Instructions for Constables appointed to the Dockyard Police Force	1834	NMM, Library L67/277
248	Admiralty to Superintendent: efficiency review	12 Nov 1840	NMM, CHA/H/37
249	Shirreff to Admiralty: fire procedure	13 May 1842	TNA, ADM1/5521
250	Demise of the Dockyard Police Force	1860	Hobbes, *Reminiscences and Notes*, p. 207
251	Police Commissioner to Admiralty: new policing body	18 Oct 1860	TNA, MEPO1/58
252	Admiralty to Superintendent: medical arrangements	10 Nov 1860	NMM, CHA/H/140
253	Admiralty Secretary to Samuel Whitbread: premises	26 Nov 1860	TNA, MEPO1/58
254	Police Commissioner to Admiralty: commencement of duties	5 Dec 1860	TNA, MEPO1/58
255	Navy Board to Admiralty: timber preservation	28 June 1815	TNA, ADM106/2267
256	Navy Board to Chatham Yard Officers: oakum preparation	22 Aug 1820	NMM, CHA/E/140
257	Navy Board to Admiralty: preserving oakum	6 July 1829	TNA, ADM106/1839
258	Navy Board to Chatham Yard Officers: oakum preparation	10 Mar 1830	NMM, CHA/H/4
259	Admiralty to Storekeeper: use of stores	7 Nov 1832	NMM, CHA/H/4

260	Admiralty to Superintendent: trials of Chilean hemp	12 Nov 1832	NMM, CHA/H/4
261	Admiralty to Superintendent: preservation of masts.	1 April 1833	NMM, CHA/H/5
262	Superintendent to Admiralty Secretary: trials of Italian hemp	15 Oct 1833	TNA, ADM1/3397
263	Experiments in Relative Strengths of Timbers	25 April 1834	NMM, CHA/H/10
264	Admiralty to Superintendent: trials in relative strengths of timbers	30 April 1834	NMM, CHA/H/10
265	Admiralty to Superintendent: Italian and Polish larch	5 Jan 1841	NMM, CHA/H/38
266	Surveyor of Navy to Board of Admiralty: alternative timber supplies	8 Oct 1860	TNA, ADM87/77

Chapter 5: Economics, Custom and the Workforce

267	Admiralty to Commissioner: dismissals	9 Mar 1816	NMM, CHA/F/29
268	Navy Board to Commissioner: overtime	6 July 1816	NMM, CHA/F/29
269	Navy Board to Commissioner: overtime	10 July 1816	NMM, CHA/F/29
270	Navy Board to Commissioner: petition	13 Sept 1816	NMM, CHA/F/29
271	Commissioner to Navy Board: reduction of sail makers	17 Oct 1816	TNA, ADM106/1815
272	Navy Board to Commissioner: reduced hours	13 Feb 1817	NMM, CHA/F/30
273	Commissioner to Navy Board: injured labourer	4 Aug 1817	TNA, ADM106/1815
274	Voluntary Apprenticeship School	1818	Dupin, *Two Excursions*, p. 65
275	Admiralty to Commissioner: working hours	8 Mar 1822	TNA, ADM1/3462
276	Petition: skill demotion	26 Sept 1822	TNA, ADM1/5132
277	Petition: earnings	6 Dec 1823	TNA, ADM106/1827
278	Order-in-Council: calculation of superannuation	19 Jan 1824	TNA, PC2/205
279	Petition of superannuated artificers of Chatham, Deptford and Sheerness yards	12 June 1824	TNA, ADM1/5133
280	Comptroller to Secretary of Navy Board: unsigned petition	17 Nov 1824	TNA, ADM106/1829
281	Admiralty Response to Petition	8 Dec 1824	TNA, ADM3/206
282	Commissioner to Navy Board: discharges	8 Jan 1825	TNA, ADM106/1830
283	Commissioner to Navy Board: help for discharged artificers	13 Jan 1825	TNA, ADM106/1830

284	Commissioner to Navy Board: discharged artificers	24 Jan 1825	TNA, ADM106/1830
285	Riggers' Petition	21 April 1825	TNA, ADM106/1830
286	Commissioner to Navy Board: injured workman	22 July 1825	TNA, ADM106/1830
287	Commissioner to Navy Board: holiday	8 May 1826	TNA, ADM106/1832
288	Commissioner to Navy Board: chapel choir	18 May 1826	TNA, ADM106/1832
289	Petition: pensions	27 Sept 1827	TNA, ADM1/5133
290	Commissioner to Navy Board: teams	24 Jan 1828	TNA, ADM106/1836
291	Admiralty to Commissioner: termination of chip money	13 Jan 1830	NMM, CHA/E/151
292	Commissioner to Navy Board: services upon which convicts employed	12 July 1831	TNA ADM106/1841
293	Yard Officers to Navy Board: infirm rope makers	15 Dec 1831	TNA, ADM106/1841
294	Plight of Dockyard Artisans	18 Sept 1832	*Rochester Gazette*
295	Yard Officers to Superintendent: anchor smiths	9 Nov 1832	TNA ADM1/3386
296	Admiralty to Superintendent: reduced working hours	3 Jan 1833	NMM, CHA/H/5
297	Superintendent to Admiralty: hours of employment	23 May 1833	TNA, ADM1/3391
298	Admiralty to Dockyard Commissioners: ending of task work	22 June 1833	TNA, ADM1/3480
299	Admiralty to Superintendent: St Clements's Day	12 July 1833	NMM, CHA/H/7
300	Superintendent to Admiralty: classification scheme	30 July 1833	TNA, ADM1/3394
301	Admiralty to Superintendent: holidays	13 Sept 1833	NMM, CHA/H/7
302	Admiralty to Dockyard Superintendents: apprentices	5 Nov 1833	TNA, ADM222/3
303	George Hammond, retired inspector of Shipwrights …		*Chatham News,* 10 July 1897
304	Admiralty to Dockyard Superintendents: working hours	11 June 1834	NMM, CHA/H/35
305	Admiralty Memorandum: classification	15 Nov 1834	TNA, ADM1/3484
306	Admiralty to Dockyard Superintendents: reaction to petitions	21 July 1835	TNA, ADM1/3486
307	Report of a Speech by William Evenden, a Dockyard Joiner	13 Dec 1836	*Rochester Gazette*
308	Public Petition: classification	13 Dec 1836	*Rochester Gazette*
309	Petition of Hired Rope Makers	5 Jan 1839	TNA, ADM1/5137

355	Warrant: appointment of Superintendent	9 June 1832	NMM, CHA/H/1
356	General Instructions for Principal Officers	18 July 1833	TNA, ADM1/3480
357	General Instructions for Foremen and Inspectors	18 July 1833	TNA, ADM1/3480
358	Superintendent to Admiralty: retirement of Master Attendant	9 July 1836	TNA, ADM1/3403
359	Admiralty to Superintendent: workforce correspondence	16 Mar 1841	TNA, ADM222/11
360	J.S. Bromley to First Lord: report on dockyard management	1847	Report of Inquiry into the Management of H.M. Naval Yards, 1860
361	Committee of Dockyard Revision: measurers	Nov 1848	TNA, ADM1/5591
362	Committee of Dockyard Revision: dockyard superintendents	14 Dec 1848	TNA, ADM1/5591
363	Surveyor of the Navy to Board: dockyard accountant	26 Oct 1855	TNA, ADM89/1
364	Yard Officers to Admiralty: measurement of works	12 Jan 1856	TNA, ADM89/1
365	Yard Officers to Admiralty: task and job	19 Feb 1856	TNA, ADM89/1
366	Isaac Watson to Admiralty: reducers	13 Nov 1857	TNA, ADM89/2
367	Comptroller to Board: supervision of labour	20 Aug 1864	TNA, ADM1/5931

Chapter 7: Central Management

368	Responsibilities of the Board of Admiralty	Dec 1787	Commissioners to enquire into Fees, f.1
369	Establishment of Committee System	8 June 1796	TNA, PC2/146
370	Duties of the Navy Board	1806	Commissioners on the Civil Affairs of the Navy: Navy Office
371	Introduction of Third Surveyor	3 June 1813	TNA, PC2/194
372	Comptroller to First Lord: increase in yard working hours	1 June 1818	BL, Add Ms 41,400
373	Minutes: Navy Board visitation	30 Sept 1819	TNA, ADM106/3233
374	Secretary of Navy Board: Review of the Committee System	1 June 1821	TNA, ADM1/3571
375	Secretary of Navy Board: retention of skilled labour	undated *c*.1822	TNA, ADM1/3571
376	St Vincent to Benjamin Tucker: dockyard administrators	11 Sept 1822	Tucker, *Memoirs of The Earl of St Vincent* Vol II, p. 425

377	Secretary of Navy Board: referral to dockyards	May 1828	TNA, ADM1/3571
378	Secretary of Navy Board: returns and accounts	July 1828	TNA, ADM1/3571
379	Comptroller's Meeting with the First Lord: constitution of Navy Board	24 Jan 1829	BL, Add Ms 41,368
380	Order-in-Council: constitution of Navy Board	30 Jan 1829	TNA, PC2/210
381	First Secretary to Comptroller: duties of Comptroller	14 July 1829	TNA, ADM1/3470
382	Comptroller to Admiral Malcolm: excessive economisers	1 June 1830	BL, Add Ms 41,398
383	Admiralty to Navy Board: naval estimates	21 Jan 1831	TNA, ADM1/3473
384	First Lord to Comptroller: naval estimates	22 Jan 1831	BL, Add Mss 41, 368
385	First Lord to Prime Minister: consolidation of departments	6 Dec 1831	Cumbria R.O., D/GN/3/1/9
386	Graham as First Lord	Feb 1832	Wade (ed.), *The Extraordinary Black Book*, p. 537
387	Melville to Sir George Clerk: uniting the civil departments	8 Feb 1832	SRO GD/2/3335
388	First Lord to House of Commons: misapplication of estimates	14 Feb 1832	*Hansard's Parliamentary Debates*, X, p. 353
389	First Lord to House of Commons: Admiralty authority	14 Feb 1832	*Hansard's Parliamentary Debates*, X, p. 354
390	Croker to House of Commons: consolidation of civil departments	27 Feb 1832	*Hansard's Parliamentary Debates*, X, pp. 800–801
391	First Secretary to House of Commons: consolidation of civil departments	27 Feb 1832	*Hansard's Parliamentary Debates*, X, p. 801
392	Civil Departments Act: abolition of Navy Board	1 June 1832	2 William IV, Cap XL
393	Secretary to Board of Admiralty: naval department offices	11 Sept 1832	TNA, ADM1/3478
394	Circular to the Surveyor-General and Accountant for Stores	14 Jan 1833	TNA, ADM1/3479
395	Secretary to Committee of Inquiry: civil departments	18 Feb 1836	Commission to Inquire into the Civil Administration of the Army, 1837
396	Business Submitted to the Board of Admiralty	Feb 1837	TNA, ADM1/3404

397	Secretary of the Admiralty: naval estimates	1 Mar 1841	*Hansard's Parliamentary Debates*, XIV, p. 655
398	Gilbert 2nd Earl of Minto: workload of Admiralty commissioners	1841	NMM, ELL/239
399	Increase of Business	1847	Barrow, *Autobiographical Memoir*, pp. 418–19
400	J.S. Bromley: report on dockyard management	1847	Report of Inquiry into the Management of H.M. Naval Yards, 1860
401	Earl of Ellenborough to House of Lords: reformed system	7 April 1854	*Hansard's Parliamentary Debates*, CXXXII, pp. 656–7
402	Admiral Duncombe to House of Commons: reformed system	12 June 1860	*Hansard's Parliamentary Debates*, CXL, p. 300
403	Constitution of Board of Admiralty	1860	Commissioners on Managing H.M. Dockyards, p. vi
404	Deficiencies in Dockyard Management	1860	Commissioners on Managing H.M. Dockyards, pp. v–vi
405	Order-in-Council: Comptroller of the Navy	23 Jan 1860	TNA, PC2/251
406	Baillie Hamilton to the House of Commons: reformed system	28 Feb 1861	*Hansard's Parliamentary Debates*, CL, p. 300
407	John Briggs: reformed system		Briggs, *Naval Administrations*, p. 32

INDEX

Note: This index should be used in conjunction with the appendices. For the period 1815–65, these provide a list of ships and other vessels built at Chatham and a list of relevant postholders. Indexed names are those appearing in the text of cited correspondence or within the introductory notes.

NAVY RECORDS SOCIETY
(FOUNDED 1893)

The Navy Records Society was established for the purpose of printing unpublished manuscripts and rare works of naval interest. Membership of the Society is open to all who are interested in naval history, and any person wishing to become a member should apply to the Hon. Secretary, Robin Brodhurst, Pangbourne College, Pangbourne, Berks, RG8 8LA, United Kingdom. The annual subscription is £30, which entitles the member to receive one free copy of each work issued by the Society in that year, and to buy earlier issues at reduced prices.

A list of works, available to members only, is shown below; very few copies are left of those marked with an asterisk. Volumes out of print are indicated by **OP**. Prices for works in print are available on application to Mrs Annette Gould, 1 Avon Close, Petersfield, Hampshire, GU31 4LG, United Kingdom, to whom all enquiries concerning works in print should be sent. Those marked 'TS', 'SP' and 'A' are published for the Society by Temple Smith, Scolar Press and Ashgate, and are available to non-members from the Ashgate Publishing Group, Gower House, Croft Road, Aldershot, Hampshire GU11 3HR. Those marked 'A & U' are published by George Allen & Unwin, and are available to non-members only through bookshops.

Vol. 1. *State papers relating to the Defeat of the Spanish Armada, Anno 1588*, Vol. I, ed. Professor J. K. Laughton. TS.

Vol. 2. *State papers relating to the Defeat of the Spanish Armada, Anno 1588*, Vol. II, ed. Professor J. K. Laughton. TS.

Vol. 3. *Letters of Lord Hood, 1781–1783*, ed. D. Hannay. **OP**.

Vol. 4. *Index to James's Naval History*, by C. G. Toogood, ed. by the Hon. T. A. Brassey. **OP**.

Vol. 5. *Life of Captain Stephen Martin, 1666–1740*, ed. Sir Clements R. Markham. **OP**.

Vol. 6. *Journal of Rear Admiral Bartholomew James, 1752–1828*, ed. Professor J. K. Laughton & Cdr. J. Y. F. Sullivan. **OP**.

Vol. 7. *Hollond's Discourses of the Navy, 1638 and 1659*, ed. J. R. Tanner. **OP**.

Vol. 8. *Naval Accounts and Inventories in the Reign of Henry VII*, ed. M. Oppenheim. **OP**.

Vol. 9. *Journal of Sir George Rooke*, ed. O. Browning. **OP**.

Vol. 10. *Letters and Papers relating to the War with France 1512–1513*, ed. M. Alfred Spont. **OP**.

Vol. 11. *Papers relating to the Spanish War 1585–1587*, ed. Julian S. Corbett. **TS**.

Vol. 12. *Journals and Letters of Admiral of the Fleet Sir Thomas Byam Martin, 1773–1854*, Vol. II (see No. 24), ed. Admiral Sir R. Vesey Hamilton. **OP**.

Vol. 13. *Papers relating to the First Dutch War, 1652–1654*, Vol. I, ed. Dr S. R. Gardiner. **OP**.

Vol. 14. *Papers relating to the Blockade of Brest, 1803–1805*, Vol. I, ed. J. Leyland. **OP**.

Vol. 15. *History of the Russian Fleet during the Reign of Peter the Great, by a Contemporary Englishman*, ed. Admiral Sir Cyprian Bridge. **OP**.

Vol. 16. *Logs of the Great Sea Fights, 1794–1805*, Vol. I, ed. Vice Admiral Sir T. Sturges Jackson. **OP**.

Vol. 17. *Papers relating to the First Dutch War, 1652–1654*, ed. Dr S. R. Gardiner. **OP**.

Vol. 18. *Logs of the Great Sea Fights*, Vol. II, ed. Vice Admiral Sir T. Sturges Jackson.

Vol. 19. *Journals and Letters of Admiral of the Fleet Sir Thomas Byam Martin*, Vol. II (see No. 24), ed. Admiral Sir R. Vesey Hamilton. **OP**.

Vol. 20. *The Naval Miscellany*, Vol. I, ed. Professor J. K. Laughton.

Vol. 21. *Papers relating to the Blockade of Brest, 1803–1805*, Vol. II, ed. J. Leyland. **OP**.

Vol. 22. *The Naval Tracts of Sir William Monson*, Vol. I, ed. M. Oppenheim. **OP**.

Vol. 23. *The Naval Tracts of Sir William Monson*, Vol. II, ed. M. Oppenheim. **OP**.

Vol. 24. *The Journals and Letters of Admiral of the Fleet Sir Thomas Byam Martin*, Vol. I, ed. Admiral Sir R. Vesey Hamilton.

Vol. 25. *Nelson and the Neapolitan Jacobins*, ed. H. C. Gutteridge. **OP**.

Vol. 26. *A Descriptive Catalogue of the Naval MSS in the Pepysian Library*, Vol. I, ed. J. R. Tanner. **OP**.

Vol. 27. *A Descriptive Catalogue of the Naval MSS in the Pepysian Library*, Vol. II, ed. J. R. Tanner. **OP**.

Vol. 28. *The Correspondence of Admiral John Markham, 1801–1807*, ed. Sir Clements R. Markham. **OP**.

Vol. 29. *Fighting Instructions, 1530–1816*, ed. Julian S. Corbett. **OP**.

Vol. 30. *Papers relating to the First Dutch War, 1652–1654*, Vol. III, ed. Dr S. R. Gardiner & C. T. Atkinson. **OP**.

Vol. 31. *The Recollections of Commander James Anthony Gardner, 1775–1814*, ed. Admiral Sir R. Vesey Hamilton & Professor J. K. Laughton.

Vol. 32. *Letters and Papers of Charles, Lord Barham, 1758–1813*, ed. Professor Sir John Laughton.

Vol. 33. *Naval Songs and Ballads*, ed. Professor C. H. Firth. **OP**.

Vol. 34. *Views of the Battles of the Third Dutch War*, ed. by Julian S. Corbett. **OP**.

Vol. 35. *Signals and Instructions, 1776–1794*, ed. Julian S. Corbett. **OP**.

Vol. 36. *A Descriptive Catalogue of the Naval MSS in the Pepysian Library*, Vol. III, ed. J. R. Tanner. **OP**.

Vol. 37. *Papers relating to the First Dutch War, 1652–1654*, Vol. IV, ed. C. T. Atkinson. **OP**.

Vol. 38. *Letters and Papers of Charles, Lord Barham, 1758–1813*, Vol. II, ed. Professor Sir John Laughton. **OP**.

Vol. 39. *Letters and Papers of Charles, Lord Barham, 1758–1813*, Vol. III, ed. Professor Sir John Laughton. **OP**.

Vol. 40. *The Naval Miscellany*, Vol. II, ed. Professor Sir John Laughton.

*Vol. 41. *Papers relating to the First Dutch War, 1652–1654*, Vol. V, ed. C. T. Atkinson.

Vol. 42. *Papers relating to the Loss of Minorca in 1756*, ed. Captain H. W. Richmond, R.N. **OP**.

*Vol. 43. *The Naval Tracts of Sir William Monson*, Vol. III, ed. M. Oppenheim.

Vol. 44. *The Old Scots Navy 1689–1710*, ed. James Grant. **OP**.

Vol. 45. *The Naval Tracts of Sir William Monson*, Vol. IV, ed. M. Oppenheim.

Vol. 46. *The Private Papers of George, 2nd Earl Spencer*, Vol. I, ed. Julian S. Corbett. **OP**.

Vol. 47. *The Naval Tracts of Sir William Monson*, Vol. V, ed. M. Oppenheim.

Vol. 48. *The Private Papers of George, 2nd Earl Spencer*, Vol. II, ed. Julian S. Corbett. **OP**.

Vol. 49. *Documents relating to Law and Custom of the Sea*, Vol. I, ed. R. G. Marsden. **OP**.

*Vol. 50. *Documents relating to Law and Custom of the Sea*, Vol. II, ed. R. G. Marsden. **OP**.

Vol. 51. *Autobiography of Phineas Pett*, ed. W. G. Perrin. **OP**.

Vol. 52. *The Life of Admiral Sir John Leake*, Vol. I, ed. Geoffrey Callender.

Vol. 53. *The Life of Admiral Sir John Leake*, Vol. II, ed. Geoffrey Callender.

Vol. 54. *The Life and Works of Sir Henry Mainwaring*, Vol. I, ed. G. E. Manwaring.

Vol. 55. *The Letters of Lord St Vincent, 1801–1804*, Vol. I, ed. D. B. Smith. **OP**.

Vol. 56. *The Life and Works of Sir Henry Mainwaring*, Vol. II, ed. G. E. Manwaring & W. G. Perrin. **OP**.

Vol. 57. *A Descriptive Catalogue of the Naval MSS in the Pepysian Library*, Vol. IV, ed. Dr J. R. Tanner. **OP**.

Vol. 58. *The Private Papers of George, 2nd Earl Spencer*, Vol. III, ed. Rear Admiral H. W. Richmond. **OP**.

Vol. 59. *The Private Papers of George, 2nd Earl Spencer*, Vol. IV, ed. Rear Admiral H. W. Richmond. **OP**.

Vol. 60. *Samuel Pepys's Naval Minutes*, ed. Dr J. R. Tanner.

Vol. 61. *The Letters of Lord St Vincent, 1801–1804*, Vol. II, ed. D. B. Smith. **OP**.

Vol. 62. *Letters and Papers of Admiral Viscount Keith*, Vol. I, ed. W. G. Perrin. **OP**.

Vol. 63. *The Naval Miscellany*, Vol. III, ed. W. G. Perrin. **OP**.

Vol. 64. *The Journal of the 1st Earl of Sandwich*, ed. R. C. Anderson. **OP**.

*Vol. 65. *Boteler's Dialogues*, ed. W. G. Perrin.

Vol. 66. *Papers relating to the First Dutch War, 1652–1654*, Vol. VI (with index), ed. C. T. Atkinson.

*Vol. 67. *The Byng Papers*, Vol. I, ed. W. C. B. Tunstall.

*Vol. 68. *The Byng Papers*, Vol. II, ed. W. C. B. Tunstall.

Vol. 69. *The Private Papers of John, Earl of Sandwich*, Vol. I, ed. G. R. Barnes & Lt. Cdr. J. H. Owen, R.N. Corrigenda to *Papers relating to the First Dutch War, 1652–1654, Vols I–VI*, ed. Captain A. C. Dewar, R.N. **OP**.

Vol. 70. *The Byng Papers*, Vol. III, ed. W. C. B. Tunstall.

Vol. 71. *The Private Papers of John, Earl of Sandwich*, Vol. II, ed. G. R. Barnes & Lt. Cdr. J. H. Owen, R.N. **OP**.

Vol. 72. *Piracy in the Levant, 1827–1828*, ed. Lt. Cdr. C. G. Pitcairn Jones, R.N. **OP**.

Vol. 73. *The Tangier Papers of Samuel Pepys*, ed. Edwin Chappell.

Vol. 74. *The Tomlinson Papers*, ed. J. G. Bullocke.

Vol. 75. *The Private Papers of John, Earl of Sandwich*, Vol. III, ed. G. R. Barnes & Cdr. J. H. Owen, R.N. **OP**.

Vol. 76. *The Letters of Robert Blake*, ed. the Rev. J. R. Powell. **OP**.

*Vol. 77. *Letters and Papers of Admiral the Hon. Samuel Barrington*, Vol. I, ed. D. Bonner-Smith.

Vol. 78. *The Private Papers of John, Earl of Sandwich*, Vol. IV, ed. G. R. Barnes & Cdr. J. H. Owen, R.N. **OP**.

*Vol. 79. *The Journals of Sir Thomas Allin, 1660–1678*, Vol. I *1660–1666*, ed. R. C. Anderson.

Vol. 80. *The Journals of Sir Thomas Allin, 1660–1678*, Vol. II *1667–1678*, ed. R. C. Anderson.

Vol. 81. *Letters and Papers of Admiral the Hon. Samuel Barrington*, Vol. II, ed. D. Bonner-Smith. **OP**.

Vol. 82. *Captain Boteler's Recollections, 1808–1830*, ed. D. Bonner-Smith. **OP**.

Vol. 83. *Russian War, 1854. Baltic and Black Sea: Official Correspondence*, ed. D. Bonner-Smith & Captain A. C. Dewar, R.N. **OP**.

Vol. 84. *Russian War, 1855. Baltic: Official Correspondence*, ed. D. Bonner-Smith. **OP**.

Vol. 85. *Russian War, 1855. Black Sea: Official Correspondence*, ed. Captain A.C. Dewar, R.N. **OP**.

Vol. 86. *Journals and Narratives of the Third Dutch War*, ed. R. C. Anderson. **OP**.

Vol. 87. *The Naval Brigades in the Indian Mutiny, 1857–1858*, ed. Cdr. W. B. Rowbotham, R.N. **OP**.

Vol. 88. *Patee Byng's Journal*, ed. J. L. Cranmer-Byng. **OP**.

*Vol. 89. *The Sergison Papers, 1688–1702*, ed. Cdr. R. D. Merriman, R.I.N.

Vol. 90. *The Keith Papers*, Vol. II, ed. Christopher Lloyd. **OP**.

Vol. 91. *Five Naval Journals, 1789–1817*, ed. Rear Admiral H. G. Thursfield. **OP**.

Vol. 92. *The Naval Miscellany*, Vol. IV, ed. Christopher Lloyd. **OP**.

Vol. 93. *Sir William Dillon's Narrative of Professional Adventures, 1790–1839*, Vol. I *1790–1802*, ed. Professor Michael Lewis. **OP**.

Vol. 94. *The Walker Expedition to Quebec, 1711*, ed. Professor Gerald S. Graham. **OP**.

Vol. 95. *The Second China War, 1856–1860*, ed. D. Bonner-Smith & E. W. R. Lumby. **OP**.

Vol. 96. *The Keith Papers, 1803–1815*, Vol. III, ed. Professor Christopher Lloyd.

Vol. 97. *Sir William Dillon's Narrative of Professional Adventures, 1790–1839*, Vol. II *1802–1839*, ed. Professor Michael Lewis. **OP**.

Vol. 98. *The Private Correspondence of Admiral Lord Collingwood*, ed. Professor Edward Hughes. **OP**.

Vol. 99. *The Vernon Papers, 1739–1745*, ed. B. McL. Ranft. **OP**.

Vol. 100. *Nelson's Letters to his Wife and Other Documents*, ed. Lt. Cdr. G. P. B. Naish, R.N.V.R.

Vol. 101. *A Memoir of James Trevenen, 1760–1790*, ed. Professor Christopher Lloyd & R. C. Anderson. **OP**.

Vol. 102. *The Papers of Admiral Sir John Fisher*, Vol. I, ed. Lt. Cdr. P. K. Kemp, R.N. **OP**.

Vol. 103. *Queen Anne's Navy*, ed. Cdr. R. D. Merriman, R.I.N. **OP**.

Vol. 104. *The Navy and South America, 1807–1823*, ed. Professor Gerald S. Graham & Professor R. A. Humphreys.

Vol. 105. *Documents relating to the Civil War, 1642–1648*, ed. The Rev. J. R. Powell & E. K. Timings. **OP**.

Vol. 106. *The Papers of Admiral Sir John Fisher*, Vol. II, ed. Lt. Cdr. P. K. Kemp, R.N. **OP**.

Vol. 107. *The Health of Seamen*, ed. Professor Christopher Lloyd.

Vol. 108. *The Jellicoe Papers*, Vol. I *1893–1916*, ed. A. Temple Patterson.

Vol. 109. *Documents relating to Anson's Voyage round the World, 1740–1744*, ed. Dr Glyndwr Williams. **OP**.

Vol. 110. *The Saumarez Papers: The Baltic, 1808–1812*, ed. A. N. Ryan. **OP**.

Vol. 111. *The Jellicoe Papers*, Vol. II *1916–1925*, ed. Professor A. Temple Patterson.

Vol. 112. *The Rupert and Monck Letterbook, 1666*, ed. The Rev. J. R. Powell & E. K. Timings. **OP** (damaged stock available).

Vol. 113. *Documents relating to the Royal Naval Air Service*, Vol. I (1908–1918), ed. Captain S. W. Roskill, R.N. **OP** (damaged stock available).

*Vol. 114. *The Siege and Capture of Havana, 1762*, ed. Professor David Syrett. **OP** (damaged stock available).

Vol. 115. *Policy and Operations in the Mediterranean, 1912–1914*, ed. E. W. R. Lumby. **OP**.

Vol. 116. *The Jacobean Commissions of Enquiry, 1608 and 1618*, ed. Dr A. P. McGowan.

Vol. 117. *The Keyes Papers*, Vol. I *1914–1918*, ed. Professor Paul Halpern.

Vol. 118. *The Royal Navy and North America: The Warren Papers, 1736–1752*, ed. Dr Julian Gwyn. **OP**.

Vol. 119. *The Manning of the Royal Navy: Selected Public Pamphlets, 1693–1873*, ed. Professor John Bromley.

Vol. 120. *Naval Administration, 1715–1750*, ed. Professor D. A. Baugh.

Vol. 121. *The Keyes Papers*, Vol. II *1919–1938*, ed. Professor Paul Halpern.

Vol. 122. *The Keyes Papers*, Vol. III *1939–1945*, ed. Professor Paul Halpern.

Vol. 123. *The Navy of the Lancastrian Kings: Accounts and Inventories of William Soper, Keeper of the King's Ships, 1422–1427*, ed. Dr Susan Rose.

Vol. 124. *The Pollen Papers: the Privately Circulated Printed Works of Arthur Hungerford Pollen, 1901–1916*, ed. Professor Jon T. Sumida. A. & U.

Vol. 125. *The Naval Miscellany*, Vol. V, ed. Dr N. A. M. Rodger. A & U.

Vol. 126. *The Royal Navy in the Mediterranean, 1915–1918*, ed. Professor Paul Halpern. TS.

Vol. 127. *The Expedition of Sir John Norris and Sir Francis Drake to Spain and Portugal, 1589*, ed. Professor R. B. Wernham. TS.

Vol. 128. *The Beatty Papers*, Vol. I *1902–1918*, ed. Professor B. McL. Ranft. SP.

Vol. 129. *The Hawke Papers: A Selection, 1743–1771*, ed. Dr R. F. Mackay. SP.

Vol. 130. *Anglo-American Naval Relations, 1917–1919*, ed. Michael Simpson. SP.

Vol. 131. *British Naval Documents, 1204–1960*, ed. Professor John B. Hattendorf, Dr Roger Knight, Alan Pearsall, Dr Nicholas Rodger & Professor Geoffrey Till. SP.

Vol. 132. *The Beatty Papers*, Vol. II *1916–1927*, ed. Professor B. McL. Ranft. SP

Vol. 133. *Samuel Pepys and the Second Dutch War*, transcribed by Professor William Matthews & Dr Charles Knighton; ed. Robert Latham. SP.

Vol. 134. *The Somerville Papers*, ed. Michael Simpson, with the assistance of John Somerville. SP.

Vol. 135. *The Royal Navy in the River Plate, 1806–1807*, ed. John D. Grainger. SP.

Vol. 136. *The Collective Naval Defence of the Empire, 1900–1940*, ed. Nicholas Tracy. A.

Vol. 137. *The Defeat of the Enemy Attack on Shipping, 1939–1945*, ed. Eric Grove. A.

Vol. 138. *Shipboard Life and Organisation, 1731–1815*, ed. Brian Lavery. A.

Vol. 139. *The Battle of the Atlantic and Signals Intelligence: U-boat Situations and Trends, 1941–1945*, ed. Professor David Syrett. A.

Vol. 140. *The Cunningham Papers*, Vol. I: *The Mediterranean Fleet, 1939–1942*, ed. Michael Simpson. A.

Vol. 141. *The Channel Fleet and the Blockade of Brest, 1793–1801*, ed. Roger Morriss. A.

Vol. 142. *The Submarine Service, 1900–1918*, ed. Nicholas Lambert. A.

Vol. 143. *Letters and Papers of Professor Sir John Knox Laughton (1830–1915)*, ed. Professor Andrew Lambert. A.

Vol. 144. *The Battle of the Atlantic and Signals Intelligence: U-Boat Tracking Papers 1941–1947*, ed. Professor David Syrett. A.

Vol. 145. *The Maritime Blockade of Germany in the Great War: The Northern Patrol, 1914–1918*, ed. John D. Grainger. A.

Vol. 146. *The Naval Miscellany*, Vol. VI, ed. Michael Duffy. A.

Vol. 147. *The Milne Papers*, Vol. I *1820–1859*, ed. Professor John Beeler. A.

Vol. 148. *The Rodney Papers*, Vol. I *1742–1763*, ed. Professor David Syrett. A.

Vol. 149. *Sea Power and the Control of Trade. Belligerent Rights from the Russian War to the Beira Patrol, 1854–1970*, ed. Nicholas Tracy. A.

Vol. 150. *The Cunningham Papers*, Vol. II *The Triumph of Allied Sea Power 1942–1946*, ed. Michael Simpson. A.

Vol. 151. *The Rodney Papers*, Vol. II *1763–1780*, ed. Professor David Syrett. A.

Vol. 152. *Naval Intelligence from Germany: The Reports of the British Naval Attachés in Berlin, 1906–1914*, ed. Matthew S. Seligmann. A.

Vol. 153. *The Naval Miscellany*, Vol. VII, ed. Susan Rose. A.

Occasional Publications:

Vol. 1. *The Commissioned Sea Officers of the Royal Navy, 1660–1815*, ed. Professor David Syrett & Professor R. L. DiNardo. SP.

Vol. 2. *The Anthony Roll of Henry VIII's Navy*, ed. C. S. Knighton and D. M. Loades. A.